The Kinsey Institute

THE KINSEY INSTITUTE

INSTITUTE

The First Seventy Years

JUDITH A. ALLEN
HALLIMEDA E. ALLINSON
ANDREW CLARK-HUCKSTEP
BRANDON J. HILL
STEPHANIE A. SANDERS
LIANA ZHOU

INDIANA UNIVERSITY PRESS

This book is a publication of

Indiana University Press
Office of Scholarly Publishing
Herman B Wells Library 350
1320 East 10th Street
Bloomington, Indiana 47405 USA

iupress.indiana.edu

*Manufactured in the
United States of America*

Cataloging information is available from the
Library of Congress.

ISBN 978-0-253-02976-8 (cloth)
ISBN 978-0-253-03023-8 (e-bk.)

1 2 3 4 5   22 21 20 19 18 17

frontispiece: Alfred Charles Kinsey. Clarence
Tripp took this photograph around the time
that *Sexual Behavior in the Human Male* was
published, ca. 1948. Photo courtesy of Kinsey
Institute Library and Special Collections.

For Wendy Kinsey Corning

Contents

Acknowledgments

It is a pleasure to have so many people to thank for this short history reaching fruition. None of us realized that this project was in our futures. Sue Carter, director of the Kinsey Institute, wanted to mark, for 2017, the seventieth anniversary of the Institute's founding. The historians amongst us realized promptly that existing Kinsey biographies or histories of American sex research did not suffice for the purpose. Too many unanswered questions loomed, and, it seemed, too much missing evidence prevented us from providing convincing explanations of key matters. Whose idea was it to found the Institute? Was it Indiana University's reliably visionary new young leader, President Herman B Wells? Was it Kinsey himself? What was its founding rationale or purpose? How was it structured, governed, and resourced? How did the university town of Bloomington, the state of Indiana, and the United States respond to this institutionalization of the field of sex research, hitherto of European rather than American genealogy? Further, if earlier Kinsey biographies and the 2004 Bill Condon movie, *Kinsey*, provided some sense of the Institute's research activities while it was led by Kinsey, the period from his 1956 death until the present, for most people, was much less clear.

Several researchers had done previous work touching one way or another on the story of the Institute's founding, early work, and activities. A seventieth-anniversary assessment, though, warranted something more systematic. It involved searching from top to bottom not only the Institute's extensive germane collections but also the Indiana University Archives, President Herman B Wells's papers and correspondence, the archives of the Rockefeller Foundation and other granting bodies, and the papers of key figures in American sex research and related clinical fields in Boston, Cambridge, New York, Philadelphia, and Washington, DC. These efforts garnered new documents, images, and texts. Some of this information came to be used for hallway display in the Institute premises and for booklets for visitors, guests, and sponsors of the Institute's work and collections.

Yet the materials we collected and appraised illuminate beyond these anniversary purposes. They permit deeper understanding, as well as fresh perspectives on the founding and subsequent development of the Institute. As we began to grasp the implications of these newly discovered records, it seemed that the seventieth anniversary presented an opportune moment to attempt to assemble a short history of the founding and further work of the Institute across its first decades. Each of us had undertaken research related to or had been associated with periods of the Institute's history. So, almost in the spirit of an experiment, each of us undertook to write first-draft chapter(s) on eras, phases, or sections of Institute history that we knew best. Then, once we could see what we had, we would revise toward a single narrative.

Historians often regard institutional histories as tedious affairs, and rightly so. Since these histories are semisponsored or maybe sullied by the whiff of being an in-house infomercial, the advance verdict can be "guilty." Of what? Boosterism. They sometimes advance an apologist voice, an unbalanced papering over, perhaps, of the problems, scandals, and mistakes. We hope we have found ways to avoid these pitfalls. Our individual histories as students, scientists, and scholars, all differently affiliated with the Institute, mean that we are committed to its most effective possible future while regretting its inglorious phases and conditions of difficulty. Yet our different generational and structural relationships with it provided us with resources to balance and critically scrutinize the perspectives we initially represented. Our collaboration involved combining our drafts into one text, then scrutinizing and revising as a whole. We asked each other hard questions. And we reached new insights from these exchanges, some of us changing our minds on issues along the way either in the light of new evidence or from the recasting of that evidence by coauthors with experience of matters narrated. We hope that these approaches and dynamics have helped us to avoid too "official" a history of the Institute. Of course, this judgment ultimately belongs to our readers.

We are indebted to the Kinsey Institute collections staff for the privilege of working with the archives and manuscripts and, not least, their invaluable assistance in navigating them. Shawn C. Wilson's knowledge of the collections and endless patience with our questions proved beyond amazing. He could not have been more generous with his time or assistance. Taylor Dean, Rachel Schend, Jack Kovaleski, and Kendra Werst tirelessly helped locate files, scan documents, and research a variety of questions, often under difficult circumstances. Anne Jones selflessly volunteers her time to help maintain the condition of the archives. We also found a warm welcome and indispensable assistance in our forays into Indiana University Archives, with its many relevant collections. Our deepest gratitude too is owed to the diverse special collections staff of many archives and repositories farther afield, including the Arthur and Elizabeth Schlesinger Library on the

History of Women in America and the Francis A. Countway Library of Medicine, Harvard University, as well as at Indiana University and its community. For their special assistance, we thank Saundra Taylor, Moya L. Andrews, Zachary Clark-Huckstep, Diana Carey, and Wendy Kinsey Corning.

Like all authors reaching this point, we owe a trail of debts to many people associated with Indiana University Press. Raina Polivka, on the eve of her departure to the University of California Press, encouraged us in the design and enlisting of this book project with the Press. Janice Frisch and Gary Dunham have been the best of editors and coaches, with unfailing faith in our shaggy collective endeavor, even in our moments of pause. Two anonymous readers offered astute and expert commentary, with an array of valuable suggestions, which we have fully embraced in the revision process. Mary M. Hill copy edited with impressive skill, shrewd insight and lightning speed; and Kate Schramm greatly assisted with down-to-the-wire problem solving and elusive details. Meanwhile, Dave Miller and his project team showed us nothing but constructive professionalism and an intriguing blend of cool (in the best sense), patience, and verve, which edged us, partly to our amazement, over the finish line. We vote them all our hearty thanks.

With six coauthors, we will spare readers the customary long lists of thanks to intimates, relatives, friends, and mentors. The precious and treasured ones who populate those lists for each of us know where they are in our affection and admiration. More than is usually the case, this book is the outcome of collective effort and support. We simply express our deepest thanks to all. If we have created a text that helps readers to understand the genealogy and timbre of the Institute in its first seventy years, our efforts will have been more than repaid.

Judith A. Allen
Hallimeda E. Allison
Andrew Clark-Huckstep
Brandon J. Hill
Stephanie A. Sanders
Liana Zhou

BLOOMINGTON, APRIL 2017

List of Abbreviations

ACK	Alfred Charles Kinsey
ACKC	Alfred C. Kinsey Collection, 1894–1956
ACKD	Alfred Charles Kinsey Directorship, 1947–56
AFG	Alan F. Guttmacher
APB	Alan P. Bell
AWF	Alice Withrow Field
AWFP	Alice Withrow Field Papers, 1909–60
CEM	Clyde E. Martin
CGH	Carl G. Hartman
CRA	Clifford R. Adams
CRPS	Committee for Research in Problems of Sex
FAB	Frank Ambrose Beach
FES	Frances E. Shields
HBW	Herman B Wells
IDS	*Indiana Daily Student*
IUA	Indiana University Archives
JB	John Bancroft
JBD	John Bancroft Directorship, 1995–2003
JHG	John H. Gagnon
JMR	June Machover Reinisch
JMRD	June Machover Reinisch Directorship, 1982–93
JRH	Julia R. Heiman

JRHD	Julia R. Heiman Directorship, 2004–13
KI	Kinsey Institute
KILSC	Kinsey Institute Library and Special Collections
KINROS	*Kinsey Institute New Report on Sex* (1990)
KIRSGR	Kinsey Institute for Research in Sex, Gender, and Reproduction
MSC	Mary Steichen Calderone
MSCC	Mary Steichen Calderone Collection
NICHHD	National Institute of Child Health and Human Development
NIH	National Institutes of Health
NIMH	National Institute of Mental Health
NORC	National Opinion Research Center
NRC	National Research Council
OSE	Oliver Spurgeon English
PDP	Prenatal Development Project
PHG	Paul H. Gebhard
PHGD	Paul H. Gebhard Directorship, 1957–81
PHS	Public Health Service
PPFA	Planned Parenthood Federation of America
RFR	Rockefeller Foundation Records, Rockefeller Archive Center, Washington, DC
RLD	Robert Latou Dickinson
RLY	Robert L. Yerkes
SAS	Stephanie A. Sanders
SBHF	*Sexual Behavior in the Human Female* (1953)
SBHM	*Sexual Behavior in the Human Male* (1948)
SL	Arthur and Elizabeth Schlesinger Library on the History of Women in America, Radcliffe Institute for Advanced Study, Harvard University, Cambridge, MA
SO	*Sex Offenders: An Analysis of Types* (1965)
SPCD	Sue Porges Carter Directorship, 2013–
WBP	Wardell B. Pomeroy
WS	William Simon

The Kinsey Institute

Introduction: Looking Back

It is the function of a scientist to discover the truth about that portion of the universe which is made of matter. It is not the function of a scientist to judge the esthetic or moral qualities of that universe. . . . [T]here is no right, no wrong, no beauty, no lack of beauty—nothing but the observed truth. . . . Any scientist who passes opinions on things spiritual or moral speaks as a theologian or as a mere man, and not as a scientist.

Alfred C. Kinsey, "A Scientist's Responsibility in Sex Instruction"[1]

A YOUNG INDIANA SOLDIER ON FURLOUGH IN 1945 wrote to Indiana University zoology professor Alfred C. Kinsey in great distress. On a date with an older woman, the soldier had attempted oral sex. Indignant, "she told me how low, dirty, mean, and contemptible I am—a pervert. Am I a fit specimen of a man after such conduct? I want to be a normal man."[2] Kinsey reassured him that there was "nothing in your experience which is in any fashion unusual or abnormal," explaining that he and other expert researchers had found such activity in 40–75 percent of married couples' histories. In addition, it is a "basic biologic situation which occurs in all the other animals related to man."[3] Another youth, a Canadian drugstore clerk, wrote Kinsey in 1948, asking to borrow a copy of the recently published *Sexual Behavior in the Human Male* because he could not afford to buy it.[4] And a marine recruit wrote from camp in North Carolina in 1953: "I was reading a book of yours and i was whant to no if you no whear i canget a book on marriage manuols. If you can help me, please let me no. I need one bad."[5]

Kinsey founded the Institute for Sex Research at Indiana University in 1947. He would continue to receive letters like these from ordinary Americans and from overseas until his death in 1956. He was an enthusiastic naturalist. Whether collecting vast samples of gall wasps—his specialty in entomology—or working in botany, hybridizing irises, daylilies, and daffodils, biology taught him a reverence for species diversity and for diversities of all kinds. That respect led him never to judge negatively behaviors naturally found among mammals and other life forms. Instead, he sought, eagerly, to study and understand all characteristics and behaviors detected within any given organism's context, which included its culture. This, after all, was the plain mission of biology. Such an approach enabled him to offer unsolicited correspondents recognition, reassurance, and, where necessary, referral for help.

This book offers a concise history of the Institute, originally named the Institute for Sex Research, from its founding until its seventieth anniversary in 2017. Its first seven decades involved dramatic transformations, sometimes in tandem with and sometimes detached from striking postwar evolution in American and broader Western erotic, reproductive, and gender patterns. The scope of this history includes the Institute's genealogy, purposes, programs, researchers, collections, publications, and development, as well as its challenges, both internal and external. As a concise history, this study is not comprehensive but rather indicative, combining both the findings of earlier scholars and new findings made in the course of our joint work for this study.

The history of the Institute intersects with that of fields researching sexuality after 1860. Institute researchers' exchanges with peer experts and scholars provide crucial context for this narrative. As well, the Institute's location, from the mid-twentieth century, in the university town of Bloomington, Indiana, inflected the Institute's work and the experiences of those associated with it. The history of the Institute, then, is an essential and illuminating part of Indiana University history. That history in turn contributes to our understanding of the modernization of the American research university.[6] In its relations with the Institute, the University has had occasion to show, in the words of its deservedly famous president, Herman B Wells, the difference between a local college and a "university of the first rank."[7]

The study of sexuality has always proved controversial. The field of sex research began in several European countries in the 1860s. Its beginnings often centered on a particular problem or sexual pattern; prostitution, venereal diseases, homosexuality, nymphomania, and masturbation anchored the field's earliest work.[8] After World War I and in the wake of fascism and specific Nazi campaigns against sexology and psychoanalysis, both sex research and clinical leadership in the field shifted to the United States.[9] Difficulties exposed by the 1930s economic depression influenced many pioneering studies of social problems. Such studies

Figure 0.1. Daffodil-edged pathway leading to the Kinsey residence, ca. 1950, Bloomington, Indiana. Alfred C. Kinsey was an avid gardener who explored horticultural diversity through hybridization of new varieties of daffodils, daylilies, and irises. Photo courtesy of Wendy Kinsey Corning.

Figure 0.2. President Herman B Wells, ca. 1954. Herman B Wells, perhaps the Midwest's most famous university president, was a keen supporter of Kinsey, the Institute for Sex Research, and both the principle and the practice of academic freedom. Photo courtesy of Indiana University Archives.

formed part of the intellectual origins of Kinsey's studies. The focus on class and "social level" central to sociology of the later 1930s and 1940s provided a favorable initial context for Kinsey's distinctive class-variegated study of American sexual behavior patterns.[10]

Such new sociological enquiries prospered during World War II. Kinsey's projects and those of his peers garnered support from authorities confronting wartime upheavals and questioning. If the social, behavioral, and clinical sciences continued to boom through the 1950s, though, other cultural forces resisted their findings and approaches.[11] Cold War domestic politics denounced relativism and behaviorism, and zealots dubbed as "un-American" research and scholarship urging "realism" about diverse mores and practices in the population at large. Instead, critics insisted on conformity to desirable norms, theories, and dogmas, enforced by whatever means necessary. McCarthyites denounced sex research as unpatriotic from the floor of Congress, charging that it undermined the American family and, thereby, national greatness. In 1954 the Rockefeller Foundation faced searing critique for supporting Kinsey's research, and a congressional enquiry threatened the removal of its tax-exempt status for facilitating such destructive research. As a result, the Foundation ceased funding for Kinsey's human sexual behavior project.

Despite reversals, Indiana University demonstrated its pride in the Institute throughout its history. On several occasions during the past seven decades, University officials publicly defended the importance of the Institute's work for science and the social good generally and for the University specifically. The University offered particular support between 1952 and 1957 when the United States Customs Service attempted censorship via suppression of imported items for the Institute collections, "libeling" them as "obscene" and scheduling them for destruction in 1956. Not only did President Wells submit an affidavit and an amicus brief on behalf of the Institute, but so too did the University's board of trustees, ultimately prevailing in a federal district court summary ruling in favor of the Institute in 1957.[12]

All this proved most consequential. Through this engagement, Indiana University became preeminent among American universities for defending academic freedom and the integrity of qualified scholarly research and researchers against prejudiced detractors. In 1968 President Wells reflected on the public relations benefits accrued from the University's support of Kinsey. Wells reported the "enormous pride" on the part of "our constituents," even those opposed to Kinsey's work, because of their "willingness to battle the Institute issue."[13]

Some may wonder at the rationale for a concise history of the Institute. Historical and biographical treatments of Kinsey and his work surely abound. Indeed, Kinsey's life and work have been the subjects of biographies and monographs from various disciplines, as well as the focus of numerous scholarly and not so scholarly articles. Despite extensive previous attention, though, controversies surrounding the Institute and its work, present from its earliest years, revived enough new attention in the 1990s and beyond to warrant reappraisal. Biographer James H. Jones's *Alfred Kinsey: A Public/Private Life* (1997) characterizes the Institute and the publications of *Sexual Behavior in the Human Male* and *Sexual Behavior in the Human Female* as the works of a deeply conflicted "homosexual."[14] This characterization of Kinsey contrasts with Jones's doctoral dissertation, entitled "The Origins of the Institute for Sex Research: A History," from 1972. Jones's dissertation offered significant information on the founding of the Institute, whereas the 1997 biography instead foregrounds speculations on Kinsey's sexual life based on anonymous and, for the reader, unverifiable sources, with attendant psychologizing.[15]

Jones's treatment of Kinsey, both lauded and decried, has produced its own set of critiques and arguments. In 1998 Jonathan Gathorne-Hardy published an alternative biography, *Sex the Measure of All Things*. Gathorne-Hardy dissented from Jones's interpretation of Kinsey's erotic preoccupations and charges of bias. In particular, he concurs with acclaimed historian Martin Duberman's rejection of Jones's claim that Kinsey was a homosexual. "By what definition?" Gathorne-Hardy quotes Duberman. "Kinsey was lovingly married for thirty-five years to Clara McMillen, and . . . their relationship was in no sense perfunctory, certainly not sexually."[16] Why might any of this matter? Because of the charge, implicit and explicit, that nonnormative desires and behavior, if established, tipped the scales and skewed Kinsey's research, the findings, or the interpretation. This assumes, of course, that normative desires and behavior did not equally confer a stakeholder position in a researcher that could be just as potentially distorting.

Alternatively, earlier biographies of Kinsey focused on the production of the male and female volumes, Kinsey's relationship with the Committee for Research in Problems of Sex and the Rockefeller Foundation, and the inner workings of the research team. Useful as these biographies were, Gathorne-Hardy judged them as "very much those of admiring subordinates."[17] While Kinsey receives attention as a historical (and American) subject, these works—including projects and articles on the technological advances that the Kinsey team used in coding and retrieving their data—do little to illuminate the workings of the Institute for Sex Research itself, that is, its founding and subsequent development after Kinsey's death.[18]

The Institute's history, as shown here, has not been the product of just one founding vision. Instead, its course tracked the postwar American cultural context and the development of sex research as a field. The broader history of the Institute to date revises ways of reading Kinsey's endeavors and illuminates the Institute's trials and perseverance.

* * *

Figure 0.3. Clara McMillen Kinsey and Alfred Charles Kinsey, who referred to each other as Mac and Prok, in their garden, ca. 1950. Photo courtesy of Kinsey Institute Library and Special Collections.

How did all of this come about? Why was Indiana University, a state college founded in 1820, the place that came to play such a central role in the history of the study of sexuality? The narrative offered here undertakes an analysis of the origins of the Institute in Kinsey, a forty-two-year-old professor of zoology who in midcareer departed into a new interview-based project seeking to quantitatively classify patterns in human sexual behavior. The first task is to place Kinsey's initial sex research in the context of earlier and wider developments in the field. The matters of the Institute's formation and establishment, its initial research trajectory, its scholarly work, and its acquisition of specialist multimedia research collections begin the story in the first chapter.

The central matter for the first decade of the Institute's work until Kinsey's death in 1956 was the production of the internationally famous and *New York Times* best-selling "Kinsey Reports"—that is, *Sexual Behavior in the Human Male* (1948) and *Sexual Behavior in the Human Female* (1953). These substantial and highly quantitative texts drew on nearly twelve thousand volunteer interviews— "sex histories," as Kinsey called them. The second chapter recounts the books' findings, as well as the methodological and mission changes embraced by Kinsey and coresearchers, during the five-year interval between them. Collections development too was a major element of Kinsey's work during the period between and after the female volume's publication, challenged by confiscation of imported photographs, publications, and objects by US Customs authorities. The chapter concludes by examining Kinsey's diverse undertakings after the 1953 female volume, particularly his commencement of a new book on abortion. The context for these books entailed the most severe challenges yet encountered by the Institute as it weathered both professional and, ultimately, political storms. Kinsey employed and attached to the Institute a broad array of experts from within and beyond the University, including linguists, jurists, criminologists, ethnographers, social workers, and photographers. From contacts made through diverse research contexts, he drew on the experience and insights of playwrights and dramaturges, dancers and choreographers, philosophers, social theorists, sociologists, and literary critics. He aimed for true disciplinary diversity in the perspectives informing projects and objectives. By doing so, he began new projects in a world of now-widened constituencies. Yet the storms unleashed in the female volume's Cold War context still raged when he died in August 1956.

The third chapter examines developments in Institute research during the decade after Kinsey's death. The long-delayed US Customs case was reanimated and throughout 1957 inspired supportive affidavit documents from an array of national experts. It also evoked a powerful and principled intervention on behalf of scientific inquiry, as well as reinforcing the necessity and wisdom of the Institute's structural independence from the Indiana University board of trustees. The terms

Figure 0.4. The Kinsey Reports. *Sexual Behavior in the Human Male* (1948) and *Sexual Behavior in the Human Female* (1953) defined Kinsey's legacy, rocketed up the *New York Times* best-seller list, and brought the Institute international fame. Photo (1953) courtesy of Kinsey Institute Library and Special Collections.

of the arguments over the right to conduct a scientific study of sexuality repay careful scrutiny, since they affected ongoing collections work by relevant experts on the Institute's staff.

Paralleling new research were efforts to complete Kinsey's unfinished works in progress. By 1965 two that he left in draft form were published. Institute researchers revised considerably, though, the framework and approach initially taken by Kinsey to both of these book projects. The methods and findings of *Pregnancy, Birth and Abortion* (1958) and *Sex Offenders: An Analysis of Types* (1965) highlight midfifties to midsixties shifts not only within the Institute as directed by Kinsey's research associate, anthropologist Paul H. Gebhard, but also within the larger field of sex research. The chapter also narrates Gebhard's deployment of advice from funders and peer professionals in undertaking a profound intellectual reconfiguration of the Institute. Outcomes included new researchers and collections staff for the advance of a very different research trajectory after the *Sex Offenders* volume.

A mighty impact of Kinsey's work was to enhance respect for the study of sexuality across the 1950s. Both researchers and studies proliferated from within many disciplines and fields. By the later 1960s, sex research had become a distinctly more "crowded field." Though represented within a broadening swath of areas, the sex research evolved toward more psychiatric and psychological orientations while also becoming more clinical and medical in its practical focus. William Masters (1915–2001) and Virginia Johnson's (1925–2013) work, as well as that of Harry Benjamin (1885–1986), John Money, and many others, signaled these field reorientations. Such foci did not necessarily synchronize with the discourses of the so-called sexual revolution and its many discontents. Assessing the Institute's work and development during these tumultuous decades is the task of the fourth chapter. Many issues became prominent, including the advent of the birth control pill and the availability of *Playboy* magazine and more diverse erotica and pornography after some relaxation of censorship laws; the rise of the women's and gay liberation movements; emerging sexual minority subcultures; early interventions of transsexual, queer, and transgender sexual identity politics; more organized commercialization of sex industries; school sex education controversies; and intensified political contention over unwed motherhood, abortion, and other birth control options. In what ways did the Institute intervene, and to what extent was its work truly engaged with these contentious areas of contemporary sexual politics? How did its efforts compare with other sex research organizations or units?

Locally, tumultuous shifts made the 1980s and early 1990s the most difficult phase in the Institute's history. After thoroughgoing reviews of its operations in 1980, reports recommended a series of critical changes. Preeminently, they called for new leadership. The priorities to follow included changes to the Institute's name, governance, staffing, administration, priorities, and relationships with the University and its faculty, staff, and students. In 1981 the Institute's name became the Alfred C. Kinsey Institute for Sex Research. Then, its first externally recruited director, June M. Reinisch, arrived from Rutgers University in 1982. A psychologist trained at Columbia University, she took the Institute in unprecedented directions in the context of the salient local and national changes that marked the Reagan era. Reinisch stressed community outreach, sex education, popular culture, and public health, with a vigilant eye on collections development and media relations. Chapter 5 examines key elements of the massive reorientation of Institute activities during the twelve years of the third Kinsey Institute director.

With the Institute renamed again in 1983 as the Kinsey Institute for Research in Sex, Gender, and Reproduction, a new era began. New scientific and collections staff appointed during the 1980s and 1990s served different research agendas, with a strong emphasis on external federal grants, despite a cultural context marked by the HIV pandemic and transformed ruminations on sexual behaviors and identities. Sex research itself became newly controversial in the middle of what historians now call "the culture wars" of the 1980s and beyond. This already difficult external context became toxic for the progress of the Institute when University community critics of Reinisch's departures from previous leadership priorities and research topics resulted in an escalating drumbeat of charges, paralyzing legal action, loss of crucial University resources, and, ultimately, Reinisch's rearly retirement in 1993.

The final chapter explores the Institute from the mid-1990s to the early 2010s. Its fourth and fifth directors sought to repair its frayed relationship with the University. Dr. John Bancroft (1994–2003) and Dr. Julia Heiman (2004–13) initiated research directions that reflected the deepening entrenchment of biomedical perspectives on sexuality across the previous quarter of a century. The mid-1990s appointment of Dutch psychophysiologist Erick Janssen, who researched variables in erotic arousal, marked this direction. Alternatively, new representations of Kinsey in sensationalized biographies, as well as retrospective critiques of aspects of his research, emerged. These were countered somewhat by a popular Hollywood biopic, *Kinsey* (2004), starring Liam Neeson and Laura Linney. Such portrayals stimulated enormous interest in Kinsey himself and raised speculations as to his own sexual practices or inclinations. Little of this outpouring, though, attended accurately to the nature of Kinsey's actual research, findings, and writings and their practical implications and impact on American, not to say international, sexual understanding.

With the new century, new research topics emerged that were responsive to fieldwide and global concerns. The treatment of sexual dysfunction, especially in aging adults, became a particularly significant area of work. Prophylactic and contraceptive error in the context of HIV/AIDS and other STDs became a strong node of Institute research, involving Indiana University researchers and core-searchers in other US universities, as well as participants from Canada and the United Kingdom. Two more foci were mood or well-being and erotic behavior and an array of psychophysiological research projects related to sexual arousal. These marked not only Kinsey Institute scientists' research but also the research of scientists at large. In a conservative 2000s congressional context, however, pressure to defund Kinsey Institute projects, even though they had already been approved by exacting national peer review, signaled the ongoing political pressures constraining sex research compared with other social, behavioral, and natural sciences. Increasingly "hot-button" cultural concerns about intergenerational sexuality, especially the sexual abuse of children, framed questions asked of and about sex research during these recent decades.

Political pressures squeezing funding have imperiled the progress and proper stewardship of the Institute's priceless collections. Their future, as Indiana University looks forward to its bicentennial celebrations, will require a new and nimble paradigm to optimize their development, preservation, and scholarly access. Meanwhile, the Internet era has posed new questions about sexuality. Singles, dating, "hook-up" culture, love, monogamy, and the nature of modern sexual and/or romantic relationships attract attention from sex researchers today. A new generation of scholars with broader and more interdisciplinary training than their predecessors permits multifaceted address of these areas in recent and ongoing Kinsey Institute research. Notable here is the combining of biology and interdisciplinary gender studies academic backgrounds in appointees, affiliates, and doctoral candidates, including Justin R. Garcia, whose interdisciplinary research focuses on the evolutionary and biocultural aspects of romantic and sexual relationships, and Amanda N. Gesselman, a social psychologist who researches the sexuality of single adults and the psychology, sexuality, and health of couples. The exciting work already produced by these young scholars portends a renaissance of new sex research that is markedly different from that of previous generations.

The book concludes with an assessment of present challenges and anticipated future directions for this venerable treasure of Indiana University. If this study marks the Institute's first seventy years, it is to be hoped that any sequel will be able to report the Institute's powerful salience in illuminating both the remaining mysteries and the entrenched problems related to human sexualities in all their diversity. Based on experience so far, sex research no doubt will continue to raise controversy. Probably it should. It is to be hoped that Indiana University will continue its long tradition of defending academic freedom for the Institute across the decades ahead and that it will see the great social utility from the Institute's research that President Wells so proudly proclaimed in the middle of the twentieth century.

1
Overlapping Foundations
(1916–1946)

Your group should be given status within the University of Indiana [*sic*] as a research Institute, probably in the Graduate School, much as our department of the Carnegie Institution works as a more or less independent research institute. You would thus have independent control of your staff, records, and library, with the advantages of University protection and accounting. . . . I think you also want complete control of the ultimate disposition of your records, and that you do not (I believe) wish to leave this entirely to the University authorities. . . . [T]his could be done by a recorded agreement between the University and yourself, setting up a special committee to care for this matter.

George W. Corner, National Research Council, to Alfred C. Kinsey, July 6, 1946, 1–2

BY 1946 ALFRED C. KINSEY REALIZED HE HAD A PROBLEM. In 1938 he had commenced undertaking interview-based individual sex histories and acquiring the data grounding previous pioneer studies by earlier peer researchers. Originally an entomological taxonomist responsible for the discovery and classification of hundreds of new species of North American gall wasps, Kinsey now had thousands of sex histories.[1] He and two coresearchers began assembling the results, the beginnings of the first Kinsey Report, *Sexual Behavior in the Human Male* (1948). These highly confidential data were added to a formidable and ever-enlarging holding of salient publications and ephemera related to erotic expression and representation that had been procured worldwide. The collections now raised preservation, storage capacity, and security concerns. What agency would keep these materials in the event of Kinsey's death or the dissolution of the project? How could he best protect the collections from fire and flood damage? What funding would support them? How could he ensure that the library and collected data would not fall into the wrong hands? Much was at stake personally, politically, and professionally.

Kinsey knew he needed support. He turned to the Committee for Research in Problems of Sex. Based in Washington, DC, and one of the specialist committees of the National Research Council, it was funded through the Rockefeller Foundation. The committee had underwritten a golden age of sex research since World War I, much of it centered on the study of animals.[2] Since 1941 the committee had provided substantial grants in support of Kinsey's study of human sexual behavior. This made it the obvious starting point in the quest for solutions. Initially, he hoped that the committee would finance the library's acquisitions, providing them with institutional stability and permanence at Indiana University. Hope gave way to dismay, however, with the news that such support would vest the committee with full disposition rights. Kinsey took his appeal directly to the Rockefeller Foundation members. In response, George W. Corner (1889–1981), pioneer embryological endocrinologist and committee member, suggested that Kinsey incorporate his project: it would remain tied to Indiana University, but Kinsey would be protected from opposing interests, whether at the university, local community, or state level, thus securing researcher control over the collections and research data. The Institute for Sex Research, then, was created at the strong urging of the Rockefeller Foundation—one of its committee members, Robert M. Yerkes (1876–1956), even coined its name.[3]

The founding of the Institute for Sex Research had a longer genealogy. Some commentators see Kinsey's sex research project and the Institute as the continuation of large fieldwork research projects emanating from well-funded institutions associated with universities or professional bodies.[4] Others portray them as the overdue inauguration of a research field valuable for understanding human behavior and solving social problems.[5] Analysts position Kinsey and the Institute either as the end of a line of researchers dedicated to large-scale taxonomic field research data or as triggers for the "sexual revolution" then ahead, with its sweeping changes and frank sexual discourses. This chapter places Kinsey, the research, and the Institute into their own historical context. To understand the development and incorporation of the Institute, it is necessary to look back to sex researchers' methods, their financial support, and the institutions they worked in during the early twentieth century.

Prior to the 1910s, most sex researchers presented their data through the case study. Thereafter, though, first questionnaires and then interviews anchored data acquisition, which was concerned with statistical prevalence and representative samples. This shift connected with another. Progressive Era social organizations and social uplift movements, as well as new doctrines, including eugenics, proved

Figure 1.1. Robert M. Yerkes was a primatologist and the chair of the Committee for Research in Problems of Sex. He is pictured here on a visit to the Institute for Sex Research, ca. 1948. Photo courtesy of Kinsey Institute Library and Special Collections.

Figure 1.2. Alfred C. Kinsey at a library bookshelf, ca. 1948. Although the collected sex histories were of major concern during the incorporation process, Kinsey made it clear that the enlarging library would also be a central component of the founding of the Institute for Sex Research. Photo courtesy of Kinsey Institute Library and Special Collections.

critical for the field's development. Sex researchers derived considerable support for research projects from associations, particularly those funded by wealthy philanthropists such as Rockefeller. Though these organizations did not directly support universities, they funded individual university-affiliated researchers and centers. Theirs were the standard research methods for social and scientific research at the time; hence, they became the accepted standard for external grant support.

The further key and immediate element in the historical origins of the Institute was Kinsey himself and his interwar project. Kinsey and his backers quickly realized that his project, which had been devised in the waning years of the 1930s economic depression, differed in scope and scale from those of previous researchers. Integral to it was a vast collection—the "sex library"—unlike any other in existence and rivaled only by Magnus Hirschfeld's collection, ransacked and burned by the Nazi regime on May 6, 1933. With this recent and traumatic precedent, Kinsey sought to combine, sustain, and steward research data, and he acquired rare books and materials as the project developed. The innovation, then, was the creation of the Institute for Sex Research as its own incorporated entity associated with Indiana University as a research institute and under the impetus of the Rockefeller Foundation and the National Research Council's Committee for Research in Problems of Sex.

From Stories to Numbers

Thanks for your note of October 16th, concerning the clinicians. ["Clinician sees only the anomalies . . . has no idea of the cross-section of the population. Have you tackled the cases in the big clinics?"] I am increasingly conscious of the way in which their opinions are warped by the quality of their sampling. Even on such a thing as names of contraceptives, clinicians have little information on what is used by the mass. They see only those cases who are already interested in contraceptives before they come to the clinics.

Alfred C. Kinsey to Carl G. Hartman, October 19, 1943

American sex research was, initially, a small and disparate field. Prior to the turn of the twentieth century, researchers in European contexts utilized the case study method and frequently focused on sexual deviance. By the interwar period, those working on human sexuality had turned to more sociological approaches.[6] Meanwhile, American sex researchers responded to national anxieties—particularly over prostitution and venereal disease—and international influences, from Freud's theories of psychosexual development and psychoanalysis to psychoneurological and endocrinological approaches with animals and humans. Kinsey disdained previous studies, finding them impressionistic and gender, class, and race biased.[7]

Figure 1.3. Gall wasp specimens, ca. 1940. Alfred C. Kinsey's first major project was studying diversity among gall wasps, tiny insects he collected, categorized, cataloged, and placed into specimen boxes. Photo courtesy of Kinsey Library and Special Collections.

Instead, Kinsey sought reliable information about sexual behavior from non-clinical informants. He wanted a secular, value-free investigation of sexual behavior of targeted groups *not* located through the process of therapy or treatment of disorder. Religious stigma, shame, and secrecy about erotic expression obstructed absolutely random samples of sexual behavior. Moreover, existing case study research did not supply adequate typologies or predictive trends. Kinsey had spent the 1920s and early 1930s climbing remote mountains and combing desert habitats collecting as many different varieties and specimens of gall wasps as possible. His zoology was taxonomic, probing interactions between the anatomy, physiology, psychology, and culture of organisms within their habitats. Gall wasp research findings informed his human sexuality research: no two individual specimens of any species were identical; therefore, normative prescriptions foundered. With the ordinariness of massive diversity within any given species, he addressed frequency issues as "average," "many," or "rare" or in terms of degrees of similarity or difference. He studied human sexual behavior identically.

Kinsey departed from his sex research predecessors by representing reported sexual behavior in statistical terms. In the language of "means," "medians," "averages," "frequencies," "accumulations," and "coefficients," he recast sexual behavior. Instead of polarizing behaviors into normal/pathological, moral/immoral, heterosexual/homosexual, and other dualisms, he plotted human sexual options and behaviors as covalent points along a natural spectrum or continuum. His hypothesis of hugely varied human sexual behavior stood to dispel many sex-polarized generalizations.

Here a paradox emerged. On the one hand, he asserted sex differences in his critique of woman-oriented sex research that omitted or pathologized male sexual experience. On the other hand, he rejected the mire of gender stereotypes, alive to the possibility that the sexes might not be so erotically different. Alternatively, he allowed that variations *within* each sex may be more significant than average differences *between* the sexes.[8]

Kinsey responded to the same context as peer researchers, both past and contemporary. He adopted newly developed sociological approaches while continuing to privilege the biological and taxonomical methods he cultivated during his work with gall wasps. In essence, he participated in the shift from individual narrative toward broader concerns with averages, patterns, and representational samples.

Late nineteenth-century sex researchers used the case study method to gather and present their evidence to their fellow researchers. They highlighted abnormal aspects of human sexual behavior and desire, capitalizing on the sensational to garner professional support while documenting, naming, and classifying sexual deviations and focusing on the psychological and biological origins of aberrant sexual behaviors and desires. Terms used to cast these behaviors often underscored sexual deviations as threats to modern society through racially coded terminology that, though applied broadly to Anglo-Saxons and Germans, nonetheless posed a threat to the white race. Richard von Krafft-Ebing, Viennese neuropsychologist, believed that he charted marks of degeneration and arbiters of the effects of modern society on the populations of Europe. While some researchers would have concurred with Krafft-Ebing, the debate surrounding the degeneration narrative would last well into the twentieth century. Britain's Havelock Ellis and, eventually, Sigmund Freud stated that same-sex desires (often the focus of early sex researchers) were often congenital and did not necessarily indicate the presence of degeneration or psychosis within an individual.[9]

Prewar and interwar American sex researchers confronted a context of heightened pathologization of sexual behavior. Pervasive fears of venereal disease affecting national troop strength and the Jim Crow decades spurred eugenics, as well as various social uplift and reform movements. Most grounded themselves in gendered and racialized narratives privileging white middle-class marriages and families. As well, matters such as "the white slave trade," free love, and feminist challenges to traditional marriage connected American sex research with activists and reform associations.

In this context, Kinsey would advance his own project by very different methods. Sex researchers addressing psychological and social aspects of human sexuality developed only small data sets, often advancing moralistic approaches. At worst, they wallowed in prescription rather than recorded actual behavior. The move away from the preceding generation of sex researchers' narrative case studies toward quantifiable data sets, then, constituted a momentous methodological shift for the field.

Initially, earlier case study projects aimed to improve outreach methods of antiprostitution and venereal disease campaigns. The International Division of the Young Men's Christian Association, for example, engaged New York doctors Paul Achilles and Max Exner to assess the current state of young men's knowledge about sex and marriage and the effectiveness of anti–venereal disease and antiprostitution literature produced by the YMCA and the American Social Hygiene Association. Both used questionnaires, presenting readers with statistical reports alongside the older method of direct anecdotal quotations from respondents. This blended approach, they believed, provided the undeniable facts that only numbers could convey while also capturing the flavor of the respondents' responses.[10]

There were, however, exceptions to the use of questionnaires and interviews in American sexology. Clelia Duel Mosher, a clinical psychologist from Stanford University who later earned her MD from Johns Hopkins University in 1900, interviewed and studied fin de siècle female college graduates. Although using a small sample, her study was one of the first instances of American sex research conducted with modern scientific standards. Examining health, menstrual cycles, and exercise, Mosher refuted claims of female workplace inferiority, rejecting also physician-prescribed inactivity during menstruation and disease-mongering approaches to female gynecology. Though Mosher and her work never attained the fame of men in the field, she influenced her successors in a new sex research trajectory that addressed distinctive populations of women.[11]

For psychologists, psychiatrists, and psychoanalysts, however, the questionnaire presented problems. American psychological researchers in university and clinical settings extended or disputed Freud's psychoanalytic theories and methods. To this end, Gilbert Van Tassel Hamilton's project, *A Research in Marriage* (1929), used interviews. He asked: "Tell me all about your sex life: I wish to know as much as possible, not merely about your sexual acts, but about all the troublesome, shameful, painful difficulties which you may have had or may now have with sexual urges." Further, he admonished his interviewees: "You must be absolutely frank with me, else this examination cannot profitably be continued." The interview proved vastly more personal, requiring the interviewee to delve deeper. Words uttered became the data. Different topics were combined: age of first learning about sex, rate of premarital intercourse, and family experiences.

Diverse informants were combined: responses comparable with others, data open to arithmetic manipulation. As Michel Foucault held, this method diversified the case study through the creation and study of the pathologized individual—a history, a past. Yet it was no longer the actual individual who mattered but rather imagining the individual as a data point in a set of infinite points. The individual only mattered insofar as he or she was positioned within a representational population.[12]

Statistical procedures loomed large in interwar studies. Psychologists sought ways to measure human personality development and behavior. The biological approach to sex research centered on animal studies, while behavioral studies privileged psychological or sociological approaches. For example, Katharine Bement Davis's study of twenty-two hundred women's sex lives used sociological approaches deployed in a questionnaire mailed to Vassar graduates. While some individual narratives populate the text, it contains profuse tables and charts offering statistical analyses and comparisons of different groups of women (with regard to employment, age, and education, among others) with control groups.[13]

Research psychologists like Lewis Terman sought rational and measurable paradigms for personality development. In *Sex and Personality* (1936), he called for a measure that "can be applied to the individual and scored so as to locate the subject, with a fair degree of approximation, in terms of deviation from the mean of either sex." He devised the Masculinity-Femininity, or M-F, Test. It featured several different subsections, including personal interests, word associations, and the Rorschach test, administered in person. He explored the extent of men's and women's alignment with a "mean" or average of masculinity and femininity. Finding unsustainable such categories as "normal" and "abnormal," Terman reported ranges of masculinity and femininity that overlapped each other, acutely so among those disclosing same-sex desire.[14]

Other psychology researchers embraced the personal interview. Columbia University psychologist Carney Landis used "a *controlled interview* [that] consisted of questions concerning the facts and phantasies related to psychosexual development." These controlled interviews asked subjects about their sexual histories, fantasies, and emotional reactions to their sexual experiences. Landis's findings on homosexual psychosexual behavior and rejection of Freudian theories impressed Kinsey, who sought his help to obtain additional sex histories. Moreover, Landis, too, found among two hundred persons wide-ranging sexual behavior and desires. He believed that similar studies would reach similar results, establishing their value to peer scientists.[15]

The interrelation between personality development and sexual expression/behavior grounded interwar sex research. The belief in universal human endowment with degrees of maleness and femaleness infused explanations for sexual variation. Landis divided the life cycle into age eras: preadolescence, adolescence, and adulthood. Comparing the psychological development of a group of 146 "normal" women and 145 women who were institution patients but who did not have severe psychological impairments, he found their development more comparable than dissimilar. Dr. Robert Latou Dickinson (1861–1950), pioneer gynecological researcher and Kinsey mentor, concurred on the mix of maleness and femaleness, as did Margaret Sanger Clinic physicians Hannah and Abraham Stone.[16]

Conversely, Kinsey took a biological approach to human male sexual behavior. His reservations about the previous half century of sexology undoubtedly propelled him toward sociological methods. He also deplored the misleading narrowness of sex research grounded only in case studies and clinical populations. Doctors, marriage counselors, hospital staff, clergy, social workers, and related professionals saw only those diagnosed or self-identifying as troubled, afflicted, diseased, or disturbed. When it came to sexual behavior, clinical frameworks provided no basis on which to conjecture the nature of sexuality at large in any given population. Instead, biases permeated clinical samples.

One problem was the preponderance of women among patients or clients of clinical services. This skewed much published research. Informants were most readily accessible from obstetrics and gynecology wards, children's hospitals, birth control clinics, religious charities, and marriage counseling offices. The overrepresentation of women led researchers to advance as human norms for sexual behavior drawn from *feminine* preferences and concerns.

Race and ethnicity presented a comparable problem. Contributors to investigations vastly overrepresented white Americans, and they discussed their sexual lives with mainly white clinicians—mostly men—who so far had penned the bulk of scholarly studies. From some regions, including specific southern or "Negro" studies, more diverse evidence occasionally emerged. Yet racial and ethnic homogeneity predominated.[17]

Finally, overwhelming class bias afflicted existing studies of sexual behavior. Drawn from fee-paying patients and clients, informants reflected experiences of the well educated, unduly grounding generalizations and assumptions embedded in sex researchers' studies. Thus, many sexual patterns remained unstudied, even unknown, in published sex research.[18]

Kinsey disdained most predecessor sex research as impressionistic and scientifically unsound. A cluster of factors grounded his criticisms. The feminine, white, Protestant, and middle- to upper-class biases of most American sex research, outlined above, had serious intellectual and methodological consequences. Most explorations of erotic lives studied the only unambiguously legal sexual encounter: marriage. This reflected the preponderance of wives among the patients and clients populating most clinical studies. Consequently, erotic patterns that took place outside of conjugal relations—meaning any sexual experiences of children, adolescents, unmarried young adults, lifelong spinsters and bachelors, persons widowed or divorced, and the elderly—in general fell outside the gaze of sex researchers. Conjugal framing foreclosed investigation: universalized heterosexual coitus became the main, normal, and representative form of human sexual activity, plotted as the rationale of marriage and perhaps undertaken otherwise in premarital and extramarital encounters, including contracted ones. Such privileging of heterosexual coitus neglected distinctive patterns pertaining to frequent erotic experiences such as masturbation, petting, same-sex relations, and "animal contacts."[19]

The challenge for Kinsey was to secure a reopening of matters presumed settled. Interwar fascism suppressed European sex research. Nonhuman sex research garnered most of the available foundation and other sources of research funding in the United States, while clinical studies dominated work with humans. Sexuality needed study in the population at large, unselected for problems or pathology. Correspondents convinced him that practices that clinicians called "aberrant" were actually familiar and common, especially among working-class men and women never likely to darken a clinician's door. The criminal justice system punished sexual practices judged deviant by upper social levels, with savage consequences for young lower-class men.[20]

Elements of Kinsey's research methods and objectives already existed in early twentieth-century research. His predecessors and peers had moved beyond the simple collection and recording of case histories while also beginning to question the validity and utility of the questionnaire in favor of the more intensive interview. Additionally, the idea of sexual expression and personality existing on a continuum was already part of the psychological explanations for personal and sexual diversity.[21] Kinsey's distinctive contribution here, derived from his extensive zoological field research expertise, was a keen understanding of the rigor required to make interviewing reliable. By this, he meant the size, scope, and extent of interviews required to sample and study any given population at large. As well, he contributed another axiomatic lesson from zoology research, namely, that variation was, in fact, natural and abundantly visible throughout the organic world. These approaches chimed in harmony with the inclination of sex researchers to plot sexual characteristics and patterns along continua of various kinds in a rejection of rigid bifurcations and rigid dichotomous norms. Expanding such approaches from animal to human sexual behavior was hardly a vast leap from existing understandings. If masculinity and femininity could exist on a continuum, then why not human sexual outlets and behavior?

American sources of funding support facilitated such conceptual innovation. Except for early attempts to study the effectiveness of eugenics literature, most sex researchers secured support from small grants awarded by the Committee for

Research in Problems of Sex, and the committee actively solicited and promoted the work of the investigators it funded. An examination of the contribution of philanthropy to the history of sex research allows better appreciation of both the opportunities and challenges presented by Kinsey's project at a crucial juncture.

Philanthropy and Sex Research

> It is not by chance that the Committee has come to give preference to neurological and psychobiological approaches to problems of sex and reproduction. Instead, this decision has been taken in attempted adaptation to two groups of fact or circumstance: one, the increasing vogue and self-dependence of hormonal studies, and two, the urgent need for more nearly adequate knowledge of sexual behavior, its conditions, modification and controls, as the basis for social guidance.
>
> Robert M. Yerkes, "Twenty-Second Annual Report: Committee for Research in Problems of Sex, Division of Medical Sciences, National Research Council for the Year July 1, 1942 to June 30, 1943" (Washington, DC, 1943), 3

Historians call the Progressive Era big philanthropy's "golden age." Individuals and families who profited from Gilded Age industrialization sought to reduce their tax burdens. John D. Rockefeller Sr., for instance, earmarked for philanthropic contribution shares of his Standard Oil Company. He envisioned a foundation that would aid in the research and amelioration of social problems, tasking his son, John D. Rockefeller Jr., to secure its establishment. The influential cofounders he assembled eventually incorporated the Rockefeller Foundation in New York City in April 1919.[22]

The initial Rockefeller Foundation projects expanded an established mission. One example was the study, treatment, and eradication of hook worm. The problem was first tackled in the South, and the Foundation then expanded its work to afflicted international sites, including China, resulting in the founding of a medical education division there. With a priority on factual research as a prerequisite for treating social problems, the Foundation expanded its focus to support US medical researchers, as well as the funding of university medical programs at home and abroad.

The Committee for Research in Problems of Sex was the 1921 brainchild of the Medical Division of the Rockefeller Foundation. Founded in collaboration with the Bureau of Social Hygiene, its general secretary, Katherine Bement Davis (1860–1935), forwarded researchers' proposals to the committee and dispersed grants to researchers. Initially, committee support targeted individuals irrespective of their professional appointment or standing. Soon, it became plain that although the group sought to fund individuals, it realized that merit-based funding alone risked the field's uneven development. The committee had shifted by 1923 to supporting applicants affiliated with laboratories or existing institutes, as well as facilitating the creation of five research institutes, some of which continued their work for over twenty years. For the most part, though, "sex problems" research emerged in other less-centralized locations.[23]

Most grants were provided to individual researchers or groups for one year. They could renew the grant for additional years. The majority of these first projects were in endocrinology and worked with animal groups, but they sought human applications. From this work came key postwar findings that attempted to find corollaries in humans and provided some of the first discoveries about the process of ovulation and the isolation and synthetic production of estrogen, progesterone, testosterone, insulin, and other hormones. Though initially seeking studies of humans, the committee resisted funding nonmedical projects. During his term as chair of the committee, though, George W. Corner, key figure in the history of the Institute for Sex Research, challenged this bias. A deep admirer of Kinsey's scientific acumen, Corner would later lobby the committee to change direction, carving a path for the direct study of human sexuality.[24]

By 1928 the Committee for Research in Problems of Sex listed twenty-one different grant-supported projects. The funding, totaling $123,180 for that year ($1.7 million in today's values), was split between biological and psychological projects usually undertaken in medical sciences institutions. Soon, support targets broadened to include projects deploying psychoanalytic and sociological methods, a testament to the enlarging legitimacy of psychology and psychoanalysis in the United States. Still, efforts to move toward direct studies of human sexuality encountered obstacles. When Gilbert V. Hamilton (1877–1943) submitted his proposed psychological study of marriage, Rockefeller Foundation officers disputed which program should support his work. The Medical Division viewed Hamilton's psychological approach as insufficiently scientific, while the committee, still wary of direct human studies, resisted a multiyear commitment. Consequently, the Bureau of Social Hygiene undertook direct support (effectively placing his work under the auspices of the Medical Division), providing $25,000 (in today's values, $346,000) for the project in 1928. Later, as Hamilton prepared to publish his study, controversy reignited. Leaders in the bureau, committee, and foundation debated open association with the study, delaying its publication. The Medical Division won, and *A Research in Marriage* was published in 1929.[25]

Hamilton's work triumphed, paving the way for more direct human studies. From its inception to 1947, the committee provided over four hundred grants. The committee's budgets suggest that it spent well over $50 million in support of researchers, making the committee the central funder of US sex research.

In 1941 Alfred C. Kinsey, Clyde E. Martin, and Wardell B. Pomeroy submitted their first application. They secured a modest $1,600 grant (worth $48,800 in 2015 US dollar values) for the first year. Thereafter, the committee increased the grant, until by 1948 it reserved for the project nearly half the annual operating budget. This constituted a significant departure from its previous funding protocols. Why? Because since the early 1940s, Kinsey's was the type of project that the committee sought to foster: its leader was a reputable tenured professor with access to university support and research materials, and the project was on an expansionist trajectory with a planned series of research outcomes, promising a scale and a social significance surpassing all previous studies.[26] With the success of Hamilton's human project, committee members saw Kinsey's project as "the next Hamilton." *A Research in Marriage* was an intensive interview study of just one hundred married couples, yet Kinsey's undertaking promised a grander scale, addressing many more questions in erotic life than its worthy predecessor. For the committee's shift to supporting human studies, though, Kinsey owed a direct debt to Hamilton.[27]

The promise of the Kinsey project confronted the committee with questions as to whether it should support sustainability in wartime. Even early in the postwar era, the committee grappled with reduced funding levels, imposing "uncertainties for fundamental research incident to the circumstances of war and of transition from war to peace." In 1946 Yerkes reported on the diversity "in the nature of research opportunities and promotional demands." Balancing between new, short-term studies and "major projects, such as Dr. Kinsey's, which require not only continuity but in some instances increasing support over an indefinite period," presented quite a problem. The solution sought was application to the Rockefeller Foundation, which then approved "$120,000 to the National Research Council for support through its Committee for Research in Problems of Sex of the work of Dr. Alfred C. Kinsey of Indiana University during three years beginning July 1, 1946," not to exceed $40,000 in any single year of the award.[28]

In terms of present-day buying power, the $120,000 grant equaled $1,459,144.62. For Indiana University, this grant assured the national and international standing achieved by Kinsey's project, instantly enhancing the research profile of the small university amidst impressive postwar expansion. President Herman B Wells, seeking to enhance his institution's research prowess by attracting high-quality professors trained at prestigious universities, evinced pride in Kinsey's progress and the scale of funding.[29]

The problem of sustainability, however, surpassed financial arrangements. Researchers before Kinsey had worked on small populations often tied to clinical settings. They had both the space and the necessary legal means to ensure confidentiality without the need of an institute. Conversely, Kinsey's project lacked the institutional support afforded those in the medical sciences. Kinsey's location in a conservative social and political context compelled him to construct protection for his data and expanding collections.

Establishing a "Sex Library"

Whatever the intent of the Research Council might be now, it seems unwise to have an arrangement which makes it legally possible for an unknown group of persons to decide the future of the library and of the other collected material.

Alfred C. Kinsey to Robert M. Yerkes, May 16, 1946

In 1920 no one would have predicted Kinsey's career trajectory. When he joined Indiana University after completing his doctoral training at Harvard, he seemed set to advance further his gall wasp studies and teach zoology and evolutionary biology classes, not destined to direct the nation's first academic sex research institute. Biographers venture personal reasons for Kinsey's interest in questions of sex (family background, his time in the Boy Scouts of America, a highly oppressive religious upbringing), but he drew some impetus from the needs of his students.[30]

Many questions about sex and marriage beset undergraduates. Since the early 1930s, marriage courses offered by friends and colleagues at various universities and colleges attracted Kinsey's attention. He soon led a group of Indiana University professors tasked with devising a multidisciplinary course offering medical, biological, legal, sociological, and psychological perspectives on marriage. The first offering in 1938, for upper-level undergraduates, engaged couples, and interested faculty and staff, received positive reviews. The sessions for students seeking Kinsey's personal advice soon evolved into "consultations," which functioned as the pilot projects that would become the foundations for the interview used to gather sex histories. In 1941, partly provoked by protests from Dr. Thurman Rice from Indiana University School of Medicine, Wells gave Kinsey an ultimatum: either teach the course or continue the research. A field researcher at heart, Kinsey took the research path without question.[31]

Relieved of his teaching duties for the marriage course (but still teaching biology and zoology courses), Kinsey devised a research team and made trips to cities such as Indianapolis and Chicago to gather sex histories. An undergraduate named Clyde Martin was the team's first member; he was later joined by psychologists Wardell Pomeroy and Glen Ramsey. Kinsey trained all of them in the interviewing techniques he had designed. These had been devised carefully as methods for obtaining sometimes elusive information during his long years of exchange with diverse social groups on whom he depended to execute his gall wasp research in habitats all over North America. He refined interview techniques further during student consultations. To optimize truthful and honest answers, Kinsey encouraged his interviewers to adjust their own language, demeanor, and behavior to best match interviewee backgrounds. For instance, interviewers might use region,

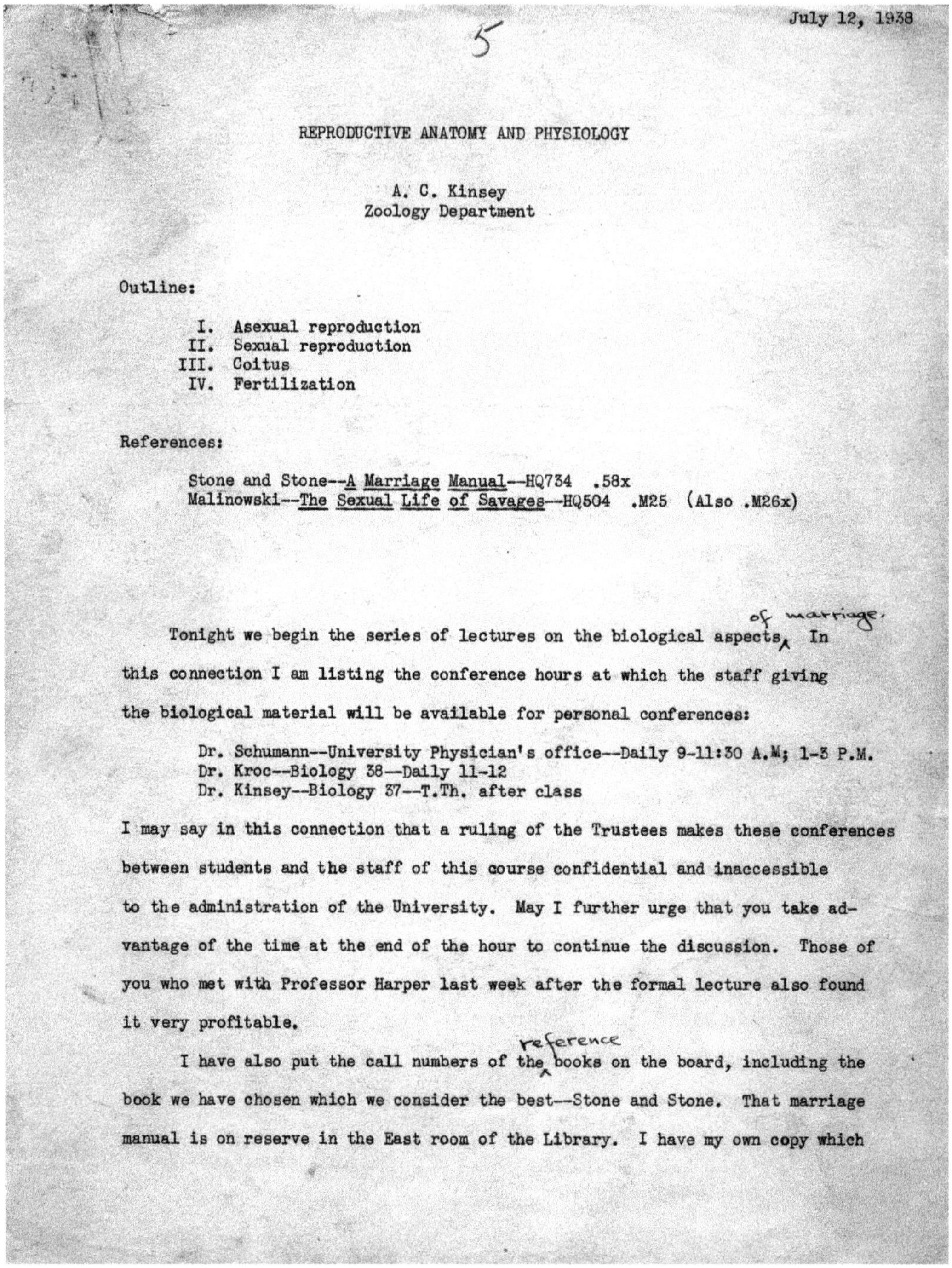

July 12, 1938

5

REPRODUCTIVE ANATOMY AND PHYSIOLOGY

A. C. Kinsey
Zoology Department

Outline:

    I.   Asexual reproduction
   II.   Sexual reproduction
  III.   Coitus
   IV.   Fertilization

References:

    Stone and Stone--A Marriage Manual--HQ734 .58x
    Malinowski--The Sexual Life of Savages--HQ504 .M25 (Also .M26x)

    Tonight we begin the series of lectures on the biological aspects. *of marriage.* In

this connection I am listing the conference hours at which the staff giving

the biological material will be available for personal conferences:

    Dr. Schumann--University Physician's office--Daily 9-11:30 A.M; 1-3 P.M.
    Dr. Kroc--Biology 38--Daily 11-12
    Dr. Kinsey--Biology 37--T.Th. after class

I may say in this connection that a ruling of the Trustees makes these conferences

between students and the staff of this course confidential and inaccessible

to the administration of the University. May I further urge that you take ad-

vantage of the time at the end of the hour to continue the discussion. Those of

you who met with Professor Harper last week after the formal lecture also found

it very profitable.

    I have also put the call numbers of the *reference* books on the board, including the

book we have chosen which we consider the best--Stone and Stone. That marriage

manual is on reserve in the East room of the Library. I have my own copy which

Figure 1.4. Marriage course lecture outline, July 12, 1938. Though not the first indication of his interest in sexuality, the marriage course proved to be a turning point for Kinsey and his research project. Photo courtesy of Kinsey Institute Library and Special Collections.

Figure 1.5. Kinsey interviewing a subject, ca. 1948. The Kinsey interview was intensive, with all data encoded on a single sheet of paper. Photo courtesy of Kinsey Institute Library and Special Collections.

class, or subculturally specific words for masturbation. The interview itself could take up to three hours of rapid-fire questioning, with built-in accuracy checks, including retakes.[32]

Kinsey added substantially to the sex library he started for the marriage course. Works in medicine, literature, biology, and sociology, among others, were his top priorities, and traveling to gather sex histories provided Kinsey with opportunities to find collectors, dealers, and agents and purchase rare books. For instance, Harry H. Freilich, a Chicago pulmonary specialist, collected literature on sexuality as a personal interest. Eventually, on successive Chicago interviewing trips, Kinsey purchased much of Freilich's collection as the doctor neared retirement and moved to Florida.[33]

Kinsey intended to create the library to ground the project, with some items collected during his time lecturing for the marriage course. Kinsey paid for these books out of his own pocket, but the costs soon became prohibitive as the size of the library increased. Dilemmas ballooned once word of his collection efforts spread. Connections in New York, Chicago, and Philadelphia soon spread word

Table 1.1. Comparison of sexual histories collected and CRPS Funding, 1941–1947

Year	Cumulative histories collected[1]	CRPS funding[2]	2016 equivalent[3]
1941	1,700	$1,600	$26,215.29
1942	3,000	$7,500	$110,821.93
1943	3,500	$23,000	$320,209.19
1944, April 1	5,500		
1944, July 1	6,100	$25,000	$342,120.74
1945	7,850	$28,000	$374,660.22
1946	10,440	$35,000	$432,300.26
1947	11,600	$40,000	$432,023.32

[1] These estimates are taken from the annual reports of the Institute of Sex Research.

[2] Funding from the Committee for Research in Problems of Sex ran on a fiscal year of July 1 to June 30.

[3] Conversions created using the CPI Inflation Calculation of the National Bureau of Labor Statistics.

of Kinsey's collection, generating keen interest from dealers, donors, and legacies. Bidding for valuable rare books could be competitive. Kinsey later recalled making rapid decisions and having to pay cash on the spot or risk losing books desired for his ever-enlarging sex library to another interested party.[34]

As well, he needed to ensure the confidentiality of thousands of interviewees. Members of the National Research Council's Committee for Research in Problems of Sex, through which Kinsey's project received Rockefeller Foundation support, gave this issue increasing attention in 1946. As Kinsey concentrated on the drafting of the male volume, his acute concerns led to a quest for a protective operating structure for these precious materials, perhaps via a designated independent incorporation. Already, whiffs of moralistic opposition and advance press prurience presented new public relations concerns for the Rockefeller Foundation as a major funder of US and international natural, behavioral, and social science research. Understanding of Kinsey's priority mission to protect the sources and resources that grounded the forthcoming first major publication from the project deepened with the committee's agreement to reimburse Kinsey the $1,400 he had spent so far on rare books, journals, photographs, and ephemera. This made the collections, technically, the committee's investment and asset.[35] Robert Yerkes, chairman of the committee, tried to assure Kinsey that the committee would not suddenly remove the library from the incorporation. Unconvinced, Kinsey reiterated his unwillingness to risk loss of ownership of the hard-won library collections in this transfer, "as long as there is specific opposition from any quarter of the National Research Council to the possibility of recognizing our incorporation," and thus title to the collections.[36]

Figure 1.6. Alfred C. Kinsey, Herman B Wells, and George W. Corner at the Institute, ca. 1948. The relationship between Kinsey, Wells, and Corner, who led the Committee for Research in Problems of Sex after Robert Yerkes retired, proved crucial to the founding of the Institute for Sex Research. Photo courtesy of Kinsey Institute Library and Special Collections.

Yet foundation legal advisors insisted, for fiscal, auditing, and managerial reasons, that entities for endowment should not be smaller than universities in general and, in this case, than Indiana University specifically. Hence, committee members proposed that Indiana University establish the institute as its own unit, with appropriate guarantees as to the independence and disposition of the data and collections.[37] The committee even offered acceptable names: Yerkes coined the Institute for Sex Research as one of three possibilities.[38]

With the committee warming to the idea of incorporation, Kinsey turned to Alan Gregg, chairman of Rockefeller's Medical Division, for advice on payment for the library. Kinsey sought $14,000 ($257,000 in 2015 values). Wells, as an ardent supporter of Kinsey, also sought expansion of Indiana University's research undertakings in putting the proposal to Gregg. The disbursement became final in 1948.[39]

Hence, it was not Kinsey's human sexual behavior research project itself that brought the Institute into being. The research did not compel an autonomous institute. Indeed, plenty of Indiana University professors undertook externally funded research projects, as did academic Rockefeller grant recipients at other universities, without the establishment of a distinctive and semi-independent research institute as a stable location for their work.[40] Rather, it was both the disposition of the confidential data created in the sex histories and the ever-enlarging collections that necessitated the founding of the Institute in the view of the project's external funders, a position readily accepted by the Indiana University president.[41]

After due negotiation with Wells, the University counsel, and his own attorney, Kinsey relinquished all of his collections to the University's newly constituted Institute for Sex Research on April 8, 1947.[42] The incorporation documents provided for a standing board of trustees of the new institute comprised of the original research staff. These individuals, the committee believed, would have the highest stakes in the continuation of the new Institute and would be the best stewards of its future. In addition to the creation of trustees, the documents outlined a continuation process in the event of the addition of new staff, the death of Kinsey and the necessity for a new director, and the appropriations of the library and research materials should the Institute ever dissolve.

The documents underscore Kinsey's deep belief in the value of his research. They detail the Rockefeller Foundation's right to acquire or disburse the library and research material in the event of the collapse of the Institute. In the event that the Foundation refused acquisition, the library and collections were to go to another high-quality research university that could ensure the preservation of the collection. Given the lengths to which Kinsey went to preserve the library, it is clear that he hoped that the Rockefeller Foundation would, in the event of dissolution, recognize the importance of the library and collected data and act accordingly or that a capable university would likewise realize the value of such a collection and acquire it for future use.[43]

With the research his top priority, Kinsey included in the incorporation documents an addendum. He relinquished his rights to the library and sold the collection of books and other materials to the Institute for Sex Research for one dollar, understanding that he would be reimbursed for nearly $10,000, with an additional $4,000 to aid in the purchase and further expansion of the collection. With the Rockefeller Foundation approval for the special grant for the library and its role in helping found the Institute, the signal of support for the research library and data collection at Indiana University was clear.[44]

With the details settled, the Institute for Sex Research was officially incorporated on April 8, 1947. Although other considerations figured into incorporation, Kinsey knew that the library was pivotal to the execution of the project. He wished to make its preservation and growth the centerpiece of the incorporation process.

— a —

ARTICLES OF INCORPORATION

of

INSTITUTE FOR SEX RESEARCH, INC.

The undersigned, being three or more natural persons of lawful age, at least a majority of whom are citizens of the United States, do hereby adopt the following Articles of Incorporation, representing beforehand to the Secretary of State of the State of Indiana and all persons whom it may concern, that a membership list or lists of the above named corporation for which certificate of incorporation is hereby applied for, have heretofore been opened in accordance with law and that at least three (3) persons have signed such membership list.

Be it further remembered that the following Articles of Incorporation and all matters heretofore done or hereafter to be done are in accordance with "An Act concerning domestic and foreign corporations not for profit, providing for fees, providing penalties for the violation thereof, and repealing certain laws," approved March 7, 1935, and all acts amendatory thereof and supplemental thereto.

1. The name of this corporation shall be....Institute for Sex Research, Inc.

(Name must include the word "Corporation" or "Incorporated" or one of the abbreviations thereof.)

2. The purpose or purposes for which it is formed are as follows:

(a) To conduct research on human sex behavior including its biological, psychological, medical, physiological, sociological, anthropological and all other aspects by continuing and enlarging the research project on said subject heretofore carried on at Indiana University under the direction of Alfred C. Kinsey with the assistance of the Medical Division of the Rockefeller Foundation, through the National Research Council, by its Committee for Research on Problems of Sex.

(b) To accept, hold, use, administer and expend income, gifts and grants of funds whether in the form of cash, securities, royalties or any other form of property or income for use in connection with such research project.

(c) To acquire, hold, own and administer research material, libraries, case histories, and other materials relating to the subject matter of said research project.

(d) To acquire, own, hold, rent, lease, sell and convey such real estate and personal property as may be reasonably necessary to the carrying out of the corporation's general purposes.

(e) To do all things reasonably incidental to the corporation's general purpose which are permitted by law.

Figure 1.7. Articles of incorporation, page 2. The articles of incorporation were much broader than a mere means to legally separate the Institute from Indiana University. They provided for the collecting and stewardship of items, letters, papers, and data relevant to the ongoing research project. Photo courtesy of Kinsey Institute Library and Special Collections.

Figure 1.8 Biology Hall (now Swain Hall East), the first home of the Institute for Sex Research, pictured here in 1938. Photo courtesy of Indiana University Archives.

Figure 1.9. The original Institute for Sex Research bookplate, ca. 1948. As a creator of plates and molds, gynecological research pioneer Dr. Robert Latou Dickinson designed a new insignia for the Institute as a gift. Photo courtesy of Kinsey Institute Library and Special Collections.

Figure 1.10. Alfred C. Kinsey, Clyde E. Martin, and Wardell B. Pomeroy, 1947, the original research team, founders of the Institute for Sex Research, and authors of the first Kinsey Report. Photo courtesy of Kinsey Institute Library and Special Collections.

Arguably, the inauguration of Kinsey's human sexual behavior collections and projects enjoyed a uniquely favorable context. Across the 1930s and early 1940s, he had already made similar arrangements for his collection of gall wasps, ensuring that the show boxes of specimens and the library would remain together. By the latter 1940s, he also led the largest sex research project in the nation, at a time when the Committee for Research in Problems of Sex sought human studies. Until Kinsey, projects had been funded by the committee with much smaller grants, without the long-term plan that Kinsey envisioned or the library he had amassed. Continuing research and the reevaluation of previous work, of course, meant that a centralized library would facilitate the project's success through a welcoming location for scholars. For its first years, all this material and the Institute's research staff had as their address Biology Hall, the east wing of Swain Hall on the Bloomington campus. Meanwhile, enthusiastic Kinsey ally Dr. Robert Latou Dickinson, a talented artist, even designed a founding bookplate for collection items.

Worldwide, the sex research community knew of the burning of Magnus Hirschfeld's library and collections in 1933 in Berlin. To redress that cultural atrocity and honor the now deceased Hirschfeld (he died in 1935) by securing the world's largest repository of sex research materials became a goal that Kinsey happily embraced. His library exemplifies the crossroads at which he and the project were founded: he collected the works of the previous generation of sex researchers, and he assured that his own work and the work of his contemporaries would be collected, cataloged, and recorded. Though Kinsey worried about the preservation of his collections and data, it was the advice and strategic planning of the Rockefeller Foundation and the Committee for Research in Problems of Sex that influenced the founding of the Institute for Sex Research at Indiana University. This unique solution to the problem of the library meant that Indiana faculty, staff, and students may access today a research collection that might not have existed at all.

The Institute for Sex Research represented more than just the incorporation of a project. It also constituted more than the legal separation of the research and the Institute from Indiana University and other political matters. A look back to the methods of sex researchers, the funding and philanthropy available for sex researchers, and Kinsey's individual disposition reveals that the Institute's foundation pivoted on preserving for future generations its collections, as well as the revered idea of academic freedom entailing the right to study sex and to proclaim that study openly. Kinsey's research methods and long-term plans for the project required the centralization and concretization of the project to ensure its permanence, protection, and capacity for continued expansion.

2
Making the Kinsey Reports
(1947–1956)

We have not understood how nearly alike females and males may be in their sexual responses. We have perpetrated the age old traditions concerning the slower responsiveness of the female, the earlier sexual development of the female, the greater extent of erogenous areas on the body of females, the idea that there are basic differences in the nature of orgasm among males and females, the greater emotional content of the female's response and still other ideas which are not based on scientifically correct data and which now appear to be incorrect.

Alfred C. Kinsey, Wardell B. Pomeroy, Clyde E. Martin, and Paul H. Gebhard, *Sexual Behavior in the Human Female*, 12

WHEN THE INSTITUTE FOR SEX RESEARCH OPENED its doors in April 1947, the "male volume" was almost complete. The January 1948 release of *Sexual Behavior in the Human Male* unleashed an avalanche of media coverage, reviews, and public interest in sex research. Immediately dubbed the Kinsey Report, its currency intensified pressure to produce the counterpart "female volume."[1]

Several strands form a portrait of the Institute during the making of the volumes soon known as the Kinsey Reports. From the hoped-for one hundred thousand sex histories, Kinsey sought to establish the contours and extent of natural sexual capacities, on the one hand, and the contribution of cultural influences, on the other—in short, a theorizing of sexual behavior that would disentangle the mammalian from the sociocultural. Sexual behaviors appeared to be part inherent and part contingent, depending on upbringing, community mores, and social group. Indeed, Kinsey emphasized conditioning, cultural learning, socialization, and education, terms he used in characterizing diverse human sexual patterns.[2] Blocked from meeting black Americans in segregated regions, his team disagreed about sampling adequacy and interpretation, the research falling short on sound African American sampling.[3] The same held for working-class female and regional sampling. Despite these key shortcomings, Rockefeller Foundation grants, book contracts, and associated researchers made the Kinsey Reports, drawn from thousands of individual accounts, possible.

The methods, findings, arguments, and implications of the 1948 male volume need examination in view of its enormous cultural impact throughout the late 1940s and beyond. It reached number two on the *New York Times*'s nonfiction best-seller list. Thousands of often moving letters arrived from members of the general public, who sought Kinsey's advice on intimate personal or family dilemmas arising from sexual or reproductive problems. He tried to answer every letter, most of which disclosed the significance that readers accorded to the Kinsey Reports. Meanwhile, he developed intense exchange relationships with diverse scholars, clinicians, journalists, writers, and other professionals. They offered data, criticisms, and advice.

These inputs altered pathways to the second Kinsey Report. With vastly different evidence and research, Kinsey penned a female volume dissimilar to the first Kinsey Report. Sex differences in behavior, irreducible to single or convincing causes, challenged his default faith in natural erotic complementarity and similarity between the sexes. New methods, arguments, and hypotheses became necessary.

The Kinsey Reports developed alongside other activities of the new Institute. As noted in chapter 1, Kinsey's collections grounded the Institute's initial raison d'être and much of its working operations. Meanwhile, Institute progress benefited from sex research bequests, as well as friendship and the support of key figures in science, letters, and culture. Contributors from abroad also assisted collections development until 1950, when US Customs confiscated imports, unleashing an unparalleled academic freedom legal case. With the 1953 female volume published, reviewed, and debated, the Institute had evolved, by then involving many constituencies. As well, it was a vibrant part of Indiana University's campus life.

The female proved much more controversial than the male volume. Partly this reflected the context of the deepening Cold War. The 1954 Select Committee to Investigate Tax-Exempt Foundations and Comparable Organizations, often known as the Reece Committee after one of its chairmen, Congressman B. Carroll Reece, excoriated the Rockefeller Foundation for its support of Kinsey's research, the committee's McCarthyist report calling sex research a threat to the American family, leaving the nation ripe for Communist takeover. With fears that its tax exemption faced peril, the foundation canceled Kinsey's research funding in late

1954.[4] From then until mid-1956, Kinsey sought alternative sources of support, but with little success.[5]

In this context, Kinsey began a new book on abortion and sexual lives. The central importance of reproduction, fear of unwanted conception, and difficulties with existing forms of birth control emerged from the 1953 rumination on nearly six thousand women's sexual histories, which had been added to existing perspectives already gleaned from the similar number of men's histories grounding the 1948 male volume. Kinsey agreed to an invitation from the medical director of the Planned Parenthood Federation of America, Dr. Mary Steichen Calderone, to present his data on criminal abortion in April 1955. Afterward, he designed a new fourteen-chapter book manuscript simply entitled *Abortion*. He secured two Rockefeller-sourced grants and began writing. His death in 1956 at the age of sixty-two ended these post–female volume endeavors.[6]

The Male Volume

Other mammals must be taken into account if we are to understand the relative effects of heredity and culture in human behavior.

Alfred C. Kinsey, Wardell B. Pomeroy, and Clyde E. Martin, *Sexual Behavior in the Human Male*, 581–82

I am surprised that you missed the point of the use of animal behavior as an explanation of what is biologically inherent behavior in the human. It looks as if 1859 Darwin, and all of the body of work which the evolutionists have done since then is still being overlooked. We have been particularly surprised to see this objection come from physicians, because every last one of them is supposed to have had training in mammalian anatomy and physiology as a basis for understanding human anatomy and physiology. Unless one is willing to discard the whole concept of evolution, one will have to accept mammalian behavior as one source of what is natural in human behavior.

Alfred C. Kinsey to Albert Ellis, August 16, 1948

Sexual Behavior in the Human Male (1948) reported on the interview-grounded sexual histories of 5,300 men who were interviewed between 1938 and 1946. Kinsey quantified diverse aspects of groups of men's experiences via the concept of the sexual outlet. Stimuli to orgasm through six sources—nocturnal emissions, masturbation, petting, coitus, same-sex contacts, and animal contacts—undergirded the volume's abundant tables and charts. Kinsey's method diverged from interwar research, centered for the most part on the study of marriage, and thereby privileging heterosexual coitus as normative. Quantification of reported orgasm rendered all outlets equal, none "the norm" or most prevalent for all. Taking a given man's lifelong sexual history, his "total sexual outlet," as Kinsey termed it, mapped an array of outlets, some featured in youth, others later in life, no two men identical.

The 1948 male volume centered on the interview and its analysis. Interviewers optimized rapport and provided assurances of confidentiality, critical with a subject that was delicate, taboo, and often beset by shame, guilt, or fear. Patterns emerged. Certain interviewees evaded, exaggerated, misled, or lied. Kinsey stressed subcultures in hypothesizing sexual behavior as learned. Erotic preferences matched pleasurable early reinforcement of some outlets, while disapproval of others produced aversion. Once established and reinforced, preferred outlets proved recalcitrant. Hence adolescent experiences shaped adult patterns. Age, then, became a decisive variable.

Quantifying outlets across sexual lives produced startling results. When reporting, as the male volume did, on the composite sexual outlets of nearly six thousand men's sexual histories, a key finding was that marital coitus accounted for only 64 percent of reported total orgasms. In other words, more than a third of men's outlets derived from nonconjugal erotic activities. Moreover, if this was the overall average, then for a significant portion of the men sampled, any conjugal percentage proved lower still. Unsolicited correspondents also convinced Kinsey that relatively few men obtained their "total sexual outlet" either from exclusively heterosexual coitus or from solely homosexual contacts. This conviction had informed his 1941 critique of simplistic endocrinal explanations of homosexuality.[7] His argument intrigued peer researchers and clinicians who also received unsolicited requests for sexual advice.

Kinsey's deprivileging of marital coitus made the full spectrum of sexual behaviors visible. Findings well substantiated Kinsey's claim of men's lifelong and diverse array of sexual outlets. His zoological background framed such diversities as natural to the human species, variably manifested in individuals. Contingent moralistic stigma, or punishment, could not eradicate the natural grounding of condemned behaviors, especially when other mammals undertook similar or comparable acts. Yet a crucial element of his analysis was the also powerful modifying influence of culture on human sexual behavior.

Adult sexual orientation appeared to follow pleasurable reinforcement of early behavior. Sexual identity inclinations might be channeled. A sixteen-year-old son of a southern tobacco farmer feared that he was homosexual. With the observation that heterosexual erotic techniques required skill and practice, Kinsey advised the boy to condition himself toward heterosexual behavior. Spend more time with girls, since often "we find that a person who has not gotten along with girls has simply never spent enough time with them socially." He suggested also

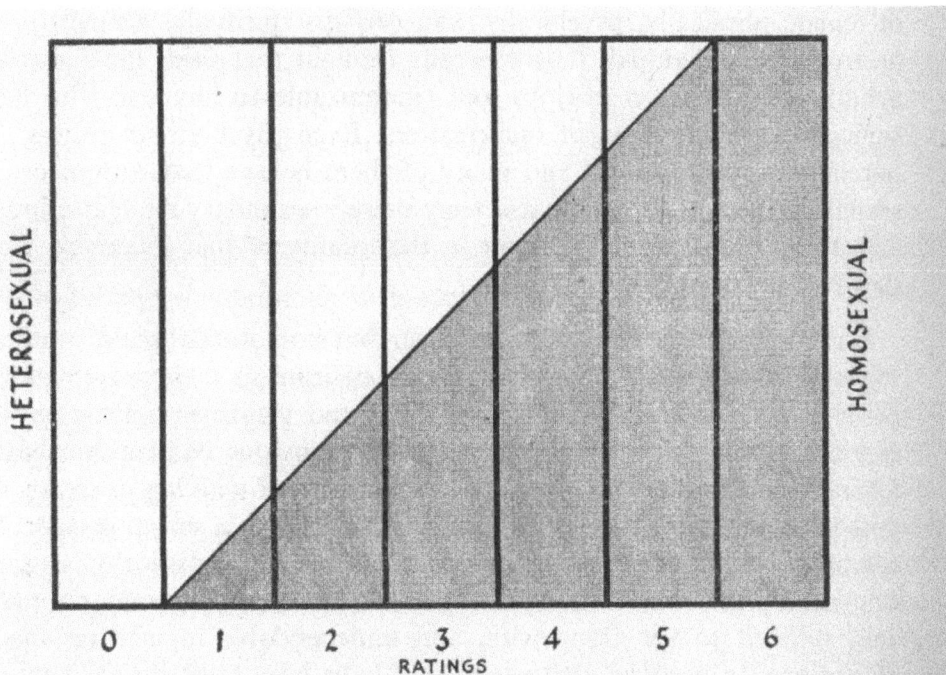

HETEROSEXUAL
HOMOSEXUAL
0 1 2 3 4 5 6
RATINGS
Figure 161. Heterosexual-homosexual rating scale
Based on both psychologic reactions and overt experience, individuals rate as follows:
0. Exclusively heterosexual with no homosexual
1. Predominantly heterosexual, only incidentally homosexual
2. Predominantly heterosexual, but more than incidentally homosexual
3. Equally heterosexual and homosexual
4. Predominantly homosexual, but more than incidentally heterosexual
5. Predominantly homosexual, but incidentally heterosexual
6. Exclusively homosexual

Figure 2.1. The Kinsey scale, 1948. One of Kinsey's innovations in *Sexual Behavior in the Human Male* was the heterosexual-homosexual scale, which measured the diversity of sexual behavior instead of classifying it into fixed and dichotomous sexual orientations. Photo courtesy of Kinsey Institute Library and Special Collections.

that a psychologist could help the boy make a heterosexual adjustment.[8] Kinsey's conviction that culture conditioned most sexual behavior enabled him to reassure troubled correspondents. If cultures constructed sexual attitudes, beliefs, judgments, and guilt, then logically such negative effects could be *deconstructed* or at least mitigated. His correspondents' erotic changes suggested that learned sexual problems could be alleviated.

Hence, Kinsey counseled against rigid classification of sexual orientations via any given choice of partner. Men and women had both heterosexual and homosexual erotic contacts—sometimes serially, sometimes simultaneously. Thirty-seven percent of men and 25 percent of women sampled reported same-sex stimuli of various kinds.[9] With the "Kinsey scale," he sought to graph wide-ranging patterns in erotic experiences, to facilitate tolerance for the diversity that interviewees and correspondents disclosed as their lived sexual lives.[10] Here Kinsey plotted same-sex and heterosexual outlets, reported by the men sampled, on a seven-point continuum, creating the most famous chart in the 1948 male volume. Due to this diversity, Kinsey willingly used "heterosexual" and "homosexual" as adjectives but not as nouns. His "scale" demonstrated an erotic range too wide for the nouns to be accurate.

War and its aftermath had profound impacts on Kinsey's informants. No uniform sexual result of war emerged. Hence he saw no need for a general theory of war sexuality. Yet letters documented postwar sexual distress for which veterans or their partners sought help. Violence emerged as an urgent problem. So common were such reports that sociologist Clifford R. Adams (1902–87) told his friend Kinsey that "the veterans' administration in Washington is quite concerned about the great number of instances of brutality they have uncovered in X-GI marriages."[11] Veteran brutality reported by Adams included "sadistic violence with fists and heavy instruments."[12] Kinsey's empathy with veteran correspondents' sexual problems caused him great distress.[13]

Economically dependent wives described their veteran spouses as insisting on undesired erotic variations. A veteran from California refused to resume the former "conventional" conjugal relationship. Instead, he insisted that his wife go to bars to solicit strangers for coitus at home, where he would conceal himself in the closet and watch in order to become aroused. Husband and wife would then have intercourse after the stranger left. Complying on many occasions because she loved him, she had hoped he could overcome this obsession. By early 1948 she had a new baby of unclear paternity, feared that she had a venereal disease, and told Kinsey that she was contemplating suicide. He immediately advised her to seek professional medical help.[14]

Another veteran husband, a Kansas father of three children, had developed new interests. His wife became disturbed by his sexual changes and frequent nocturnal absences. Eventually, she hired a private detective, writing Kinsey about the results:

> I suspected my husband was running around and staying with boys. . . . As a wife my husband has always said I was satisfactory in our sexual relations. . . . I have never accused him. In my mind I felt it to be like a drug that he must have once in a while. I was willing to share him that way . . . just so I could have him, because I love him, not for sexual reasons only. . . . Three weeks ago he stayed out night after night. . . . I asked him what was wrong. Then he told me he would leave, just like that . . . no fuss, very casually. . . . Why write to you? I don't know. You are studying this problem. You know more about it than I. Is there a cure? Do or can men or women conquer this? Do they get too old for it? . . . Please say you can help.[15]

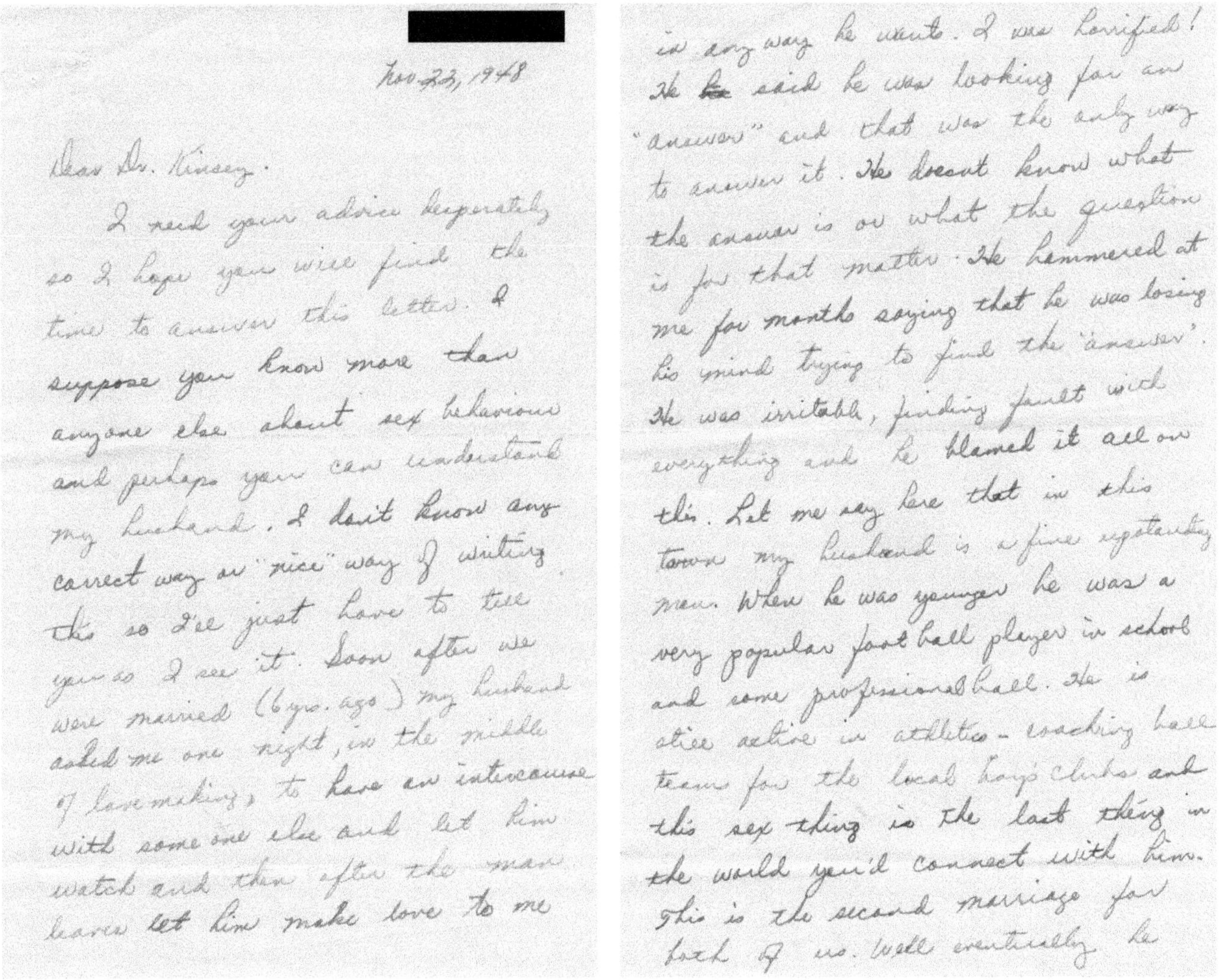

Nov 22, 1948

Dear Dr. Kinsey,

I need your advice desperately so I hope you will find the time to answer this letter. I suppose you know more than anyone else about sex behaviour and perhaps you can understand my husband. I don't know any correct way or "nice" way of writing this so I'll just have to tell you as I see it. Soon after we were married (6 yrs. ago) my husband asked me one night, in the middle of lovemaking, to have an intercourse with some one else and let him watch and then after the man leaves let him make love to me in any way he wants. I was horrified! He said he was looking for an "answer" and that was the only way to answer it. He doesn't know what the answer is or what the question is for that matter. He hammered at me for months saying that he was losing his mind trying to find the "answer". He was irritable, finding fault with everything and he blamed it all on this. Let me say here that in this town my husband is a fine upstanding man. When he was younger he was a very popular foot ball player in school and some professional ball. He is still active in athletics — coaching ball teams for the local boys' clubs and this sex thing is the last thing in the world you'd connect with him. This is the second marriage for both of us. Well eventually he

Figure 2.2. Letter from an unhappy wife to Alfred C. Kinsey, November 22, 1948. This is one of thousands of unsolicited "Dear Dr. Kinsey" letters from people seeking advice for sexual and birth control problems. Many of these letters described World War II veterans' problems resuming marriage, family life, and other relationships. Photo courtesy of Kinsey Institute Library and Special Collections.

Kinsey urged her to find a physician, a psychiatrist, or a clinical psychologist.[16]

Whether men were veterans or not, though, Kinsey found that age, class (or social level, as marked by educational attainment), and religious piety operated as powerful conditioning forces in men's sexual patterns. Least-educated men proved least "restrained," having frequent coitus from age fourteen, marrying at the earliest ages—the reason, often enough, an unexpected pregnancy. These young husbands often were adulterous during the childbearing years of marriage. Unnatural and counterproductive criminalization or stigmatization of nonmarital sexuality—including its outcome of out-of-wedlock childbearing—imposed needless hardship on the sexually active young. They might experiment with same-sex contacts in adolescence at the height of their biological sex drive, but male adults sought coitus and "rapid intromission," most reporting that they did so within two minutes, seeing extensive nongenital love-play as pointless, unnatural, and even unhygienic! Kinsey defended all this as natural and mammalian.[17]

To upper-level men, these lower-level erotic preferences seemed nonsensuous and impoverished. Alternatively, Kinsey portrayed lower-level men's patterns as natural and uninhibited by culture, dismissive of women's problem with the average man's "three minute coitus." Kinsey found that inhibited upper-level men began coitus late, making their infidelity, a majority male pattern, more a middle-aged behavior than it was for less-educated men. He deplored medical men's authority over sexual problems, their narrow range of sexual outlets leading them to condemn other sexual subcultures. Thereby, doctors' minority mores restrained the majority, causing much injustice.[18]

When it came to religion, Kinsey's findings confounded predictions. Many expected, for instance, that Catholicism would prove to be the most erotophobic of American faiths. Instead, theology itself predicted little at all about men's sexual behavior. Irrespective of nominal doctrine, it was degree of piety that influenced sexual behavior. The more pious, observant, and engaged with any given faith a man was, the less diverse and less extensive his total sexual outlet. Conversely, whatever their nominal creed, the least pious men had a greater rate and range of lifelong sexual outlets than the most pious.[19] Religion exemplified a larger pattern. Kinsey often found that nonbiological forces patterning different social groups functioned repressively. In the male volume, he portrayed cultural variables and institutions as inhibitors of greater sexual outlet, with the exceptions of erotica, pornography, and related visual representations.[20]

Most reviews of the male volume praised its achievements.[21] That said, critics attacked the failure to achieve national coverage, with the Midwest, the mid-Atlantic states, and the Northeast overrepresented and too few subjects from the West and the South.[22] One of the many hostile correspondents, from whom Kinsey received "hate mail," seized on this fact. As a proud southerner, he denounced interviewees' morality: "You won't find such people in the South outside of reform schools. . . . They nor any of our neighbors were any such trash as you describe in your book. Maybe Indiana is filled with such people."[23]

Alternatively, intellectual and professional women detected male bias: "I'll admit I saw red over the . . . *Male* book for I thought it often sounded impatient . . . with the female contingent."[24] So wrote Greenwich Village poet and critic of science Ruth Herschberger to Kinsey. Her book *Adam's Rib* (1948) satirized scientific misogyny with regard to gender and sexuality and was hailed as a feminist counterpart to (indeed, a critique of) the first Kinsey Report.[25] Despite her criticisms, however, she allowed Kinsey an interview and helped him to obtain interviews with several of her Greenwich Village friends—writers, artists, actors, doctors, publishers, and civil servants. Though female histories had accumulated since 1938, in-depth analysis, and augmentation of the sample, awaited completion of the male volume. Then everything would change.

Turning to Women

> On the human female . . . orgasm probably involves the whole nervous system in any individual case and the psychological background of the individual has a tremendous lot to do with the nature of the response. Certainly, the clitoris is rich in nerve endings and the vagina has apparently none, except in the anterior wall directly at the entrance. But the labia, the anus, the mouth and its adjacent lips, and still other parts of the animal's body are richly supplied with nerves.
>
> Alfred Charles Kinsey to Frank Ambrose Beach, January 23, 1950

In the fall of 1947, with the male volume in press, Kinsey turned to women. Until then, the female volume had been intended to complete the project begun with the male volume. While Kinsey restated this intention, it no longer seemed possible. The male volume had propounded a new way of analyzing sexual behavior, arguably establishing its own *male* norms. Those norms, at least initially, framed the team's approach to the female data. The parameters soon shifted away from those structuring the 1948 text.[26] Some take the five-year gap between the two volumes to show Kinsey's disinterest in women's sexualities relative to other subjects. Indeed, historians, biographers, and insiders describe Kinsey as "a bit of a misogynist," depicting the 1953 female volume as a necessary chore, the second half of the same project, delayed by detours into projects of greater interest—especially prison sexuality, sex offenders, and homosexuality.[27] This account is irreconcilable with the deep rumination, diverse consultations, and wider investigation that Kinsey and his associates undertook with regard to women's sexual lives during the late 1940s and early 1950s. One of the most significant of these associates was Emily Hartshorne Mudd (1898–1998), founder of the Marriage Council of Philadelphia, introduced to Kinsey in 1943 by pioneer gynecological researcher and clinician Robert Latou Dickinson. Mudd referred scores of clients to Kinsey to give him their sex histories. She was a friend, a defender, and, at times, a devastating critic whom he greatly respected and whom he tried to recruit several times to the Institute as a researcher.

Institute activities in this period suggest a different, richer picture. Kinsey's sex research project underwent methodological scrutiny and widened expert input. The result was significant new findings and daunting interpretive challenges, some at odds with the earlier male volume. These reconfigurations, arguably still

Figure 2.3. Dr. Emily Hartshorne Mudd, 1952. Kinsey credited Mudd with sending him more interviewees than almost anyone else. Family ties and her faculty post at the University of Pennsylvania obstructed Kinsey's efforts to lure her to Bloomington. They planned a book on spousal erotic adjustment and sparred often over methodology, the value of "paired reporting" (i.e., interviews with both sexual partners), and gendered assumptions inflecting research questions and interpretations. Photo courtesy of the Kinsey Institute Library and Special Collections.

Figure 2.4. W. H. Auden at the Institute, ca. 1950. British poet W. H. Auden was a fervent admirer of Kinsey's work. On a 1950 visit to the United States he came to Bloomington to meet Kinsey and tour the Institute and library. Photo courtesy of Kinsey Institute Library and Special Collections.

in progress, required more time, but diverse pressures compelled the 1953 publication of the female volume. Explaining sex differences in sex behavior emerging from the data became all-important. It had become clear that the main analytical grids and arguments of the male volume, especially those bearing on social level and sexual behavior, would not apply equally to women. The mission began to change. The more Kinsey posed new questions, the clearer his own ignorance became. The female volume unleashed a massive reorientation in his understanding of the nature of sexuality itself.

Nearly half of the interviews with women were added between 1947 and 1951.[28] Kinsey also capitalized on new sources of female interviewees among professional women who were his friends and colleagues. Several of these helpful colleagues loomed very large in the making of the second Kinsey Report. These women, who were some of his most important collaborators, have little or no place in the existing Kinsey literature, so firm has been the view of his lack of interest in "females."[29] These researcher and clinician colleagues excelled in hitherto male-dominated fields. They were well-educated, sophisticated urbanites, reflected in their views of sexuality and human relationships. Their fields of work garnered many interviewee prospects for Kinsey—clients, patients, patrons, students, and friends.[30]

Meanwhile, Kinsey also assimilated materials bequeathed by Robert Latou Dickinson. This immense bequest, formalized in 1946 and fully acquired after Dickinson's death in 1950, ignited major changes in Kinsey's thinking about female sexuality. He undertook new research, advised by expert gynecologists, obstetricians, marriage counselors, psychiatrists, and lawyers. Their advice and critiques struck at the core of his central quantitative method, namely, counting orgasms as a proxy for sexual events constituting "total sexual outlet." Clinically speaking, women's frequent anorgasmia in coitus (but not otherwise) in a culture normatively confining women to conjugal coitus via double sexual standards that rendered all else unrespectable made orgasm a poor proxy for women's sexual experience.[31]

Soon enough, Kinsey became aware of the hostility of the psychoanalytic fraternity to his sex research project. While he found their more dogmatic claims absurd—such as the notion of sexual sublimation, or estimates that over 80 percent of American women suffered from "frigidity" (a common term for anorgasmia)—such claims highlighted the contentions still surrounding the basic physiology and anatomy of women's sexual functioning. Kinsey denounced the reckless use of theory that was unconnected with actual sex research but that was nonetheless used to ground psychoanalytic claims that he found to be both misogynist and unscientific.[32] From these "frigidity wars" of the 1950s came the fiercest enemies of his research. They articulated implacable opposition to his sex histories–based research project, insisting on the superior expertise and authority of psychiatry and psychoanalysis over all matters sexual.[33] Kinsey countercharged that these clinicians argued like hysterical, dogmatic fanatics without a shred of robust scientific or empirical evidence to support their essentially "theological" position.[34]

Interview data alone could not resolve these contentious areas. Kinsey undertook corporeal investigation of erotic functioning and tactile sensitivity in 1950–51, with the assistance of six clinical gynecologists, most of them friends of Dickinson. They tested over a thousand of their own (consenting) patients, and their data allowed Kinsey to reevaluate a number of conflicting claims, including the erotic role of the cervix and anterior vaginal walls as sources of vaginal lubrication and other secretions generated in sexual response, as well as to generate systematic scientific data on the tactile sensitivity of different parts of the female genitalia. Though he had already dismissed the so-called vaginal orgasm as an impossibility in the male volume, this clinical testing confirmed the clitoro-vulval locus of stimulation and arousal.[35] The discrepancy between women's high rates of orgasm with masturbation compared with coitus became more intelligible. This research was a major factor in making the female volume so different from its 1948 predecessor.[36] As he would soon explain in the 1953 female volume, men needed to approach women differently from the usual ways reported by both sexes. He speculated on both technique and ambiance of sexual encounters most likely to be satisfying to most women. His portrait of woman-oriented sexuality stood in marked contrast with accounts of men's coital methods. Women preferred

> a considerable amount of generalized emotional stimulation before there is any specific sexual contact. They usually want physical stimulation of the whole body before there is any specifically genital contact. They may especially want stimulation of the clitoris and labia minora, and stimulus which after it has begun, is followed through to orgasm, without the interruptions which males . . . often introduce into heterosexual relationships. . . . Heterosexual relationships could become more satisfactory if they more often utilized the sort of knowledge which most homosexual females have of female sexual anatomy and female psychology.[37]

Following lively exchanges around this new work, Kinsey embarked on a new design for the female volume. He reevaluated existing literature and offered new data on the anatomy, physiology, endocrinology, neurology, and psychology of female arousal and orgasm.[38] These were the subjects of the final chapters of the text, comprising nearly a third of it, and had no counterpart in the 1948 male volume. Much of the medical and scientific content of the female volume was new, sometimes very new, to its author. His approach to women's sexuality diverged from the previous Kinsey Report's portrait of men's erotic lives.

The existence of the 1948 volume meant that female data received comparative rather than autonomous analysis. Yet the male volume, as the first report, lacked the benefit of the intellectual influences of figures converging on Kinsey and Bloomington, so crucial in the making of the very different female volume. The male volume hewed close to Kinsey's zoological background, resembling his late 1930s and early 1940s gall wasp taxonomy work. By contrast, the research for the female volume confounded predicted female patterns. The data supported only some of Kinsey's earlier hunches. Meanwhile, new findings needed explanation. The 1953 female volume centered on sexual differences, foregrounded questions of gender, and pondered unresolved claims of nature versus culture in shaping sexual behavior.

Interviewees, peers, and consultants portrayed reproduction and birth control as central preoccupations in women's sexual lives. Women wondered about the safety and effectiveness of new spermicidal creams and jellies. These products had high failure rates, a fact that informed Kinsey's advocacy of decriminalized abortion.[39] New York sterility specialist Dr. Frances Shields (1983–1964) was especially important in the development of Kinsey's practical knowledge of and policy suggestions on reproductive and birth control matters. He admired her research on menstruation, ovulation, and fertility patterns, as well as that on artificial insemination. She enhanced his appreciation of clinical perspectives for illuminating matters left unresolved by interviews.[40]

As the draft text took shape, word of Kinsey's preliminary findings aroused interest among zoologists and animal sexuality researchers. Always engaged with animal and human comparisons, Kinsey initiated dialogue between zoologists, psychologists, gynecologists, and obstetricians. Yale animal psychologist Frank Beach (1911–88) was central in this regard. Coauthoring a book on animal sexual behavior and exploring implications of orgasm—and its absence—for females of many species, Beach became intrigued by the evolutionary theory implications of orgasm in *Homo sapiens* females but its apparent lack in other mammals and species.[41]

In addition to these multidisciplinary exchanges during the period between the Kinsey Reports, the Institute investigated both female and male sex offenders, research that was undertaken in tandem with the analysis of the female data and the drafting of the female volume. Progress accelerated when in 1950 Kinsey secured the services of criminal justice ethnographer Alice Withrow Field (1909–60), the Institute's first female research associate.[42] Field had been research director of New York City's Wayward Minor Court, renamed Girls' Term in 1940 (to combat the stigma of criminality), and her approach to women's and girls' diverse sexual lives unsettled the 1948 male volume's portrayal of female sexuality just as Kinsey was working on his intensive analysis of female interview data, new clinical data, and further multidisciplinary medical research. Field inspired considerable revision of Kinsey's understanding of young women's sexual experiences.[43]

New legislation, including the "sexual psychopath" laws, identified only men as sex offenders. This legislation cast adult women and children of both sexes as the hapless, passive victims of psychopathic, lower-level men.[44] By contrast, Kinsey

Figure 2.5. Dr. Frances E. Shields, ca. 1947. New York infertility specialist Frances E. Shields was a colleague who forwarded Kinsey interviewees, assisted him in networking with fellow clinicians, edited both the male and female volumes, and was perhaps the person most responsible for making Kinsey aware of the potential contributions of theater, ballet, and the performing arts to sex research. Photo courtesy of Kinsey Institute Library and Special Collections.

Figure 2.6. As the 1948 publication of *Sexual Behavior in the Human Male* loomed, Institute staff, pictured here, had the arduous task of creating the index. Photo courtesy of Kinsey Institute Library and Special Collections.

came to understand "sex offenders" as a broader category than is usual today. Through dialogue with Field, he included prostitutes, "wayward" girls, abortion providers and their clients, and those in same-sex erotic contacts. In addition to rape, he examined noncoital sexual assault, exhibitionism, "public sex" or "lewdness," voyeurism, incest, prohibited intergenerational encounters, and bestiality. Criminal justice systems targeted most nonmarital and nonprocreative sexual activities and associated practices. For Kinsey, sexual behaviors judged offensive deserved investigation to illuminate the production of "offendedness." Poignant, angry, confused, and desperate letters from people who had been targeted by police and had often been subjected to barbaric treatment by the criminal justice system dramatized outraged mores. He was moved to try to help.[45] Bemused, he noted the puzzling claim that offenders committed crimes "against nature," as if nature was a victim.[46] He visited prisons, especially in California, and lectured widely, sometimes to vast audiences.

Figure 2.7. Kinsey lecturing at the University of California, Berkeley, 1949. This image captures the enormous public interest in Kinsey's research and findings; nine thousand people attended this lecture. Photo courtesy of Kinsey Institute Library and Special Collections.

Many if not most sex offenses warranted deregulation, destigmatization, and privacy. Consensual erotic encounters between teenagers or between adult persons of the same sex exemplified the negative face of official responses, as did the treatment of unwed mothers. Abortion was illegal and thereby subject to corruption, graft, and politically motivated policing to the detriment of women and girls. And these women and girls, like homosexual men, were at risk of being blackmailed.

With this array of new inputs percolating through Kinsey's work on the second report, he decided to jettison much of the male volume's structure and framework. The second volume's content reflected his lively engagement with a distinguished group of researchers, clinicians, intellectuals, academics, officials, creative artists and performers, and other professionals. It became a midcentury rumination on the meaning of sexuality itself in the light of its strenuous representation by both mainstream and subcultural stakeholders. Though thousands of ordinary men's sex histories had formed the empirical backbone of *Sexual Behavior in the Human Male*, that volume was a more closed, discrete, and coherent study than the *Human Female* volume. Questions and findings that had been central to the male volume wobbled before questions and findings raised in the second volume. Kinsey told confidants that of the two, the 1953 *Human Female* volume was "a much better book."[47]

Figure 2.8. Alfred C. Kinsey and Cornelia Otis Skinner, 1949. Skinner, a popular comedian, came to Bloomington to visit Kinsey in 1949. Kinsey's obvious pleasure in Skinner's company was one of the bright spots in his experience of executing his exacting research project. Photo courtesy of Kinsey Institute Library and Special Collections.

The Female Volume

> The current position of women has been acquired only after some centuries of conflict between the sexes. . . . There are still male antagonisms to her emergence as a co-equal in the home and social affairs . . . down to the present day, there is more heat than light in most attempts to show that women are the equal of men or that the human female differs in some fundamental way from the human male. It would be surprising if we, the present investigators, should have wholly freed ourselves from such century-old biases and succeeded in comparing the two sexes with complete objectivity which is possible in areas of science that are of less direct import in human affairs.
>
> Alfred C. Kinsey, Wardell B. Pomeroy, Clyde E. Martin, and Paul H. Gebhard, *Sexual Behavior in the Human Female*, 567

The female volume addressed the central problem motivating Kinsey's whole undertaking. Why, when the sexes were so comparable, analogous, and similar in key biological domains, were they so different in their sexual behavior? As a biologist, Kinsey was less troubled by those aspects of difference that appeared to be mammalian than by those he attributed to culture, conditioning, mores, and customs. Although he readily identified cultural elements, he described rather than explained them. While his way of posing the problem of sex differences tended to unify women as a single group with various attributes, his data disclosed significant differences among women that cried out for alternative analysis. Pressure to publish the long-awaited female volume forced Kinsey to leave key problems half-posed and unsolved. What were his findings about the sexes?

By publishing the white male data first in the 1948 volume, Kinsey established, in addition to a white norm, a masculine norm for understanding sexual behavior. He overlooked the epistemological implications of taking the orgasm—the typical experience of men but often not women—as the measure of human sexual experience. Women's main sexual patterns had no autonomy in this framework, appearing instead relative to men's. Despite Kinsey's oft-repeated claims of detachment and scientific objectivity, loaded androcentric questions and assumptions handicapped his efforts. This bias was nowhere more apparent than in Kinsey's choice of language, terms, and mode of formulating reports and discussion.[48]

By 1953, after benefiting from six years of extra research and many intervening experts, the female volume was less interview based and less orgasm centered. Class and, to some extent, age either disappeared or, in historian Paul Robinson's words, "were mere shadows of their former selves."[49] Kinsey jettisoned the male volume's class analysis, perhaps because the female data diverged inexplicably. University-educated women had more diverse outlets and more orgasms than least-educated women. A quarter of women admitted adultery, 13 percent same-sex eroticism, while masturbation remained important for most women lifelong. The most orgiastic of the female informants had pursued teenage sexual experiences, especially petting. Women had greater erotic variation than men, invalidating deterministic explanations for higher male total orgasm counts.[50] Kinsey called the alleged "vaginal orgasm" an anatomical impossibility, accusing psychoanalysts of perpetrating a myth of mass female frigidity.[51]

Instead, Kinsey found the sexes analogous in both structure and function. No anatomical, physiological, or hormonal distinctions proved sufficient to explain the sexed orgiastic discrepancy.[52] Though he entertained neurological and psychological hypotheses, he ultimately gestured toward cultural arrangements, later called "gender." His achievement here was in exposing these explanatory lacunae. Yet the limits of his zoological training forestalled adequate explanation of these sexual differences and their cultural habitats, making the female volume uncertain and unfinished, if arguably more intriguing than the 1948 volume.

The female volume addressed a Cold War cultural context. The narrative challenged sexual illiberalism, urged decriminalization of sexual behaviors, and advocated tolerance for sexual diversity amidst prosecution of homosexuals and imposition of draconian sexual psychopath legislation.[53] Its depiction of coitus was melancholy.[54] Contrary to much received wisdom about sex differences in erotic life, Kinsey reported the sexes to be essentially similar or comparable in anatomical and even endocrinal characteristics. Yet, by the measure of orgasms from any and all sources of stimulus, men had vastly more of what Kinsey called "total sexual outlet." Explaining this sex difference became a vexing and central problem.

By measuring and contextualizing women's orgasms and sexual experiences, Kinsey rejected coitus as the best practice for quantifying women's rates of orgasm. He baldly stated that a large amount of women's sexual activity, especially coitus, remained anorgasmic. By contrast, most men preferred coitus above other outlets, almost always proceeding to orgasm. Hence, coitus was a feasible proxy only for *men's* arousal rates, while women routinely endured intercourse without orgasm. Heterosexual activities, he concluded, do not provide a good measure "of the female's innate capacities and desires."[55] Ineffective male techniques made coitus an unreliable measure of female sexual desire and capacity. Scientifically, the outlet to measure was whichever one women freely chose without coercion and most reliably led to orgasm. Kinsey found that outlet where sex researchers Wilhelm Stekel and Dickinson had found it three decades earlier: autoeroticism.[56] It proved the most effective and illuminating measure of women's desires and sources of orgasm across the sexual life, confirming too the clitoro-vulval locus of female orgasm. Little of women's autoerotic practices centered on deep vaginal penetration.

Class, specifically the lower-level educational group, did not predict greater sexual outlet in women, as it had among men. In fact, higher education predicted greater outlet and range among women, a finding reported but underread in Kinsey's narrative.[57] The male volume's analysis proved inapplicable to the female data, with women more significantly sharing common problems, patterns, and experiences. While male sexual patterns seemed variegated by class and age, female trends were less so.

These profound sex differences presented vast interpretive challenges. Kinsey's dismal portrayal of heterosexual coitus from women's perspective did not greatly differ from that advanced by Dickinson and other forebears. Yet Kinsey had hitherto offered bracing criticism of earlier accounts of women's conjugal erotic unhappiness. After his considerable resistance, Mudd, Robert Laidlaw (president of the American Association of Marriage Counselors and later chief of psychiatry at Roosevelt Hospital in New York), and other clinicians persuaded him that sexual technique and relationship counseling could improve sexual lives. Laidlaw and Mudd reiterated this when visiting Bloomington in 1952 to act as content editors of the draft book manuscript on behalf of Kinsey's medical publisher, W. B. Saunders.

As yet, historians have paid scant attention to the volume's intervention in 1950s debates about sexual difference. The five long final chapters of the 1953 text,

Figure 2.9. Alice Withrow Field, ca. 1951. Field, a criminal justice analyst and author of works on gender and law in the Soviet Union, Britain, and the United States, became the first female research associate of Kinsey's project. Her input into his sex offenders work was critical and probably facilitated his 1955 testimony before Sir John Wolfenden's Departmental Committee on Homosexual Offenses and Prostitution. Photo courtesy of Kinsey Institute Library and Special Collections.

comparing the sexes in terms of anatomy, physiology, psychology, neurology, and endocrinology, formed over a third of the 863-page book. Kinsey positioned these chapters at the end of the text, as if they provided the resolution to a troubling set of findings: first, that women and girls had fewer sexual outlets than men, and second, that nowhere was sexuality more problematic for women than in the most approved and prescribed form—heterosexual coitus. Yet women's anatomical and physiological functioning was either identical or analogous to men's, while hormonal differences did not point conclusively toward sex differentiation in types of sexual outlets.

The chief area of marked sex difference seemed to be in the domain of psychology. Here, Kinsey reached a critical explanatory crossroads: either he could accept women's reportedly lesser arousal from psychological, especially visual, stimuli as an artifact of cultural conditioning, or he could seek a biological explanation for this reported difference. On balance, he favored the latter, despite compelling evidence for the former. He sought a biological grounding for sex differences in erotic life, perhaps sex differences in the cerebral cortex processing of arousing psychological stimuli. In short, according to critics, Kinsey sought a "female brain."[58]

This quest for one inherent explanation showed the limits of Kinsey's training and predisposition. If he recognized gendered outcomes of conditioning, then methods for further investigation, to him at least, seemed amorphous. Though he became attuned to sociocultural origins of sex differences after the male volume, he retained his former disciplinary bias. His investment in sex dimorphism (and often, as its apparent corollary, the misogyny and sexism that had incensed Kinsey's feminist critics) showed in his attempt to reconcile divergent, even competing, explanations of sex differences in the psychology and neurology chapters, respectively.[59]

The complexity of assessing Kinsey's legacy for women in the female volume and beyond, however, confronts the reader sharply. While we may justly recoil at his theory of the "female brain" and other textual commentary, his unstinting efforts to expose "the myth of the vaginal orgasm" can hardly rate as misogynist or sexist. In the 1950s frigidity wars in the professional literature that raged around his text, Kinsey moved decisively beyond his earlier defense of mammalian two-minute coitus as "natural." The female evidence convinced him that sexual life was problematic and unsatisfying for women; more significantly, it was unsatisfying for reasons that were not inherent but rather cultural and contingent.

Human Female disclosed Kinsey's deepening multidisciplinary grappling with incommensurate explanations for vast sex differences in "sexual outlets" or erotic experiences.[60] In particular, the unsolved problem of pregnancy and birth control preoccupied him while he was completing the female volume. Informant women made all too clear the inhibiting force of the fear of undesired pregnancy in their sexual histories, an issue often not grasped by women's male sexual partners.

Figure 2.10. Dr. Robert Laidlaw, Alfred C. Kinsey, and Emily Hartshorne Mudd, 1952. Kinsey's publisher, W. B. Saunders, hired both psychiatrist Robert Laidlaw and marriage counsellor Emily Hartshorne Mudd to go to Bloomington in 1952 and work as editors of the manuscript of *Sexual Behavior in the Human Female*. Here they are pictured questioning a particular passage. Photo courtesy of Kinsey Institute Library and Special Collections.

Kinsey wrote to contacts at contraceptive companies like Ortho with women's feedback on product effectiveness and acceptability limitations.[61] Though birth control campaigners contended that contraception could eradicate abortion, Kinsey found that women using contraceptives secured abortions if their contraceptive methods failed.[62] The one did not eradicate the raison d'être for the other.

As well, he came to appreciate the agonies of women desiring to conceive but without success. Kinsey's preparation for the female volume intensified his attention to the broad range of reproductive issues. This imperils his characterization as uninterested in women's supposedly repressed sexualities and their uncongenial preoccupations with conception, fertility, and maternity.[63] In an early to midcentury research context in which biology was the original discipline of many sex researchers, Kinsey was the one least likely to minimize the significance of reproduction. His original expertise as the world authority on the gall wasp of North America entailed the evolutionary study of egg-laying females of the species, which he studied in the full diversity of their environmental adaptations.[64] In the Department of Zoology, Kinsey taught the courses on biological evolution, a subject matter made palpable through patterns in reproduction. Sex research, then, only deepened his predisposition to take reproduction very seriously.

The *Human Female* volume, then, mapped a radically transitioning research undertaking. Only in the most formal ways did it join a clear space alongside the 1948 *Human Male* volume as its "other half." The second volume's challenging questions, even if not also persuasive and definitive, deployed new methods and evidence, reasons alone for its marked differences from the first volume.[65] Moreover, far from being a grinding and overdue next chore, the second volume was a quantum leap in Kinsey's conceptualization and analysis of human sexuality.

Endings Unfinished

> I'm so sorry that the pump is misbehaving. I hope you can happily adjust to a less active life. Perhaps this is what your younger staff members need to put them on their toes. What a pity that none of them is imbued with ambition and ability to raise money!! It is certainly a very special quality which you possess.
>
> Frances E. Shields to Alfred C. Kinsey, July 27, 1956

By the time Kinsey read this wry get-well note, he had less than a month to live. Heart trouble had emerged after a stress-filled three years. This final phase of his life entailed controversy over the female volume, including blistering professional reviews, hidden vendettas, and adverse lobbying, culminating in the 1954 McCarthyist congressional enquiry threatening the Rockefeller Foundation's tax-exempt status over its support for sex research. The foundation ceased its grants to the Institute, putting in peril both existing and planned projects, including a new book on abortion.[66] Meanwhile, as Kinsey continued the crucial work of building the library and archives collections, a contentious dispute with US Customs authorities over the right to import and study sexually explicit materials ignited expensive litigation. President Herman B Wells, Kinsey's longtime colleagues, and, perhaps most impressively and independently, the Indiana University board of trustees rallied to the defense not only of Kinsey's work specifically but also of the broader issues of academic freedom raised by the case. Sadly, Kinsey did not live to see the final legal push or results.

The Cold War context proved hostile to the 1953 female volume. Critics denounced as a slander on American womanhood the report that half of all women had premarital sex and a quarter had extramarital sex, while 13 percent had same-sex sexual outlets.[67] Criticism of Kinsey's projects, launched by clinicians with antithetical approaches, sharpened. Psychoanalysts, Kinsey's most vehement opponents, read interviewees as patients who were incapable of true testimony. As Kinsey told a colleague, psychiatrist Oliver Spurgeon English, the attacks "by

Figure 2.11. Conference on animal studies, Amherst, Massachusetts, December 1954. A "who's who" of friends and foes were assembled at a key annual conference when news of Rockefeller's cancelation of Kinsey's funding was becoming known. Pictured are Alfred C. Kinsey, Paul H. Gebhard, Wardell Pomeroy, Clyde E. Martin, Lawrence S. Kubie (a vocal Kinsey critic), John Money, and Frank A. Beach, among others. Photo courtesy of Kinsey Institute Library and Special Collections.

the psychoanalysts (not by psychiatrists in general), by selfmade statisticians and by certain theologians have led the Rockefeller Foundation to decide that they do not want to support sex research at all."[68] Kinsey's old nemesis, Viennese analyst Dr. Edmund Bergler, published a scathing and tendentious psychoanalytic critique of the female volume.[69] Entitled *Kinsey's Myth of Female Sexuality* (1954), Bergler's book accused Kinsey of endangering American women's mental health by normalizing their neuroses, manifested in an epidemic of primary frigidity. Responsible action would have been to steer this majority of female adults to the psychoanalyst's couch to learn to have "vaginal orgasms" and forget clinical claims of the clitoro-vulval locus of women's erotic arousal.[70]

Kinsey was alarmed to see notable figures like Karl Menninger in Bergler's camp. More generally, medical ignorance of and hostility toward sex research boded ill for the future.[71] Later, Emily Mudd recalled that the attack on Kinsey's research and integrity by Bergler, Lawrence Kubie, and others in the psychoanalytic lobby was an assault from which he never recovered. Thereafter, he was an angry, disturbed, obsessed man who was preoccupied with vindication and a refutation of unfounded charges.[72]

* * *

Even so, Kinsey pushed forward. The impetus for his planned volume on abortion came partly from outside the Institute. Even before the 1948 male volume was published, as word of his research spread, prominent doctors and other experts, including Robert Latou Dickinson, Abraham Stone, Christopher Tietze, and officials from the Planned Parenthood Federation of America and its local branches, repeatedly asked Kinsey for any data he had on contraception use and incidence of induced abortion. Few if any statistics existed.[73]

Kinsey had raw data. Men and women mentioned their contraceptive and abortion experiences as part of sex histories. He deflected demands from peer scientists and clinicians by promising to publish those data at some point. The female volume, though, had priority.[74] Once the female volume appeared in 1953, petitioners resumed. Inspired by the 1953 text, Dr. Calderone urged him to present his abortion data for the first time to a professional audience at a planned 1955 conference on criminal abortion.[75] She wrote to Kinsey that "we might look rather foolish if we had a conference on this problem and . . . discovered that the problem to all intents and purposes did not exist or at least did not exist in amounts sufficient to warrant efforts to solve it."[76] Kinsey's work was essential, then, to determining the existence and scope of criminal abortion and its causes.

Calderone and Kinsey differed in their views. She called abortion a public health problem, comparable with venereal diseases or other preventable epidemics such as tuberculosis.[77] Furthermore, "abortion *per se* is a wasteful and destructive process, actually a disease of society—and . . . it is a shameful thing to allow any disease to exist in this day and age, for which we have some preventive measure available."[78] Kinsey undertook to contribute "objective data" to the conference, but he would not agree that abortion was a disease of society, nor would he, without evidence, concur with Calderone's assumption that contraceptive use would eradicate abortion.[79] Similarly, Kinsey disdained many delegates' approaches to abortion. He dissented from an early draft of policy recommendations from the conference, in particular, the assumption that abortion exerted a "grave influence" on the "physical and mental health of the nation. Such data do not exist in connection with the abortion cases that we have studied." Similarly, he rejected labeling abortion a "disease of society" and any analogy drawn with venereal diseases. Doctors had been ignorant as to effective treatment of the latter, whereas the "abortion problem is primarily one of the refusal of physicians to perform abortions." He had not seen evidence to support the claims that abortion was a "traumatic" experience for a woman or that sex education and a wider knowledge of contraception would reduce the number of unwanted pregnancies and the incidence of abortion.[80]

Kinsey disputed medical delegates' tendency to pathologize abortion recipients. One delegate claimed that abortion revealed an "imperfect inter-adaptation of the woman and her environment" and "almost always" indicated a "disordered family, economic, or social situation."[81] In other words, physically and mentally healthy women in well-adapted families did not seek abortions. By contrast, Kinsey's data suggested that economic factors underlay most demand. Though abortion was hardly a preferred family planning method, it seemed "inconsistent for a Planned Parenthood group to suggest that planning of the size of a family represents illness or imperfect inter-adaptation." He insisted that "the abortion problem is primarily dependent upon unrealistic state laws, and the failure of the medical profession to view the matter in more than a moralistic light."[82]

Such views confirmed Kinsey's resolve to write the abortion book as his next priority. His unfinished draft targeted unrealistic abortion laws and medical hypocrisy. Both men and women, among his eighteen thousand sex histories, had provided considerable detailed information about abortion. He decried arbitrary police crackdowns at the behest of ambitious district attorneys seeking higher office. Selective and erratic regulation of this heavily demanded illicit medical service turned on corruption and extortion from providers. If a woman or couple were determined that a pregnancy would end, Kinsey observed, this usually came to pass. Even though abortion laws were rarely enforced, the widespread resort to illegality impaired social ethics and mocked the rule of law.[83] Meanwhile, he observed, women desperate to terminate an unwanted pregnancy and unable to secure a safe abortion ranked among the most psychologically disturbed people he had encountered in all his sex research work.[84]

Kinsey always classified prisoners convicted in relation to abortion as sex offenders. This acknowledged abortion's long legislative association with obscenity laws, notably, prosecutions of abortifacient suppliers, alongside pornographers, via the notorious Comstock Act (1873), which targeted mail-order businesses.

Moreover, criminal law amendments in many states criminalized pregnant women's resort to auto-abortion. In addition, abortion demand was related to the sexes' negotiations of their sexual lives and undesired outcomes, especially given the overrepresentation of abortion as the outcome of pregnancy for single women compared with wives, discussed further below. Where those selectively convicted were third-party providers of abortion services, they readily resembled scapegoats for a broader cultural hypocrisy.

Shortly after Calderone's conference in April 1955, Kinsey undertook a range of activities. In Britain in October 1955 he testified for Sir John Wolfenden's Committee on Homosexual Offenses and Prostitution, urging repeal of draconian British sodomy sentences and those for other sex offenses.[85] As well, he visited Wormwood Scrubs prison, the usual destination of men sentenced to custodial terms for homosexual offenses. Then he visited experts in various European countries and became convinced that a study of European sexual behavior should be undertaken.[86] His further planned book on sex offenders had him interviewing prisoners at Alcatraz and other prisons, as well as testifying against sadistic calls for castration of those convicted. Yet his thinking about parties to abortion as sex offenders led him to begin a new book that he entitled, simply, *Abortion*.

The table of contents for the book on abortion showed a plan for fourteen chapters. The book's format resembled that of the male and female volumes. Age and marital status loomed large as key quantitative parameters for pregnancies occurring, live birth rates, spontaneous abortions, and those intentionally induced. Despite his colleagues' resistance to the use of the admittedly incomplete "Prison Histories" and "Negro Sample," Kinsey intended a full chapter on each. Moreover, he mapped a chapter correlating abortion and educational level and another entitled "Parental-Occupational Class" and its relation to abortion. Further, another chapter was to address changed abortion rates by women's decade of birth, demonstrating rising demand among women born after 1920 compared with their forebears. National incidence and transnational comparisons provided another focus, as did access and aftercare in the context of the continued illegality of all nontherapeutic abortion. Finally, he proposed to address sterility and a range of other outcomes.

The draft chapters, dated July 28, 1956, suggest the text that might have eventuated. Like the previous Kinsey Reports, the discussion in the abortion book centered on variables of age, marital status, birth decade, education, race, and religion. He targeted the sexual genesis of unwilling pregnancy, setting abortion patterns in the context of coital frequency, sterility and fertility, and relevant cultural mores. The typescript consisted of two chapters, "Chapter III: Relation to Marital Status" and "Chapter IV: Correlated with Age at Marriage," and included Kinsey's annotations. Age was a proxy for biological factors (capacity to conceive);

Figure 2.12. Mary Steichen Calderone, ca. 1930. Calderone, daughter of modernist painter and photographer Edward Steichen, was medical director of Planned Parenthood Federation of America. She was the only person to succeed, of the many who tried and failed, in persuading Kinsey to process and present at a conference his findings on induced criminal abortion. Later she was at the center of a storm over schools and sex education after she founded the Sex Information and Education Council of the United States (SIECUS) in 1967. Photo courtesy of Schlesinger Library, Radcliffe Institute, Harvard University.

Kinsey outline

ABORTION

Table of Contents

Chapter

I   Factors Leading to Abortion

II   The Sample

III   Relation to Marital Status

      a.   Pregnancies

         Females   _(N = no. of ♀ who ever preg. in that stat_
         Rate _per female_
         Active Incidence   _Accumulated incidence_   _(N = no. of ♀ wh._
         Frequency distribution by 5 year periods   _had C in that marital status_

      b.   Live births

      c.   Spontaneous abortion

      d.   Induced abortion

IV   Correlated with age at marriage   _OUT PREG_   _RELIGION_

V   Relation to Decade of Birth   _OUT PREG_   _INTERVIEWER_

VI   Relation to Educational Background _OUT PREG_   _EVER SEPAR. WID,_

VII   Relation to Parental-Occupational Class _OUT_

VIII   Abortion in Negro Sample

IX   Abortion in Prison Histories

X   Sterility Cases

XI   Estimates for U. S. Population - by Christopher Tietze

XII   Abortion in Other Countries

XIII   Obtaining an Abortion

XIV   Physical, Psychologic, and Social Outcomes

Figure 2.13. _Abortion_ table of contents, July 1956. Kinsey had planned many projects beyond the first two Kinsey Reports. The contents page of a planned book on abortion, shown here, differed considerably from the one included in _Pregnancy, Birth and Abortion_ (1958), published after Kinsey's death. Photo courtesy of Kinsey Institute Library and Special Collections.

social constraints (access to contraception and abortion); and a combination of biological, psychological, and social concerns (frequency of coitus). Just as sexually active adolescent males who were barred from a legitimate sexual outlet sought illicit, illegal, or disapproved sources of orgasm, so those sexually active girls unfortunate enough to become pregnant faced grim choices. Whereas in the male volume, education, which defined social levels, predicted varying ranges and extent of sexual outlet, in the abortion book, marital status predicted varying reliance on abortion. Single minors had the greatest abortion incidence relative to pregnancy rates, just as lower-level males reported highest sexual outlet. Wives occupied more prosperous and secure positions—by analogy, the upper social level—than single women. Like men at the lower social level, who had the highest rate of sexual outlet, so single women had the highest rate of abortion.

Kinsey noted that half of women sampled, irrespective of class level or education completed, had premarital coitus. Yet only between 10 and 30 percent of them became premaritally pregnant. Such low rates could reflect relative infertility in adolescent women and men, found across cultures, though "male vanity" and men's overblown claims to ageless potency had oriented infertility scrutiny toward women, so that study of male infertility remained far from comprehensive.[87] Moreover, frequency of coitus was a major factor in the odds of conception, and "only a small percentage of the unmarried females have coitus frequently enough to ever become pregnant."[88]

Some evidence suggested, so Kinsey reported, that perhaps orgiastic women had greater odds of conceiving than anorgasmic. It was unclear, though, whether this was because orgasm was a proxy for relative coital frequency. The research of Kinsey's colleague Dr. John Haman with sterile women seeking to conceive disclosed proportionally lower rates of orgasm than among fertile women, leading Kinsey to believe that the whole issue needed more research. These apparent correlations, however, suggested that demand for abortion might be greatest among the most erotically active heterosexual women. Abortion rates might even be one kind of proxy for high sexual outlet in some women.

Contraception did play some role in holding down pregnancy rates among the unmarried. Kinsey wanted to ensure that its role was not overstated, however, since many factors obstructed its effective access and use, especially among the young. Propagandists held that it could remove the demand for abortions. Such a position assumed access and reliability (not so often the experience of teenagers), implicitly generalizing options for wives, presumably in an effort to discourage teen sexual activity. He called such assumptions puritanical and erotophobic.

Kinsey assailed the unjust medical practices that produced very different outcomes by age. Pregnant teenage girls had a higher rate of live births than older single women due to the refusal of "the medical profession in particular, to provide induced abortions as frequently as they will provide them for an older unmarried female." He was enraged by the treatment of so-called wayward minor girls and sexually active unmarried women. "It would appear," he ventured, "that our present mores are intent on magnifying the number of teenage unmarried mothers and increasing the number of illegitimate children who have *teenage* unmarried mothers." Older women had greater capacity to secure medical cooperation, while doctors, by contrast, "will provide no such help for the unmarried pregnant girl in her teens."[89]

Part of the reason physicians refused to help women secure abortions, he observed, was the "ease" and "consistent insistence" with which psychoanalysts characterized abortions as "traumatic experiences from which the female will never recover."[90] Allowing this experience to older unmarried women who could afford to pay for the procedure but not to young teenage girls was bizarre, for they were hardly more fit to be mothers of children. They encountered major obstacles to "social adjustment," a particular concern of the American Law Institute.[91] Kinsey likewise condemned state-level legislation prohibiting the sale of contraceptives to minors, increasing teenagers' difficulties in preventing pregnancy. Such restrictions reduced access to abortions and enhanced the odds of live births. Physicians upheld abortion laws in uneven ways and often refused an abortion to those who most needed it. Doctors were particularly unwilling to abort "wayward girls," a group acutely vulnerable to unwanted pregnancy.

Despite these obstacles, 74 percent of unwillingly pregnant minors secured abortions. Combined with the higher rates for older unmarried women, the abortion rate for single women was 93 percent. While married women as the numerically largest group pregnant in any year had the largest *actual* number of abortions, only 33 percent of them terminated. Hence, among all pregnant women each year, single women had the highest incidence of abortion. Kinsey observed that social stability relied on a hypocritical nonenforcement of existing abortion law in order to prevent "some hundreds of thousands of illegitimately fathered children added to the population."[92] Indeed, he asked further about the "AngloAmerican bent for closing our eyes to the realities and hoping that in some fashion our social organization will muddle through."[93]

Other features of Kinsey's abortion analysis continued themes from the female volume. His findings on the impact of both decade of birth—in effect, the gradual liberalization of sexual mores—and degree of religious piety resurfaced as factors in the odds of conception, the use of contraception, and the recourse to abortion. Also, he expanded on the dilemma of religiously devout young women, who were as vulnerable as young men to sexual arousal and natural desire via cerebral cortex stimulation, leading to spontaneous coitus and unplanned pregnancy. In other words, pious young women would resolve not to have premarital coitus. They would then succumb on impulse to natural desires on a date without contraceptive preparation. Therefore, the most pious women who believed most strongly that it was wrong for them to have coitus could have multiple unwelcome pregnancies and then seek abortions: "The clergyman's daughter will end up with three or four pregnancies just because she is so sure it is wrong to have premarital coitus."[94] This all too ordinary situation made Kinsey skeptical about Planned Parenthood's contraception versus abortion dichotomy, or the hypothesis that accessible contraception would erode demand for abortion. Instead, single women's unwelcome pregnancies confirmed his belief that shame and moralism created barriers to healthy sexual adjustment.[95]

* * *

The loss of external funding was a bitter blow to Kinsey. Only he had a full-time tenured faculty position. His research associates with young families faced retrenchment, as did other Institute staff. Fund-raising efforts proved substantially fruitless. Grounds for further concern seemed to snowball. The Institute, established as a protective University unit for stewardship of sensitive data, records, and resources, had existed for less than a decade. When the Institute was incorporated, the Rockefeller Foundation channeled support of almost half a million dollars in today's values to it annually, while healthy royalties from the male and female volumes optimized, Kinsey hoped, progress toward his diversifying intellectual and research goals. Though the research data and collections, as shown above, precipitated the creation of the Institute, the University's support for its new unit remained unspecified. In the crisis unleashed by the outcome of the Reece Committee enquiry, Kinsey sought clarification of "formal action" taken by the University's board of trustees "regarding the relations between the University and the Institute for Sex Research," adding that he and President Wells had agreed that "if the status is not sufficiently clear, it may be appropriate to consider the possibility of taking some formal action now."[96] The archivist found only approval of the "Articles of Incorporation," on May 26, 1947, while Wells could recall "no other discussion by the Board on this matter during the most recent years."[97]

In late June 1956 Kinsey received notice from US Customs authorities that his impounded "libeled" imports were about to be destroyed, unleashing bemused and widespread national coverage.[98] Just over a month later, he was hospitalized. Alfred Charles Kinsey died from congestive heart failure on August 26, 1956. For the Institute, a momentous consequence of his death that would shape its future for the next quarter of a century of its history resulted. Paul H. Gebhard became the Institute's next executive director.

3
Finishing the Mission
(1957–1965)

There is hardly another area in human biology or in sociology in which the scientist has had to fight for his right to do research, as he has when he has attempted to acquire a scientific understanding of human sexual behavior. It is incomprehensible that we should know so little about such an important subject as sex, unless you realize the multiplicity of forces which have operated to dissuade the scientist, to intimidate the scientist, and to force him to cease research in these areas.

Alfred C. Kinsey, "The Right to Do Sex Research," August 1956

KINSEY CALLED HIS LAST ESSAY, DISCOVERED only after his death, "The Right to Do Sex Research."[1] He outlined his passionate belief that scientists had an *obligation* to further understandings of human sexual behavior and, through that knowledge, to combat the religious zealotry, moralism, and ignorance that had hurt so many people. Kinsey had heard the emotional pleas of his students at Indiana University, of homosexuals, of prisoners, and of thousands of ordinary people who had written to him over the years, and his work was driven by compassion as much as by scientific curiosity. He had also heard gratitude from those who felt less alone, even "normal," for the first time in their lives after reading the male and/or female volumes—the Kinsey Reports.

His compassion for ordinary people, particularly those who were often labeled deviant, sick, or criminal, led him to feel the obstacles to sex research deeply. The accusations of the Reece Committee and the subsequent withdrawal of funding by the Rockefeller Foundation, the actions of the US Customs Service, the FBI's investigation of the Institute's staff, and, more generally, the shrill Cold

War mindset that connected sex research with Communism left Kinsey feeling defeated and deeply saddened. Some of his closest friends even said that he died above all of a broken heart. On the other hand, in his last days Kinsey remained as driven and determined as ever, working frantically in spite of doctors' warnings that he would die if he did not take care of himself.[2] In his later biography of Kinsey, Wardell B. Pomeroy wrote that "morale was low for a time and there was a general feeling of disorganization."[3] There is no doubt that the Institute faced a multitude of problems.

Counterweights also figured. The remaining Institute staff, as well as Herman B Wells and other Indiana University officials, felt the immensity of Kinsey's legacy. They and the trustees of Indiana University fully believed that the mission was worth continuing, even as the Institute faced extreme difficulties. Although Kinsey had been notoriously inept at making fund-raising appeals in person, his name carried a great deal of weight in scientific communities.[4] Still, the already difficult task of securing external support funding could only intensify after his death.

Moreover, as noted above, the "Customs case" loomed. Just before Kinsey's death, the secretary of the treasury had finally notified the Institute that it was not exempt from laws that prohibited importing obscene materials just because they were going to be used by scientific researchers, guaranteeing that the long-standing dispute between the Institute and US Customs would go to court, a lengthy and expensive prospect with potentially wide-ranging consequences.[5] Losing the Customs case would have meant much more than the loss of a few photographs. It would have called into question the legal status of all sex research by codifying in law the idea that no one had the right to obtain "obscene" materials, even for scientific or research purposes. The case loomed large as the concrete manifestation of all the opposition facing sex research in Cold War America.

In the meantime, the Institute had to face the more mundane problems of leadership and day-to-day research goals. The agenda Kinsey laid out in 1955 in the last Institute annual progress report before his death would have been considered ambitious by the standards of any research institute, let alone one that had little money beyond the small contributions of private donors and dwindling book royalties. The goal was still to gather one hundred thousand histories (around eighteen thousand had been completed in nearly eighteen years of work), which would be used for twenty-three projects, at least nine of which were planned as full-length monographs.[6] Although many of those publications were supposed to derive from data that the Institute had already collected, researchers had only begun actual writing for one and data tabulations for two others. Kinsey himself had written two chapters for a book on abortion; several staff members were analyzing data on homosexuality for a project entitled "The Homosexual-Heterosexual Balance"; and preliminary analysis was under way for a study of sex offenders and sex offenses, a subject about which Kinsey had written a number of essays and lectures.

The first step was establishing new leadership. Wardell Pomeroy and Paul Gebhard discussed the matter and decided that they should codirect the Institute. Indiana University stepped in, however, and determined that the executive directorship should go to Gebhard, while Pomeroy took up the role of director of field research. Pomeroy was, as he put it, "naturally hurt at what appeared to be a rejection," though he supposed that Indiana University's decision was because Gebhard held a full-time appointment in his home department, anthropology, while Pomeroy did not.[7]

Meanwhile, Clyde Martin, who had been at the Institute as long as anyone—and significantly longer than Gebhard—felt altogether slighted because he was not included in the decision-making process at all. Pomeroy called the slight "unintentional" and said it occurred simply because he and Gebhard had been sharing the major work with Kinsey. His view here, however, may indicate that he and Gebhard respected Martin's contributions less, either because he lacked an advanced degree or because he was primarily in charge of data analysis rather than interviewing and writing.[8] Whatever the case, Martin left the Institute a few years later to pursue an advanced degree.

The restructuring of the Institute generally had the effect of distributing decision-making powers among more people. Cornelia Christenson was added as a trustee, as was Professor Theodore Torrey, chair of the zoology department. In addition, zoology agreed to set aside the equivalent of Kinsey's salary in order to pay for outside consultants to visit and advise the Institute. Whereas Kinsey had determined the research agenda and made most Institute operational decisions, a consensus emerged as to the benefits of a team approach and contributions from outside experts.

This is not to say that Gebhard, as executive director, did not take control and innovate. Many of the changes he made were gradual. One of his first decisions, however, had a drastic and immediate impact on the direction of the Institute's research: he turned to the government for funding. In 1957 the National Institute of Mental Health (NIMH) rescued the Institute from financial collapse, but it also—as Kinsey had feared—made demands, both implicit and explicit, on the Institute that changed everything from researchers' methodology to their governing structure over the subsequent fifteen years. The NIMH, as well as other branches of the Public Health Service (PHS), to which the Institute later applied for funding, wanted practical, useful answers to the specific problems faced by clinicians and public policy makers. Primarily, this meant that it wanted research on sexually abnormal or deviant people, on prominent social problems, and on criminals; the broad understanding of the sexual behaviors of humans as such, to which Kinsey had devoted his research, was simply not to be a priority. This change in direction was obvious in the next two books published by the Institute, *Pregnancy, Birth*

Figure 3.1. Dr. Paul H. Gebhard, pictured here in 1957, became the second director of the Institute for Sex Research in 1956. He would be the longest-serving director in the Institute's history. Photo courtesy of Kinsey Institute Library and Special Collections.

and Abortion (1958) and *Sex Offenders: An Analysis of Types* (1965), and even more so in the projects proposed by Institute staff after 1965.

Nearly as significant for the future of the Institute as gaining funding was winning the Customs case. The "test case," *United States of America v. 31 Photographs*, finally went to court on August 4, 1956, just a few weeks before Kinsey's death. In the minds of the Institute, its lawyers, Indiana University trustees, and the several other parties who filed amicus curiae briefs, the issue at hand was the grand and abstract notion of academic freedom. Was the Institute free to gather materials necessary to its research without interference by the government, even if those materials were considered "obscene" or "lewd" when in the hands of ordinary citizens? In its decision, the United States District Court of Southern New York explicitly set aside the question of academic freedom in favor of ruling on the definition of "obscenity," a question that was in fact being considered in courts all over the country at the time. The case nevertheless became a landmark in legal precedence because it defined academic researchers as a separate category of actors who, because of their scientific perspective, would not be subject to the pernicious influences of obscene materials.

The direction of the Institute and its research during the first half of the Gebhard era was influenced by competing factors. The staff felt the obligation to continue with Kinsey's work, but practical financial demands, the legal uncertainties of the Customs case, and the intervention of the University administration qualitatively changed the research and the publications that resulted from it. Gebhard, who had long thought that Kinsey paid too little attention to the anthropological, sociological, and psychological aspects of sexual behavior, lent a different cast to the Institute's 1960s work. *Sex Offenders* in particular was a very different study from the one that Kinsey had envisioned in collaboration with Alice Field. The nine years after Kinsey's death were still somewhat transitional because of the ongoing efforts to complete Kinsey's unfinished work, but in them lay the seeds of the more drastic changes that Gebhard would introduce after 1965.

United States of America v. 31 Photographs

The result [of the Customs case] has been to establish a clear-cut affirmation of the principle that the subject matter of objective scholarly inquiry is not an object of federal prohibition. This principle has obvious implications for freedom of the mind in many fields, and it is noteworthy that, although Judge Palmeri decided this case on statutory grounds, he took occasion to indicate that, were he compelled to reach a different result under the statute, serious doubts of the constitutionality of the law would have been presented.

Harriet F. Pilpel, "Summary," June 16, 1959, 5, in Customs case documents compiled by Greenbaum, Wolff and Ernst

Kinsey always insisted that the Institute's collections anchored research into human sexual behavior. By the time of his death, the "sex library" had long been the most extensive in the country and probably in the world. He sought materials from as many different cultures and historical periods as possible because he believed that a full understanding of sexual behavior demanded scrutiny of the wide variety of human sexual thought and representation. Touting the Institute's progress on the library in 1948, Kinsey wrote: "A sex library, unlike a library in any other subject, must draw material from a diversity of fields. Not only must biology, medicine, psychology, psychiatry, and other sciences be represented, but also material from purely literary sources, from the Classics, from modern fiction, from poetry, from art, from law, from religious literature, and from many other fields."[9]

Kinsey and his colleagues also collected a wide array of erotic and pornographic images, pictures of lewd graffiti from bathroom stalls, sex toys and contraceptive devices from across the globe, indeed, anything else sex related that they could reasonably acquire. The very first item cataloged in the Institute's artifact collection was a set of eight Glanskap "male diaphragms"—condoms—complete with instructions on correct usage.

In acquiring such materials, Kinsey and his colleagues acted in a legal gray area. At the time, the Comstock Act (1873) prohibited sending obscene materials through the US mail. Many states banned publishing and distributing obscene materials of any kind.[10] Prior to the US Supreme Court's 1965 decision in *Griswold v. Connecticut*, it was illegal in some states, for instance, to use or to distribute information about contraceptives. The law proving most problematic for the Institute, though, was the 1930 Tariff Act. The "Smoot-Hawley" Act, better known for significantly reducing tariffs on imports and, arguably, contributing to economic problems of the Great Depression, included a provision that made it illegal to import any obscene or immoral materials. This act tasked Customs officials with seizing and destroying such materials.[11] Kinsey feared that this dispute with Customs, in addition to costing perhaps $20,000 to $30,000 in legal fees, would do "considerable damage to our capacity to obtain the necessary material to study human sex behavior."[12]

The Institute's contest with the US Customs Service began in 1950. According to some accounts, Kinsey had an informal agreement with the usual Customs official in Indianapolis, who ignored packages destined for the Institute. In November 1950, however, that official was on vacation, and his temporary replacement seized a mixed imported shipment addressed to the Institute—an eighteenth-century French novel, a book by humorist Gershon Legman, a Victorian "spanking novel" called *The Memoirs of Dolly Morton*, and several other "grossly obscene" texts.[13] Though Kinsey and others believed that scientific researchers were exempt from

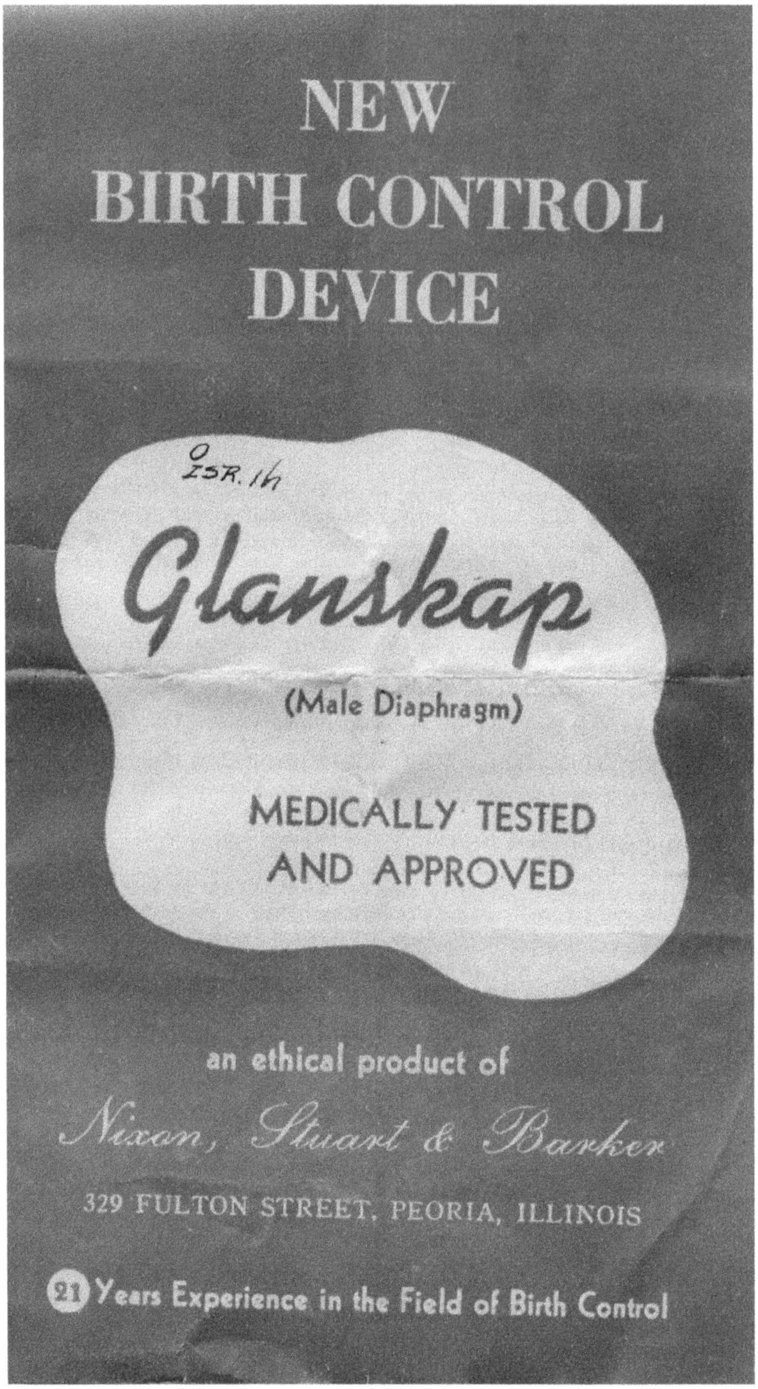

Figure 3.2. Glanskap condoms. Data and printed material were not the only items added to the Institute collections. Pictured here is the instruction manual for a "male diaphragm," recorded as ISR1—the first such item to be cataloged in the newly created Institute Library and Special Collections in 1947. Photo courtesy of Kinsey Institute Library and Special Collections.

Christine Jorgensen Reveals

Is She A Woman?
What About Her Love Life?
Can She Become A Mother?

An intimate glimpse into the personal life of the worlds most sensational celebrity.

Figure 3.3. Christine Jorgensen became a media sensation with her transition narrative and, by extension, added fame to Harry Benjamin, Jorgensen's medical advisor in the United States. She is pictured here advertising a "tell-all" interview. Photo courtesy of Kinsey Institute Library and Special Collections.

laws that restricted access to obscene materials, such an exemption had been neither codified in statutory law nor tested in courts.

The Institute had retained a high-profile New York law firm that was well known for civil rights cases—one of the named partners, Morris Ernst, was a cofounder of the ACLU—before the release of the male volume, and the Institute asked the firm to find a way to obtain the seized materials and, if possible, to ensure that future shipments would not be subject to such seizure. Initially, the lawyers at Greenbaum, Wolff and Ernst sought to bring a "test case" to the courts. In 1952, however, that case was put on hold as they decided to appeal to the secretary of the treasury, who, within the provisions of the 1930 Tariff Act, had the discretion to make exceptions for books of established scientific merit. The secretary, unfortunately, failed to act until 1956, when he denied the Institute's application, saying that the matter should be decided by the courts.[14]

Harriet Pilpel (1901–71), the lawyer then in charge of the Institute's case, reverted to the idea of a test case. In the months prior to Kinsey's death, she worked with Paul Williams, the US attorney for the Southern District of New York, to bring the case before the courts. The most significant result of that negotiation was that the libel suit that the government filed would be against "31 photographs 4¾ × 7 inches in size, and various pictures, books, and other materials," instead of against the Institute itself; the Institute would act as the claimant, but it would not be subject to legal penalties if the government won. This did not mean that the stakes were not high. If the Institute lost, all of its research materials, including, potentially, its data, could have been subject to all of the other laws restricting obscene materials in Indiana and throughout the country.

The Institute and its lawyers—and the trustees of Indiana University, who filed an amicus curiae brief supporting the Institute's claims—did not seek to challenge obscenity laws as such. They framed their case instead as a defense of the rights of researchers. A few days before the government officially filed its suit, Kinsey told a reporter that the case was "a real test of the right of scholars to have access to their materials." One of the lawyers involved in preparing the Institute's claim told the same reporter that the government's action was "the most severe blow in our country's history against freedom of scientific inquiry . . . a direct attack on freedom of access to the factual material on which all scientific research must be based."[15] Pilpel argued the case, for the most part, on these grounds.

The decision in the case, then, was a little bit anticlimactic. As with most court decisions, Judge Edmund L. Palmeri's opinion could be read in several ways. Pilpel chose to see it as a clear-cut victory for researchers. Palmeri, however, based his ruling not on any protections for scholars or academics but on the definition of obscenity. In fact, he explicitly wrote that the question of "'academic freedom,' much bruited in the oral argument by the claimant, does not arise in this case."[16] He ruled instead that the materials in question were not obscene and should not have been seized on that basis. The logic by which Palmeri determined that explicitly pornographic images were not obscene seems a little convoluted, but his ruling was very much in line with a plethora of case law. In June 1957 the US Supreme Court, in *Roth v. United States*, had decided that any material that on the whole appealed to the prurient interest of an average person should be considered obscene and therefore subject to legal restriction.[17] Researchers were not "average people," Palmeri said; therefore, precedence from several earlier cases came into play. The material in question would not appeal to the prurient interest of "all

Figure 3.4. Attorney Harriet Fleischl Pilpel, ca. 1955. Pilpel, a prominent First Amendment attorney, would help lead the Institute through the Customs case, ending in 1957. She is pictured here visiting the research team in Bloomington. Photo courtesy of Kinsey Institute Library and Special Collections.

those whom it is likely to reach," the standard set down in *United States v. Levine* in 1936.[18] Just as a naked body is not obscene in a medical textbook but would be if "wantonly exposed in the open market," pornography is not obscene in the hands of a scientist.[19]

Also, in *Roth*, the Court held that a California statute that made it illegal to send obscene materials through the mail did not violate the First Amendment protections of free speech because obscene materials, by definition, held no redeeming social value, and the First Amendment only protected speech and ideas that contributed to public discourse in some way (however objectionable those ideas might be to the mainstream of public opinion). That aspect of the ruling was significant in *31 Photographs* because if obscene materials, by definition, have no redeeming social value, then materials that do have such value—or that are used to contribute to the good of society—must not be obscene. However tautological such an argument might be, it led Palmeri to the conclusion that the purpose for which something is used must be considered when determining if it qualifies as obscene or not.

Palmeri cited several cases supporting his decision. All converged on the proposition, however, that no material is obscene per se; obscenity must always be defined with reference to a "beholder" and the interest or purpose of that beholder.[20] The ruling was undeniably a victory for the Institute and for sex researchers more generally. It placed the Institute on solid legal footing when it came to its collections and library. The ruling indirectly became significant when Institute researchers solicited diaries and sex calendars from research subjects. Gebhard, Pomeroy, and others assured those wishing to contribute that they would not be subject to laws restricting mail, since any mail directed to the Institute was exempt. On the other hand, the decision rested on the Institute's assurance that its library and archival collections would not be widely available and would only be used by qualified researchers employed by the Institute. The win, then, had two effects: while it set a legal precedent that, many hoped, legally codified the right to do sex research, the wording of the ruling made some at the Institute even more cautious about allowing outside researchers access to the Institute's data, library, and collections.

The latter aspect of this decision still loomed in the background when, just a few years later, the NIMH urged Gebhard to open the doors of the Institute and allow a wide variety of scholars to access the Institute's data and collections. By and large, Gebhard agreed with the goal, but throughout his tenure he proceeded with extreme caution, sometimes expressing his fear that outside scholars could easily damage the reputation of the Institute if they were allowed too much latitude with the Institute's materials. On the other hand, the Customs case was among the reasons Gebhard felt forced to turn to the NIMH for funding in the first place.

Figure 3.5. Dr. Harry Benjamin, ca. 1950. Benjamin was a leading endocrinologist working on transsexuality research. He corresponded regularly with Kinsey and would later donate his collection to the Institute. Photo courtesy of Kinsey Institute Library and Special Collections.

Figure 3.6. Cornelia V. Christenson and William Dellenback photographing collections. Christenson, hired to assist in the later stages of the female volume, would become a research associate and later publish the first biography of Kinsey. She is pictured here with William Dellenback, the Institute's photographer, making photographic file records for sculptures and other fragile three-dimensional objects, many still in storage, in the Institute's collections. Photo courtesy of Kinsey Institute Library and Special Collections.

Although Indiana University had taken on much of the financial cost of the case, it had further drained the Institute's already overburdened budget.

Pregnancy, Birth and Abortion

> The reasons for induced abortion are, and have been, legion in human history. Usually the motive is powerful and compelling, as in instances where poverty or ill health is involved, or where a birth would result in serious social complications. In other instances the motive is, to western minds, trivial: for example, some women on the island of Lesu abort because pregnancy interferes with dancing, which is one of the chief pleasures of life.
>
> Paul Gebhard, Wardell Pomeroy, Clyde Martin, and Cornelia Christenson, *Pregnancy, Birth and Abortion*

In Gebhard and his colleagues' hands, the volume that would become *Pregnancy, Birth and Abortion* (PBA) diverged from Kinsey's original plan and chapter drafts. It included only one chapter on induced abortion, while the remainder of the book was about reproductive behavior more generally. Some of Kinsey's ideas remained, but by and large they were buried within the broader and more descriptive concerns. On abortion law, the book's only statement was that there was a "widespread difference between our overt culture as expressed in our laws and public pronouncements and our covert culture as expressed in what people actually do and secretly think," as with laws concerning most types of sexual behavior. The authors noted that police and other officials often allowed known abortionists to practice because "it is felt that there is a need for their services." Here no trace of the heat of Kinsey's critical draft can be detected.[21]

Paul H. Gebhard, Wardell B. Pomeroy, Clyde E. Martin, and Cornelia V. Christenson wrote the text of *PBA*. Moreover, Dr. Christopher Tietze, an outstanding demographer and statistician, served as a consultant. The book was not based on any new data (there was little funding and less time for field research), which posed problems but also added benefits. Since, according to the authors, Kinsey had set out to study sexual behavior, not pregnancy and its outcomes, "this particular piece of research might be described as peripheral to our main interests."[22] Not all of the histories included data on pregnancy, particularly the earliest in the sample. On the other hand, the sample was enhanced by an accurate view of pregnancy and its outcomes outside marriage, for which there were few data at the time. The sample was also interesting in that it included, for the first time, the "negro" sample, allowing the authors to add another dimension to their comparisons. The data on prison women, too, were unprecedented in the existing literature. The sample allowed for a wide view of reproductive behavior as it related to an array of issues precisely because pregnancy, birth, and abortion had not been the main goal of the existing histories.

Although some in the press called *PBA* an "explosive" new "K-bomb," it received nothing like the media attention that had accompanied the Institute's first two volumes.[23] Not surprisingly, the press, including *McCall's* magazine, which had exclusive rights to preview the volume before publication, focused on "unwanted pregnancies" and abortion. The opening page of the *McCall's* article asked: "How many American women get pregnant before marriage? Is this figure higher among the 'upper class'? . . . among the strongly religious? . . . among the younger generation? How many have become 'shotgun brides'? How many have abortions? How many women die from or are permanently injured by abortion? Who performs abortions and how much do they cost?" The report, according to *McCall's*, proved that abortion was "a modern social problem of far greater scope than most people ever would have dreamed."[24] Only a few paragraphs in the article said that *PBA* examined how many women get pregnant, whether they were married or not, and the outcomes of those pregnancies.

The final text of *PBA* contained fewer than forty pages specifically devoted to abortion. As the last chapter and some appendices, this material corrected common misconceptions. For example, most reports from sampled informants depicted the experience of abortion as neither physically nor psychologically traumatic.[25] On the other hand, Kinsey's pointed frustration and sense of social injustice were largely absent from the volume. Some of the issues in which he had expressed the most investment during the 1955 Planned Parenthood conference and after, such as the causes of women seeking abortion and his trenchant critique of corrupt law enforcement, received only watered-down treatment in *PBA*. And the abortion chapter offered no exploration of the tantalizing hypotheses sketched in the 1956 text. Instead, the book's chapter structure and arrangement of material echoed the first Kinsey Reports. The team had analyzed the interviewee sample by marital, racial, and social/civil status—"The Single Woman," "The Married Woman," "The Previously Married Woman," "The Negro Woman," and "The Prison Woman"—as the chapter divides.

Within each chapter a basic format arranged the analysis: "Pregnancy" and "Outcome of Pregnancy." Rich with finely differentiated tables that specify trends for each category of pregnant woman, the 1958 text did confirm a key Kinsey finding outlined in his 1956 draft. Married women, as the majority of women pregnant in any year, had the largest net number of induced or nontherapeutic, and thus illegal, abortions. They also had higher odds of securing approval for therapeutic or legal abortions. Interestingly, too, doctors more often believed wives reporting their abortions as spontaneous in the context of about three-quarters of net conceptions in married women ending in childbirth.[26] Why would this supposedly natural event befall single pregnant women far less frequently? It seems unlikely that marital status would affect rates here, but it could certainly affect perception.

Conversely, by the 1940s, induced abortion was the commonest outcome of pregnancy among single women sampled. Wives in the Institute sample reported that about a quarter of conceptions resulted in induced illegal abortion. For single women, the rate was closer to two abortions for every live birth. The authors took this to be a marker of the great stigma attached to unwed motherhood, especially in white population groups.[27]

Once the book had been published, Gebhard turned to the daunting task of completing the research and preparations for the long-planned sex offenders study. In 1959 he made two crucial hires on whom he greatly depended for the next six years. Alan Blaine Johnson, a computer expert and data manager, became a central resource for compiling and interpreting quantitative data. The other hire was John H. Gagnon, a sociologist trained at the University of Chicago and a notable later exponent of the concept of the social construction of sexuality. He joined the research staff in 1959 before he had submitted his doctoral dissertation. Soon he provided invaluable momentum in the completion of the sex offenders study, lodging successful grant applications and later, in 1965, persuading his graduate

Figure 3.7. Dr. John H. Gagnon, ca. 1961. Gagnon became the first new researcher hired by Gebhard. He was recruited in 1959 specifically to assist with the completion of *Sex Offenders* and new projects the Institute started in the mid-1960s. Photo courtesy of Kinsey Institute Library and Special Collections.

school colleague William Simon to join the Institute as a researcher after Simon's decade of work with the National Opinion Research Center.

Even as the Institute staff girded themselves for completing this last part of Kinsey's original mission, Gebhard looked ahead, and with quite some anxiety. No longer did private foundations seem willing to fund sex research. The 1954 Reece inquiry sent a thoroughly chilling message about the risks of angering the partisan foes of sex research. Government had to be considered a principal likely funder, but acquiring this support would require different approaches and strategies not hitherto undertaken by Institute researchers. The NIMH and PHS as major funders of cognate fields needed to understand Institute work for there to be a chance of researchers securing their support. So Gebhard petitioned for an evaluation of the Institute setup via a formal "site visit," or external review. Throughout the 1962–63 consultant visits and evaluations, Institute staff—Gebhard, Gagnon, Christenson, and Johnson—became aware that it was they who had to understand NIMH work in any campaign for research funding. The shoe proved to be on the proverbial other foot.

The NIMH Review

> I am sorry we are not offering NIMH a bright new package designed to be in complete accord with what we know is wanted. Our package represents our compromise with harsh reality: it's going to take us three years to free ourselves from servitude to the twenty-five years of accumulated data and habit and make ourselves the masters rather than the servants of the Institute.
>
> Paul H. Gebhard to Philip Sapir, October 13, 1963

One of Gebhard's first decisions as the newly minted executive director of the Institute was to turn to the PHS for funding. Kinsey had preferred private foundations and individual donors, since they were less likely to try and influence the direction of research than government agencies. However, two years after the Reece committee, it was clear that philanthropic foundations like Rockefeller would not promptly overcome fears of congressional reprisals if they resumed support for sex research. The Committee for Research in Problems of Sex had awarded a couple of small grants—$3,000 and $5,000, or $25,807 and $43,012 in today's values—for the abortion study.[28] Other individuals, Hugh Hefner among them, offered some donations, but the Institute was relying largely on dwindling royalties from the Kinsey Reports and on government bonds that Kinsey had purchased for a "rainy day." Even with Indiana University providing facilities and some researchers partly paid by their home departments, Gebhard estimated that the Institute needed around $75,000 (approximately $593,000 today) each year to carry out its research program.[29] Even that number meant a substantial reduction in field research. Private foundations simply were not, Gebhard concluded, offering grants that would cover those kinds of expenses.

Arguably, Kinsey's wariness about government funding proved justified. While significant research funding of various kinds existed, three factors influenced permissible disbursement. First, each agency held autonomous objectives and concerns and expected research projects to match its agenda. Second, political mandates—including those from the president—impacted agency agendas. Third, Congress could veto or restrict agencies' budgets to register disapproval of proposed research projects and researchers, a powerful influence on research receiving public support. Project proposals were rarely funded outright. PHS officials and outside experts reviewed each one, a process that garnered critiques of every aspect of the proposed research. Frequently, the Institute had to revise and resubmit proposals. Once the Institute did receive funding, PHS officials regularly visited the Institute to check on project progress and offer yet more advice on proceeding. While such visits were, in many ways, collaborative, further funding depended, of course, on the evaluation lodged.

To test the waters, in 1957 the Institute submitted proposals for two projects: the "heterosexual-homosexual balance" and a study of sex offenders and offenses. Although the NIMH offered support for the sex offender project for three years—$42,000 in year one, $44,000 in year two, and $46,000 in year three (today equal to $371,000, $379,000, and $396,000, respectively)—from the outset the NIMH urged the Institute to adjust its priorities. In explaining why the NIMH had given only about half the support requested for the Institute's homosexual-heterosexual balance project, Philip Sapir, chief of the research grants and fellowship branch, wrote that it was because "the major interest" of the research team "was in correcting popular misconceptions about the bipolarity of sexuality" instead of focusing on the contributions their work could make to "developmental psychology and psychiatry."[30] The NIMH, in other words, was less interested in homosexual activities and more interested in (primarily) homosexual people, their psychological development and makeup, and the ways mental health professionals could best treat them.

This critique signaled beyond the one specific research project at issue. Sapir urged the Institute researchers to reevaluate all of their operations and methodologies so that they would remain relevant. The NIMH wanted useful, practical information from the researchers they funded. Researchers needed to do more than illuminate realities and problems; they needed to aid progress and solve problems. Sapir implored Gebhard to make the Institute less insular and secretive, to collaborate with other researchers, and to educate both students and other professionals.

Neither the research projects nor the library and collections mattered unless the Institute acted, transmitting relevant knowledge and expertise. Indeed, he warned the researchers that Kinsey's insistence on complete confidentiality and his unwillingness to share data from unfinished research (in the form of articles and lectures) posed a serious barrier to their productivity and, therefore, their ability to secure new funding.[31]

In response, Gebhard solicited further expert opinion. "We are currently in the midst of introspection and planning concerning the future of our research," he wrote to one expert, Dr. William Caudill. "We'd like to cast a critical eye on everything from our methodology to our taste in office furniture."[32] The review process took nearly a year and a half. The Institute paid an array of consultants, as well as NIMH officials, for two to three days of visits, prognosis, and brainstorming. Suggested changes did not proceed from scientific or research problems that Institute staff encountered. The NIMH insisted that changes must precede the Institute securing support. The interests of Congress, Presidents Kennedy and Johnson, and the political and social climate more broadly drove the shape of these changes.

In unison, the first priority the consultants and NIMH officials urged was using the data collected since 1938. Most of those data had not yet been truly analyzed; Kinsey had estimated that only 10 percent of the data grounded the male and female volumes. The consultants also recommended allowing outside researchers to have access to the data, which Kinsey had adamantly opposed on the grounds that he had promised absolute confidentiality to all of his subjects.[33] NIMH experts responded warmly to this prospect; indeed, the only grant request from 1962–63 that was fully funded was for the "data retrieval" project. Over the next five years, the Institute staff—researchers, as well as the archivists and librarians—devoted a significant amount of time to transferring interview data to tapes and IBM cards, making them amenable to rapid sorting and tabulation.

The consultants could see value in new Institute projects and methods. Such undertakings, though, should only begin following completion of current projects, especially the *Sex Offenders* volume. In the meantime, Institute researchers should examine existing data on specific groups of people (transvestites and homosexuals were at the top of the list) or specific abnormalities and inadequacies, with a strong favoring of the problem of impotence. Output should privilege quantity, especially via refereed scientific journal articles, over long monographs, which could be years in the making. A consequence of this mode of completion, analysis, and professionalized output might be, as a long-term goal, a distinctive new theory of human sexuality and sexual development.[34] In his summary of the advice of Dr. Fred Strodtbeck (1919–2005), a psychologist from the University of Denver, Gebhard's notes from the meeting included this one: "The only significant contribution other than the raw empirical data which [illegible] made by the Institute has been the use

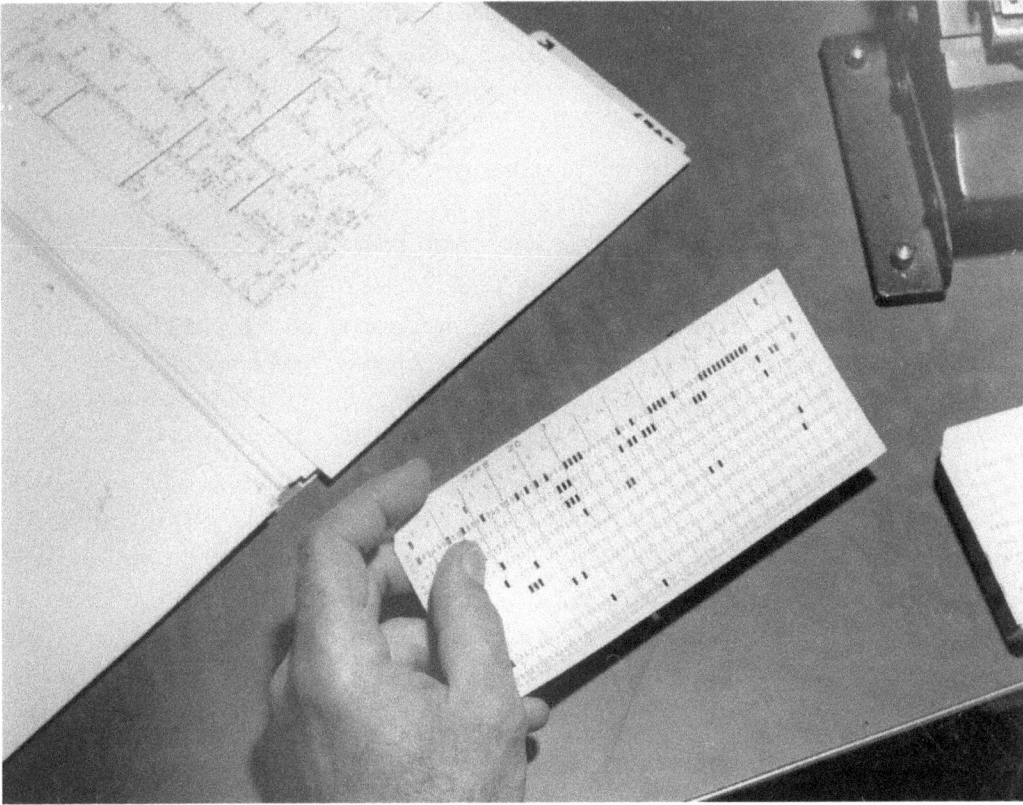

Figure 3.8. A punch card and a sex history, ca. 1948. A major development during the final stages of data crunching was the Hollerith machine. Data from the sex histories were punched into punch cards and sent through the machine. Photo courtesy of the Kinsey Institute Library and Special Collections.

of the orgasm as the unit act for counting human sexual experience. Even so, our work has become simply known as the Kinsey Reports, indicating a description of a body of data rather than as in the case of Newton or Morton whose names are then attached to their theoretical orientation and laws of experience."[35] This observation was not necessarily a criticism of Kinsey's work. Strodtbeck argued, however, that Kinsey had started at ground zero and, by necessity, had accumulated data on Americans' sexual experiences. Now it was time for the Institute to interrogate reasons for sexual behavior and the meanings that people attached to their experiences. As an example, Strodtbeck argued that while it is interesting to know that one-third of all the males in America had at least one orgasm in homosexual contact, it would be "even more interesting to know what the genesis of homosexuality was and how it varied in different sets of persons."[36]

Other consultants echoed Strodtbeck's advice. They contended that the Institute's large body of accumulated data suggested solutions to social and individual problems, if they were used to ground theoretical understandings of sexuality, with particular focus upon sexual abnormalities and inadequacies. In addition, such theories would allow the Institute to respond to current events and advocate social policies. A theoretical understanding of the genesis of homosexuality was newly necessary in light of contemporaneous social and political events that made homosexuality a visible "problem" in American culture.[37]

Specific research plans ranked as of only secondary importance to these consultants. Institute researchers had proven records for solid, valuable research. Instead, advice highlighted the structure and operations of the Institute and its nonresearch activities. Consultants urged the creation of an advisory board and a board of governors, greater use of external consultants, and teaching. Reviewers contended that the staff spent too much time talking only to each other without generating new ideas. The Institute had always been run by trustees who were also researchers. Time better devoted to research was wasted on administrative tasks, signaling poor management. Such tasks consumed over half of Gebhard's time, time that was instead needed to complete *Sex Offenders*, which should have been his top priority. The researchers diverged their precious time and effort to questions and problems outside their specific fields of expertise. Interactions with fellow experts with related interests but different skills would prove much more productive. Continual, two-way interaction with other experts would make the Institute more efficient and would help spur creativity.[38]

Consultants' third recommendation concerned teaching. Institute staff had not taught classes or given seminars on sexuality since Kinsey, at the insistence of President Wells, resigned from the marriage course in 1940. In his history of the Institute from 1956 to 1982, Gebhard wrote: "1962: NIMH demands that we teach sex courses to students and staff in Psychiatry at the Indiana University medical school. Consequently, president Wells drops his ban on our teaching and encourages us."[39] Philip Sapir was indeed emphatic in saying that the Institute staff, as leading experts in the field of sexual behavior, should advance sex education and incorporate human sexuality in medical school curricula. The future doctors and psychiatrists of the world needed to know how to help their patients with sexual problems, and they were entirely unprepared by their medical education to do so.

Other consultants agreed and suggested that, in addition, Institute researchers should all teach courses on human sexuality in their home departments at both the undergraduate and graduate levels. It was no longer necessary, they said, to hide from the outside world in order to prevent controversy, and, in fact, students had reached a point where they hungered for reliable information about sexuality not only for their personal lives but also in service of understanding human cultures and history.

All of the consultants concurred that Institute work had stagnated. In large part, they attributed this stagnation to a reluctance to engage with the world outside of the Institute's doors. Things had changed since 1948. In the context of what is commonly described as the "sexual revolution" (which, according to the media at least, Kinsey had launched), researchers had much less to fear in public. Consultants also agreed that sex and sexuality were public social and political issues or problems to which the public expected sex researchers to seek solutions.[40]

The advice of these consultants determined the direction of the Institute for nearly two decades. Almost all of its activities received scrutiny in the process of this review. Gebhard sought to plan new research projects, as well as a new, more theoretical methodology. He also sought the guidance of research psychologists and psychiatrists such as Dr. John Benjamin, who studied transvestism at the University of Denver Medical School, and Dr. Strodtbeck. On Sapir's advice, though, Gebhard also solicited input from advisors who, though not sex researchers, understood the operations of well-funded research institutes. In particular, he consulted oncologist Dr. Michael Shimkin (1913–89), famous for establishing the link between cigarettes and cancer. As well, Gebhard greatly valued Johns Hopkins genetic epidemiologist Dr. Abraham M. Lilienfeld (1920–84), with his extensive survey research and his daunting record, "a minimum of twelve grants of his own going at any one time, probably totaling in any one year over half a million dollars."[41] Gebhard chose other consultants from the NIMH or the PHS. The Institute desperately needed dollars, but Sapir held firm: those dollars awaited demonstrable change in the Institute's direction.

Significantly, most of the consultants were either medical doctors or psychologists and psychiatrists from medical schools. By contrast, principal Institute staff represented the social science fields of anthropology and sociology. Even Wardell Pomeroy, the only Institute staff member with any expertise in psychology, pursued a PhD rather than an MD. Philip Sapir and the NIMH's emphasis on "useful" and "practical" knowledge meant that the Institute researchers needed advice on how to make their research valuable to clinicians—practicing psychologists, marriage counselors, doctors, social workers—whose interest in sex research related directly to their patients and clients. Dr. Lilienfeld, an MD in the public health department at Johns Hopkins University, even recommended that the Institute hire a medical doctor with epidemiological experience, especially since "the attack by congress on health research is on specific projects, not on medical research." Dr. Strodtbeck, who had visited the Institute multiple times as a member of the NIMH grant review teams, accused the Institute of being outright hostile toward clinicians and insisted that it redress this bias.[42]

Gebhard gave responses at once optimistic and pessimistic. In the midst of it all, he wrote to Sapir that "looking at ourselves through our consultants' eyes" was a "painful sight." A few years later, however, he wrote again to say he was extremely grateful for all of the advice, lamenting not seeking such a review years earlier.[43] For the most part, he embraced the consultants' suggestions and was particularly excited about developing a firm theoretical stance with reference to the genesis and development of sexuality. He doubted, however, his capacity and that of the Institute as a whole to change direction quickly enough.[44] Perhaps Gebhard was still feeling the wounds of the 1950s, starting with the Reece committee and followed by the Customs case. Insufficiency of resources for meeting financial and institutional expectations heightened his anxieties over the Institute. His notes on the site visit included the following: "It might be useful to change the name of the Institute and not talk about sex research, but rather to describe ourselves as an Institute for social biology. This would reduce our vulnerability to Congressional investigation, and it would also not flaunt our role in the face of the community." He added that if the name were changed to something nonsexual and therefore less controversial, people might bequeath donations to the Institute in their wills.[45]

Gebhard took nearly three more years to finish *Sex Offenders*. While he was doing so, other Institute staff initiated minor changes. The data retrieval project was their biggest success, as well as their start on allowing researchers to use the data, library, and archives. Elizabeth Egan, then head librarian, began to adapt the Dewey Decimal System so that the library and collections could be more comprehensively cataloged and accessible to outside researchers. The Institute staff cautiously opened the doors halfway. Not until 1966 though did they truly embark on major changes and new research projects.

Sex Offenders

> But it is difficult to find logic in our culture vis-à-vis adult heterosexuality. On the one hand, we stress and encourage the development of heterosexual behavior—the literature, the advertisements, the movies, everything relentlessly dins the order: be sexually attractive, find romance, get a mate! On the other hand, we strive to prevent heterosexual coitus, the logical end-product of the social campaign for heterosexuality, in any situation other than legal marriage. We tread on the accelerator and brake simultaneously; this may result in the desired speed, but it is difficult on the mechanism.
>
> Paul H. Gebhard, John H. Gagnon, Wardell B. Pomeroy, and Cornelia Christenson, *Sex Offenders: An Analysis of Types*, 108

A sex crime panic gripped the United States in the 1930s and 1940s. Legislators across the country passed "sexual psychopath laws." Such laws had as their premise that most or all sex-related offenses signaled a potentially violent, even homicidal psychopathic condition that required treatment; their focus was not to criminalize particular behaviors but to harshly treat a category of people. Kinsey and Alice Field understood sex offenses broadly—they included prostitutes, "wayward" girls, abortion providers and their clients, and those in same-sex erotic contacts, as well as those committing rape, noncoital sexual assault, exhibitionism, "public sex" or "lewdness," voyeurism, incest, prohibited intergenerational encounters, and bestiality—but they understood such crimes as different acts, not as symptoms of a pathology or any other overall condition.

Sex Offenders: An Analysis of Types (1965), like its 1958 predecessor, *Pregnancy, Birth and Abortion*, straddled the line between the "Kinsey era" and the "Gebhard era." It was the last major Institute publication that was strongly taxonomic in approach. It also was the last based primarily on the eighteen thousand interviews collected during Kinsey's lifetime, thus continuing much of the same methodology. The study was, however, very different from the one that Kinsey had begun planning even before the 1948 male volume was published. Gebhard and his colleagues—John Gagnon, a sociologist who had joined the Institute in 1959, just after *PBA* was published, Pomeroy, and Christenson—narrowed the scope of the study to men ages sixteen and older who had been convicted of, relatively speaking, a select few offenses.

Most crucial, *Sex Offenders* correlated behaviors and personality or identity categories. It was the first Institute book to do so, reflecting promptly the impact of the NIMH consultants' recommendations. This amounted to a huge methodological shift. It was also rather shaky, since this approach would have implications for the method and research. The descriptions were, as Gebhard and the team wrote, "necessarily rather impressionistic" because they had little data on psychological factors and because they did not have a working theory of sexual etiologies. Still, their reconfigured treatment of the sex offender material embraced a move toward some of the themes that would predominate in the Institute's research in the latter half of Gebhard's directorship.[46]

The sex crime panic that had led to passage of so many sexual psychopath laws in the 1930s and 1940s had formed the backdrop of Kinsey's work on the subject. By the time Gebhard took the lead on the project, though, panic had eased, and the United States had entered a somewhat more "liberal" era. The category "sex crime" itself fragmented. The slippery term had included everything from rape to adultery, from abortion to consensual homosexual acts, from contraceptive use to producing indecent literature, but in the 1960s the media began to distinguish between varieties of crimes and degrees of severity. Similarly, courts and legislators became more wary of their own slippery categorizations. Many sexual psychopath laws were repealed or revised over the course of the 1960s and 1970s, partly because psychologists and academics began repudiating legislators who claimed that solid psychological theory supported their legislative efforts.[47] At the same time, elements within the civil rights movement publicized racism in sex crimes prosecution, effectively combatting the journalistic stereotype of black offenders against white women and sometimes portraying sex offender laws as new forms of lynching. Contemporary popular narratives portraying a single sexually "deviant" act as signaling violent psychopathology declined.[48]

Sex Offenders participated in and advanced these trends. Much media coverage of the book claimed that it proved that sex crimes were rarer and sex offenders less violent than previously believed. The crazed sex fiend was a "figment of journalistic imagination," newspapers across the country reported. Drugs and pornography did not cause sex offenses, violence and murder associated with sex crimes were extremely rare, and sex laws were too harsh and out of step with reality.[49] *Sex Offenders* gained relatively little media attention, though it garnered favorable and appreciative reviews, and it reinforced the already popular ideas that not all kinds of sex crimes were the same and that consensual activities between adults in private should not be criminalized.

The simple goal of *Sex Offenders* was to answer several key questions: "Are the sexual histories or social backgrounds of sex offenders different from those of non-offending individuals? Do persons with the same sort of illegal sexual behavior, whether convicted or not, have similar sexual and social histories?" The book answered these questions, but it did so with reference to a very small number of sex offenses, primarily because of the narrow definition of "sex offense" that the authors used: "an overt act committed by a person for his own immediate sexual gratification which (1) is contrary to the prevailing sexual mores of the society in which he lives, and/or is legally punishable, and (2) results in his being legally convicted."[50] Crimes like prostitution, bigamy, abortion, and any number of paraphilias were not, therefore, included. Neither were women, since "women are rarely charged with, and still more rarely convicted, of sex offences other than prostitution."[51] If Kinsey and Field's general vision for the study remained, the successor team excluded from the final book much of their sample and many of the offenses and offenders they had studied. *Sex Offenders* was entirely devoted to men in prison.

More tellingly, the categories of analysis changed. Crimes were divided into "types" according to criteria of "basic psychological and sociological importance: whether the offence was directed at a person of the same or opposite sex; whether that person was a child, minor, or adult; whether he or she was genetically or socially closely related to the offender; whether the relationship was by consent or forced; and whether or not physical contact was involved."[52] Many offenders acted opportunistically or situationally, but other crimes were the result of particular personality traits. This effort to draw conclusions about the personalities of offenders was the strongest indication that Gebhard and the other authors had moved far away from Kinsey's vision and toward a psychological framework and methodology for understanding sexual behavior.

Kinsey had never given credence to either personality or identity as relevant categories of analysis. In one of the most famous sections of the male volume, he wrote that "the world is not to be divided into sheep and goats. Not all things are black, nor all things white. It is a fundamental of taxonomy that nature rarely deals with discrete categories. Only the human mind invents categories and tries to force facts into separate pigeon-holes."[53] His data and experience proved the lack of fixity in lifelong human sexual behavior. Hence, rigid sexual categories more served enforcement of social mores than accurate individual description.

Gebhard and his colleagues did not suggest that all sex offenses were the result of either personality traits or identity. Yet large groups within their study occupied such categories. For example, a large proportion of their heterosexual offenders against children were classified as pedophiles, distinct from those who offended against children for opportunistic or situational reasons or because more appropriate partners were unavailable. Similarly, they made a distinction between those with a marked homosexual orientation and those who committed homosexual offenses for other reasons. Gebhard and the other authors did not try to delve into the psychological causes or other etiologies of pedophilia or homosexuality. Indeed, they argued that to do so would be futile, since so little was known on the subject. Their analysis indicated that in some people such factors were the principal causes of their offenses, an argument that Kinsey would never have made.

The Institute team's belief in fixed personalities and identity categories led Gebhard and the other authors to specific conclusions about sex crime laws and prosecutions. They claimed that "within the foreseeable future, there will be no great reduction in the number of sex offenders unless our laws are changed." Their most significant conclusion was that there were, broadly, two classes of offenders. First, there were those whose behavior was "statistically normal, motivated by desires which most laymen and clinicians would consider within our cultural norms." These offenses were "normal" but for a variety of reasons were inappropriate or punishable. Heterosexual adultery between consenting adults and occasional opportunistic peeping would be the best examples. Significantly, these offenses were not caused by any kind of pathological personality traits. The other class consisted of behavior that was statistically rare and "outside our cultural norms and/or pathological." All offenses involving force, offenses against children, incest, exhibitionism, and compulsive peeping fall into this category. These behaviors did, at least much of the time, indicate a pathological personality. The authors recommended expending minimal resources on the first class of offenders, since their acts did not threaten social organization or cause psychological damage to any great degree. Their recommendations adhered to the same philosophy as

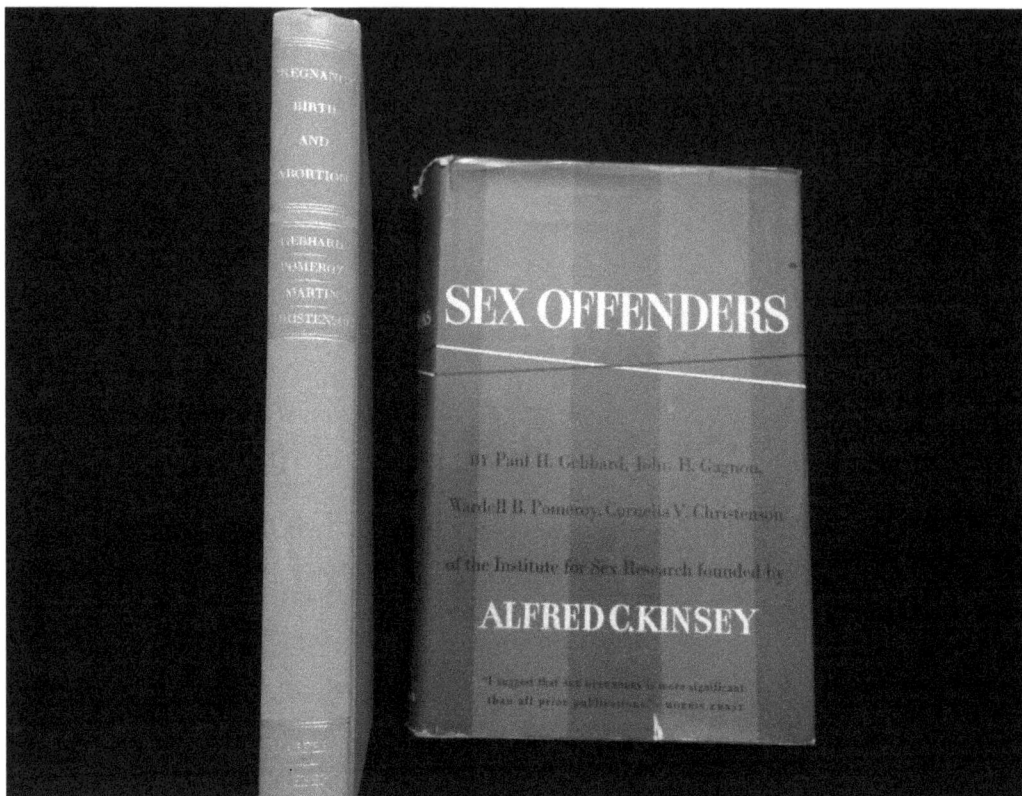

Figure 3.9. *Pregnancy, Birth and Abortion* (1958) and *Sex Offenders: An Analysis of Types* (1965) completed the Kinsey-era monograph projects. Photo courtesy of Kinsey Institute Library and Special Collections.

that of the American Law Institute and the Wolfenden report in England: "What two or more consenting adults did sexually in private should not be governed by statute law."[54]

Significantly, homosexual contact between consenting adults did not fit into either class of offense, since it was outside of social norms but statistically normal. It was frowned on but it did no actual harm to the individuals involved. Since homosexuality had no reproductive consequences "to form a legitimate concern of society," the authors concluded that laws against homosexual activity "are designed not for the protection of person or property but for the enforcement of our cultural taboo against homosexuality."[55] That cultural taboo was partly expressed by a belief that homosexuality was a product of a pathology—it was classified as one by the American Psychiatric Association until 1973—but the idea that homosexuality was instead a fixed identity, not a pathological personality type, was gradually spreading in the mid-1960s.

* * *

Sex Offenders completed the projects that Kinsey had left on the drawing board. Though plenty of other projects—such as a volume on marital adjustment to be coauthored with Emily Mudd and a volume on European sexual behavior—had been under discussion or on wish lists or projected plans, it was abortion and sex offenders that had him put pen to paper before his death. Both had reached a peak of concern and depth of analysis during the first decade of the Institute's existence, and Kinsey's efforts had been quickened by analysis of the female volume data and the contributions of peer scientists, clinicians, and professional contacts who enlarged his intellectual and methodological horizons. Meanwhile, the Customs case outcome, which Kinsey did not live to see, opened up a new phase in collections development.

As noted above, the tenor of the 1958 and especially the 1965 volumes differed markedly from the books planned by Kinsey. Their altered methods, focus, and rhetoric signaled the sea change under way at Gebhard's instigation as the new executive director. These volumes partly responded to his understandings of a changing external environment for the Institute's work. The Institute was no longer the recipient of significant private foundation funding of its projects and philosophical direction, and support on a scale sufficient for both the research staff and their projects and the crucial development and management of collections would not be forthcoming from Indiana University. In assessing their options, Institute staff realized that government grants via various authorities and disbursers appeared to be the only viable path forward.

Hence, Institute researchers could no longer chart their own missions, directions, and methods. The NIMH site visit between the two final Kinsey-inaugurated books made that perfectly clear. If Gebhard somewhat tactlessly spoke ill of the dead, describing himself and Institute colleagues as slaves or servants of the founder's vision, the decade ahead would show if the path he chose molded them not into the master of his aspirations but instead into servants of new masters.

4
Navigating Sexual Revolution
(1966–1981)

Now we are revising our schedule of questions. Lots of questions have been answered—we are past the stage of counting noses and orgasms. The second step is to study sex in terms of its meanings to the individual, the interaction between individuals and society, sex in its emotional and psychological context.

Paul H. Gebhard, quoted in Alton Blakeslee, "Many Follow in Kinsey's Inquiring Footsteps," *Arizona Republic*, January 23, 1968

The increasing significance of the sexual in modern life has been greeted with joy by a few, despair by a few, and an ambivalence by the many. . . . This experience of change, especially with respect to the mass media and the freedom of discussion of sexual activity, has led to a belief in the existence of a sex revolution. What may be revolutionary or may set the stage for revolution, however, is the eager willingness of the society to embrace the idea that a revolution is going on.

William Simon and John Gagnon, *The Sexual Scene*, 3–4

WHAT DID THE AGE OF AQUARIUS, WOODSTOCK, the Stonewall riots, the Miss World protests, free-love hippies, and the civil rights and Black Power movements mean for the Institute? Late fifties and early sixties sexual icons—Hugh Hefner, Masters and Johnson, and Helen Gurley Brown—and the 1960 release of the contraceptive pill had framed the writing of *Pregnancy, Birth and Abortion* (1958) and *Sex Offenders* (1965), bespeaking a new kind of popular concept of sexual subjectivity. The Playboy and the Single Girl demanded and consumed sexual fulfilment as desirable for health and happiness. Did these early 1960s understandings, elaborated below, permeate the sexual attitudes and behavior of the next generation, the young people found on university and college campuses and street corners and in bars, shopping centers, discos, rock concert audiences, diners, and roadhouses in the late 1960s and 1970s?

Answers to this question seemed uncertain. With both youth and sexuality in the spotlight, contention ignited diverse sexual politics both nationwide and overseas. Especially from 1968 onward, matters such as censorship, unwed mothers, no-fault divorce, abortion law reform, homosexuality, prostitution, pornography, androgyny, feminism, cohabitation, and nonmonogamy inflamed public debate and pushed legislators for action and professional experts for explanations or prognoses. The traditional languages of sexual deviance and immorality confronted the languages of victimless crime and adult entitlement to consenting erotic privacy.[1]

With the original Kinsey mission completed, the Institute seemed well positioned to capture the moment. This chapter explores the second phase of Paul H. Gebhard's directorship, from 1966 until 1981. John H. Gagnon started this phase by hiring Chicago graduate school colleague and sociologist William Simon, both men civil rights activists and attuned to the moment's youth protests.

Yet Gagnon and Simon shared with Gebhard a skepticism about the actuality of any "sexual revolution." They decided to study the sexual behavior and attitudes of youth on campuses. In a singularly obdurate stance, Institute researchers determinedly debunked claims that a sexual revolution engulfed 1960s and 1970s America. Gebhard insisted that behaviors and attitudes remained unchanged, believing that a "strong vein of conservatism" pervaded the culture.[2] Most of their subjects condemned extramarital sex, prostitution, and homosexuality, as well as casual sex unmoored from relationships. The pill did not launch an avalanche of either premarital or extramarital heterosexual activity. Nor did college students suddenly increase their rates of casual sex, most associating first or early coitus with love, if not marriage. Gagnon and Simon's "Youth Study" data revealed sexual behavior comparable with their parents' generation. Purported changes actually continued "long existing trends."[3] Collectively, Institute researchers attributed the myth of a sexual revolution to freer media discussion of sexual activity.[4] According to Institute data, amassed between 1965 and 1980, existing attitudes about sexuality and sexual behaviors dated from before Kinsey began taking sex histories. Changes in the 1960s and 1970s were neither more rapid nor deeper than they had been in previous generations. Officially, then, skepticism ruled.[5]

Team grant applications ensued. One centered on youth and sexual development. Others treated aspects of homosexuality and the processing and accessing of the original Kinsey era interview data and related collections development. These projects dominated Institute research activity throughout the late 1960s and early 1970s, as outlined below.

Figure 4.1. Cornelia Christenson, Paul H. Gebhard, John H. Gagnon, and William Simon, ca. 1966. With the recruitment of sociologist William Simon, the reconfigured research team set about applying, mostly successfully, for a new set of research grants on new projects. Photo courtesy of Kinsey Institute Library and Special Collections.

The Institute's studies, however, did reflect changes in understandings of sexuality, the function and purpose of sex in individuals' lives, and what it meant to be a sexual person. Institute researchers responded to popular ideas, common theories, and stereotypes and to the public's perception of social problems. In some instances they were at the forefront, debunking stereotypes and advocating ideas that were not yet popular. More often, though, their language and understandings of sexuality paralleled or even lagged behind broader cultural shifts of the era. This was particularly evident in the evolution of the Institute's most ambitious projects, each of which eventually took a decade or more to complete, key ones remaining unpublished. Significant among these was the proposed study of youth on college campuses, the oft-purported laboratory of erotic experimentation.

New ways that Americans discussed sexuality challenged the Institute.[6] Broadly, sex researchers responded to—and contributed to—two cultural trends.

In the first place, the media, filmmakers, advertisers, and even some sex educators, doctors, and psychologists glamourized and idealized sexuality and "sexiness." An active and "good" sex life became necessary to individual physical and mental health and happiness. Various authorities expected sex researchers to solve a multitude of sexual problems impeding sexual fulfillment or at least the quest for ideal sex lives. Simultaneously, women, homosexuals, transsexuals, and other groups loudly protested prevalent cultural perceptions of their identities, expecting constructive responses from sex researchers. More and more, discourses depicted sexuality as, by definition, an identity that encompassed nearly every aspect of life instead of a behavior or an activity, as Kinsey had understood it. Sex researchers, including Institute staff, made gradual shifts toward identitarian over behavioral framings of sexuality throughout the 1960s and 1970s.

Yet sexual explicitness did not make sex research easier or more secure. Funding remained scarce and was freighted with sponsor agendas. Academic sex researchers insisted that their research was not simply "sexy." They could provide useful data to the government agencies that provided much of their funding. Further, sex researchers became more specialized, with individual researchers, clinics, and institutes occupying smaller niches. By the mid-1960s, studying the sexual histories of Americans in general was no longer an option. Instead, sex researchers found themselves compelled to address sexual problems, the medical or psychological problems of specific segments of the population.

The Institute's research methods changed. A proposed study of college students emphasized the relationship between social and cultural pressures, sexual behaviors, and psychological health. Similarly, proposed projects on homosexuality addressed it through the prism of psychology and psychosexual development—approaches never previously characterizing Institute research. Such studies removed focus from behaviors as such, investigating instead the emotional and social meanings of those behaviors for individuals. In a cultural climate portraying sexual fulfillment as both an ideal and a necessity, authorities and funders tasked sex researchers with solving obstructions to this outcome.

Meanwhile, collections activities surged. Gebhard and research associate Cornelia Christenson devised a new monograph series centered on scholarly use and dissemination of items in the collection. The first published, of which the team was very proud, was Columbia University literary scholar Steven Marcus's highly influential work *The Other Victorians* (1966).[7] This book augured a new phase of collections development, opening the door to scholars, as per the recommendation of the NIMH consultants. Such moves pleased the University. Three more volumes followed, including Christenson's biography of Kinsey.

By 1980, though, Institute fortunes had taken a drastic turn. Developments in the fate of both funded research projects and collections projects warrant narration

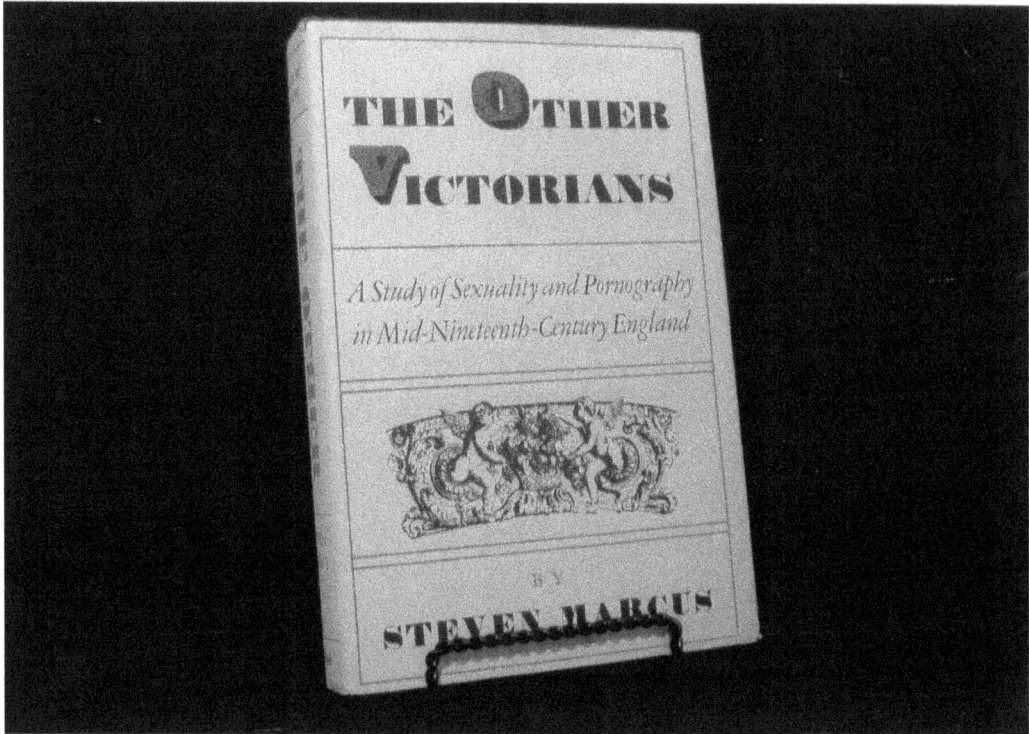

Figure 4.2. Book cover, Steven Marcus, *The Other Victorians* (1966). Marcus was one of the first researchers from outside the Institute to use the Institute's collections. This famous book has become one of the standards of sex research literature in the humanities for its treatment of Victorian-era pornography. It launched a new series of Institute monographs, Studies in Sex and Society, published with Basic Books. Photo courtesy of Kinsey Institute Library and Special Collections.

and analysis in context. According to a stinging description in the local press, the Institute had become "moribund," quoting a University officer, while its director, so the charge went, had "mothballed" the precious Kinsey collections to the point of virtual inaccessibility.[8] The Institute was a closed fortress and, more and more, a poor fortress at that. Two review committees, one internal, one external, urged drastic changes, including "opening the doors" and reinvigorating and restructuring the Institute's operations, its mission, and its relation to the University. What was the genealogy of such a thorough rebuke, and how justified should readers today find the criticisms leveled at Institute leadership?

The Playboy and the Single Girl Meet Modern Youth

The "Kinsey Report" was the first extensive scientific study of United States sex practices. Unquestionably, it affected behavior, even as it reported it. America's sexual hypocrisy was out in the open—we had been preaching one thing and practicing another. The country's puritanical zealots, who had successfully sustained the image of sex as sin by keeping it in the shadows, suddenly found that someone had let the sunshine in. And in the bright light of day, sex didn't seem so terrible to most of us.

Hugh Hefner, "The Playboy Philosophy—Editorial Part 3," *Playboy* 10, no. 2 (February 1963)

To what degree, if any, and in what direction have the sexual attitudes and practices of college students changed? This is fundamentally the question: is there a sexual revolution occurring on American campuses, or is there simply a continuation of a long-term secular trend noted by Kinsey, *et al.*, 1948, 1953?

William Simon and John Gagnon, "Youth Cultures and Aspects of the Socialization Process. A Grant Proposal Submitted to the National Institute of Mental Health and the National Institute of Child Health and Human Development," 5

The "Gebhard era" truly began in 1966. Ten years overseeing work begun by Kinsey ended with the publication of *Sex Offenders*. Now Gebhard would take the Institute in an entirely new direction. New methodologies, new kinds of data, and new research questions and approaches would advance.[9] The Institute could enter a new phase, one truly Gebhard's to direct. Unshackled from outdated research, researchers could address cultural concerns of the moment. Projects could incorporate—or challenge—changing understandings of sex and sexuality.

Befitting this new era, in 1967 the Institute moved from its third home in Jordan Hall, where it had been located since 1955. Refurbished offices in Morrison Hall, originally a student dormitory, became its new address. And after having endured twenty years with an impermanent institutional identity, Gebhard had at last secured job security. The Department of Anthropology undertook full funding of his salary, now that he was a tenured member of the faculty.[10] The next decade became, according to Gebhard, the busiest and most productive in the Institute's history. With Hugh Hefner promising $70,000 ($592,000 today) and the commitment from the NIMH of $174,000 (worth $1,298,000 today) awarded for two years, as well as good prospects for grants ahead for studies of youth and sexual attitudes and of the impact of sex education, the team looked forward with optimism.[11]

New Institute projects were all, to a degree, grounded in psychological theories. Paradoxically, though, psychology itself was not the academic background of Institute researchers. As they sought to understand broad processes of socialization and the impact that culture and community had on individuals' sexual behaviors and attitudes, they took for granted the idea that people were psychologically predisposed toward particular sexual behaviors and desires. Hence, the focus became the factors propelling the erotic outcomes of these predispositions rather than the study of sexual behavior itself.

Figure 4.3. Morrison Hall, formerly a dormitory, became the Institute's fourth home in 1967. The collections have been subject to water damage from numerous leaks in the roof and ceilings and from floods caused by plumbing failures. Photo courtesy of Kinsey Institute Library and Special Collections.

Nonetheless, a theorizing of sexuality as a fixed component of personality traits and identity, already clear in the *Sex Offenders* study, soon underpinned all the work of Institute researchers. They simultaneously examined sexuality at the individual, family, community, and cultural levels, always maintaining that factors of each impacted all the others. This approach defined research begun at the Institute during the remainder of Gebhard's directorship, even though, unlike under Kinsey, researchers no longer worked as one unified team. To strengthen the psychology and psychiatry pitch of their social science offerings, researchers resolved to hire a psychologist. In 1966 they recruited Alan P. Bell, a newly minted Columbia University psychology doctorate and Simon's brother-in-law, whom Gebhard called "a former coffee-house priest."[12] Still, the mixture of sociology, anthropology, and psychology seems not to have resulted in an interdisciplinary "metalevel" of inquiry, with sometimes-telling disciplinary grumblings about respect for one discipline's methods over others.[13]

Figure 4.4. Alan B. Johnson, Paul H. Gebhard, Martin S. Weinberg, and Alan P. Bell, ca. 1970. Unlike the Kinsey directorship, the Institute staff worked on smaller projects rather than one "Institute" project across the 1970s. Photo courtesy of Kinsey Institute Library and Special Collections.

What lay ahead? How would this group of young postdoctoral and assistant professor appointees, joined in 1968 by Associate Professor Martin S. Weinberg, a sociologist of sexuality and deviance from Rutgers, work together under the direction of the nearly fifty-year-old veteran of the Kinsey era in the tumult of 1966 to 1970? What understanding of the current era did they bring to the Institute's research activity? Did they identify with their disciplines of origin, or did location in the Institute allow them to forge different academic identities? And what contributions would be possible for the humanist, Cornelia V. Christenson, originally a research assistant hired by Kinsey?

* * *

Late 1960s Institute projects reflected popular national discourses on sex and sexuality. Research team members wanted to know whether adults actualized the ideals of the Single Girl and the Playboy. Were these figures merely popular fantasies? Did youth and adults identify with the Single Girl and the Playboy, striving to live the lifestyles they represented? Simon and Gagnon's project, "Youth Cultures and Aspects of the Socialization Process," known simply as the Youth Study, examined whether a sexual revolution was occurring on college campuses. They explored comparative rates of change in sexual behaviors against Kinsey's findings for previous generations, as well as attitudes toward sexual behavior.

Helen Gurley Brown's book, *Sex and the Single Girl* (1962), and Hugh Hefner's magazine, *Playboy*, invoked iconic and aspirational sexual identities. With alluring and glamorous prescriptions for the type of heteroerotic modernity enjoyed by young, urbane, white, wealthy men and women who had active sex lives, sexiness anchored the lifestyles Brown and Hefner promoted even while protesting the status quo. Carefree fun, experimentation, glamour, and rebellion appealed to the restless "baby boom" generation. Hefner's "philosophy" began developing years before the first issue of *Playboy*, combining individuality, freedom, fun, intellectuality, motivation, and hard work. "The Playboy Philosophy" was part advertising campaign, part social theory, and part political manifesto.

The Playboy was an icon. Intelligent, witty, carefree (yet driven and hardworking), nonconforming (yet patriotically conservative, extolling free enterprise, democracy, and individual liberties), he was a successful man for whom life was fun, exciting, and—yes—sexy. The Playboy was also an "idea man," contributing to an American Renaissance and part of a generation bent on both social and sexual revolution. "America has come alive again" through overthrowing the "puritanical prudishness and hypocrisy" that for too long had controlled and deadened the minds of men. The Playboy, then, combined a particular version of heterosexual masculinity with the most ideal (according to Hefner) model of a responsible and engaged American citizen.[14]

The Single Girl was the woman who dated the Playboy. Intelligent and hardworking, she was the carefree, charming, fun, sexy woman who could hold the interest of men who would otherwise have been bored either by their wives or by other less sexy women. The Single Girl was looking for a man to marry, but in the meantime she sought fun and fulfilling affairs. Brown's book held that "sexiness," rather than restraint, was natural. Each girl began life "naturally sexy," but "all her growing up years she will be exhorted to keep her dress down, her knees crossed, her thoughts pure, never to let anybody touch her *there*." The sexy woman has relearned to enjoy sex, with Brown offering the education.[15]

Sex and the Single Girl and *Playboy* illustrated hallmark American debates about sex and sexuality. First, sex and sexuality were matters of personal, physical, and psychological health. This individualism differed from marriage manuals and sex research discourses that positioned "normal" sexuality as a component of an ideal marriage. Second, Single Girl and Playboy functioned as identity categories. They described types of people with particular personality traits. If not the only available heterosexual identities, they were important ones within the heterosexual typologies. Third, the Playboy and the Single Girl normalized a high level of sexual responsiveness and sexual satisfaction. This did not hinge on more sexual contacts or partners; it meant that enjoying sexual contact and feeling sexually satisfied underwrote a healthy life.

As the Institute's projects became more focused on the psychological and social adjustment of individuals, researchers absorbed these theories about sexuality. Sexual satisfaction became a matter of individual health. They examined the developmental factors fostering or obstructing "normal"—by which they meant ideal, not common or average—or healthy sex lives. Alternatively, they defined "asexual" as an indicator of poor sexual adjustment or even pathology.[16] Although not producing a taxonomy of heterosexuality, they treated "heterosexual" and "homosexual" as identity categories, the former inhabited by a diversity of individuals, the latter inhabited by diverse types (in a drastic departure from Kinsey's understanding of sexuality). Among both heterosexuals and homosexuals, subjects who were described as normal, well adjusted, and even happy reported high levels of sexual satisfaction. Among the prominent messages of the sexual revolution was that sex—good sex—was necessary for every individual. The Institute embraced this belief.

The premium on sexual fulfilment as health had immediate consequences. Sex researchers, along with 1960s and 1970s sex educators and marriage counselors, joined the quest for practical solutions to sexual problems and abnormalities. Even the initial studies of William Masters and Virginia Johnson, which examined "normal" sexuality, made therapeutic goals paramount. *Human Sexual Response* (1966) began with the "challenge" issued by Robert Latou Dickinson in 1925: scientists, he argued, overly fascinated by "the bizarre and the extreme, the abnormal and the diseased," needed instead to provide "succinct statistics and physiologic summaries of what we find to be average and believe to be normal." Forty years later, this challenge remained, according to Masters and Johnson. Even with progress on psychological and sociological aspects of sexual behavior, unless physiological research advanced, "psychologic theory will remain theory and sociologic concept will remain concept." Treatment of human sexual inadequacy called for "reliable physiologic information in the area of human sexual response."[17] The axiom of pleasure as the bedrock of individual health grounded their research on the physiology of orgasm.[18] Obstructions to sexual pleasure, physiological or psychological, required clinical treatment, generating professionalized sex therapy, with sexuality now a matter of lifelong individual health.[19] This medicalized understanding displaced couple- and family-centered interwar to postwar marriage counseling.

The Institute's Youth Study integrated enquiry into the sexual revolution with the study of young adult identity. Simon and Gagnon, both trained as sociologists but deeply influenced by psychological theory, decided to examine the sexual behaviors and attitudes of college students as a way of understanding processes of maturation, sexual adjustment, and personality development. "Youth" became the

Figure 4.5. Virginia Johnson and William Masters, pictured in their St. Louis clinic, are often portrayed as the successors of Kinsey. Their therapeutic work on sexual physiology in a medical school setting was very different from Kinsey's scientific expertise and institutional facilities. Photo courtesy of Kinsey Institute Library and Special Collections.

period between adolescence and adulthood, or, roughly, age eighteen to twenty-two. Their study would interview 1,100–1,200 college and university students to explore behavioral changes.

The project's central research question was: "Is there a sexual revolution occurring on American campuses, or is there simply a continuation of a long term secular trend noted by Kinsey et al.?" Were Americans right to believe that sexual patterns, attitudes, and norms were rapidly changing? Sex researchers converged on such questions, as did mass media. Debate over the sexual revolution anchored political and social activism. Diverse groups asserted different definitions of "sexual revolution" in seeking to explain such revolutionary change. Simon and Gagnon, like other sex researchers, defined the term "sexual revolution" as rapid and significant changes in behaviors and attitudes. Via various tests, most researchers relegated the sexual revolution to the status of a myth.

The study also sought to refine theoretical understandings of psychosocial development during youth. This aspect made use of current theories in developmental psychology, particularly those of Erik Erikson and Abraham Maslow. Both Erikson and Maslow were original members of the human potential movement, which positioned the individual as an active participant in his or her own psychosocial development. Maturation, in other words, was the result of working toward specific goals or commitments to personal style and identity, a process that became known popularly as "self-actualization."[20] Simon and Gagnon hypothesized that the "management of sexuality" was key to this maturation and socialization process and that developing a sexual identity was necessary to successfully become an adult.[21] In a palpable change in direction away from sexual behaviors, NIMH officials advised placing sexuality "in the broader context of the socialization process," since, though it is important, "it is not the only (and perhaps not even the most important) contributor to the socialization process in college."[22] Hence, replotted survey questions spanned a wide array of subjects, from grades to friendships, leisure activities to professional goals, and, above all, subjects' feelings about themselves and their lives. Questions on dating history, for example, targeted its impact in other domains. Did a subject's confidence in his or her dating life correlate with confidence in a classroom or during a job interview? Did anxiety about sexual prowess interfere with finishing assignments or participating in sports activities?[23] All this deflected attention away from the Kinseyan focus on sexual behavior itself.

Despite their skepticism about the characterization "sexual revolution," Simon and Gagnon did note some changes among youth. College students, women in particular, showed greater enjoyment of their first experiences of intercourse, which Gebhard attributed to changes in attitudes. "It is becoming respectable to be an admittedly sexually responsive female," and both men and women experienced less guilt over their sexual activities than they had twenty years earlier.[24]

The study design and premises reflected predominant 1960s and 1970s *sexual* understandings of sexuality. The assumption that "youth" was a distinct time of life or category of people with common characteristics was itself a product of the baby boom generation. Similarly, defining adulthood as an identity that one must achieve correlated with the popular idea that sex, sexuality, and "sexiness" were components of a whole lifestyle in which wittiness and the proper application of makeup, to use some of Brown's examples, were indicative of a specific sexual identity. The single girl's identity was never only defined by what she actually did in the proverbial bedroom. At least as important was her presentation of herself in social spaces and her feelings about sex and sexuality. Simon and Gagnon noted that the "management of sexuality" was a key part of the "developmental process that culminates in adulthood," which was determined by and determinative of individual personality.[25]

This was precisely the kind of theorization that the NIMH reviewers had recommended in 1963. Simon and Gagnon were working toward a generalized theory of sexually normal versus deviant adults. The project also fulfilled the mandates set down by Presidents Johnson and Kennedy and by Congress. They were applying scientific methods to social problems, as Johnson had famously pledged. In tandem, their work sought useful sexual etiologies for clinicians and law and policy makers.

Yet Simon and Gagnon were not long for the Institute. In the heady campus and nationwide politics of 1968, these dynamic young scholars had options. Both Gagnon and Simon involved themselves in student politics. Gebhard recalled that in 1966 "a popular rock group, the Fugs, and Alan Ginsberg decide[d] to visit IU to honor Lindesmith (an IU sociologist drug supporter) and ISR. They came uninvited. They shocked the university at several lectures." An irate dean of faculties wrote to Gebhard "saying that ISR cannot give public events," unhappy to learn that Simon headed Students for a Democratic Society, "but Simon is appointed in Sociology."[26]

No doubt Bloomington seemed far from the epicenter of antiestablishment politics and culture. More crucial, the independent status of the Institute meant that it lacked the resources of an academic department. Gebhard had little chance of retaining and advancing talented researchers when he had no tenurable job to offer and only lean salaries compared to other universities. Just as the loss of Rockefeller funding impelled Kinsey to try to reopen the Institute's legal and economic relationship with the University in 1956, Gebhard too sought to achieve a merger with Indiana University. No longer did he wish to be at the mercy of the annual grant cycle.

Several times, from 1966 onward, Gebhard attempted to negotiate a changed Institute-University relationship. The objective was to stabilize and permit planning in years when grants proved lean. President Elvis Stahr (president 1962–1968) proved amenable and sympathetic, agreeing that the University would ensure permanent base budget funding with tenure lines in home departments, as well as University funding for a head librarian, an archivist, a curator, and administrative assistants to the director.[27] With this plan, essentially, the researchers would have employment certainty. External grants would determine the balance of teaching to research in their work pattern each year. One condition was new governance by an advisory committee of interested and expert faculty. Plans moved slowly, however, with several elements to resolve. In July 1968 Gebhard informed the president of the Rockefeller Foundation that its continued status as recipient of the library and special collections in the event of the Institute's incorporation ending now presented a problem. The reason, he said, was that the Institute currently was in the process of affiliating even more closely with Indiana University and wished to retain the collections.[28] Meanwhile, he and the University counsel negotiated terms on which the Institute might move to another institution, with the University requesting a five-year notice period. Everything halted, however, in 1968, when Stahr, an environmentalist, resigned to lead the National Audubon Society.

So Gebhard had to begin again with Stahr's successor, political scientist Joseph Sutton. Willing enough to consider the new plan of enlarged University support for the Institute, Sutton would proceed only if the board of trustees henceforth seated mainly University officials and administrators to oversee the increased resource investment. Simon opposed this stipulation.[29] Soon, he was gone.

Gebhard described Gagnon as lured to a tenurable post by ally Professor Stanley Yolles at the State University of New York, Stony Brook, while Simon returned to the National Opinion Research Center in Chicago. There were a number of hints of discord within the Institute for some time prior to their resignations, including office politics, affairs, vendettas, and fired clerical workers.[30] Gebhard sent all Institute members a memo commanding them to desist from gossiping about internal conflicts.[31] Gagnon and Simon were replaced by Martin S. Weinberg and by Colin Williams in 1971. Each of these efforts ended in disputes over contracts.

Slow progress in 1968 and 1969 stopped in 1970.[32] An insuperable obstacle emerged: "The idea of merging with IU is dropped. Cliff Travis, the IU attorney, says IU prefers the status quo." By this time, a twelve-seat advisory board of faculty and deans was in place.[33]

Homosexual Subjectivities

Homosexuality encompasses far more than people's sexual proclivities. Too often homosexuals have been viewed simply with reference to their sexual interest and activity. Usually the social context and psychological correlates of homosexual experience are largely ignored, making for a highly constricted image of the persons involved.

Alan P. Bell and Martin S. Weinberg, *Homosexualities*, 25

Postwar homosexuality researchers addressed two questions: What caused homosexuality? And what might be an accurate typology of homosexuals? Hypotheses proliferated, but few agreed on classifications. Careful parsing of the personality, identity, and history of homosexuals would be, it was assumed, particularly important in clinical practice.

The Institute was well positioned to explore such questions. Hypotheses could be paired with resources. Along with library and archival materials, researchers had a multitude of contacts in homosexual communities, as well as considerable and as-yet-unused Kinsey research data. Their interest was sharpened by current attention to homosexuality throughout mainstream American culture. Many who identified themselves as homosexuals were interested in a fuller understanding of homosexuality. During the early 1950s homophile groups emerged that were committed to enhancing an understanding of same-sex-desiring persons and to providing support for those struggling in a hostile sexual culture.[34]

Federal government interest in this "problem" meant research resources. Stanley Yolles, director of the NIMH until 1970, created a task force to "tell him what we ought to be doing about homosexuality."[35] He appointed Evelyn Hooker, most notable for developing several psychological testing instruments for determining the psychological adjustment of male homosexuals, as director. Careful to avoid any appearance of bias, Hooker brought together a diverse team of experts in psychiatry, law, anthropology, religion, and sexology, including the Institute's own Paul H. Gebhard. Far from groundbreaking on either policy or public opinion, although it did call for the decriminalization of some homosexual acts, the task force's main recommendation was for increased support for research. The Institute was well placed to receive that support.[36] Yet the context of this NIMH "deep concern" identified homosexuals as abnormal or deviant, even pathological. Such a framing of enquiry could not have been more different from Kinsey's 1940s and 1950s approach as demonstrated in the continuum of the Kinsey scale. His efforts had become a legacy, a historical artifact with little impact on contemporaneous thinking.

That said, Institute researchers designed three ambitious projects related to homosexuality. In 1965 Gebhard and Gagnon had proposed a four-year study of homosexual communities officially entitled "Patterns of Adjustment in Deviant Populations." The NIMH initially approved the study in full. Congressional cuts, however, blocked full support.[37] After submitting a revised request in 1967, researchers began an Indianapolis pilot study, as well as initial interviewing in Chicago later that year.

The second project was funded in 1968 and involved Gebhard, Alan P. Bell, and Martin S. Weinberg. Its mission was a three-year examination of San Francisco communities. The plan was for the project to build on data from the "Chicago Deviance" study. A third project, also proposed in 1968, was an attitudes study. Affiliated researcher Albert Klassen proposed a study entitled "Attitudes towards Selected Forms of Deviant Behavior." He sought to ascertain national opinions on homosexuality compared with other forms of illicit or taboo behaviors and to help establish classifications and etiologies of homosexuality. His three-year study secured NIMH funding. Its interviews would be conducted by the National Opinion Research Center (NORC) rather than Institute staff. A further project also continued under Institute auspices. When Weinberg joined the Institute staff in 1968, he directed a small study of homosexuals in Denmark and the Netherlands for a cross-cultural analysis and a study of homosexuals who were dishonorably discharged from the military.[38]

The Deviance Study that Gebhard proposed in 1965 was largely ethnographic. According to him, too much emphasis had been placed on the etiological factors that predisposed individuals to enter homosexual communities without enough attention to subsequent development. He hypothesized that the management of sexuality, and thus the mental health of homosexuals, would be greatly influenced by participation in a "community of fellow deviants."[39] Gebhard was interested in the structure and operations of these communities just as much as in the individuals who inhabited them.

The theoretical understanding of sexuality in this proposal was similar to that of the Youth Study. The homosexual community, like colleges, provided the context in which young people learn to socialize their sexual drives and to "love as well as to copulate." Both heterosexuals and homosexuals "who are not successful in managing the duality of purely physical sexuality and socialized sexual conduct may run the risk of serious pathology," but "the homosexual has fewer resources with which to solve this problem."[40] Homosexuals would learn behavioral norms and take on specific roles appropriate to the social context.[41]

Gebhard located sexual contact as only one aspect of a homosexual identity and life. The sexual outlets of homosexuals did not concern him, even though, conceivably, they were relevant to various community roles he sought to analyze. Instead, for him, homosexuality was an "existential" condition, with "outlets and gratification" not "immediately sexual" available in homosexual communities. Thus, an individual homosexual might become more "socially homosexual."[42] Gebhard's concern was with the social rather than the erotic aspects of homosexual identity, mapping the degree to which he declined Kinsey's behaviorism and resistance to sexual identity categories.

To undertake this study, the Institute needed an interview that targeted psychological data. Here was part of the rationale for the hiring of Bell, an expert in devising and using psychometric devices to study personality in relation to social conditions. Though he was a self-described counseling psychologist, his work resembled social psychology.[43] His first task was to help develop the questionnaire for the Deviance Study. Bell proposed using existing objective psychological testing instruments in conjunction with questionnaires so that researchers could correlate behavior and psychological characteristics. If such tests proved flawed for sustaining claims for personality distinctions between homosexuals and heterosexuals, they might serve for classifications of homosexuals, their roles, the varieties of pathology involved, and modes of treatment that would be useful.[44]

Members of homosexual communities raised prompt objections to psychological or other classifications. "Experts" had often used such constructs to denigrate homosexuals as sick or deviant. Bell resisted such homophile objections. He was concerned less with judging whether homosexual roles indicated sickness and more with asking, "Are there patterns of early relationships, of needs and self-images, etc. which can differentiate people according to their sexual adjustments?"[45] Bell's interest was in homosexual adjustment. Amidst the Chicago study, he developed

Figure 4.6. Alan P. Bell. Expert consultants and external funding agencies urged the Institute to incorporate psychological and even clinical approaches to sex research. Bell was recruited to provide such research expertise. Bell, pictured here in the late 1960s, studied homosexual subjectivities, roles, and personality adjustment. Photo courtesy of Kinsey Institute Library and Special Collections.

a psychometric index of adjustment coordinating with the Rotterdam Incomplete Sentences blank test.[46]

The initial multicity scope of the study soon contracted. The NIMH offered only half the funding requested, permitting an Indianapolis pilot study, with a full Chicago-based study of about five hundred people. When, soon after, the NIMH announced more funds for homosexuality research, the Institute proposed the San Francisco study, "A Study of Deviant Socialization." If methodologically like the Chicago study, it differed by including female and nonwhite subjects and twice as many subjects (twelve hundred). Interviewing family members of subjects was also a further and later stage in the research plan.[47]

Alan P. Bell and Martin S. Weinberg eventually published *Homosexualities: A Study of Diversity among Men and Women* (1978) and, along with Sue Kiefer Hammersmith, *Sexual Preference: Its Development in Men and Women* (1981), both based on data from the San Francisco study. The former was concerned with a typology of homosexuality, while the latter was concerned with etiologies of homosexuality and individuals' development into the types delineated in the first volume. Most research in the area, Bell and Weinberg claimed, had been concerned only with how homosexuals as a group differed from heterosexuals. Most claimed distinctions derived from stereotypical factors, such as degrees of masculinity or femininity, "active" or "passive" erotic roles, or extent of exclusivity in homosexual contact. By contrast, the San Francisco study considered a much greater array of "the various features of homosexuality." The authors measured, among many other things, such dimensions as homosexuals' overtness, sexual frequency, cruising patterns, nonsexual involvement with partners, sexual techniques and problems, and any regret about homosexual identity.[48]

A typology emerged. In *Homosexualities*, researchers divided subjects into "close-coupleds," those who lived together monogamously; "open-coupleds," those who lived together but were sexually nonmonogamous; "functionals," who were sexually and socially well-adjusted singles; "dysfunctionals," who were troubled socially, sexually, and psychologically; and "asexuals," who either chose to have little sexual contact or could not find sexual partners easily. The asexuals were not so often exclusively homosexual. The typology rested primarily on three correlating factors: sexual gratification, social adjustment, and psychological adjustment.[49] Bell and Weinberg could not say what proportions of the homosexual community fit into each category, since, as they carefully admit in the book, their sample was not representative, nor could it be.[50]

Bell, Weinberg, and Hammersmith generated no distinct etiological theory of homosexuality. Instead, their aim was to refute common psychological and sociological theories of the etiology of homosexuality. While documenting several commonalities in the development of homosexual persons, they proffered no

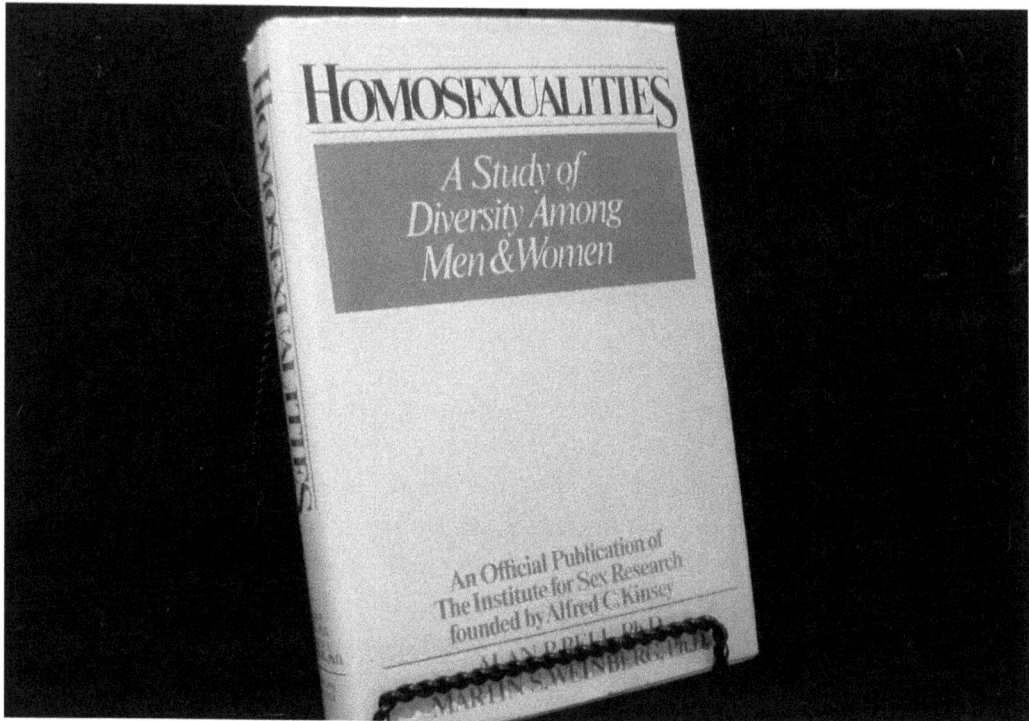

Figure 4.7. Book cover, Alan P. Bell and Martin S. Weinberg, *Homosexualities: A Study of Diversity among Men and Women* (1978). The culmination of ten years of research, *Homosexualities* studied diversity among homosexual populations, refuting many unsubstantiated stereotypes and biases. Photo courtesy of Kinsey Institute Library and Special Collections.

conclusions as to homosexuality's *causes*, leaving the implication that it was a fixed identity comparable with race. Homosexuals might simply be born that way, in which case, causes could not be found, as commonly assumed, in life experiences or psychological development.

The third study of homosexuality, "Attitudes towards Selected Forms of Deviant Behavior," differed from the Chicago and San Francisco deviance studies. It focused less on homosexuality and more on public opinion about it. The Attitudes Study evolved. The initial proposal was for a study of adult attitudes toward homosexuality compared to attitudes toward other forms of sexual behavior. An early draft proposal, probably written by Klassen, suggests limited goals.[51] A second, more expansive draft followed the recruitment of affiliated researcher Eugene Levitt, a clinical psychologist at the IU Medial School. Klassen and Levitt increased the proposal's appeal to the NIMH by centering attention on Americans' attitudes toward any sexual behavior that was "considered a serious social and/or psychological problem and sufficiently prevalent to cause societal concern."[52] These behaviors included premarital and extramarital sex, masturbation, prostitution, incest, and child molestation, in addition to homosexuality. Institute collaborators integrated legal concerns by investigating sex laws that criminalized common sexual behaviors. In tandem, the Presidential Committee on Obscenity and Pornography sought the Institute's cooperation, which made attitudes toward erotic materials a new secondary goal of the Attitudes Study.

Levitt and Klassen took as stipulated that the attitudes of average Americans would—or should—have an impact on clinical practice, law, and public policy.[53] Social reactions to homosexuals impacted their mental and social well-being. It was necessary to know the extent to which the public understood homosexuality in order for public policy and education efforts to be effective. The study would be national in scope, and Levitt and Klassen intended to integrate questions regarding "the extent and nature of homosexuality in the adult population of the United States." They could identify adults according to "variations of homosexuality in their experience" and investigate "some factors antecedent, and perhaps etiologically related, to homosexuality."[54] They would collect data on childhood sex play, family psychodynamics, and sociocultural conditioning and correlate them with data on sexual satisfaction and gratification, the results of which would be potentially illuminating. These data could then be used in conjunction with data from the San Francisco and Chicago studies to establish correlates between homosexual behavior patterns and "characteristics secondary to homosexuality" and to refine, in effect, a taxonomy of sexual identity and correlative etiological antecedents.

The Attitudes Study, then, was designed to nationally mirror prominent and widely popularized expert debates. With delays, however, came further project evolution. Another newly affiliated Institute researcher, Colin Williams, undertook the project in the mid-1970s and reverted to the initial focus of the study. That is to say, he examined whether, as of 1970, when collecting the data, American sexual standards had undergone a radical or revolutionary shift. By 1980 Williams had a complete draft, and it was under consideration for publication.[55] The first chapter, "The Notion of the 'Sexual Revolution,'" included a historical analysis of reasons for the 1960s popularity of the idea of a sexual revolution:

> The idea that a "sexual revolution" is occurring or that sexual morality is breaking down is not one that is unique to present-day society but has enjoyed a vogue at various times not only in our past but in the histories of other societies. Such an idea seems to emerge in conjunction with unsettling social changes, for example, during and after wars. It should not be surprising, therefore, that the idea surfaced again in the United States in the late 1960s. . . . Amidst . . . convulsions in the social fabric, the idea of radical ("revolutionary") changes in the sexual sphere seemed logical enough.[56]

The idea, Williams wrote, was too imprecise to verify. How could one establish whether or not a sexual revolution had occurred—or was occurring—if the notion itself could not be defined and criteria could not be established? Most scholars asking the question attempted to answer it behaviorally, insufficiently attentive to meanings of that behavior or its associated values.[57]

Entitled "American Sexual Standards," the slightly revised 1981 draft then traced changes in America's mores and attitudes. Researchers defined these "sexual standards" as the "moral strictures which give meaning to sexual acts" and the total sociological context within which sexual expression and behavior occurred.[58] Whether changes were "revolutionary" or not was not for them to say. They could measure, though, the degree to which public morality departed from traditional sexual norms. Attitudes toward homosexuality illuminated broader changes, functioning as a symbolic touchstone for understanding American sexual standards as a whole.[59]

Contrasts between the Attitudes Study of 1968–70 and "American Sexual Standards" of 1981 closely paralleled changes in both public and expert concerns about homosexuality. Debates in the 1960s around etiology and classification withered, eclipsed by ruminations on consequences for others of homosexual "lifestyles" or "orientation." The American Psychiatric Association had removed homosexuality from its list of psychopathologies by the time of Williams's draft. The public, often prompted by shrill conservative voices like that of Anita Bryant's "Save Our Children" campaign, asked what homosexuals' behavior might do to others—especially children—rather than what homosexuals might do within their own communities.

All three 1960s and 1970s Institute homosexuality studies jettisoned Kinsey's vision. He did not countenance the term "deviant," except in its most technical sense as a departure from a norm, which, for him, homosexual behavior was not. These studies proposed examining homosexual *people*, whereas Kinsey's interest was in studying homosexual *behavior* in all people. Significantly, in the San Francisco Study, a small percentage of respondents reported significant sexual feelings toward and/or contacts with members of the opposite sex (Weinberg and Bell even used an adapted version of the Kinsey scale to rate their feelings and experiences), but they were all included in the homosexual sample. Presumably, this is because all of these people in some way participated in the "homosexual community" from which the sample was drawn or otherwise self-identified as homosexual. Either way, heterosexual desires, feelings, and contacts were understood as variations among homosexuals, not as data indicating that the category "homosexual"—or even "bisexual," for that matter—might be problematic in the ways that Kinsey had described so long ago.[60]

The shifts and evolutions of these studies from the 1960s to their late 1970s and 1980s incarnations reflected the successes of the homophile, gay liberation, and gay rights movements. The most striking shifts occurred in the language used to describe homosexuality. By the late 1970s terms like "sexual preference" and "sexual orientation" had entirely superseded "sexual deviance" among sex researchers and in much of mainstream culture. Institute publications largely followed, rather than led, cultural trends.[61]

Opening the Doors

Among scholars around the world the library of the Kinsey Institute is regarded as the most important sexological library in the world. Scholars everywhere are deeply appreciative of the access that they have to it from afar, via its information service, and of the welcome they are given as visiting scholars, despite the overcrowding and strain of extra work on the staff.

John Money and Anke Ehrhardt, "Report on the Institute for Sex Research, Indiana University," 10

While the research staff undertook new projects, collections too underwent a period of marked development. The full staff numbered twenty during Kinsey's time. By the early 1970s it fluctuated between forty and fifty, not including graduate students and interns.[62] In part, this increase reflected multiple simultaneous projects. Much of it was due to NIMH support for making Institute data and the library and collections accessible to scholars and for increased teaching and training activities. The NIMH reviewers had told the Institute, in effect, that it would become irrelevant if it did not open its doors, share information with other researchers, and get advice and consultation from external experts.

Gebhard made extensive, although always cautious, strides in this direction. The data retrieval project, supported by the NIMH, made Institute data available to researchers while maintaining confidentiality of research subjects. A "core support" grant, also from the NIMH, made it possible to hire new librarians and information services staff, who created and published a new classification system for the library and fulfilled requests for data and bibliographies; the library was opened to "qualified researchers," and the Institute sponsored a monograph series of works based on materials found there; and the Institute staff began teaching classes on sexuality within the University, as well as a regular summer seminar for medical students and other professionals.[63] In 1966 the Institute recruited a number of Indiana University faculty to form an advisory board that would give advice on Institute operations and activities. Throughout the late 1960s and early 1970s the Institute hosted a number of consultants to advance research projects. In the context of the so-called sexual revolution, many believed that it was time for the Institute to become less insular, without risk of scandal or other repercussions.

Still, Gebhard never relinquished his concern about the reputation of the Institute, nor did he forget the legal battles and congressional hearings that had plagued the Institute in previous decades. He vetoed a planned book on erotic comic books because he and his collaborator, Eugene Levitt, could not agree on presentation. Levitt wanted a coffee table book that would highlight the art, whereas Gebhard favored a more "serious," scientific treatment of the materials, more in line with the Institute's other publications.[64] When scholars first applied to participate in the monograph series, Gebhard wrote to the advisory board, concerned that the planned publications all addressed pornography, giving the public the impression that "the Institute is producing a continual flow of sexually titillating literature."[65]

In 1968 Gebhard established a board to evaluate researchers wishing to use the library and archives. The Customs case ruling had said that many library materials were only not obscene in the hands of qualified researchers. Gebhard repeatedly consulted lawyers and University faculty and administrators for advice on precisely what the Institute could and could not do with its collections.[66] He was even more cautious than Kinsey had been. Ironically, this was because of, not in spite of, the sexual revolution. Gebhard believed that the visibility of sexual matters in the public sphere indicated a kind of obsessive prurience on the part of the public, making him anxiously protectionist toward the general public, the media, and other scholars.[67]

The NIMH initiated the most extensive "door opening" of the Institute. It granted support toward the Institute becoming an international clearinghouse for information on all sex-related matters. The first grant was for the five-year data retrieval project that began in 1963, just after the NIMH review. The project involved transferring interview data, without identifying markers, to computer tapes so that the Institute could quickly process marginal tabulations for outside researchers. In theory, then, a researcher could request information on any kind of sexual behavior that was covered in the Kinsey era interviews, and the Institute could provide statistics and demographic breakdowns for that behavior. In practice, the Institute rarely had sufficient resources to respond to the scale of demands. Later, the Russell Sage Foundation provided a grant for a related project, and the Institute eventually published *The Kinsey Data: Marginal Tabulations of the 1938–1963 Interviews Conducted by the Institute for Sex Research* (1979).

Even more significant was the library core support grant of $135,000 per year beginning in 1970. In the short term, this enabled the Institute to hire several new librarians and assistants and to create a full-time position for an information services coordinator, who would respond to requests from outside scholars and researchers.[68] The longer-term purpose of the grant was threefold. First, the Institute would become a central information clearinghouse, appropriate since the library and collections were already the largest in the country, if not the world. Second, the Institute would copy many of its materials and deposit them with other libraries and with the NIMH. This was largely a safeguard against something disastrous happening to the library, which had extensive holdings unavailable anywhere else.

Figure 4.8. Elizabeth Egan with two members of the library staff, ca. 1970. The Institute's collections staff not only fielded ever-increasing expert and general public demands for information but also developed a thesaurus for sex research while working on the grant to process the Kinsey data into a still confidential but accessible format for other researchers. Photo courtesy of Kinsey Institute Library and Special Collections.

Third, the Institute librarians would create a classification system for the library that would be comprehensible to and accessible by outside scholars.

This last goal was the most complicated, but it was also the most important. Classification systems controlled the vocabularies central to all research fields. Such tools marked sex research as a valid and established academic research field. Previously, Kinsey had organized the library archives by gradually developed subject headings pertaining to specific topics arising in the human sexual behavior project. When used only by Institute staff, this organization sufficed. It was less navigable for outside researchers. Moreover, collections expansion presented great challenges. By 1971 the library held a total of 27,539 volumes in addition to extensive archival, art, film, and artifact collections; a decade later, these totals had increased to over 59,000 volumes, 25,000 pieces of art, 50,000 photographs, and thousands of objects, film reels, ephemera, and microfilms.[69] No system existed to catalog these materials, particularly erotic items, which were excluded from Library of Congress and other classification systems. And many erotic or "obscene" materials had only incomplete or falsified bibliographic information. The Institute librarians, therefore, had to make organizational systems to classify the holdings.[70]

In the 1960s Elizabeth Egan, then head librarian, had begun to adapt the Dewey Decimal System to accommodate Institute materials. She kept the basic classes used by the system but applied them to sexuality. For example, the 500s, which in the Dewey Decimal System are "pure sciences," would become scientific and social science studies of sexual behavior. In the early 1970s Ruth Beasley, the new information services coordinator, and Rebecca Dixon, head librarian, continued Egan's work. In addition, JoAnne Brooks and Helen Hofer were put in charge of compiling the master subject index, which would eventually be published as *Sexual Nomenclature: A Thesaurus* (1976). The terms of that index were partly borrowed from Kinsey's subject heading list, but they were expanded to provide hierarchical relationships between precoordinated terms. Dixon, Beasley, Brooks, and Hofer drew on new 1970s guidelines for creating thesauri published by the National Information Standards Organization and the Education Resources Information Center (ERIC).[71] Though the librarians borrowed from the Library of Congress, most of the new thesaurus terms were based on the library materials themselves.

One key difficulty was in establishing terms both familiar and yet nonjudgmental, in the Kinseyan tradition. For example, "Erotica" covered a wide range of materials, some intended to sexually stimulate the reader or viewer, while "Pornography," a narrower term, was freighted with moral and legal connotations. Similarly, Dixon and Beasley chose "Sex Variations" rather than "Sex Deviations" or "Sexual Deviance" to indicate behaviors that were outside the statistical norm.[72]

Along with *Sexual Nomenclature*, the Institute published *Catalog of the Social and Behavioral Sciences, Monograph Section of the Library of the Institute for Sex Research* (1975) and *Catalog of Periodical Literature in the Social and Behavioral Sciences Section, Library of the Institute for Sex Research* (1976). These navigation tools were important for visitors to the Institute library and archives. They became authoritative for those developing libraries of sex and sexuality, providing tools for librarians encountering materials that had rarely been cataloged. Even though sex research had greatly expanded, researchers lacked basic tools available to researchers in other fields until the catalogs and thesaurus were published. "Researchers in any one area, such as psychology, usually tapped only the resources that existed in their own area," librarian Rebecca Dixon said. "Now a psychologist doing research can know what the sociologist, the anthropologist and other researchers are doing in the field as well."[73] The catalogs helped facilitate the kind of multidisciplinary study so valued by Kinsey from the outset of his devising the collections while also manifesting the field's scholarly infrastructure.

A persistent further problem for the collections was infrastructural. The upper floors of Morrison Hall, the Institute's home since 1967, had been part of a student dormitory, rather than a building purpose built for academic offices and teaching spaces. As one of the earliest University buildings, it had, and still has, a leak-prone roof, sorely tested each spring, placing precious items at clear and palpable risk. An electrical problem compounded the problem in February 1978. Rather than evacuate, leaving confidential data and irreplaceable collections insecure and at risk of burglary, Gebhard sought permission to remain in the building. His description of working conditions was graphic: a repeated and serious leak above the library ceiling could not be repaired until the spring thaw. In the meantime, he explained, daily monitoring took place. Books would be shifted and plastic covers placed, while watchful eyes monitored new leaks. Gebhard explained that the staff was managing by torchlight.[74]

* * *

Teaching also made the Institute accessible to the University community. Gebhard and other Institute staff had begun teaching sexuality classes to the psychology department of the medical school in the early 1960s and to Bloomington campus graduate students in anthropology, sociology, and psychology in a cross-listed seminar from 1970. That latter class developed into a human sexuality minor a few years later. In 1972 Indiana University recruited a committee to develop a class on human sexuality for 150 undergraduates, offered from 1973; Gebhard was the primary professor, and he brought in several other Institute staff members to lecture within their disciplines. These efforts helped boost the number of visitors to the library as well. The 1973–74 annual report of the Institute notes over two hundred visitors and specifically states that the number of undergraduates from Indiana University who used the library had more than doubled that year.

The Institute did its most significant teaching, though, outside Indiana University's normal class schedule. The NIMH prompted "summer seminars," sponsoring between twenty-five and thirty-five students, primarily educators in medical schools, each year. For the first few years, the seminars trained medical school professors to develop human sexuality curricula. Later, more participants came from social work, nursing, and psychology, but the focus remained on training to teach human sexuality. In 1975 the focus shifted toward training those in clinical practice. The Institute instructors chose applicants, limited to 135 students yearly, by their likely impact within their respective professions. Significantly, they also chose applicants who delivered services to the working class and the poor, to minority groups, and to mentally and physically handicapped persons, reasoning that in these areas clinicians and educators would assist those in most need.[75] The Institute, therefore, played a considerable role in professional sex education during

Figure 4.9. Summer seminar cohort, 1970. The Institute offered summer seminars as an instructional program for medical and other professionals working with sexuality. These programs involved intensive, one- to three-week training from Institute staff members. Photo courtesy of Kinsey Institute Library and Special Collections.

the ten years the seminars were offered. Such efforts expanded the influence and reach of the Institute among professionals in many disciplines.

Simultaneously, though, by the mid-1970s internal strife, research project delays, and external factors hampered Institute outreach. Later Institute trustee Dr. Eugene Eoyang remarked after Gebhard retired in 1987 that "by the 1970s, the Institute was not merely discreet, it was moribund."[76] Now emeritus professor of anthropology, Gebhard vehemently refuted the statement, citing the data retrieval project, the library classification system, the summer programs, and a multitude of publications (mostly journal articles). It would have been more accurate, he said, to call it "healthy, though not flamboyant."[77] Internal documents show, however, that this was not his view at the time.

"Moribund" and "Mothballed"?

I feel that we have produced high quality publications, service, and teaching. . . . However, we have fallen badly behind schedule in certain projects. With regard to . . . obtaining grants and other external funds, we have been satisfactory in obtaining monies for the Information Service, Summer Program, and Library, but we have not submitted any research grant proposals within the last five years because we were still completing prior research projects whose grants had expired.

Paul H. Gebhard, "Director's Report for I.U.B. Research Review," 3

Even if the cultural changes of the 1960s and 1970s should not be called a sexual revolution, the era offered possibilities and opportunities for the Institute. In the late 1960s Gebhard and his team made energetic responses to those opportunities. Perhaps because researchers undertook too many projects simultaneously, though, they proved unable to maintain momentum, and so projects remained unfinished. In 1974 Gebhard took a dismal view of Institute progress: "All research grants have now expired. . . . Those projects which require the expenditure of money (virtually all for salaries) are being funded from the Institute's own money."[78] He sought to suspend roles and services, though he doubted that the scale of information demands from the public could allow services to be fully "mothball[ed]."[79]

Gebhard resisted seeing any "serious problem" finishing projects. Yet he outlined several issues that promised considerable delay. The Institute's researchers failed to complete and publish the Youth Study, the Chicago study, and a study of the effects of sex education. Meanwhile, Gebhard promised a manuscript of the data retrieval project within a year, though its publication awaited another five years. The Attitudes Study was delayed because neither Klassen nor Levitt found time to complete it and because "communication and coordination between the two investigators has been difficult."[80] The San Francisco project and the Attitudes Study would eventually be published after many more delays.[81] Further, the NIMH had taken a turn. Gebhard explained that "with regard to funding sex research, the immediate future is gray, if not darker. NIMH has been battered politically and has less money; NSF [the National Science Foundation] has shown no interest in sex."[82] Other sex research foundations were struggling, a comparison that Gebhard hoped would soften the criticisms of the Institute: "The Center for the Study of Sex Education in Medicine was temporarily saved by a Commonwealth grant . . . and SIECUS is near bankruptcy."[83] Stressed by but resigned to the plight in which he found himself, Gebhard told Institute trustees that finding additional funding would be unlikely. "Federal grants for research will very probably be withheld," he wrote, "until we put out some major publication on the San Francisco homosexual study and the attitude survey." Still he held out hope that "if we have manuscripts for these in publishers' hands, we can again approach the government for research grants."[84]

After 1975 the library and archives experienced significant cuts as well. The archival staff, which had been slowly decreasing, was cut entirely, and "the archival function [was] virtually suspended." Librarian positions and the information services coordinator position were cut to half time. Ruth Beasley moved to take charge of the summer program, which, after considerable uncertainty, received additional funding in 1975 and was continued through 1979.[85] The *Indiana Daily Student* reported bluntly, "Funds Drop: Kinsey Institute Must Limit Services." The information services department would be effectively cut, and requests would be answered "with a copy of whatever is requested. This contrasts to the fairly complete information package now sent."[86] The library too would have to limit assistance to scholars and students.

Delayed publications, extended and expired grants, internal conflicts, and the poor state of the library led some to question the continued housing of the Institute at Indiana University. Other universities expressed interest in becoming the Institute's home. With the failed merger in 1970, researchers contemplated options. Meanwhile, at the request of its Office of Research and Graduate Development, the University appointed both internal and external review committees on the Institute. Both suggested that significant changes would provide momentum. Their far-reaching recommendations would have ongoing effects down to the present.

The internal review from 1980 noted that "both the heritage of the Institute for Sex Research and its possibilities for the future argue strongly that its existence be continued and its essential activities reinvigorated."[87] Keeping the Institute at Indiana University would mean a number of changes, some drastic. Both review committees recommended wholesale changes in leadership, governance, and operations.

The first recommendation was to make the Institute more recognizable. High international and national regard, according to the internal review, was "rooted in the original work of Alfred C. Kinsey." And that regard remained, notwithstanding the more recent blows to the Institute's research reputation "relative to its earlier period." The causes were plain: "failure to meet in a timely fashion obligations to bring work to completion," as well as remaining "aloof from innovative approaches to sex research." Informally, the Institute for Sex Research "is 'the Kinsey Institute' to a great many persons," an identification that "traces back to the 'old' days of Kinsey—a reputation for care, honesty, and probity in conducting its activities."[88] The reviewers argued that it was time to assert these associations by identifying the name "Kinsey" and the Institute. Proper honoring of his achievements had never happened. Though Gebhard undertook to coordinate a festschrift in Kinsey's honor shortly after his death, it never materialized. When Cornelia Christenson published a Kinsey biography in 1971, followed by one published by Wardell Pomeroy in 1972, Gebhard saw these as superseding the need for the long-promised festschrift.[89] One way to finally honor him, committee members held, "is through renaming the Institute the Kinsey Institute for Sex Research. We recommend that this be done."[90] The external review, headed by John Money, a prominent medical psychologist from Johns Hopkins, and Anke A. Ehrhardt, then associate professor of clinical psychology at Columbia University, concurred in the renaming, made official in 1981.[91]

Reviewers suggested fundamental structural changes. They ranked new leadership the top priority. Gebhard's unusually long incumbency, twenty-four years and counting as director, made him the most enduring influence over Institute characteristics and direction of any director before or since. The sixty-three-year-old Gebhard told reviewers that he was tired and lacked the energy to implement recommended changes, a seemingly accurate assessment.[92] Prerequisite for any long-overdue reorientation, then, would be a new director, recruited from an open search that was national and international in its reach.[93]

The second zone needing urgent change concerned governance. The board of trustees should be disbanded and replaced by a board comprised of members outside Institute staff. Put differently, the researchers should not govern themselves. Certainly, they should be represented through an executive committee, to whom the board of trustees should be responsive. The board, though, must retain ultimate power over policy decisions.

A third and telling recommendation concerned scientists and research associates. Reviewers urged researchers to return to their home departments. A new system of formal affiliation should be set up for scholars doing research on sexuality. In other words, researchers would no longer be directly employed by the Institute. Since the Institute's capacity to pay salaries depended on research grants, this system would create a more stable professional environment for researchers and, ultimately, the Institute.[94]

These three changes were all instituted over the next few years. Money and Ehrhardt saw them as preparatory for a larger desirable development. They urged Indiana University to incorporate the Institute into its existing structure and create a new interdisciplinary Department of Sexology.[95] As outlined in chapter 1, a legal separation between the Institute and Indiana University protected the interview data and the collections from moralistic state or federal political interference, such as censorship or suppression of materials liable to be found "offensive" or "distasteful." Yet this separation had been tested by the 1950–57 Customs case. Its outcome reaffirmed Kinsey's founding mission, namely, that to understand human sexual behaviors and desires, their full cultural manifestations had to be seen and scientifically studied toward better understanding, even when, at different times and in different contexts, specific behaviors or practices might elicit widespread distaste or even fear. There had to be a repository that could hold and steward

Figure 4.10. John Money, pictured here, most significantly introduced the concept of "gender" to sex researchers and undertook pioneering and controversial work on transsexuality. He served as one of the external reviewers of the Institute in 1980. Later he donated his papers and case files to the Institute and established a named research fellowship for Institute scholars. Photo courtesy of Kinsey Institute Library and Special Collections.

these materials, sometimes the only known surviving instances of them, so that they would not be forever lost.

Hence, Money and Ehrhardt contended that in order to regularize the Institute's long-standing relationship with the University, a sexology research and teaching department should be established. It should be governed, resourced, and accountable just like any other University department. Such a development would solve two problems. First, it would provide a more stable relationship between the two entities, giving the University oversight and direct capacity to protect the Institute, as it so effectively did in the Customs case, even though it was not legally required to intervene at all. Second, a department structure would create tenure lines, which the new director could use to attract top talent to study and conduct research from Indiana University. Money argued that here Indiana University had the option of becoming the world's premier research university for the study of sexology.[96] It would need to offer both undergraduate and graduate degrees. While the Institute was internationally well known, Indiana University owed its international reputation largely to its association with the Institute. Combining the two would raise the international profile of Indiana University.[97]

Concurrently, researchers at several universities attempted something similar, including Money at Johns Hopkins. He, as much as anyone, knew the difficulties of creating an interdisciplinary department of sexology in the climate of the late 1970s. His own Sexual Behaviors Unit never managed to move out of the medical school. Medical school links with the Institute faced the challenge of being on different campuses separated by fifty miles. Neither Indiana University's Office of Research and Graduate Development nor Institute directors after Gebhard seem ever to have embraced this goal.

The 1980 reviewers' remaining recommendations related to the information services and to library and other collections. Though the evidence of unproductivity had been damning for Gebhard and the team, it was the state of the library and archives that received the strongest outcry from reviewers:

> A major reason for arguing the importance of the continued existence of the Institute is its library, collection of art and artifacts, and information service. . . . We have noted that the state of the Institute's library and archives constitute an emergency. . . . A tour of the library reveals appalling conditions. The collections are bursting at the seams. Gift materials, recent acquisitions, and archival materials are unopened, stacked in closets, corners, on window sills. Valuable art works are stuffed, unprotected, into tightly filled drawers of map cases. Roof leaks have caused water damage to irreplaceable collections. It is an understatement to say that these holdings are too valuable to permit their loss through neglect.[98]

The library had, at one point, enjoyed wide use among Indiana University and external scholars. This forced Gebhard to admit that the expiry of the core support grant meant that much of the library and archives staff had to be cut, and the archives were put into "mothball status," a term Gebhard used derisively to characterize the haphazard storage of items, as if tucked away for the winter. From the external review, Money noted that sex researchers who might normally donate their collections had to consider the risk involved in trusting them to current Institute collections stewardship.[99] The roof leaks Morrison Hall experienced every spring, requiring the regular practice of covering shelves and stored items with sheets of plastic, compounded a sense of literal physical jeopardy.[100] Meanwhile, the internal reviewers urged a collections committee to devise salvage and preservation strategies. That committee made a significant suggestion: incorporate the collections into the main Indiana University library system. Finally, echoing the 1963 NIMH review, they argued that the library and collections should be open to more scholars and students, as should the rest of the Institute.[101]

Money and Ehrhardt tackled the recommendations for the collections somewhat differently. They believed it was impossible to address the collections apart from two related issues: the need for stabilization and best practices, and the legal standing of the collections. Extolling the precious and irreplaceable nature of the holdings, they implored the University to provide conditions for stability, professional stewardship, and innovative development. Lack of funding had long meant that most elements of the collections, meaning archives, manuscripts, photographs, films and videos, art, newspapers, and ephemera, languished in low-grade storage, unprocessed, uncataloged, inaccessible, and in real physical peril. "Ideally," they urged, "the library and collections of the Kinsey Institute should have an endowment for their proper housing, permanent safekeeping, and scholarly utilization, as well as for their expansion and updating." Without this, they ventured, gifts of "the personal papers and archives of great sex researchers" were more an embarrassment than the invaluable asset they should be in the otherwise most appropriate auspices for such scholarly materials.[102]

What were the options? The external reviews did not believe that integrating the collections into the existing Indiana University library system was a feasible option. They observed the vulnerability of materials on sex to theft and vandalism in all libraries, including medical libraries, "unless they are put in maximum security storage." Hence, Institute collections would always require their own "maximum security quarters . . . guaranteed inaccessible to censorship and litigative interference." These conditions were assured legally by establishing the collections under the permanent custody of the corporation. "This is their present status, and it should remain unchanged."[103]

These reviews presented an unmistakable critique of Gebhard's stewardship of the Institute. His defensive reactions could only have been expected: "Since giving the Institute over to a new director is like offering my child for adoption, I want to be certain of the quality of the individual." He argued that he should be central to the new search for a director and that "he/she be on probation for a year and subject to annual appointment by the Institute's Board of Trustees for several years thereafter."[104] Though he did not want to seem like he was "dragging his feet," he wrote that he did not "want to abdicate until the 'non-research' trustees and I are presented with a really good candidate. I think the 'non-research' trustees (Remak, Yamaguchi, Christenson, Torry) and I should retain our prerogative of voting (along with new trustees) on a new director."[105]

Gebhard also wanted to maintain influence over who would be appointed to the new board of trustees. It must be done carefully "so that we do not inadvertently [commit] suicide," he wrote, and he emphasized that the new board could not legally be appointed by the Office of Research and Graduate Development; new members must be voted in by the current board.[106]

Regarding the library, Gebhard argued vehemently against it being incorporated into the main Indiana University system. His primary concern was the confidential material: "A serious problem has not been addressed by either review committee. I feel responsible for the highly confidential information entrusted to Kinsey and later to me, and I would like to see safeguards made before I give up legal control over such information and material."[107] He should be given, he argued, sole control over these materials until a solution could be found. He argued further that the doors were, in fact, open but that the Customs case and some of the Institute's agreements with police departments (who donated some confiscated materials) restrained it; the Institute had neither the staff nor the space to solicit users or adequately screen the credentials of potential users.[108]

* * *

The University removed Gebhard from the directorship and returned the remaining research associates who had joined the Institute during the 1960s and 1970s to their tenure home departments. No longer would the Institute employ and supervise researchers directly. Instead, faculty had to be appointed to academic departments and affiliated from that framework. The Gebhard era and the so-called sexual revolution came to a close simultaneously. On November 10, 1981, in the midst of a search for a new director and a new mission, the Institute for Sex Research officially became the Alfred C. Kinsey Institute for Sex Research.[109] The renaming of the Institute was commemorated through a well-attended conference with leading figures in sex research in attendance, including Harry Benjamin, Frank Beach, Mary Calderone, Anke Ehrhardt, and Richard Green. Robert Kolodny and John Money also attended, as did John Gagnon.

The event proved momentous. It functioned, perhaps inadvertently, as a preliminary canvassing for possible nominees to the soon-to-be-created new director shortlist. Gebhard, invited "to draw up a list of persons to be considered for the new director," later reported listing four: John Bancroft, Anke Ehrhardt, Richard Green, and June Machover Reinisch. "John Bancroft and Anke Ehrhardt declined to be considered and finally only Richard Green and June Reinisch remained," Gebhard wrote. According to his version of the transition narrative, the selection of Reinisch was almost happenstance: "I had placed June on the list without knowing much about her, but she was famous for getting a million dollar grant."[110]

Gebhard could not see a fit successor. His responses to reviewers that the new director be on probation for a year and be subject to "annual appointment by the Institute Board of Trustees for several years thereafter" were telling.[111] As he gravely assured all stakeholders, "It is not going to be easy to find a good new director." As the third director would find out soon enough, after more than a quarter of a century as the second director, her predecessor would not pass the torch easily.

5
Initiating Paradigm Shifts
(1982–1993)

In much of today's science, there is a powerful polarization of the biological and the sociobehavioral disciplines. Very few scholars cross the equator of learning and become equally knowledgeable at both poles. . . . To find one of these few people is a challenge confronting the University's search committee. The person may very well be a woman, since that would redress the masculine bias that has characterized the Institute in the past. There may be a temptation to favor a person with an M.D. instead of a Ph.D. qualification, but that would narrow too much the research horizons of the Institute . . . toward pathology and treatment. That would be a disaster for the Kinsey Institute and for sexological scholarship in general, for medical schools already give over-representation to research in pathological sexology at the expense of healthy sexual functioning.

John Money and Anke Ehrhardt, "Report on the Institute for Sex Research, Indiana University," 12

THE 1980 EXTERNAL REVIEW OF THE INSTITUTE called for extensive changes. For too long, the reviewers contended, the Institute had remained insular. Despite the advances that Kinsey made in his own approaches to the challenges of the female volume, his coresearchers disdained new angles of enquiry connecting sexuality and sustained gender analysis. Dismissals of gender and sexual politics pervaded Institute culture, weakening research quality and constraining Institute relevance in a changing world. This underpinned John Money and Anke Ehrhardt's observation of "masculine bias." Research productivity, collections conditions, morale, and staffing patterns all suffered. Externally recruited leadership seemed the only way to secure the drastic and durable change needed for the Institute's survival.[1]

Between 1982 and 1993 June Machover Reinisch initiated new leadership paradigms. She sought to transform the Institute into a research, teaching, and outreach entity comparable with other Indiana University institutes and academic units. Through internal changes, a heightened public profile, and federally backed research initiatives, the Kinsey Institute attempted fundamental change toward patterns urged by the NIMH in the 1960s but left undone during the 1970s. The methods Reinisch and her team used to make the Institute and sex research more generally available to the public included television appearances, popular news articles, and even a Kinsey Institute–produced sex research column syndicated for national newspapers. The Institute's research undertook directions consonant with broader paradigm shifts in the field.

Soon, the Institute faced one of its biggest challenges: the HIV/AIDS crisis of the 1980s. In the context of the epidemic, the Institute and its researchers quickly added HIV/AIDS research to their agenda, making the Institute a central clearinghouse for sex research and sexual health information. While researchers in medical facilities across the country scrambled to understand the new disease that seemed to cause rare cancers among gay men in urban populations, Institute researchers relayed information and created the space for professionals to discuss the impact of HIV/AIDS on various communities.

Raising the public profile and opening the doors of the Institute to the public were no small challenges. The cultural and political response to the HIV/AIDS crisis—most notably, the public denial of the crisis from nearly every level of government, including then president Ronald Reagan—was but one dimension of the cultural and political sea changes of the 1980s. Increasingly vocal opponents of sex research, especially from the religious Right, gained traction. AIDS was God's punishment visited on the wicked. During the 1970s, campaigns like Anita Bryant's "Save Our Children" openly attacked sex researchers, especially those who viewed homosexuality as a natural variant of the sex instinct. Ironically, although the Institute had seemed apolitical and had debunked the intense sexual politics of the so-called sexual revolution, the AIDS crisis catapulted it inescapably into the eye of the sexual politics storm. In such a context, the Institute's visible public profile created opportunities and challenges as it spoke to those who sought scientific answers to their sexual problems and received criticism for their work.[2]

Ultimately, however, reversals of fortune came in the late 1980s and early 1990s, less from external opponents—though they certainly made their mark—than from members of the University and local and state constituencies that were unreconciled to the changes Reinisch instigated. The previous director was seemingly her most vigilant critic.[3] According to critics, Reinisch took the Institute in entirely the wrong direction. In spite of internal and external obstacles, though, the Institute made unprecedented advances during Reinisch's tenure. The collections, described as an "emergency" by the 1980 review committee, needed urgent attention, and she made them a central focus. Access to the library, archives, and art and artifacts became a key goal. Moreover, the researchers affiliated with and external to the Institute used the collections in new ways, highlighting the public relevance of sex research. This was no easy task in an increasingly vociferous conservative cultural climate both within and beyond the University.[4]

Reinisch took a three-pronged approach. First, she sought international exchanges. She worked in conjunction with other internationally renowned sex researchers to host annual symposia on topics of contemporary concern to academic, medical, and lay communities. From these emerged high-quality interdisciplinary scholarship. Her second focus was the collections. She worked to expand services and access to foster increasingly creative use of the collections by researchers, faculty, students, and the public. This positioned the collections as a central resource through which the Institute could build constituencies for a sexually knowledgeable public culture. Third, Reinisch inaugurated a vastly expanded Institute presence and intellectual impact through use of the popular press, radio, television, and other print and electronic media. Through these three areas, Reinisch sought to enhance the Institute's national profile and international reputation.

* * *

The critical review of the Institute presented in 1980 stressed the need for momentum. With new hires working from their home departments and as affiliated faculty within the Institute, Reinisch coordinated research teams able to respond to a field that had become, over the past three decades, keenly medicalized.[5] Her own research reflected these developments. She had earned her doctorate with distinction from Columbia University in 1976 and worked and trained with distinguished field leader John Money at the Johns Hopkins Hospital Psychohormonal Unit since 1970. With her hire, the Institute halted sociological and ethnographic research in the embrace of medical and psychological approaches to sexuality. Her research focused on the effects of prenatal exposure to hormones via maternal medical treatment on subsequent sex- and gender-related development in humans. She also had extensive collaborative experience in animal studies, since her prenatal hormone research required randomized experiments, illegal for humans. Her impressive publication record included four articles published in *Science* and two published in *Nature*, two of the world's most prestigious multidisciplinary scientific journals. Her current grant with the National Institute for Child Health and Human Development, entitled "Long-Term Consequences of Prenatal Exposure to Hormones," had received just over $1 million in funding through 1985.[6] Prior

Figure 5.1. Portrait of Dr. June Machover Reinisch, ca. 1982. Reinisch became the Institute's third director in 1982. A psychobiologist, she took medical and public health approaches to sex research partly in response to the HIV/AIDS crisis, prioritizing internationalism and expert consultation. Her unprecedented stress on outreach, public sex education, external promotion, and public relations departed from previous Institute leadership and so was locally controversial. Photo courtesy of Kinsey Institute Library and Special Collections.

to her appointment at the Institute, she had taught at Rutgers, the State University of New Jersey, for seven years in the Department of Psychology.[7]

The external review of the Institute urged governance changes to better integrate the Institute within Indiana University. Reinisch promptly reformulated its advisory and executive boards. Instead of solely internal membership, her new boards seated both Indiana University faculty and world-renowned sex researchers. Hence, the newly structured board of trustees comprised faculty and administrators who were affiliated with the University but external to the Institute. Though highly invested in the success of the Institute within Indiana University, they had no sex research expertise.

Reinisch also formed the Scientific Advisory Board. Moreover, she secured additional external members for the board of trustees to gain psychoneuroendocrinological, sexual science, fund-raising, and publishing expertise.[8] Such experts willingly served and devoted their time. They testified that it was their respect for the legacy of Kinsey's vision that secured their service: the Institute was an object of esteem.[9] Indeed, both 1980 reviews suggested that the name of the Institute be changed from the Institute for Sex Research to honor its founder. At the end of Gebhard's directorship the legal name was changed to the Alfred C. Kinsey Institute for Sex Research. After Reinisch's arrival a variant of the name suggested by Money and Ehrhardt was implemented, the Kinsey Institute for Research in Sex, Gender, and Reproduction, reflecting the fact that most people referred to it as the Kinsey Institute and that its purview was to include sexual aspects of gender and reproduction.

Reinisch made the reviewers' call for enlarged access to the Institute a central element of its mission going forward. "Consistent with its mission to promote sound research on and education about sexuality," the external reviewers believed the new director should be charged with expanding knowledge about and access to the resources of the Institute "to any serious scholar seeking to use them," increasing outreach and visibility to the broader research community internal and external to Indiana University and the public. Expanding access required properly caring for, conserving, and preserving the collections and making those resources more widely known within and outside the University. With the reorganization of the Institute and the former researchers back in their home departments, there was no longer a core research staff of Indiana University faculty within the Institute. Instead, any faculty member with an interest in sex research could apply to and be appointed by the director as research associates without release time from teaching duties unless they could "buy out" their time with grants. Project leaders who had received grants or some other source of funding through the Institute could hire personnel for their specific projects for the duration of that funding.

Before accepting the position of director, Reinisch developed a five-year plan and then negotiated with the University for the resources to accomplish it. Her recommendations for expanded, renovated, and unified physical space for the Institute also had to be negotiated and implemented. The Institute attained University approval for significant expansion and renovation of its space in Morrison Hall, home to the Institute since 1967. The third floor and half of the second floor were renovated in tandem with the original space on the fourth and fifth floors. These renovations included temperature and humidity controls.

By the 1984 annual report to the board of trustees of the Institute, Reinisch could report that many of the expanded programs and goals had been achieved. These, she noted, were due in part to Indiana University's continued "philosophical and financial support." Even with the structural changes at the Institute, Reinisch commended her small staff's performance "above and beyond any normal expectations with regard to hours or responsibilities for over 2 years."[10]

After reaching its most stagnant point in 1980, the Institute would quickly restore its productivity. Along with creating an active program of scientific research and publishing, Reinisch also worked to position the Institute as a hub for interdisciplinary dialogue on topics of vital importance to the field and society through conferences and workshops. She implemented an affiliated scholars program to include a broader range of people and research topics, beginning also the Institute Series—edited volumes highlighting multidisciplinary perspectives on topics of interest to the field. Such work, however, would have little impact, she believed, if it was kept within the confines of academia.

Sexual Health / Public Health

> The urgency of the current AIDS crisis and the demands from various public and private sources has forced the Institute to redirect some of its energy and resources to meeting these needs. Understanding the potential for the sexual transmission and spread of HIV . . . requires the study of the interaction across many segments of our society. Any misinformed effort to see sexually-labeled groups as separate and independent from one another flaunts these facts and hides from the potentially deadly reality.
>
> June Machover Reinisch, annual report (1989, 8)

Reinisch's appointment shifted Institute research toward both psychoendocrinology and sexual public health. The latter attended to broader factors in human health and development, such as environmental effects on the body, barriers to health care, and population and community-level health assessments. Reinisch

Figure 5.2. Institute staff, ca. 1983. Reinisch hired new staff members to the Institute, including biopsychologist Stephanie A. Sanders, technical analyst Thomas Albright, and head librarian Doug Freeman. Other new staff members performed research, collections development, education, outreach, and administrative support functions. Photo courtesy of Kinsey Institute Library and Special Collections.

had her own project along these lines called the Prenatal Development Project. The project, along with its federal funding, was relocated to the Institute, bringing much-needed grant assistance. She hired Stephanie A. Sanders, whom Reinisch had mentored at Rutgers, as a research associate and, initially, as the science assistant to the director. Sanders, a developmental biopsychologist, worked on menstrual cyclicity and women's sexuality, with additional duties on the prenatal project.

This project was the most complex and ambitious research project undertaken at the Institute during this era. This was clear from external funding and data collection.[11] Collaborative studies with researchers at the Institute and at the Psykologisk Institut, Kommunehospitalet, and Rigshospitalet in Copenhagen, Denmark, received a series of NIH grants. The prenatal project examined the long-term developmental consequences of maternal treatment during pregnancy with hormones and drugs, which alter the prenatal environment. The studies elucidated the impact of different exposures to these substances on offspring behavioral, cognitive, personality, social, and physical development, especially sexual and psychosexual development. During the data collection period, a number of key literature review articles and chapters, many of which were invited papers, were published that contributed theoretical models for understanding the interaction of biological and social variables in gender development and critically evaluated the content, strengths, and limitations of existing research.[12] Reinisch and Sanders also explored previous prenatal project data sets based on established samples of American subjects who were prenatally exposed to a synthetic progestin with a masculinizing potential and a synthetic estrogen with a feminizing potential. They compared these subjects with their unexposed same-sex siblings. Numerous publications have relied on the project's databases, which will continue to be utilized well into the future. The prenatal project held promise in helping solve long-standing questions about the relationship between prenatal environments and sexual development.

Meanwhile, other, more sociological questions about sexual and public health loomed large. National- and state-level concern over teen pregnancy pervaded public health debates. Teen pregnancy and birth rates proved substantially higher, and contraception use significantly lower, in the United States than in other developed nations.[13] As James Trussell noted, "One out of every 10 women aged 15–19 becomes pregnant each year in the United States. Of these pregnancies, five out of every six are unintended—92% of those conceived premaritally, and half of those conceived in marriage."[14] In December 1983 the Institute conducted its first data-gathering conference, the first Kinsey Dialogue, "Adolescent Life Styles." Seventeen high school seniors from nine diverse US regions came to act as participant observers. They discussed their own and their peers' and communities' views of teen pregnancy, as well as teenager-parent interactions, sex education, sex behavior, love, pregnancy, contraception, sexually transmitted diseases, marriage, dating, masculinity, femininity, and parenthood. This event piloted the third Kinsey Symposium in 1986, entitled "Adolescence and Puberty."[15]

Such events signaled the way in which the Scientific Advisory Board altered Institute interests and activities. A concerted effort to respond to broad topics and seek expertise beyond Institute personnel marked Reinisch's directorship. The outcome was a consistent scholarly interdisciplinarity that exceeded previous endeavors.

Such organizational changes grounded work for Reinisch's second primary goal: raising the public profile of the Institute by opening the research and collections to other researchers and the public. Access to information about sex was just as important for the educator as it was for the lay population. In the conservative context of the 1980s, the Institute faced significant challenges. Conferences and workshops marked Reinisch's tenure as director. Prominent too were data-gathering meetings and workshops to discuss future research directions and facilitate interdisciplinary and international collaborations. These accented the Institute's leadership role in the field. Indiana University sponsored these meetings and the resultant publications, fostering collaboration, interdisciplinarity, and theoretical and methodological inquiry. Conference topics for the Institute Symposia Series, selected in consultation with the Institute's Scientific Advisory Board, were those "of the utmost contemporary concern to the academic, medical, and lay communities." These invitational symposia permitted internationally renowned scholars from diverse disciplines to exchange and integrate perspectives on issues of mutual interest.

Central among these was the Institute Symposia and their resultant edited volumes in the Institute Series. Conference attendance itself was limited in order to facilitate productive cross-disciplinary dialogue. Following the conference, speakers finalized their chapters in light of the discussion at the symposium. These chapters were then included in edited volumes published by Oxford University Press. These books disseminated information to a wide audience of academics as well as educated lay persons. And by partnering with Oxford and having members of the advisory board who were knowledgeable about publishing, these conferences marked a departure from previous Institute operations and publications. No longer did Institute publications emanate only from in-house researchers. Instead, scholars from diverse backgrounds and fields published the Institute's edited volumes. The hope was that the Institute would become not only a center for discussing sexual health issues but also a key disseminator of sexual health knowledge.[16]

The Institute Symposia Series reflected 1980s cultural and political concerns. Women's movement advocacy inflected the first symposium, "Masculinity/Femininity: Basic Perspectives." Representing a wide range of perspectives became a common theme among the symposia, which were based on psychological, neuroscientific, evolutionary, behavioral, and developmental/psychosocial/cultural methods. The authors raised critical issues in methodologies and definitions, and they presented a complex picture of the intricacies of the interaction between biology and environment in behavioral differences between females and males and how such differences are interpreted.[17]

Other topical issues, such as heterosexuality/homosexuality, adolescence, and puberty, comprised the following years' conferences. Cross-disciplinary work diversified approaches and enlarged the numbers of conference delegates. Meetings and publications identified continuing research agendas, such as sexual orientation, childhood sexual development, and issues for public health officials on both topics.[18]

The Kinsey Institute library and collections became the interdisciplinary hub of sex research information that Alfred Kinsey had envisioned. NIMH recommendations had suggested that more openness and renewed commitments to scholars outside of the Institute would help it become the key sex research facility in the nation. Achieving this goal took nearly twenty years of effort. This interdisciplinary work would be needed in the face of a new public health crisis.

These in-house initiatives marked the early 1980s. Structural reorganization, new faculty, and renewed relationships with Indiana University topped the agenda. Meanwhile, West Coast doctors were reporting rare forms of cancer among gay men, most commonly Kaposi sarcoma lesions. What was initially termed gay-related immunodeficiency disease (GRID) would later be called human immunodeficiency virus (HIV) and then lead to a condition called acquired immunodeficiency syndrome (AIDS). Between 1981 and 1985 HIV spread nationwide, affecting some three million people and causing innumerable deaths within gay and straight communities. Slow state and federal government responses intensified the crisis. Its perceived link to socially ostracized and oppressed communities bred official resistance to acknowledging HIV/AIDS as a public health crisis, soon a pandemic, with devastating effects.[19]

Americans' friends and family members died in unprecedented numbers. In urban queer communities in New York, women and men started the AIDS Coalition to Unleash Power (ACT-UP). Through direct-action protests and propaganda campaigns, members of ACT-UP sought to educate communities about HIV/AIDS and pressure local, state, and federal officials to fund research on HIV/AIDS and provide services for those living with the disease. Other groups, such as Gay Men's Health Crisis, started as a means of providing services to patients and families of those affected by the disease, creating a grassroots response to the crisis.[20]

By the late 1980s, AIDS overtook teen pregnancy as the primary societal concern involving sexuality. In light of the emerging pandemic, in 1988 the surgeon general of the United States, C. Everett Koop, directed the creation and mailing of the Public Health Service's brochure *Understanding AIDS* to 107 million households in the United States, promoting public awareness of the importance of sexual behaviors as related to health and raising public awareness of the importance of studies of sexual behavior.[21]

The onset of AIDS initiated a major shift in Institute focus. In an effort to become a "leading source of timely and accurate scientific information about sex, gender, and reproduction in the minds of other researchers, educators, public officials, the media, and the general public," the Institute sought closer networks among experts.[22] As the crisis developed, many scientists joined the research effort, although most of them had no training in the assessment of the sensitive and complex topic of sexuality. Accurate assessment and sophisticated understanding of patterns of sexual behaviors and identities across various groups were imperative for understanding the spread of the virus and the development of appropriate behavioral interventions, then the only means to curb viral transmission. The Institute sought to foster collaboration between sex researchers and AIDS researchers

Figure 5.3. Reinisch addressing a plenary panel during the "AIDS and Sex" conference in 1987. Photo courtesy of Kinsey Institute Library and Special Collections.

and educators in an interdisciplinary and public dialogue. Its researchers proposed identifying levels of risk in understudied groups, highlighting important methodological issues such as the need for increased specificity in recording sexual behaviors and noting (especially for risk assessment) that sexual behaviors occur across seemingly distinct groups; in other words, those who identify as either gay or straight frequently had sexual contacts outside their identity category.

Soon the Institute became the international flagship of sex research. Yet unlike the Institute's remote or skeptical postures during the sexual revolution, Reinisch held that responsiveness, especially to changing public health concerns, was imperative. Hence, she abandoned the original plan for a 1987 conference in favor of a symposium devoted to HIV/AIDS. It would prove to be the Institute's largest ever conference. Supported by the National Institute of Allergy and Infectious Diseases, the National Institute of Child Health and Human Development, and Indiana University, its delegates included Dr. Bruce Voller, a leading biologist, AIDS activist, and cofounder of the National Gay and Lesbian Task Force, and Michael Gottlieb, first to report AIDS cases to the Centers for Disease Control in 1981.[23] Reinisch reallocated resources to address this unforeseen and urgent

Figure 5.4. The "AIDS and Sex" conference was one of the best attended in Institute history. Pictured here are William Masters, Virginia Johnson, Frank Beach, and Paul Gebhard, among others. Photo courtesy of Kinsey Institute Library and Special Collections.

public health crisis. Benefits accrued in new cooperative alliances with funding agencies. The Institute "established a reputation for facilitating accurate and timely exchanges of AIDS information among scientists, the media, and the general public on a worldwide basis," Reinisch testified before the Presidential Commission on the Human Immunodeficiency Virus Epidemic in early 1988.[24] Institute HIV/AIDS work then stepped firmly into the public realm, offering comprehensive information on sexual health and the ongoing crisis of HIV/AIDS.

For the Institute to make its most effective public impact, however, the collections needed urgent and extensive support. Reinisch had begun the necessary improvements to modernize the library and archives collections and their storage conditions. The Institute's enlarging profile made those improvements more pressing than ever.

Collections Enrichment and Outreach

Roof leaks have caused water damage to irreplaceable collections. Collections of serials, unrivaled in any other collection, in newsprint are rapidly deteriorating; without archival microfilm copies being made, these will be forever lost. Given crowded conditions, and the absence of personnel to supervise use of materials, security against theft of or misuse of them is minimal. The cataloging system for art works and ephemeral publications follows no established lines. . . . Printed materials, phonograph records, tapes are not properly stored, and will be lost unless appropriate copies are made and used instead of fragile originals.

Sheldon Stryker, Chair, Institute for Sex Research Review Committee, to George Springer, Research and Graduate Development, February 26, 1980, 9–10

Reviewers in 1980 lamented the state of the collections by the end of Gebhard's directorship. Money and Ehrhardt stressed the library's and archives' international standing with scholars, who described them "as the most important sexological library in the world." Scholars, the reviewers noted, received warm welcomes and painstaking staff assistance "despite the overcrowding and strain of the extra work on the staff."[25] If the collections were to be properly used, they needed renewed attention. Like the external reviewers who stressed the importance of the Institute's collections to Indiana University officials, Reinisch maintained that the collections were the heart and soul of the Institute. Directors and researchers and their projects would come and go. What remained for posterity were library materials, archival and historical records, art, artifacts, film, sexual histories, and data.

Upon her arrival, the collections had been effectively closed for five years. Reinisch worked to implement significant changes in assessment, conservation, and cataloging/indexing of the Institute's unique materials. Her priority was scholarly and public access. She created and filled the position of head of collections and services with Douglas Freeman in November 1983. This new position replaced that of head librarian and permitted the reintegration and central administration of different portions of the collections, which had been treated by Gebhard's staffing patterns as entities separated by media or genre. As well, she hired a full-time editorial assistant in 1984 to meet the increased demands for literature searches, to organize letters, and to assist with the newspaper column and staff public appearances.[26]

Proper stewardship also demanded thorough investigation of the collections' physical safety and security. "Brick and board" shelves had to be replaced with proper shelving, which would also provide storage for "books stacked in piles on the floor." James Kennedy, then Indiana University chief of police, and George Huntington of the Indiana University Police installed climate control systems to regulate temperature and humidity, as well as alarms and smoke detectors linked to Indiana University security services.[27]

These enhancements required massive resources. Meanwhile, Thomas Solley, director of the Indiana University Art Museum from 1971 to 1986, identified the most valuable items in the collection, as well as those most in need of preservation. Other museum staff offered advice on photography cataloging and initiated preservation of fragile artifacts, while James Riley from the Rochester Institute of Technology advised on photographic preservation. He recommended short-term and affordable preservation measures that would ensure the continuance and preservation of the art and artifacts. More valuable items were matted and framed or stored in boxes. Meanwhile, staff tackled new organizational methods and arrangement of the Institute's own historical operational archives, as well as of donated materials, confidential correspondence files, and restricted materials of various types. Attempts were made to obtain all materials relating to Dr. Kinsey from Bowdoin College, Stevens Institute, and the faculty of the Department of Biology. Indiana University archives retained their materials.

Gebhard had only allowed collections access to a few select scholars. Alternatively, mostly through the Institute monograph series, Reinisch facilitated new use of the archives and collections through the research associates program. Instituted in 1982, this program brought together a diverse range of scholars from both the humanities and the sciences. Funded projects were selected from proposals and represented a new range of scholars who were previously underrepresented at the Institute. Along with increased external scholar users, researchers helped organize the collections and created new bibliographies for future scholars' use.[28] Other researchers sought to use the archived data collected from the Kinsey and Gebhard directorships. Homosexuality came into new focus in the wake of the post-1974 American Psychiatric Association's removal of the category "homosexual" from the *Diagnostic and Statistical Manual*.[29] Professor Joseph Harry of Northern Illinois University reevaluated earlier data, especially the perceived rise in suicide rates among homosexual men. Similarly, Margaret Intons-Peterson of the University of Houston scrutinized psychological effects of sex education literature in curtailing the effects of violent pornography.

These works, using the Institute's collections and data, established a new pattern of collections research. The impact of the collections, therefore, reached far beyond the confines of the Institute itself and became a central resource for a number of groundbreaking works in sex research outside of the hard sciences and the fields now represented by Kinsey Institute staff. In return, these efforts attached the Institute's name to more peer-reviewed and scholarly works, further securing its political, academic, and cultural reputation. Visiting scholars came from Australia, Denmark, Spain, Sweden, West Germany, and many locations in the United States for varying periods of time to use the collections and collaborate with

Institute researchers and programs.[30] Visitors Mary Ziemba-Davis and Craig Hill, for instance, later joined the Institute staff with publications related to the prenatal project, sexual orientation, high-risk sexual behaviors, and sexual health.[31]

Donors remained key supporters of the collections. As well, collections staff regularly submitted grant applications to federal agencies and private foundations. For example, a National Endowment for the Humanities grant was obtained by Freeman to fund an art cataloger and to bring to the Institute a group of six internationally recognized consultants from various humanities disciplines to appraise the art and artifact collections' significance for their fields of study. They unanimously agreed on the importance of the collections as a resource, requiring a permanent curator and an acquisitions budget.[32] To initiate at least some progress here, given insufficient budgetary resources, a series of graduate assistants began to serve collections needs, one as curator of the art, photography, and artifact collections. Each assistant made significant inroads into cataloging and organizing the backlog of unprocessed materials, improving access, storage, and display.

Reinisch conceptualized the Institute's library as the centerpiece of the corporation, helping all parts of the Institute work smoothly together while also reaching out to other researchers, institutions, and the public. Collections and staff anchored the success of two major public service projects sponsored by the Institute. The first was widespread public access to factual information about sexuality. The second was Reinisch's internationally syndicated newspaper column, underwritten by a popular sex education book. These activities attracted extensive media attention. Not since the publication of the Kinsey Reports in 1948 and 1953 had the Institute been so much in the public eye.[33]

Information services and the library anchored information provision. From research and outreach functions, preparation required for the newspaper column ("The Kinsey Report"), and the upcoming publication of *The Kinsey Institute New Report on Sex* (*KINROS*), demands on collections and staff increased. Increased public and media visibility generated by the newspaper column only further enlarged pressures. Concomitantly, information services answered telephone and mail inquiries and handled requests from Institute research staff and Indiana University faculty and students while also lending films and other materials for Indiana University faculty class use, assisting visiting scholars to the Institute and to Indiana University, helping identify speakers and materials for conferences by the Institute and state and nonprofit agencies in Indiana, compiling standard bibliographies, providing tours to classes and visitors to Indiana University, working with other libraries, managing paperwork, recording statistics, and filing.

The thrice-weekly internationally syndicated newspaper column, "The Kinsey Report," with United Feature Syndicate, launched in February 1984. This undertaking greatly enlarged the tasks of collections staff in their efforts to provide answers to readers' questions based on the most current biomedical, social science,

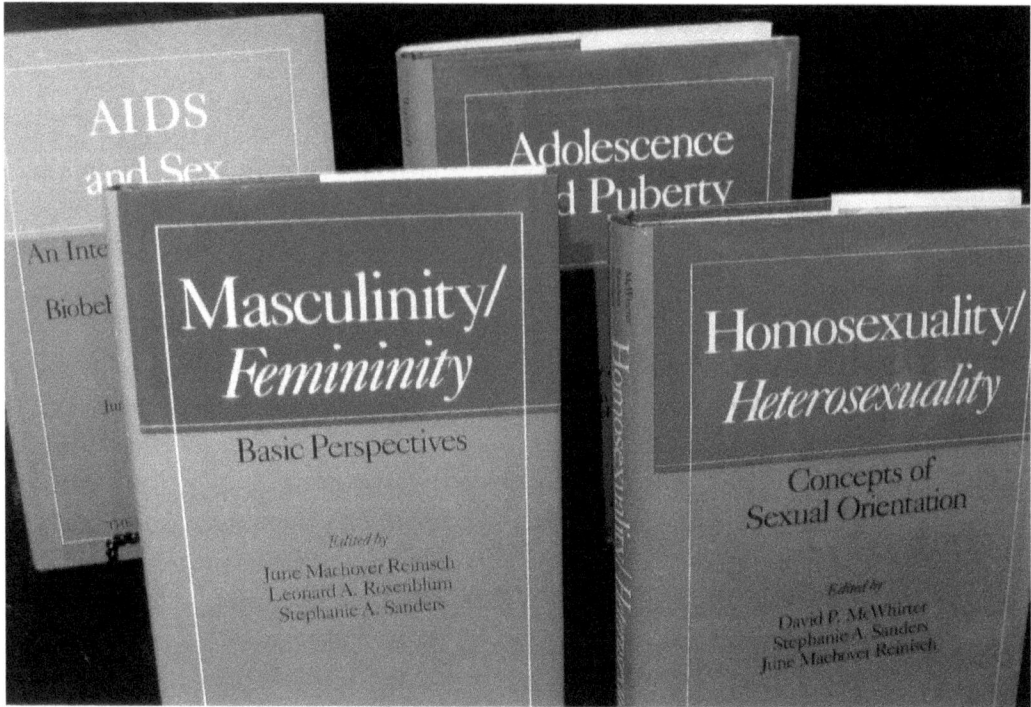

Figure 5.5. The summer symposia provided the source material for several edited collections from the Institute between 1982 and 1994. Photo courtesy of Kinsey Institute Library and Special Collections.

and scientific research available, not personal advice or opinion. The purpose was to increase the public's knowledge of sexual health and behavior, gender, and reproduction. Reinisch authored the column with writing assistance from librarian Ruth Beasley. Numerous outside experts helped assure accuracy.

Many feared that the column would enmesh the Institute in controversy. Others saw it as a welcome source of public sexual health information, with support letters received far outweighing criticism. Editors of newspapers carrying the column reported that readers overwhelmingly hoped to keep the column running in their daily press. All of these good reports on the Institute column told Reinisch and the research team, as well as sex researchers worldwide, that the public was looking for scientific and factual sexual health information. Even with the rise of the New Right and a renewed conservatism gaining in politics during the 1980s, any fears about a public backlash toward the Institute or Indiana University were allayed.[34]

This Institute outreach brought research from a wide array of scientists and scholars to a global public. "The Kinsey Report" reached thirteen million readers a week in Argentina, Australia, Canada, Chile, Colombia, India, Iran, Spain, Turkey, the United Arab Emirates, the United Kingdom, and Venezuela. In the

United States the column was syndicated in Anchorage, El Paso, Baton Rouge, New York City, San Francisco, Detroit, and, of course, Bloomington, Indiana.[35]

By 1992, the column's writers had answered more than 2,600 reader questions. Meanwhile, each year thousands of letters arrived, analysis of which revealed that most readers were seeking information about basic aspects of sexual and reproductive health and function rather than more unusual aspects of sexual behavior. Letters from readers helped influence the focus of the column. Approximately equal numbers of men and women ranging in age from eleven to one hundred wrote with their sexual health questions. "Regular analyses of the letters received reveals, not surprisingly, that female readers are most concerned about sexually transmitted disease and female genital problems," Reinisch reported, "while males most often are concerned with erection problems and the appearance and size of their penis and testicles."[36]

The newspaper column not only provided the public with scientific sexual health information but also gave researchers at the Institute a pool of letters and contacts that could serve as a source of information about the public's concerns about sexuality. Like other outreach undertaken by Reinisch and the Institute's team, the column demonstrated the public's interest in sexuality despite cultural and political opposition to public discussion of sexuality and sexual health.

That public interest was to be served further by a popular sex education book. *The Kinsey Institute New Report on Sex: What You Must Know to Be Sexually Literate*, or *KINROS*, as Institute researchers called it, was an updated version of the original Kinsey Reports. The book utilized a question-and-answer format, with over 650 questions. New advances in sexology told against simply reusing the newspaper columns. New writing and rewriting would be required to incorporate the latest research.

The book reflected early 1990s sex research transformations. It provided an increased focus on public health and an integration of sexual health with other components of health and well-being. Compared to the column, the book format afforded more space to elaborate on key topics. It included relevant illustrations from the Institute's internationally famous art collection, as well as charts and diagrams specifically created for the book.

The first chapter focused on results of the Institute / Roper Organization National Sex Knowledge Survey. The eighteen questions aimed at assessing whether questions the public sent to the Institute accurately reflected senders' knowledge about human sexuality.[37] This survey was conducted by a nationally reputable opinion research center, the Roper Organization, during face-to-face interviews with a representative sample of 1,974 Americans in the fall of 1989.

Arranged by topic and subdivided by common questions received by the Institute, *KINROS* sought to address pervasive sexual ignorance. Once Institute researchers acquired and processed the results, Reinisch and Beasley reported that

Americans had failed. Roper results indicated that American adults demonstrated ignorance about, or else erroneous understandings of, many sexual topics, including AIDS and other sexually transmitted diseases, contraception, homosexuality, erection problems, extramarital sex, and menopause. More than 55 percent were unable to answer even half of the eighteen Roper questions correctly. These results corroborated Institute researchers' impression from letters to the column that there was a lack of comprehensive or even basic sex education in the United States, whether through school sex education classes, health care providers, or the media in general. This impression underpinned the educational outreach attempted by the newspaper column and *KINROS*. The book, then, would answer some of the thousand questions the Institute received.[38]

The concerns and knowledge lacunae found in the general public had a longer genealogy. *KINROS* findings echoed ignorance and problems found in Kinsey's interviewees some forty years earlier. "Am I normal?" was by far the most common question. And like previous book-length Institute reports, *KINROS* presented sexual facts and data in neat tables. Like Kinsey's volumes, the book declined to take a political stance on sexual matters (except for nonconsensual sex), undertaking merely to present factual information.[39]

Nonetheless, differences from earlier Kinsey volumes proved telling. While many letters the Institute received during the 1980s resembled the "Dear Dr. Kinsey" letters of forty years earlier, some of the writers' concerns had changed. For example, correspondents expressed considerably more concern and asked more questions about sexually transmitted infections and diseases than those writing to Kinsey in the 1930s, 1940s, and 1950s. No doubt, this reflected the HIV/AIDS crisis and, perhaps, a popular culture more saturated in sexual imagery than sexual knowledge. Further, *KINROS*, while providing sexual facts based on Institute work and the work of other researchers, reads more like *Our Bodies, Ourselves*, the groundbreaking book published by the Boston Women's Health Book Collective in the early 1970s, with subsection titles providing quick information for the reader about sexual intimacy and sexual problems. Moving quickly from basic anatomy (of which Reinisch and Beasley note many Americans were ignorant), later chapters are titled "The Sexual Adult," "Sex with a Partner," "Unfinished Development and Sexual Mismatches," and "Sexually Transmitted Diseases."[40]

KINROS explored these topics more directly than any previous Institute volumes. Kinsey's zoological and sociological interests converged on sexual behavior rather than the study of cultural narratives, discourses, emotions, or identities surrounding sex. By 1990 the outlet as the prime measurement of the sexual event was no longer used in Institute research. Instead, readable, accessible information on a variety of topics—not just instances of orgasm—was the aim. With three successive printings and serials in magazines such as *Self, Men's Health Newsletter*,

Prevention, *New Woman*, the *National Enquirer*, *Complete Woman*, *Child Magazine*, *Woman*, *American Woman*, and *Cosmopolitan*, *KINROS* was considered by the Institute as a successful attempt at outreach.[41]

Controversy and Transition

To my knowledge, that Department [Psychology] never produced any item of significance with the exception of the over-valued and outrageous B. J. Skinner and June Reinisch. Hooray for June! Unlike helpless students, the Big Boys have shoved and she has shoved back, much to their chagrin.

George B. DeKalb, alumnus, *Indiana Daily Student*, January 30, 1989

During the later 1980s Reinisch's focus was the Institute's public profile. Hence, in addition to work on her own research projects, she attended to the public outreach portions of her strategic plan. Many found the new face of the Institute refreshing. Others, though, proved less than pleased with the Institute's new direction.

In 1987 the dean of research and graduate development, Morton Lowengrub, received six anonymous letters. Signed by "Alfred," they charged Reinisch with mismanagement and misconduct. So began a year of meetings, internal reviews, scandalized press reviews, and ultimately Reinisch coming under fire from the University. Reinisch's predecessor, Paul Gebhard, utilized correspondence and newspaper interviews to claim that she had misdirected resources for travel, media appearances, and furniture to the neglect of the collections. He approached the chancellor with his complaints, charging that Dean Lowengrub's friendship with Reinisch made Lowengrub likely to ignore Gebhard.[42] In fact, Lowengrub appointed a five-person internal review committee to investigate. Their report accused Reinisch of mismanagement of grants and insufficient research productivity. In early 1989 Indiana University asked for her resignation. However, according to the legal advice she secured, only the Institute's board of trustees could fire her, since the Institute was a separate, autonomous corporation.[43]

So Reinisch refused to resign. Many in the Indiana University community and within the Institute supported her, arguing that an orchestrated plan had sought her removal without just cause. Reviews undertaken appear not to have followed Indiana University protocol, prompting criticisms from University faculty in letters to both the dean and public newspapers.[44]

Accusations flew by letter and public media. The international reputation of the Institute, which Reinisch had spent so much energy building, provided the support network that she and the Institute needed. An international group of researchers, many of whom had served on the Scientific Advisory Board under

Reinisch, wrote Indiana University expressing their support of Reinisch and their skepticism of the review that resulted in the request for her resignation.[45]

Amidst all this contention, the collections suffered reverses. The three librarians were abruptly reassigned to other University units, effectively closing the Institute library and collections. After this happened, in 1990 the Institute hired Margaret Harter as head of information and reference services and Liana Zhou as head of technical services.[46] As the previous librarian had left in the middle of a major renovation, Harter and Zhou faced the daunting task of reestablishing a library that had been "mothballed" for nearly two years. With no staff in the library, unprocessed materials had been mixed with materials stored in boxes throughout the four floors of the Institute, and previous librarians had left no "maps" or other guides to indicate where items were located. The new librarians also worked with Indiana University Libraries to automate the Institute's library catalog and integrate it with the Indiana University system, making the resources of the Institute more accessible to scholars around the world.

All this damaged the public image of the Institute. Even as its researchers and staff sought to recover, external attacks came from the evangelical Right. Around the time of publication of *KINROS*, a new attack on Alfred Kinsey's research led to litigation. In 1981 Judith Reisman, an American conservative academic, supported in her views by the Rutherford Institute, the Heritage Foundation, the Family Research Council, and members of state and national legislatures, made allegations about Kinsey's research and ethics.[47] In 1988 conservative columnist Patrick Buchanan's syndicated newspaper column reiterated Reisman's charges. Then in 1990 she published the book *Kinsey, Sex, and Fraud*.[48] She and her co-author alleged that the content of Kinsey's 1948 male volume proved that he had abused children to collect data and that he fraudulently analyzed and presented his data on homosexuality.[49] It was a sign of the changing times that anyone would believe such charges, despite the male volume's vast sales since 1948 and thus its unprecedented scrutiny by scientists, media, and the public for more than thirty years.

The Institute and the University issued a joint press release, rejecting Reisman's allegations as unfounded. Leaders of both entities declined media invitations to appear with Reisman. Instead, the Institute and the University provided publicly available information on Reisman's credentials and background. Reisman sued for defamation of character and infringement of her First Amendment rights. Upon its adjudication, though, the case was "dismissed with prejudice." This meant, as with all cases dismissed "after adjudication on the merits," that thereafter "the plaintiff is barred from bringing an action on the same claim. Dismissal with prejudice is a final judgment and the case becomes res judicata on the claims that were or could have been brought in it."[50]

* * *

In 1993 Reinisch retired as director emerita. During her term she had implemented a new organizational direction for the Institute and sought to make the Institute *the* public resource for sexual health information. While she brought in her own funding for the Institute, her work and that of the Institute's members enhanced Institute resources and attracted more external scholars working across disciplinary lines. The revitalization of the library and archives became central to her research programs, especially during the HIV/AIDS crisis, and the Institute grew to a national prominence that had been occluded since Kinsey's directorship. Controversies at the end of her tenure, however, would slow the progress and work of the Institute. By 1993 a new director was needed to guide the Institute forward.

Stephanie A. Sanders became interim director from 1993 to 1995. She continued in-progress research projects and reopened the Institute library and archives. As well, she extended outreach in several important ways. Crucial here was teaching. Sanders began designing new courses for and contributing to the curriculum development of the College of Arts and Sciences' women's studies program. Though nationally and internationally women's studies had long aspired toward interdisciplinarity, scientific expertise proved elusive in most universities and colleges. As an accomplished biopsychologist, Sanders formed a crucial bridge between Kinsey's legacy and the Institute, on the one hand, and women's studies at the University, on the other. She did this during the years that women's studies evolved toward intellectual reconfiguration as gender studies, moving toward department status through establishing new degree programs, new faculty appointments, fund-raising, and new faculty governance. Similarly, Sanders collaborated with colleagues in other campus schools to develop and extend an interschool graduate minor in human sexuality. Here she worked closely with Professor William Yarber from the school now called the School of Public Health.

Sanders's pressing assignment was the quest for a new permanent Institute director. She worked with Indiana University, the Institute's board of trustees, and the Scientific Advisory Board to find a new director. John Bancroft, a British psychiatrist and former member of the Scientific Advisory Board, assumed Institute leadership in late 1995. Under his direction, new avenues of sex research commenced, continuing Reinisch's major emphasis on the public along with new projects on sexual practices and behaviors with potentially immediate application for the public.

6
Turning Outward
(1994–2016)

I told the [Indiana University] Trustees that, as a public university, we must protect scientific research, regardless of how controversial it may be to particular individuals, groups or segments of society. I felt this principle was inviolate since no state university can thrive if it is beholden to special interests. . . . Today, more than a half-century after that initial conversation with our Trustees, my feelings have never been stronger.

Herman B Wells to Indiana Governor Frank O'Bannon, January 27, 1998

THE NEW INSTITUTE DIRECTOR WAS A LONG-STANDING FRIEND. John Bancroft, a psychiatrist and senior researcher at the British Medical Research Council's Centre for Reproductive Health, based at the University of Edinburgh, had long served on Reinisch's Scientific Advisory Board. He agreed to become the Institute's fourth director in 1995. A difficult context greeted him. While he achieved considerable gains for the Institute, outlined below, he and the Institute staff struggled against difficulties well above and beyond their control. Looking outward, connecting with the widest combination of constituencies possible became essential for the Institute's ongoing viability.

Continued political and social pressure brought the Institute and its funding under fire. As historian Dagmar Herzog has noted, the conservatism that began in the early 1980s deepened across the 1990s.[1] The so-called culture wars pervaded American life, with a negative impact on financial support for sex research. Despite the booming Clinton-era economy, funding for sex research was scarce, deterred also by renewed attacks on the Institute from conservative self-proclaimed "culture warriors."[2] By the turn of the twenty-first century, the main funding body for sex research—the National Institute of Mental Health—would see its projects, and, by extension, the projects of the Institute, come into question.[3] Bancroft decided to retire to the English countryside in 2003.

The fifth Institute director, Dr. Julia R. Heiman, also faced a tough political climate. The challenges pressed the ever more painfully declining budgets that attended the great recession of 2007 onward. Like so many other states, Indiana slashed university funding. Research branches of the University became foremost targets for crippling base funding cuts, and these branches were thereafter expected to cover their overhead expenses with the indirect costs of external grants.[4] Heiman's efforts to negotiate better conditions and resources for the Institute while pursuing innovations and global perspectives on sex research dilemmas despite straitened resources, with an insistent focus on scholarly excellence, repay particular attention here.

As ever in its history, the Institute struggled to find a way to survive. Nevertheless, its researchers and staff for the past twenty years have turned outward, often needing to find ballast and vindication, sometimes while enduring local opposition. Repeatedly, consultants and critics have enjoined previous directors to open the doors of the Institute and raise the public profile of its work and researchers. Both Bancroft and Heiman sought to integrate an international and comparative perspective into the Institute's projects, while they and their staffs traveled widely as advocates for sex research.

Turning outward could also be a local campus endeavor. To seek full integration of Institute researchers into appropriate campus departments that match their expertise was an important development. For example, Stephanie A. Sanders designed and offered successful interdisciplinary undergraduate and graduate classes on gender, science, and sexual differences in the new Department of Gender Studies in the late 1990s. She later accepted a joint half-time appointment. In 2004–2005 she successfully won tenure, in 2007 she became a full professor, and in 2015 she was awarded both the Peg Zeglin Brand Chair of Gender Studies and a Provost's Professorship. Since then, with initiatives begun by Heiman, joint hires of Institute researchers in partnership with University departments have been undertaken with great success. Beyond shared costs, such outward-looking developments have integrated the Institute more into the life of the campus via teaching and graduate supervision, as well as brought new perspectives into the Institute's research culture.

Budgets and space constrain implementation of the best Institute aspirations. A 2004 external review of the Institute noted that many of the central components of Institute activities and instrastructure were understaffed and underfunded.[5] A core task of this chapter is to trace the Institute's efforts to maintain its mission in the face of external pressures and, predictably, falling short. Indeed, impressionistic speculations are inevitable, especially in relation to known events or apparent trends for which the evidence needed to securely document and understand their formation or circumstances is not yet archived and available to researchers. Judgments about the accomplishments and developments of the last fifteen years await fuller context, with appropriate sources of evidence to sustain reliable historical interpretations in the decades ahead.

Beginning to Pivot

The Kinsey Institute . . . has objectives, at least in part, which are wholly consistent with the aims and objectives of Indiana University—the collection of materials of interest to scholars, the provision of access to these materials, the Institute research objectives in the area of sexuality, gender, and reproduction, and the contribution to teaching of both undergraduates and graduates with the University. The specialized field of the Institute . . . requires a broad interdisciplinary approach which does not conform to conventional academic department structure, but does lend itself to special Institute structure.

John Bancroft to John Ryan, May 16, 1995

When Dr. John Bancroft arrived in 1995, the Institute was preparing to celebrate its fiftieth anniversary. Amidst the festivities, however, Bancroft had a raft of important goals to implement. First among them: renewing, negotiating, and, as far as possible, clarifying the relationship between Indiana University and the Institute. This entailed considerable effort to restructure the Institute's inner workings and budgets, its mechanisms of accountability, and the reach of its activities and proper concerns. Using his own clinical background, he created the Institute's first Sexual Health Clinic as a significant new component in the Institute's mission. He received sufficient resources to build support staff, including a full-time art curator post, and eventually further support staff. Changed objectives and technologies mandated a review of library and archives objectives. Liana Zhou and Shawn Wilson began the posts today known as director and associate director, respectively, of the Kinsey Institute Library and Special Collections. These appointments restored levels of professionalism and innovative initiatives in collection stewardship, acquisitions, and development and in donor relations. After enduring periods of mothballing and neglect, the collections were again open for business, facilitating serious multidisciplinary study of sexuality, gender, and reproduction.

Yet as Bancroft worked on these new goals amidst the celebration plans for 1997–98, the Institute found itself once again at the center of controversy. External pressures began early in Bancroft's tenure, imposing a chill over Institute research. In December 1995 a freshman Republican congressman from Texas,

Figure 6.1. Portrait of John Bancroft. Bancroft, a longtime friend of the Institute and a member of its Scientific Advisory Board, became the Institute's fourth director in 1995. Photo courtesy of Kinsey Institute Library and Special Collections.

Steve Stockman, introduced House Bill 2749 with the support of the Family Research Council. Called the Child Protection and Ethics Act, the bill called for an investigation into past Institute research. Further, the bill would terminate funding of federally funded institutions teaching sex education influenced by the original Kinsey data. Despite considerable media attention, the bill proceeded no further.[6]

That the bill was introduced at all, however, illustrates the comparatively adverse context in which the Institute and Bancroft were operating. Even during the 1980s turn to conservatism, the Institute enjoyed an autonomy and public success that few thought possible, especially considering conservative activists' attacks. The 1990s, however, unleashed new anxieties. Federal research grant allocations underwent unprecedented politicization, especially for public health projects. The religious Right appropriated many of the ideas of sex research critics, reviving a new wave of panic over crimes against children, highlighted by media attention to the 1996 murder of JonBenét Ramsey.[7] The Family Research Council, for example, attempted to discredit the Institute by reviving Judith Reisman's charges that Kinsey obtained data through child sexual abuse, postulated in its documentary production *The Children of Table 34*.[8]

In response to these controversies, Bancroft prioritized renegotiating the Institute's relationship with Indiana University. He characterized the existing relationship as "anomalous" in letters to the Institute's council and to then president John Ryan. The Institute needed new bylaws, according to Bancroft, that would establish clear procedures regarding Institute members (namely, the director, associate director, and researchers) and the provenance of the collections and archives. The recent controversies made the establishment of such protocols all the more pressing, as it was clear the Institute would continue to come under fire.[9]

Bancroft proposed splitting the Institute into two different entities that would be treated as one. First, the Kinsey Institute would retain its affiliation with Indiana University, which would supply the funding for salaries and hire staff and personnel. This portion would fall under what the University calls an "external agency agreement." This arrangement would "normalize" the Institute and put it in line with other institutes on campus, providing stability to the Institute in difficult grant years. Second, the Institute would carry on as it had for many years: it would remain a 501(c)(3) nonprofit organization that would own the collections and archives, keeping the collections, data, art, and artifacts as an independent corporation beyond state supervision. The new board of trustees would oversee the nonprofit portion of the Institute and have regular correspondence with Indiana University officials.[10]

The Institute's board of trustees and Indiana University passed the new bylaws just in time for the beginning of the fiftieth-anniversary celebration and undoubtedly brought relief to the Institute's staff and researchers. In effect, an extra layer

Figure 6.2. Institute staff, 2002. Under Bancroft, new staff roles and appointments matched changes in the organizational structure of the Institute. Photo courtesy of Kinsey Institute Library and Special Collections.

of protection for the Institute had been created, placing a barrier between the outside political climate and the collections while also protecting the Institute from financial failure, as grant funding for sex research was becoming scarcer. Further, the extra support allowed the Institute to turn outward, addressing once again the public's sexual health concerns.

First, however, local celebrations were in order. The Institute's fiftieth-anniversary celebration included an art exhibit, *The Art of Desire: Erotic Treasures*

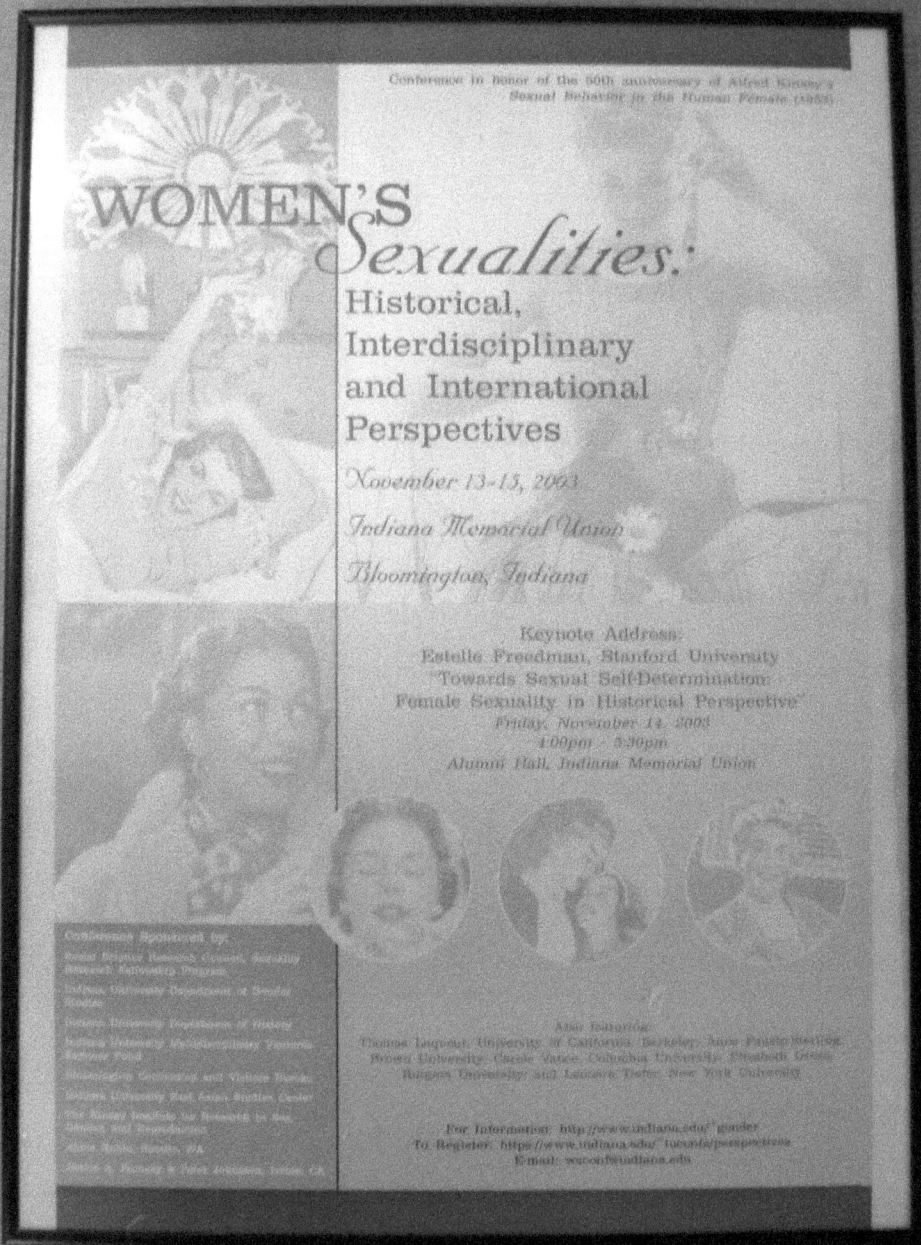

Figure 6.3. Poster from the conference "Women's Sexualities: Historical, Interdisciplinary and International Perspectives," 2003, featuring prominent lectures from interdisciplinary perspectives on women's sexuality in celebration of the fiftieth anniversary of the female volume. Photo courtesy of Kinsey Institute Library and Special Collections.

from the Kinsey Institute, and the rerelease of Kinsey's original volumes, *Sexual Behavior in the Human Male* and *Sexual Behavior in the Human Female*, both with new introductions by Bancroft. In addition, Indiana University Press republished *The Kinsey Data: Marginal Tabulations of the 1938–1963 Interviews Conducted by the Institute for Sex Research*, a volume of over five hundred tables from the original Kinsey data. During the fall of 1998, a number of events brought the celebration to a culmination, including a panel of Institute researchers discussing the changes in sex research over the last fifty years and a keynote address by researcher and activist Leonore Tiefer.[11] Five years later, a year of events celebrated the fiftieth anniversary of *Sexual Behavior in the Human Female*, including a film festival, art exhibitions, performances, lectures, and seminars and culminating in a national conference, "Women's Sexualities: Historical, Interdisciplinary and International Perspectives," November 13–15, 2003, with campus-wide sponsorship and collaborative organization.

* * *

Celebrated milestones did not deter renewed efforts against sex research by opponents in the Indiana state legislature. Republican state representative Woody Burton introduced a resolution calling for an investigation into the research of the Institute and for withdrawal of state-level funding. Simultaneously, conservative Republican state senator John Waterman introduced a bill calling for the withdrawal of appropriated state funding from the Institute. In an unusual twist of state politics, the Burton resolution was passed as a formality by the Indiana House of Representatives but buried among other inactive state bills and resolutions. In 1999 Representative Burton made a final unsuccessful attempt to reinvigorate his resolution. The Senate bill proposed by Waterman never proceeded beyond the original proposal.[12]

Such threats to Institute research funding made reaching out more important. Bancroft aimed to strengthen Institute ties to Indiana University. The Institute also needed to convince the public that sex research was, in fact, an important aspect of public health and had implications for people's everyday lives. At first, the Institute continued Reinisch's initiatives of hosting symposia and conferences and publishing the Kinsey Institute Series. In further outreach, Bancroft put his clinical training expertise to use, in 1995 developing the Kinsey Institute Sexual Health Clinic on the Bloomington campus.[13] The clinic provided individuals and couples with diagnostic assessment, counseling, and treatment. Problems addressed included sexual functioning (e.g., erectile problems in men and orgasm problems in women), sexual and gender identity development, consequences of sexual assault or abuse, and the treatment and care of transgender persons. The overarching aim of the clinic program was to approach human sexuality psychosomatically, in other words, exploring the interaction of psychological and physiological processes within individuals' sexual lives. The clinic emphasized improving the quality of an individual's sexuality and sexual life, not just resolving problems. As one of the first clinical services to serve transgender people in Bloomington during the 1990s, the clinic provided holistic counseling and transition-related care. Additionally, the clinic offered services at a reduced rate with "no intent of making a profit"; clinical fees ranged from $15 for Indiana University students to $60 for a one-hour psychotherapy session.[14]

The clinic augmented research efforts. Despite external pressures, the Institute was able to maintain and even enhance productivity. External pressures, however, did not rest for long. Renewed assaults on Institute research led to different outreach tactics, including educating the Institute's friends and colleagues, as well as the public.

Testing Outreach

We need to understand how they are thinking. . . . Then we can begin to intervene more effectively.

Dr. Erick Janssen, *New York Times*, November 9, 2004

Institute members had made good-faith efforts to connect with Indiana University staff, students, and faculty throughout the 1990s. Meanwhile, renewed agreements with Indiana University fostered increased research productivity. Indeed, Institute staff published over sixty articles, monographs, and essays between 1997 and 2003. In 1998, however, yet another legislative effort to defund the Institute's projects began. What the Institute, and Bancroft especially, realized was that looking outward—making the case for sex research—had to have national and not just local horizons. The controversy of 1998 would provide Bancroft the opportunity to do just that by responding to conservative attacks on the federal appropriations of the NIMH. Though the Institute made a convincing case, its efforts would have to continue well into the next directorship.

Research at the Institute from 1997 through 2003 focused on data collected from the Sexual Health Clinic. Projects addressed pharmaceutical treatments of sexual dysfunction such as Viagra while also responding to ongoing debates about sexual education. Bancroft and other researchers wrote articles, for example, on women's sexual health, sexual response, and treatments for menstrual pain. As one of the first clinics of its kind in Indiana, however, the group was well positioned to evaluate practical, methodological, and theoretical problems in the treatment of women's sexual health from a clinical perspective.[15]

Figure 6.4. The condom use research team. One Institute research project with major impact is still ongoing: investigation of the causes, significance, and consequences of condom use error. The condom use research team, pictured here, includes Stephanie Sanders, Cynthia Graham, and William Yarber. Photo courtesy of Kinsey Institute Library and Special Collections.

Other researchers focused on sexual health and well-being, particularly among the college-aged. Stephanie A. Sanders, for example, explored the potential high-risk behaviors of college students and the ways in which sexual partners negotiated the use of condoms. Studies on condom use made significant interventions in debates about sexual education. Despite advances in treatment, HIV/AIDS was still a significant health risk, and the Institute's researchers argued that knowing more about the negotiation of sexual behaviors and practices between partners would help public health officials to construct better sex education outreach programs. In addition, students were now being trained as research assistants at the Institute. As a result, Institute researchers published papers detailing their work in sex research education.[16]

These efforts sought also constructive intervention into late 1990s and early 2000s sex education. Condom use studies, for example, aimed to inform sexual health outreach programs targeted to specific communities. Debates about the usefulness of such research intensified. Like the McCarthyist efforts to undermine tax-exempt organizations during Kinsey's time as punishment for supporting sex research since the 1940s, opponents of sex research who challenged the federal appropriation of the National Institute of Mental Health and the projects it supported had a comparable objective.

Institute researcher Erick Janssen's project "Mechanisms Influencing Sexual Risk Taking" came under direct attack. His was among four studies singled out from hundreds of projects slated for National Institutes of Health (NIH) funding and targeted in a proposed amendment to a House appropriations bill. Republican congressman Pat Toomey from Pennsylvania called for the withdrawal of funding from projects the congressman and his committee deemed "not worthy of taxpayer funds," despite rigorous NIH scientific peer review. Rev. Peter Sprigg of the Family Research Council asked in a *New York Times* article on the debate, "Using government dollars to pay for people to watch porn? I wonder how many Americans would be comfortable with that." Janssen, however, wished to remind *New York Times* readers that his study was about more than pornography. "All of the public health messages . . . are designed on the presumption that people behave rationally," he told the *Times*, "but many of them don't." After a spirited debate, the amendment was defeated by only two votes. This close margin underscored the tension between social and political conservatism and sexual science research, even in light of the dire need for increased behavioral research regarding HIV/AIDS. Janssen argued that "in order to understand how best to design [public health] messages, we need to understand how [people] are thinking."[17]

Janssen was not alone in his desire to know more or his concerns about the political climate in which sex researchers found themselves. The same *New York Times* article interviewed other sex researchers in the United States, asking for their opinion about the relationship of sex research to the religious Right. Dr. Gilbert Herdt from San Francisco State University told the *Times*, "I have been in this field for 30 years, and the level of fear and intimidation is higher now than I can ever remember." And John H. Gagnon, former Kinsey Institute researcher and professor emeritus at the State University of New York at Stony Brook, said, "We've all learned to play the euphemism game, where we code words to disguise studies."[18]

This highly politicized and public process imposed a new challenge. Institute scientists needed to describe the significance of sexual science research to the general public, finding new ways to communicate with lay audiences whose tax dollars supported the research. Previous directors had secured positive external appraisal of Institute research, archives, and collections. Intensified electronic media since the millennium, however, made the evaluation process constant, favoring conservative opposition voices. Indeed, Janssen observed that to be effective, "we have to educate our advocates." From here the Institute would plan to make its mark not only in research but also in accessible public discourse as trusted knowledge. Bancroft underscored the duty to translate: "We have a responsibility to communicate the significance of what we're doing, in a way that makes sense to the layperson. We take this responsibility seriously. It's an important part of *our job*."[19]

Sex researchers resisted congressional efforts to curb NIH's support for sexual health and science research. In March 2004 the Coalition to Protect Research, the American Psychological Association, the American Association for the Advancement of Science, the Decade of Behavior, and more than forty other organizations convened the first ever congressional briefing, titled "Lost in Translation: Public Health Implications of Sexual Health Research—a Congressional Briefing." This was the first time sexual research scientists and politicians had gathered. As one presenter, Thomas Coates of the David Geffen School of Medicine at the University of California, Los Angeles, stated, "When scientists are silenced and they can't criticize one another, the science can't get better," referring to congressional circumnavigation of the peer-review process.[20]

Outwardly, the Institute held together. Moreover, its members looked outward to join the debate about sex research in Congress. The effort proved successful, yet the chill inflicted on the Institute and on sex researchers nationwide was palpable. The effects on sex research would last well into the next directorship as funding for sex research, even when "coded" to meet funding standards, became harder to secure. When John Bancroft retired in 2003, soon returning to Britain, a search had already secured a new director: Dr. Julia Heiman.

Sexual Health Worldwide

From the beginning, I've been interested in how sexuality changes, either on its own or with some kind of external effort. How do we come up with newer and better ways to measure aspects of sexuality? . . . I'm interested in how sex fits within other aspects of a person's life, instead of conceiving of it as separate from the other ways people function, think, or feel.

Julia R. Heiman, research statement, Kinsey Institute website

Julia R. Heiman, a clinical psychologist, became the fifth Kinsey Institute director in June 2004. A former colleague of Gagnon at the State University of New York at Stony Brook, Heiman gained praise and widespread attention early in her career with her unique approach to women's sexual health. Her work took an innovative approach to self-help in the 1976 book *Becoming Orgasmic: A Sexual Growth Program for Women* with coauthors Leslie LoPiccolo and Joseph LoPiccolo.[21]

Heiman joined the Institute at a moment of increased attention occasioned by the feature-length film *Kinsey* (2004). Heiman's initial goals for the Institute seemed eclipsed by Hollywood hoopla. An Indiana University press release in

Figure 6.5. Portrait of Julia R. Heiman. Heiman, from the University of Washington, Seattle, an authority on women's sexual health, became the Institute's fifth director in 2004. Photo courtesy of Herbert Ascherman.

Figure 6.6. Panel on the film *Kinsey* (2004). Julia R. Heiman joined the Institute just as a major feature-length film about Kinsey debuted, directed by Bill Condon. Pictured here is Heiman with Condon and producers discussing the film. Photo courtesy of the Office of the Vice President and General Counsel, Indiana University.

April 2004 announcing Heiman's appointment reported her top priority was to "maintain and grow" the Institute's research and collections and archives. Then vice president for research Michael McRobbie characterized Heiman as "a leader in the field of sexuality scholarship, and we're delighted that she is bringing her energy and talents to work at the Kinsey Institute."[22]

The goals of "maintain and grow" would prove to be lofty. Despite the increased publicity the film *Kinsey* generated, Heiman joined the Institute as the United States was still recovering from the events of 9/11. Heiman, too, noted continued adversity toward sex research, recounting that "national and local 'political' factors have gained in intensity, surfacing with any positive attention." For example, in the midst of the film's overwhelmingly positive reception, conservative voices attacked actor Liam Neeson for taking on the role of Kinsey and criticized the film more broadly.

Looking globally, Heiman knew an expanded vision would "also add new dimensions to managing the external political environment." She sought to remake the Institute through a number of strategic initiatives that would reshape it to be more in line with business models. She reunited the governance boards

Figure 6.7. Institute staff, 2008. The Institute staff was augmented in the middle 2000s. Shawn C. Wilson, associate director of the Kinsey Library and Special Collections, is pictured here, among others. Photo courtesy of Kinsey Institute Library and Special Collections.

separated by Bancroft into a single Kinsey Institute board of trustees. External reviews designed to help identify and shape these goals revealed that many of the Institute's component parts were underfunded and understaffed. Though many at the Institute remained hopeful, the great recession starting in 2007 would damage universities across the nation. The result was a cut in support from the University, support that had provided a critical lifeline for the Institute.[23]

In spite of these external pressures, the Institute embraced the mission of researching sexual health worldwide. Distinct from previous directors like Reinisch, Heiman's priority was less raising the Institute's public profile than enhancing its reputation as a worldwide leader in sexual health research and resources. She wanted the Institute to become an authoritative source for sexual health knowledge, aided by its quality research and its unique archives and collections.[24]

These stated goals required an expansion of Institute research fields. Global perspectives were critical. Heiman hired Virginia Vitzthum as a senior researcher. Vitzthum's work spanned many different countries, including Germany, Bolivia, Mongolia, Greenland, Iceland, and the United States. In addition, the Institute attempted to build on the international success of the *Kinsey* film by working directly with journalists to help convey sexual health data and education through the media. For instance, in the fall of 2006, a joint Kinsey Institute / Poynter Institute seminar with several news outlets in attendance, including *USA Today*, *WebMD*, the *Chicago Tribune*, *Glamor Magazine*, and *ABC News 20/20*, resulted in a paper, published in the *Journal of Sex Research*, detailing how sex researchers could engage with journalism to have a wider impact.[25]

Locally, the Institute partnered with a team of technology specialists with the support of Indiana University for the 10 Million Lives Project. Heiman and associate director Stephanie A. Sanders, in conjunction with Erick Janssen and the Indiana School of Informatics, worked to launch a multidimensional sexual health data collection platform through the Kinsey Reporter app. The app allows people from around the world "not only [to] report on their sexual behavior and experiences, but also to share, explore, and visualize the accumulated data." In 2012 Heiman told the *Advocate*, "People are natural observers. It's part of being social, and using mobile apps is an excellent way to involve citizen scientists."[26]

Finally, in 2014 the Institute achieved one of its goals toward incorporating a global approach to sexual health. The Institute attained the United Nations' Non-Government Organization Special Consultative Status. While there have since been shifts in institutional priorities, the Institute's NGO status represented an opportunity to work with international leaders at the intersection of sexual health and human rights. The culmination of the Institute's global perspective resulted in a proposed International Fellows Training Program.[27]

From 2004 to 2017 the Institute has faced a tumultuous cultural backdrop and operational context. Funding cuts have forced its directors and researchers to find new avenues of support. Such challenges, however, have only obliquely limited the Institute's goals as advanced by Heiman. Her research in basic human sexual health and behavior continues to be a top priority, marking a shift away from medicalized sexual health to a project more grounded in the Institute's history of exploring human sexual behavior. Projects that seek definitions of "having sex" and the Kinsey Reporter app, though controversial, highlight the continued need for basic data on behavior, emphasizing a standard knowledge base from which sexual and public health concerns, both nationally and internationally, can be better addressed.[28]

One marker of outward partnership was the 2013 joint hire of Dr. Justin Garcia as an assistant research scientist / assistant professor in the Department of Gender Studies. With his interests in evolutionary behavioral sciences, gender studies, behavioral biology, intimate relationships, sexual behavior, romantic love, social/sexual monogamy, and sexual and reproductive health, Garcia has reoriented Institute research toward Kinsey's original concern with sexual behavior in a biological and cultural context. Along with research on singles culture, "hooking up," and Internet dating, he is also leading a team of over fifty faculty members

Figure 6.8. Dr. Justin Garcia, an evolutionary biologist, joined the Institute in 2012 in a joint appointment with the Department of Gender Studies. He received tenure in 2017. Garcia investigates dating, hook-up culture, and online dating, as well as sexual violence on university and college campuses. His courses include Modern Love. He directs Institute education and outreach initiatives. Photo courtesy of IU Communications.

campus-wide in a project exploring national needs for best-practices policy on rape and sexual violence at universities and colleges nationwide.

* * *

Just as Institute research resumed a focus on human sexual behavior, the archives and collections also readopted Kinseyan priorities. As the second strand of Heiman's strategic plan, the collections served to attract external researchers while also acting as an outreach mechanism through edited publications of the Institute's holdings. Kinsey sought as many of the papers, manuscripts, and data materials of his sex research predecessors as possible; his acquisitions of rare manuscript holdings of other researchers include those of Havelock Ellis, Robert Latou Dickinson, Magnus Hirschfeld, Carney Landis, Harry Benjamin, and others. Under Zhou's initiatives, holdings have expanded to include the papers of significant pioneer postwar sex researchers from the twentieth century. These include the Albert Ellis Papers, the John Money Collection, and the William Masters and Virginia Johnson Papers, as well as the records of the Society for the Scientific Study of Sex and, more recently, the Helen Fisher Collection.

The work of Liana Zhou, library and archives director, and Shawn C. Wilson, manager of library and user services, has greatly optimized external scholars' use of the library and special collections. Despite diminished funding for sex research during the early twenty-first century, sexuality studies across the arts, humanities, and social sciences continue to enlarge and prosper. Clear within many disciplines, notably history, sociology, anthropology, fine arts, and literary and film studies, key recent scholarly works have used the collections. Still, a vast portion of the archives remains unexplored due to a lack of processing resources. Nonetheless, as more scholars begin to use the collected papers of sex researchers held at the Institute, they will have the acquisition directives of the Heiman directorship to thank for their preservation.

Several initiatives centered on the collections developed during the early 2000s just as funding for sex research was decreasing. Under the leadership of Zhou, the Institute expanded both the 20th Century Sex Researchers' Archives and the initiative for building the Women Sex Researchers' Archives.[29] The Polyamory Collection centers on sexual community formation and engagement. Through these initiatives, the collections have garnered significant support. In the process of working with donors, the Institute has created new research endowments, promoting researchers' work with the collections, the continued preservation of the photographic collections, and the expansion of the art collections with the work of contemporary artists.[30]

Through strategic and long-standing partnerships with Institute donors, scholars, publishers, and the Indiana University community, Zhou has expanded

Figure 6.9. Dr. Virginia Johnson. In 2012 the library acquired the extensive Masters and Johnson Papers. They have been added to the manuscript collections of twentieth-century sex researchers but, like so much of the extensive collections, remain to be fully processed and accessioned. Johnson is pictured here sometime in the 1960s. Photo courtesy of Kinsey Institute Library and Special Collections.

Figure 6.10. Dr. Helen Fisher, a biological anthropologist, is a senior research fellow at the Kinsey Institute; a member of the Center for Human Evolutionary Studies in the Department of Anthropology, Rutgers University; and chief scientific advisor to the Internet dating site Match.com. Her donated papers join the Institute collections of notable twentieth-century sex researchers. Photo courtesy of Adam Tinsworth / One Man & His Blog.

preservation and digitalization efforts, including establishing a new digitization lab to make the collections more accessible to scholars unable to travel to the Institute. John Money's estate provided funding to establish in 2009 the John Money Fellowship, which supports scholars' research with the collections.[31] Since 2015 Zhou has been assisted in her stewardship of the collections by the new collections advisory committee. Its expert members are drawn from the Lilly Library, the Wells Library, the Grunwald Gallery of Art, the Department of History, the Department of Gender Studies, Institute collections donors, the Media School, and Indiana University Press.

Through these efforts, the Institute has enabled increased access to the collections by streamlining student authorization, reaching out to scholars on campus and beyond, and collaborating with Indiana University departments, libraries, and the Indiana University Cinema. Endowments and planned gifts have sustainably increased, as have donations of archival materials. With the support of Shawn Wilson, the use of the Institute's library and collections has increased to between four and five hundred registered users per year.

Figure 6.11. Recent books researched in the Kinsey Institute Library and Special Collections. The addition of new collections means increased access for researchers. Photo courtesy of Kinsey Institute Library and Special Collections.

The Institute has also sought expanded access to the Institute's art holdings and growing art collection. In 2006 the Institute held its first-ever Juried Erotic Art Show. Art curator Catherine Johnson-Roehr received 195 submissions from around the globe, of which thirty-eight were selected by Betsy Stirratt, director of the Grunwald Gallery of Art at Indiana University, for the nearly three-month show, which drew more than eight hundred gallery visitors.[32] The Juried Erotic Art Show became an annual event at the Grunwald starting in 2007.[33] By 2013 the exhibition featured ninety-four pieces selected from 923 submissions.[34] The final show, for which over 700 pieces were submitted, was held in 2014. One consistent benefit derived from the juried art shows was that many of the contributing artists donated their art pieces in order to expand the contemporary holdings of the Institute's collections. These new holdings in turn resulted in more exhibitions, increasing from three to six per year.[35]

To match the "global" initiatives of the Institute, library staff responded to international requests for items from the Institute's holdings. Requests included five George Platt Lynes photographs loaned to the Musée d'Orsay in Paris as part of an exhibition entitled *Masculine/Masculine: The Nude Man in Art from 1800 to the Present Day*, which was then presented at the National Museum of Art in Mexico City. Additionally, the Institute loaned items such as a letter written by Freud regarding homosexuality to the Wellcome Trust in London as part of its exhibition *The Institute of Sexology*, the first United Kingdom exhibition dedicated to pioneers in the study of sex.[36] The array of projects the collections staff undertook, locally and internationally, did not go unnoticed. The juried art shows were a success, and collaboration with other institutions was arguably at its highest point in the Institute's history.

* * *

Heiman achieved several new initiatives for the Institute. These included organizational growth and development, global expansion with the Non-Government Organization Special Consultative Status, acquisition of art and archival collections, and considerable research and donor funding. Her tenure as director ended in the late fall of 2013. She remained as faculty in the Department of Psychological and Brain Sciences. Associate Director Stephanie A. Sanders again became interim director while Indiana University and the Institute board of trustees conducted a search for a new Institute director.[37]

The search committee appointed biologist Sue Porges Carter as the sixth Institute director and Rudy Professor of Biology. Carter is a renowned expert in behavioral neuroendocrinology, and her research background and expertise in the physiological mechanism of social bonding mark yet another notable shift from the Institute's previous research agenda. In particular, her interests in love, bonding, and monogamy offer a new node of concentration. In her first year as director, Carter recrafted and expanded the Kinsey Institute's mission, "exploring love, sexuality, and well-being," redirecting the emphasis from global sexual health. Instead, her focus is on biological factors associated with love, nurture, and well-being across the lifespan. Carter's appointment also introduced an active animal behavior laboratory, including animal models, specifically using prairie voles to examine social monogamy. As the Institute celebrates its seventieth year on the Indiana University campus and as Carter commences her third year as director, she has commissioned several initiatives to mark the occasion.

* * *

Contrary propositions seem clear even from this nearsighted vantage point of writing a history down to the present. Even as the Institute since 1994 has looked outside its walls and neighborhood, local challenges have persisted. In part, the roots of these challenges lie in the ongoing contentiousness of the subject matter

Figure 6.12. Sue Carter, ca. 2015. In 2014 Carter, a distinguished biologist who is famous for her work on oxytocin, love, and bonding, became the sixth Institute director. Her focus is on relationships and attachment in a wide variety of biological and social contexts. She has initiated several key initiatives in honor of the Institute's seventieth anniversary. Photo courtesy of Herbert Ascherman.

of sex research. Opponents want to censor sex research or refuse to provide a place for it at all, and certainly not in the setting of a Research I state university. President Herman B Wells's entreaties for academic freedom to pursue knowledge, wherever it may lead, leave those opposed to sex research unmoved. That implacably opposed constituency emerged with the publication of the Kinsey Reports as a classic reaction formation.[38] It has regularly reconstituted itself, issue by issue, as sexual politics contention points shift.

One element of the opposition would pit religion, sometimes used synonymously with morality, against science, and in various ways. Scores of pious citizens wrote to Kinsey, threatening him with hellfire for corrupting the young with salacious publications and proving thereby that he must be a Communist! A Catholic archbishop in Indianapolis urged President Wells to dismiss Kinsey for propounding findings likely to undermine accepted moral codes.[39] Contrary to those expecting some religions to be more "erotophobic" than others, Kinsey found that the specifics of the faith mattered less for sexual outlets and behavior than the degree of piety or extent of religious observance. The more pious, the less extensive and less diverse the sexual outlets reported, and vice versa.[40]

The opposition of certain religious movements and trends has proved consistent throughout the Institute's existence. The most vocal form of that opposition emerged in the early 1950s in the wake of the female volume and the Cold War, but Gebhard experienced another intense spike during his directorship in the mid-1970s. The so-called religious Right in cultural politics, embodied in figures like Anita Bryant, took aim at sex research, including the Institute, claiming such cultural forces unleashed the sexual revolution, women's liberation, *Roe v. Wade*, and the "gay lifestyle."[41] The Institute was a ready scapegoat for those discontented with changes in later postwar sexual patterns and erotic lives. Gebhard held that these trends greatly intensified during the Reagan years, with the 1980s HIV/AIDS pandemic strengthening anti–sex research constituencies.[42] Reinisch found that the array of targets reconfigured themselves, changing to pornography, especially child pornography and pedophilia. The Reisman books, among other critics, accused Kinsey of criminal experiments on children, unleashing media storms and bitter disputes that carried over into Bancroft's 1990s and even Heiman's 2000s at the Institute. Once again, a puritanical and erotophobic effort to suppress knowledge has been on full display in recent congressional interference in the scientific peer-review process.

If sex research and piety have been counterposed to each other, another consistent theme in the Institute's history has been collisions with representatives of professional or cognate fields. In these contests, clinicians of various specialties have figured prominently. Kinsey's first encounter began in 1938 with Thurman Rice from the University Medical School. Rice insisted that only medical men had the qualifications necessary to teach or research sexual matters with appropriate authority and decorum. Psychoanalysts also objected to the entire tenor of Kinsey's research, claiming it was simply unsound because it was insufficiently attentive to the determining role of the unconscious. Other professionals discomfited by Kinsey's emphasis on a wide diversity of sexual behavior asked, "What about love?" Love, Kinsey replied, was the concern of poets and philosophers. Not that it was unimportant, just that it was not amenable to scientific investigation.[43] This pattern of displacement or diversion away from the erotic, the sexual, continued during Gebhard's directorship, when government funding bodies attempted to overturn Kinsey's approach to sexual behavior in favor of a psychological and clinical study of "deviance," their officers urging a decentering of physical sexual behavior itself. Gebhard himself considered abandoning a focus on sexuality in order to secure funding from increasingly censorship-inflected funding bodies. Preeminently, though, these battles amounted to turf wars over authority in the context of a decisive medicalization of sexuality across the postwar to early twenty-first-century period: surgery, drugs, therapies, counseling; sexuality as a health entity that should be sanitized, regulated, normalized, contained. The battle lines remain drawn.

* * *

The Institute has weathered recent challenges. Even with the raft of unresolved problems outlined above, it once again seeks to open its doors to a global community of scholars, public health professionals, and anyone else seeking answers about sex and sexuality. Throughout bouts of social and political scrutiny throughout the mid-1990s to 2016, Institute directors, researchers, and staff have continued to claim new ground and navigate troubled waters filled with social and political opposition. The Institute's long-standing impact on and continued significance to both public and cultural discourses are evident in the immense public support it has received over the past seven decades. The research and collections underscore the notion that conducting, recording, and preserving evidence on the human condition is essential, no matter how controversial. Academic freedom continues to be the cornerstone of Indiana University values and is critical to rigorous scientific inquiry. The Kinsey Institute continues to be an internationally recognized authority for sex and sexuality research, as well as one of the most extensive collections of cultural and historical artifacts, depicting and describing human sexual behaviors, desires, fantasies, and identities.

Conclusion: Looking Forward

I want to reassure all members of the Kinsey community that the Kinsey Institute is a highly valued part of Indiana University's academic mission. Both historically and currently, the importance of the research conducted at the Kinsey Institute is valued and appreciated. . . . As demonstrated by the commitment of senior level expertise to the Kinsey Board, I have been and continue to be committed to the success of the Kinsey Institute.

Michael McRobbie, President, Indiana University, to Professor Amy Applegate, Chair, Kinsey Institute Board of Trustees, July 25, 2016

Six institute directors—three men and three women—have faced similar challenges in the first seventy years of the Institute's existence and work. They found themselves charged with creating, pioneering, and stewarding, in their different ways and in different ratios, a fledgling interdisciplinary field while defending the very existence of an Institute that has faced denial and repudiation. Other fields of science and humanities enquiry encounter nothing like the ferocity of interests arrayed against the study of sexuality. On the contrary, cancer research, for instance, garners not only financial support but also a collective sense of hope that a dreaded disease will be cured. Criminology, pediatrics, gerontology, all peopled by natural and social scientists, address widespread and everyday problems. By default, their institutional and professional value is self-evident. As a rule, their practitioners and exponents need to neither explain nor justify their research undertakings and endeavors.

Sex researchers, from Krafft-Ebing to the present, have also addressed widespread and everyday problems of vital importance. Yet they have enjoyed little to no default legitimacy, no matter how stellar their scientific, humanistic, scholarly, or clinical record. Sex research has always proved controversial. As attorneys say, we can take this as stipulated. The field's late nineteenth-century European founders faced religious and moral objections. Their anecdotal work featured case studies centered on sexual deviance. World War I improved the field's fortunes. Maimed and shell-shocked veterans, many with venereal diseases, found it difficult to resume their former lives with their families and to establish new relationships. Eugenicists sounded the alarm about birth defects and genetic erosion. Sex researchers worked in the Netherlands, France, Britain, the Soviet Union, and Japan, but Germans led in research initiatives, seeking positive outcomes in treatments, counseling, law reform, and policy changes.

Shock and astonishment then greeted news from Berlin in May 1933. Famous sex researcher Dr. Magnus Hirschfeld, director of Berlin's Sex Research Institute, was targeted by Hitler's SS and assaulted, kicked, beaten, and left for dead in the street. He never fully recovered before his death in 1935. Raids on his premises removed patient records, data files, photographs, books, offprints, and other materials. Researchers and clinicians all over the world expressed indignation. In the United States, Dr. Robert Latou Dickinson, founder of the American Gynecological Association, deplored the intellectual losses and the ability of totalitarian regimes to halt further European advances. Philanthropist John D. Rockefeller, long concerned about prostitution, venereal diseases, birth defects, and sex education, financially underwrote much of the initial shift of sex research leadership from Europe to the United States in response to the call of prominent researchers like Dickinson, George W. Corner, Robert Yerkes, and Alan Gregg. All these research pioneers mentored and sponsored Alfred C. Kinsey's sex research. Through the Committee for Research in Problems of Sex and the National Committee on Maternal Health, interwar sex research concentrated on problems in marriage and on the sexual and reproductive behavior of primates and other mammals.

Kinsey, an Indiana University zoology professor, began reading all the sex research publications he could find. President Herman B Wells had agreed that Indiana University would offer, like other colleges, a course on marriage for engaged undergraduates. As a taxonomist and world expert on the diversity of the gall wasp of North America based on his collection of millions of samples, Kinsey rebuked the small size and unrepresentativeness of samples cited in sweeping generalizations about human erotic norms. Born in 1894, Harvard-educated Kinsey sought to research sexual behavior not as selected from married couples or unhappy wives darkening clinicians' doors but at large, across diverse habitats and cultural contexts.

And so in 1938 Kinsey began his sex research project. He sought to map the full spectrum of human sexual behavior, much of which faced criminal sanctions, social stigma, or personal shame. The quest for large samples that would

Figure 7.1. Clara McMillen Kinsey gardening, ca. 1950. Photo courtesy of Kinsey Institute Library and Special Collections.

be unbiased by diagnosis, condemnation, or pathology led to new methods. He adopted the initially ingenious *quantitative* measure of the "sexual outlet." An individual's total sexual outlet was the sum of his or her erotic contacts, actions, or fantasies resulting in orgasm. This simple method counted all sources of outlet disclosed through sex histories, and it deprivileged marital coitus as normative.

Kinsey used diverse variables to interrogate his findings from the eighteen thousand sex histories completed between 1938 and 1956. These variables included class, social status, education level, age, sex, race, religion, marital status, and region as advanced by 1930s and 1940s sociologists. He found massive behavioral and experiential variations, rendering subcultural erotic behavior, expression, and representation critically important. Interviews alone could not explain sexual behavior. Kinsey collected multidisciplinary holdings, seeking items from book agents, peer researchers, and veterans serving overseas. Moreover, he wished to acquire works dispersed by fascist regimes, thereby building a safe, scholarly repository for sex researchers. In short, he sought to honor the founders of the field of sex research in the aspiration to reassemble earlier collections and data sets.

Impressed by the innovativeness of Kinsey's new methods, the Rockefeller-funded Committee for Research in Problems of Sex began to award him grants. From an initial 1941 equivalent of about $80,000 today, grants from 1947 to 1954 equaled nearly $500,000 a year in today's values. Further, by 1946 Kinsey had spent, in current values, $150,000 for what Rockefeller officials called his "sex library" (the foundation reimbursed him in 1947). He was finalizing *Sexual Behavior in the Human Male* (1948) and was concerned about preserving the confidentiality of his sex histories and the safety of his collections from the "book burners," whether in the legislature, the churches, or the local community. Understanding these real concerns, the chair of the Rockefeller-funded committee after the retirement of Robert Yerkes, George W. Corner, urged a solution: create a separate entity that could be firewalled from local, political, and institutional mandates and that would protect the interests and confidentiality of informants, data, and other erotic materials acquired. Primatologist Robert L. Yerkes coined the name Institute for Sex Research, the name used until 1980. Dickinson designed the bookplate, and President Wells was pleased with the Institute's formal legal independence, as was the University board of trustees, which voted its approval in the spring of 1947.

The Kinsey Institute's founding raison d'être, then, was the welfare and confidentiality of its collections and data. Put differently, the importance of the collections and data brought the Institute into existence. The human sex behavior project alone made no such requirement, with no such proposal. The Institute's holdings, which are concerned with sexual behavior and its cultural representations, include a vast rare books section, journal offprints, newspapers and news cuttings, magazines and periodicals, diverse ephemera, institutional archives, data and manuscripts from sex research and clinical pioneers, and extensive photographs. They currently measure 9,523.72 linear feet, while films, visual art, and material objects run at 1,821.09 linear feet. Library collections account for 80 percent of annual user demands, while art and artifact users form about 5 percent of collections patrons. Yet the tiny collections staff of the Institute were "hard-pressed," as a 2008 external review put it, to manage the outreach projects, collaborations, and local demands of students and researchers. The external review committee wrote, "Regarding the staffing need for the Kinsey collections . . . it was noted that the current staff are barely able to manage the everyday needs of the collections, with little or no time for preservation and planning for the collections."[1] The numbers in the report easily demonstrate the demands on the collections staff. In 2007 alone there were 170 in-person research visits, more than 600 visits and requests from Indiana University undergraduates, and over 1,500 inquiries via telephone. The report noted that visitors came from a "wide range of disciplines," from "art and art history to history, sociology, biology, [and] psychology," among others. In emphasizing the importance of the Institute's collections, the external reviewers observed that the collections are "the ultimate interdisciplinary unit on campus."[2]

Though staffing has waxed and waned, the Institute collections still function with only one full-time librarian, one administrator, one curator, a handful of hourly staff, and volunteers and students. Yet annual visits to the collections expand each year, and the staff continue to serve researchers from a broad range of disciplines for whom Institute collections are essential to their work. Digitization projects are ongoing, as are special collections processing, rearrangement, and cataloging. As discussed in chapter 1, the Rockefeller Foundation was the chief funder of Kinsey's sex research. Apart from the salary paid to the head librarian, a position created by the University in 1967–68 after negotiations with Gebhard twenty years after the Institute's founding in 1947, collections functions and costs have always had to be met by privately raised resources. This means that acquisition, stewardship, conservation, production, and supervised use of special collections have, for the most part, depended on donations and subsidies from researchers' hard-won grant monies. All these tasks are executed by a largely impermanent casual labor force that has been trained in-house. Lack of assured budget line items of any collections functions has bedeviled proper professional planning and development.

In an interview in 1968, President Wells recalled that the Institute's independent legal status was unusual at the time. The University normally acted as the single point of contact and disbursement for externally funded research projects. Yet Wells reiterated the wisdom of the arrangement when pressure groups and the general vicissitudes of politics threatened independent research generally and the right to study sex in particular.[3] One such moment came in the early 1950s, and it was left unresolved until 1957. The US Customs Service confiscated, "libeled" as obscene, and scheduled for destruction a collections shipment: thirty-one Japanese nude photographs, some eighteenth-century French erotic novels, some erotic story scrolls, and a small Japanese phallus sculpture. Though the case's litigant was the Institute for Sex Research, President Wells and the board of trustees insisted on participating. Not only did First Amendment attorney Harriet Pilpel challenge the Customs Service, but also the board of trustees' Indianapolis firm, Barnes, Hickam, Pantzer and Associates, submitted a powerful twenty-five-page amicus brief. Wells later recalled that the board never wavered, despite its challenging course, holding that "on this issue would be determined whether or not we would be a University of the first rank or simply another teacher's college. . . . They never moved," he reported, from their firm defense of academic freedom, even when faced with intensive "bigotry and whatnot." Everyone remembered the Nazi books and photos burning.[4]

Nonetheless, the consistent pattern of "moral" objection to sex research has greatly influenced and obstructed its funding and, thus, its intellectual advancement. In lean times, with waning external support, no one can be surprised that individual directors initiated reopening the question of the Institute's relationship with the University. Kinsey did so, as discussed in chapter 2, when the Rockefeller Foundation funding ceased in 1954 under political pressure. With three research associates and several support staff thereby in danger of losing their jobs, Kinsey clearly hoped that the University would be unwilling to see this outcome and step in.

Kinsey's successor as director, Paul Gebhard, grappled with the same problem. After the 1962 NIMH site visit, he contemplated changing the Institute's name in order to obscure the nature of the research undertaken and mislead the pious and the moralistic, the would-be censors and suppressors of sexual information and education, with a view to securing research grants and private donors. With the 1965 publication of *Sex Offenders* and the 1966–68 securing of large grants and new researchers, the question of the Institute's relationship to Indiana University was reopened. President Elvis J. Stahr favored a merger. This would mean that the University would fund Institute researchers and collections professionals as department faculty members in their areas of expertise. To this end, he required a faculty advisory board and underwrote departmental funding of the Institute researchers. Advice to his successor, President Joseph Sutton, from the University counsel, however, favored retaining "the status quo," presumably a wish to keep the collections at arm's length and protect the University from embarrassment. This advice may also have registered the force of local or state pressure group politics.

That same status quo permitted June Reinisch to refuse to resign as director in 1989. Yet it also diminished the Institute when, amidst the crises that dogged the end of her term as director, the University removed and relocated Institute library staff, effectively halting scholarly use of the collections and the public information services she had prioritized. Though Director John Bancroft found the relationship between the Institute and the University dysfunctional and initially sought repair and greater closeness, the political storms of the 1990s and early 2000s and the need to defend and protect the Institute effectively forced him in the opposite direction. His efforts moved toward strengthening the insulation of the independent corporation from emboldened anti–sex research activists. Though Liana Zhou as Director of Library and Special Collections succeeded in securing some sources of private support for collections throughout the 2000s, Director Julia Heiman remained disappointed and frustrated by the leanness of available resources as she confronted serious base budget cuts and insufficient funds to support both research staff and proper stewardship of the collections. By the time Sue Porges Carter became the sixth director in 2015, the Institute was in striking range of its seventieth anniversary. The enfranchised board of trustees was a changed entity. It had altered in this way: from predecessor boards entirely comprised of Institute researchers in 1947, to twelve University faculty interested in the Institute's work by 1967, to a board without any enfranchised Institute researchers as full members at all and instead almost entirely peopled by University administrators and officials by 2016. This was quite the transformation, the kind President Sutton had envisaged in 1967–69 in exchange for economic security and stabilization.

* * *

Indiana University gave the Institute a dramatic anniversary present. On November 30, 2016, the Institute board of trustees voted to merge with Indiana University, abolishing the 1947 independent incorporation absolutely and completely. Henceforth, as with other research institutes, the University has full control over governance, hiring, firing, funding, evaluation, infrastructure, services, and, above all, the ownership and stewardship of the collections.

As noted above, we are in the midst of these changes. The necessary range of evidence is not yet available to offer a feasible interpretation of the reasons for this merger being effected at the end of 2016 rather than, say, in 1993, when Reinisch departed, or at some other moment. Given the political volatility of recent decades, already outlined, what does such a merger now portend? Is the same spirited defense of academic freedom, the one that informed Herman B Wells's intervention in the 1950s Customs case, motivating this merger? Will the University be willing and able to protect the research and the collections both in the current moment and

It's almost official: Kinsey Institute to merge with IU

By Michael Reschke
812-331-4370 | mreschke@heraldt.com

It looks like the Kinsey Institute for Research in Sex, Gender and Reproduction finally will be part of Indiana University.

The IU board of trustees unanimously approved merging the institute with the university during an academic affairs and university policy committee meeting Wednesday afternoon in the Indiana Memorial Union's Alumni Hall. The action item must be approved at the board's business meeting today, but with all board members serving on all committees, it's likely to pass.

Jackie Simmons, IU's vice president and general counsel, acknowledged most people probably thought the institute, which is located on the Bloomington campus, was already part of the university, but she said it has been a legally separate entity since it was created in 1947.

Founder Alfred Kinsey wanted to keep the institute separate because he was worried his research notes might become public, Simmons said. Specifically, he worried his notes could be used to out people who were gay. Now, Indiana's public records law includes an exemption for research materials, Simmons said.

Despite the separation, the Kinsey Institute is housed in Morrison Hall, and IU pays the salaries for all of its employees. Simmons said IU can make contributions to other educational entities and nonprofits, which is what it was doing with the Kinsey Institute. However, because they were legally separate, the two entities had to enter into contracts for things such as information technology support. Merging the two will eliminate needless impediments, she said.

Follow @MichaelReschke on Twitter today for meeting updates.

Figure 7.2. "It's Almost Official: Kinsey Institute to Merge with IU." Just as 2016 was coming to a close, the Institute and Indiana University Foundation announced that the final steps of a merger were under way. For the first time since its creation seventy years ago, the Institute will no longer have a completely independent status. Pictured here is a headline from the Bloomington-based *Herald Times* from December 1, 2016. Photo courtesy of Robert Zaltsberg / *Herald Times*.

in the Institute's next seventy years? Is this a bright new moment, when the collections, often called one of the University's crown jewels, at last have the chance to secure proper support in a stable, secure, and appropriate physical setting and with fully professional conditions of administration, scholarly use, and access?

Historians study transformation over time in specific contexts, analyzing influences, factors, and forces in play. Alternatively, historians rarely are good predictors of the future. Few ever would have predicted some developments presently under way, for instance, in state politics around sexuality and birth control. Historically, though, Indiana University has led the fight to protect sex histories and "the sex library" and to establish the right to study sex. Like most rights, this one needs maintenance and reinforcement, especially when state and local political developments are inauspicious. The history of sex research generally and that of the Institute in particular do show that there are foreseeable reasons to expect this field of research to remain controversial compared to, let us say, particle physics. The resurgence of external political opposition to sex research projects during the directorships of Reinisch in the 1980s and early 1990s and Bancroft in the late 1990s and early 2000s provided forceful reminders of cultural forces standing to be arrayed against research and education related to sexuality.

Such contention has kept the field relatively poor. Just as in the past, the collections of historical and multidisciplinary sources that ground sex research, its study and genealogy as a field, require serious investment. Such collections rarely can pay for themselves. This is especially true for precious sex research collections held in the archives of the Institute itself, including the papers of field pioneers Havelock Ellis, Robert Latou Dickinson, and the Masters and Johnson Collection, which either their St. Louis institutions, the Arthur and Elizabeth Schlesinger Library on the History of Women in America, or the Francis A. Countway Library of

Medicine of Harvard University might have expected to acquire. That the Institute secured them is a tribute to collections staff and the deep operational grasp of field developments, as well as the building of relationships of trust over the long term. It is our sincere hope that moving forward for the Institute's next seventy years will entail the full realization of the collections' momentous significance and their resourcing and management.

Even with uncertainties and unsolved problems, the seventieth anniversary of the Institute is an occasion for joy. Kinsey himself may never have imagined it would still be in operation sixty years after his death. He also may never have dared hope that its trustees would have reason to be confident that the independent incorporation that began our short history might no longer be needed by 2017. Future historians will have to chart the sequel to this merger—its genealogy, meaning, and consequences.

Introduction

1. Alfred C. Kinsey, "A Scientist's Responsibility in Sex Instruction," 1, National Association of Biology Teachers, Philadelphia, December 1940, Alfred Charles Kinsey Directorship, 1947–56 (ACKD), V: Speeches and Lectures, Kinsey Institute Library and Special Collections (KILSC).

2. WHM to Alfred Charles Kinsey (ACK), September 13, 1945, ACKD, I: Correspondence, KILSC. (Initials are used throughout this book to maintain the confidentiality of people who wrote personal letters to Kinsey.)

3. ACK to WHM, September 21, 1945, ACKD, I: Correspondence, KILSC.

4. RA to ACK, December 14, 1948, ACKD, I: Correspondence, KILSC.

5. DCB to ACK, November 25, 1953, ACKD, I: Correspondence, KILSC.

6. See Jonathan R. Cole, *The Great American University* (New York: Public Affairs, 2009). For an update on longer outcomes, see David Ekbladh, *The Great American Mission: Modernization and the Construction of an American World Order* (Princeton, NJ: Princeton University Press, 2010).

7. Thomas D. Clark, typescript of interview with Herman B Wells (HBW), "Kinsey and the Kinsey Institute," Bloomington, January 1968, 6, Kinsey Institute for Sex Research, Indiana University Archives (IUA).

8. See Erwin J. Haeberle, ed., *The Birth of Sexology: A Brief History in Documents* (New York: United States Consortium for Sexology, 1983); and Vern Bullough, *Science in the Bedroom: A History of Sexology* (New York: Basic Books, 1994).

9. See, for instance, Heike Bauer, *English Literary Sexology: Translations of Inversion, 1860–1930* (New York: Palgrave, 2009), 128, 148.

10. See, for instance, F. S. Chapin, *The Measurement of Social Status by the Use of the Social Status Scale* (Minneapolis: University of Minnesota Press, 1933); A. B. Hollingshead, "Human Ecology and the Social Sciences," in *An Outline of the Principles of Sociology*, ed. Robert E. Park et al. (New York: Barnes & Noble, 1939), 65–168; W. L. Warner and P. S. Lunt, *The Social Life of a Modern Community* (New Haven, CT: Yale University Press, 1942); and W. L. Warner and L. Srole, *The Social Systems of American Ethnic Groups* (New Haven, CT: Yale University Press, 1945).

11. See Elizabeth Evanston, "Social and Economic Change since the Great Depression: Studies of Census Data, 1940–1980," *Focus* 11 (Fall 1988): 1–11.

12. Greenbaum, Wolfe and Ernst, "*AD. 189–50: United States District Court of Southern New York, v. 31 Photographs, 4–3/4 Inches in Size and Various Pictures, Books and Other Articles. Institute for Sex Research, Inc. at Indiana University,*" 320–45, series B: 1957–81, Paul Henry Gebhard Directorship, 1957–81 (PHGD), VII: Operations Records, a. Legal, KILSC.

13. Clark, interview with HBW, 21.

14. James H. Jones, *Alfred Kinsey: A Public/Private Life* (New York: W. W. Norton, 1997), 79, 170, 270, 272, 307, 380–83, 387, 425, 790n61.

15. See Jonathan Gathorne-Hardy, *Sex the Measure of All Things: A Life of Alfred C. Kinsey*, American ed. (Bloomington: Indiana University Press, 2000), viii. See also Jones, "The Origins of the Institute for Sex Research: A History" (PhD diss., Indiana University, Bloomington, 1972); Jones, *Alfred Kinsey*, xii, 4, 58, 72, 75, 379.

16. Gathorne-Hardy, *Sex the Measure of All Things*, 83.

17. Ibid., vii.

18. See Donna J. Drucker, *The Machines of Sex Research: Technology and the Politics of Identity, 1945–1985* (New York: Springer, 2013); and Drucker, *The Classification of Sex: Alfred Kinsey and the Organization of Knowledge* (Pittsburgh, PA: University of Pittsburgh Press), 20

1. Overlapping Foundations (1916–1946)

1. See Louise Rosenberg and Saul Rosenberg, "Notes on Alfred C. Kinsey's Pre-sexual Scientific Work and the Transition," *Journal of the History of Behavioural Sciences* 5, no. 2 (April 1969): 173–81; Theodore M. Brown and Elizabeth Fee, "Alfred C. Kinsey, Pioneer of Sex Research," *American Journal of Public Health* 93 (June 2003): 896–87; and Donna J. Drucker, *The Classification of Sex: Alfred Kinsey and the Organization of Knowledge* (Pittsburgh, PA: University of Pittsburgh Press, 2014), 13–31.

2. Examples of publications from these projects include T. L. Chamberlin, W. U. Gardner, and Edgar Allen, "Local Responses of 'Sexual Skin' and Mammary Glands of Monkeys to Cutaneous Applications of Estrogen," *Endocrinology* 28, no. 5 (May 1941): 753–57; P. A. Duncan, Edgar Allen, and J. B. Hamilton, "The Action of Testosterone Propionate on Experimental Menstruation in the Monkey," *Endocrinology* 28, no. 1 (January 1941): 107–11; Frank R. Lillie, "Bilateral Gynandromorphism and Lateral Hemihypertrophy in Birds," *Science* 74, no. 1,920 (1931): 387–90; W. L. Williams, K. F. Stein, and Edgar Allen, "Reaction of Genital Tissues of the Female Mouse to the Local Application of Colchicine," *Yale Journal of Biology and Medicine* 13, no. 6 (July 1941): 841–46. See also Robert M. Yerkes, "Social Behavior of Chimpanzees: Dominance between Mates, in Relation to Sexual Status," *Journal of Comparative Psychology* 30, no. 1 (August 1940): 147–86; Yerkes, "Conjugal Contrasts among Chimpanzees," *Journal of Abnormal and Social Psychology* 36, no. 2 (April 1941): 175–99; and Yerkes's magisterial *Chimpanzees: A Laboratory Colony* (New Haven, CT: Yale University Press, 1945). See also Edgar Allen, ed., *Sex and Internal Secretions: A Survey of Recent Research* (Baltimore, MD: Williams & Wilkins Company, 1932).

3. See Robert M. Yerkes (RMY) to Alfred Charles Kinsey (ACK), June 15, 1946, Alfred Charles Kinsey Directorship, 1947–56 (ACKD), I: Correspondence, Kinsey Institute Library and Special Collections (KILSC).

4. See Drucker, *The Classification of Sex*, 4–5.

5. See Paul A. Robinson, *The Modernization of Sex: Havelock Ellis, Alfred Kinsey, William Masters and Virginia Johnson* (Ithaca, NY: Cornell University Press, 1989),

42–49; and Stephen Garton, *Histories of Sexuality: Antiquity to Sexual Revolution*, 1st ed. (New York: Routledge, 2004), 203–6.

6. See Janice M. Irvine, *Sex and Gender in Modern American Sexology* (Philadelphia: Temple University Press, 1990), 21–32.

7. See Alfred C. Kinsey, Wardell B. Pomeroy, and Clyde E. Martin, *Sexual Behavior in the Human Male (SBHM)* (Philadelphia: W. B. Saunders, 1948), 30–31, 197, 222, 263, 323.

8. See Alfred C. Kinsey, Wardell B. Pomeroy, Clyde E. Martin, and Paul H. Gebhard, *Sexual Behavior in the Human Female (SBHF)* (Philadelphia: W. B. Saunders, 1953), 39.

9. Richard von Krafft-Ebing, *Psychopathia Sexualis: Eine medicinisch-psychologische Studie*, 2nd ed. (Stuttgart: Ferdinand Enke, 1891); Havelock Ellis and J. A. Symonds, *Das konträre Geschlechtsgefühl*, trans. Hans Kurella, 1st ed., Bibliothek für Socialwissenschaft (Leipzig: Georg H. Wigand's Verlag, 1896); Ellis, *Sexual Inversion: A Critical Edition*, ed. Ivan Crozier (New York: Palgrave Macmillan, 2008); Sigmund Freud, *Drei Abhandlungen zur Sexualtheorie*, 2nd ed. (Leipzig: Franz Deuticke, 1910).

10. See Max Joseph Exner, *Problems and Principles of Sex Education: A Study of 948 College Men* (New York: Association Press, 1915); and Exner, *The Rational Sex Life for Men* (New York: Association Press, 1917). See also Paul Stronge Achilles, *The Effectiveness of Certain Social Hygiene Literature* (New York: American Social Hygiene Association, 1923).

11. Clelia Duel Mosher, "Hygiene and Physiology of Women," 1912, survey of forty-seven women, Stanford Digital Repository, http://purl.stanford.edu/sr010vc5273. See also Kara Platoni, "The Sex Scholar," *Stanford Alumni*, March–April 2010, https://alumni.stanford.edu/get/page/magazine/article/?article_id=29954.

12. See Gilbert Van Tassel Hamilton, *A Research in Marriage* (New York: Albert and Charles Boni, Inc., 1929), 22; and Michel Foucault, *The History of Sexuality*, vol. 1, *An Introduction*, trans. Robert Hurley (New York: Vintage, 1990), 43.

13. On her use of the questionnaire, see Katharine Bement Davis, *Factors in the Sex Lives of Twenty-Two Hundred Women* (New York: Harper and Brothers, 1929), xii–xiii, and on the different categories and data tables, see ibid., 1–37.

14. See Lewis M. Terman and Catharine Cox Miles, *Sex and Personality: Studies in Masculinity and Femininity* (New York: McGraw-Hill, 1936), 3, vi.

15. See Carney Landis, Agnes T. Landis, and M. Marjorie Bolles, *Sex in Development: A Study of the Growth and Development of the Emotional and Sexual Aspects of Personality Together with Physiological, Anatomical, and Medical Information on a Group of 153 Normal Women and 142 Female Psychiatric Patients* (New York: Paul B. Hoeber, 1940), 51, xii, 91–92.

16. See Robert Latou Dickinson and Laura Beam, *The Single Woman: A Medical Study in Sex Education* (Baltimore, MD: Williams and Wilkins Company, 1934), 214; and Hannah M. Stone and Abraham Stone, *A Marriage Manual: A Practical Guide-Book to Sex and Marriage* (New York: Simon and Schuster, 1935), 278.

17. See, for example, *SBHM*, 75–76, 393. See also Siobhan B. Somerville, *Queering the Color Line: Race and the Invention of Homosexuality in American Culture* (Durham, NC: Duke University Press, 1999), 29–38.

18. See, for example, *SBHM*, 7–8.

19. Ibid., 19, 23–34.

20. ACK to Carl G. Hartman (CGH), October 19, 1943, ACKD, I: Correspondence, KILSC.

21. See Terman and Miles, *Sex and Personality*, 239–45. Terman divided his "homosexual" male informants into active and passive groups and compared them to "normal"

subsets of high-school-age men and women and "normal" military men. While the ranges for each group have a definite peak, there is a broad range in each group that overlaps with each other. Though not explicit, Terman's data suggest that active homosexual men rated more masculine, in fact, than their "normal" military counterparts while still indicating a range of scores. See also his discussion of range and overlap in Lewis M. Terman, *Psychological Factors in Marital Happiness* (New York: McGraw-Hill, 1938), 267, 343.

22. Waldemar A. Nielsen, *The Big Foundations* (New York: Columbia University Press, 1972); and Mark Dowie, *American Foundations: An Investigative History* (Cambridge, MA: MIT Press, 2001).

23. "First Annual Report of the Committee for Research on Sex Problems of the Division of Medical Science, National Research Council" (Washington, DC, 1923), 13–14. On the first research centers the committee supported, see Sophie D. Aberle and George W. Corner, *History of the Committee for Research in Problems of Sex* (Washington, DC: National Research Council, Committee for Research in Problems of Sex, 1950), 54–55.

24. Aberle and Corner, *History of the Committee*, 76–80; and Vern L. Bullough, "The Rockefellers and Sex Research," *Journal of Sex Research* 21, no. 2 (May 1985): 117–18.

25. "NRC—Committee for Research in Problems of Sex," projects, RG 1.1, series 200, box 40, folder 461, Rockefeller Foundation Records, Rockefeller Archive Center, Washington, DC (RFR). On the debate about Gilbert van Tassel Hamilton, see Aberle and Corner, *History of the Committee*, 78–79; and Bullough, "The Rockefellers and Sex Research," 120–22. On funding from the Bureau of Social Hygiene for Hamilton, see "NRC—Committee for Research in Problems of Sex," 4.

26. Aberle and Corner, *History of the Committee*, app. E, 9; and see "Twenty-Seventh Annual Report of the Committee for Research in Problems of Sex" (Washington, DC, 1948); "Twenty-Eighth Annual Report of the Committee for Research in Problems of Sex" (Washington, DC, 1949).

27. "Twenty-Second Annual Report: Committee for Research in Problems of Sex, Division of Medical Sciences, National Research Council for the Year July 1, 1942 to June 30, 1943" (Washington, DC, 1943), 1–2; "Twenty-Fifth Annual Report: Committee for Research in Problems of Sex, Division of Medical Sciences, National Research Council for the Year July 1, 1945 to June 30, 1946" (Washington, DC, 1946), 1, 4–5.

28. "Twenty-Fifth Annual Report," 5, 11.

29. See, for example, Herman B Wells (HBW) to ACK, June 14, 1941, March 30, 1945, ACKD, I: Correspondence, KILSC. See also James H. Capshew, *Herman B Wells: The Promise of the American University* (Bloomington: Indiana University Press, 2012), 7.

30. Apart from Jonathan Gathorne-Hardy, *Sex the Measure of All Things: A Life of Alfred C. Kinsey* (Bloomington: Indiana University Press, 1998), and James H. Jones, *Alfred Kinsey: A Public/Private Life* (New York: W. W. Norton, 1997), other biographies are Cornelia V. Christenson, *Kinsey: A Biography* (Bloomington: Indiana University Press, 1971); and Wardell B. Pomeroy, *Dr. Kinsey and the Institute for Sex Research* (New Haven, CT: Yale University Press, 1982).

31. See, for example, Alfred Kinsey, "Reproductive Anatomy and Physiology" (lecture), ACKD, IX: Manuscripts and Collections, a. Alfred C. Kinsey Collection, 1894–1956 (ACKC), KILSC.

32. On Kinsey leaving the marriage course for research, see ACK to HBW, September 10, 1940, ACKD, I: Correspondence, KILSC. On the addition of research team members, see, for example, Pomeroy, *Dr. Kinsey*, 86–89, 97–105. And on the interview process and training, see Gathorne-Hardy, *Sex the Measure of All Things*, 170–71, 174–81; and see *SBHM*, chap. 2, esp. 42–43.

33. For details of Freilich's negotiation of early postwar period book sales to Kinsey, see ACKD, I: Correspondence, Freilich, KILSC.

34. "Thirtieth Annual Report, Committee for Research in Problems of Sex, Division of Medical Sciences, National Research Council: July 1, 1950–June 30, 1951" (Washington, DC, 1951), 6. On Magnus Hirschfeld's library, see Ralf Dose, *Magnus Hirschfeld: The Origins of the Gay Liberation Movement* (New York: Monthly Review Press, 2014); Elena Mancini, *Magnus Hirschfeld and the Quest for Sexual Freedom: A History of the First International Sexual Freedom Movement* (New York: Palgrave Macmillan, 2010). On Kinsey's arrangement with Indiana University for the preservation of the gall wasps and collected library, see ACK to RMY, May 16, 1946, ACKD, I: Correspondence, KILSC.

35. HBW to Alan Gregg (AG), May 23, 1947, ACKD, I: Correspondence, Rockefeller Foundation, KILSC.

36. George W. Corner (GWC) to ACK, June 20, 1946; ACK to RMY, May 16, 1946; GWC to ACK, July 5, 1946; and ACK to RMY, May 16, 1946, all in ACKD, I: Correspondence, KILSC.

37. GWC to ACK, July 6, 1946, 1, ACKD, I: Correspondence, KILSC.

38. RMY to ACK, June 15, 1946, 1, ACKD, I: Correspondence, KILSC.

39. HBW to ACK, April 11, 1947, ACKD, I: Correspondence, KILSC; and AG to HBW, May 23, 1947, ACKD, I: Correspondence, KILSC. See also Norma S. Thompson to HBW, September 19, 1947, Rockefeller Foundation, Indiana University Archives (IUA).

40. There were other institutes on Indiana University's campus before the Institute for Sex Research. One was the Institute of Criminal Law, later called the Institute for Criminal Law Administration, a clearinghouse for researchers in other departments of IU to coordinate and share research. See "Minutes of the Board of Trustees of Indiana University, 8 September 1936," IUA, http://webapp1.dlib.indiana.edu/iubot/view?docId=1936–09 -http://www.indiana.edu/~crimjust/history.php. The other was the Institute for Training for Public Service in the Department of Government. See "Minutes of the Board of Trustees of Indiana University, 14–15 October 1944," IUA, http://webapp1.dlib.indiana.edu /iubot/view?docId=1944–1014.xml&chunk.id=d1e120&toc.depth=1&toc.id=d1e120 &brand=iubot&text1=institute&op1=and&op2=and&field1=text&field2=text&field3 =text&fromYear=1920&toYear=1950&startDoc=21#. Lastly, the Waterman Institute for Scientific Research was established through a gift to IU of $100,000 in 1915 and established in Indianapolis, Indiana. The Office of the Vice President for Research at IU reports that the gift has supported the research of nearly two dozen researchers and is currently used to support endowed chairs for the university in physics and psychological and brain sciences. See http://ovpr.indiana.edu/funding/ovpr-funding-programs/luther-dana -waterman-professorship/. The Institute seems to have been the first to function much like research institutes continue to do today.

41. HBW to AG, May 23, 1947; ACK to HBW, April 11, 1947 , ACKD, I: Correspondence, KILSC.

42. ACK to RMY, April 27, 1947, ACKD, I: Correspondence, KILSC.

43. "Original Certificate of Incorporation," April 8, 1947, ACKD, VII: Operations Records, a. Legal, KILSC.

44. "Twenty-Seventh Annual Report"; ACK, "1948 Studies in Human Sex Behavior: Progress Report," April 1, 1948, ACKD, VII: Operations Records, b. Reports, KILSC.

2. Making the Kinsey Reports (1947–1956)

1. See, for instance, Abram Scheinfeld, "Cold Women and Why," *Argosy*, June 1948, 21, 104–105; "Petting Is on the Increase, but Percentage Non-virtuous Women Remains about Same," *Ames Daily Tribune*, January 5, 1948, 8; "Report on Kinsey," *New York Herald Tribune*, April 4, 1948, Alfred Charles Kinsey Directorship, 1947–56 (ACKD), VI: Newsclippings, a. *Sexual Behavior in the Human Male* (1948), Kinsey Institute Library and Special Collections (KILSC).

2. Alfred C. Kinsey, Wardell B. Pomeroy, and Clyde E. Martin, *Sexual Behavior in the Human Male (SBHM)* (Philadelphia: W. B. Saunders, 1948), 307.

3. Jonathan Gathorne-Hardy, *Sex the Measure of All Things: A Life of Alfred C. Kinsey* (Bloomington: Indiana University Press, 1998), 233, 261.

4. The final majority report of the Reece Committee did not accuse the Institute or Kinsey himself of un-American activities but called his work "pseudoscientific" and held that the Kinsey Reports subverted national morality. It also charged the Rockefeller Foundation with support for subversive activities, urging it to police itself more carefully. See, for example, United Press, "Probers Find No Hint Sex Is Un-American," *Washington Post*, January 7, 1954, 9; "House May Call Kinsey: Unit Is Asked to Investigate His Financial Backing," *New York Times*, January 7, 1954, 21; C. P. Trussell, "Power of Grants Scored in Inquiry: Dr. Hobbs Says Beneficiaries Have Adverse Effect on Politics and Morality," *New York Times*, May 20, 1954, 26; "Calls Kinsey's Sex Studies a Bad Influence," *Chicago Daily Tribune*, May 20, 1954, B17; C. P. Trussell, "Foundations Help Subvert Country, House Study Says," *New York Times*, December 20, 1954, 1, 20; Murrey Marder, "House Group Splits on Foundation Probe," *Washington Post and Times Herald*, December 20, 1954, 1, 2; Rodney Crowther, "Foundations Advised to 'Reform' at Once," *Sun* (Baltimore, MD), December 20, 1954; "Excerpts from Reports on Congressional Investigation of Tax-Exempt Foundations," *New York Times*, December 20, 1954, 21; "Reece Says Foundations Breed Socialist Menace: Democrats Hit Report as a 'Crackpot' View Goodwin Signs, but Dissents from Findings of Majority," *Daily Boston Globe*, December 20, 1954.

5. Mary Steichen Calderone (MSC) to ACK, November 16, 1954, Addendum, 7315081M35, Mary Steichen Calderone Collection (MSCC), Arthur and Elizabeth Schlesinger Library on the History of Women in America, Radcliffe Institute for Advanced Study, Harvard University, Cambridge, MA (SL).

6. US Customs, "Notification of Intent: Destruction of Libeled Materials, July 24, 1956," ACKD, VII: Operations, a. Legal, KILSC.

7. Alfred C. Kinsey, "Homosexuality: Criteria for a Hormonal Explanation of the Homosexual," *Journal of Clinical Endocrinology* 1 (May 1941): 424–28.

8. KDM to ACK, October 1, 1948, ACKD, I: Correspondence, KILSC.

9. *SBHM*, 623; Alfred C. Kinsey, Wardell B. Pomeroy, Clyde E. Martin, and Paul H. Gebhard, *Sexual Behavior in the Human Female (SBHF)* (Philadelphia: W. B. Saunders, 1953), 452–53.

10. *SBHM*, 638. See, for instance, Paul A. Robinson, *The Modernization of Sex: Havelock Ellis, Alfred Kinsey, William Masters and Virginia Johnson* (Ithaca, NY: Cornell University Press, 1989), 16–19; James H. Jones, *Alfred Kinsey: A Public/Private Life* (New York: W. W. Norton, 1997), 530–32; George Chauncey, *Gay New York: Gender, Urban Culture, and the Making of the Gay Male World, 1890–1940* (New York: Basic Books, 1994), 70–71; and Gathorne-Hardy, *Sex the Measure of All Things*, 194, 217.

11. Clifford R. Adams (CRA) to ACK, May 13, 1946, ACKD, I: Correspondence, KILSC.

12. CRA to ACK, November 22, 1948, ACKD, I: Correspondence, KILSC.

13. Gathorne-Hardy, *Sex the Measure of All Things*, 303.

14. ACK to CRA, November 1948, ACKD, I: Correspondence, KILSC.

15. AM to ACK, November 18, 1948, ACKD, I: Correspondence, KILSC.

16. See ACK to AM, December 2, 1948, ACKD, I: Correspondence, KILSC.

17. *SBHM*, 580–81.

18. Ibid., 388, 336–37, 333.

19. Ibid., 79, 212, 263, 393–94, 465–76, 473–87.

20. Ibid., 3, 22, 58, 165, 335, 365, 374, 393, 477, 486, 510, 542–47, 574–75.

21. For an overview of reviews, see Miriam G. Reumann, *American Sexual Character: Sex, Gender, and National Identity in the Kinsey Reports* (Berkeley: University of California Press, 2005).

22. *SBHM*, 5–6.

23. SYM to ACK, July 6, 1948, ACKD, I: Correspondence, KILSC.

24. Ruth Herschberger to ACK, September 1, 1953, ACKD, I: Correspondence, KILSC.

25. See "Woman Writer Takes the Male Apart," *Long Beach Independent*, April 12, 1948, 4.

26. See Paul H. Gebhard and Alan B. Johnson, *The Kinsey Institute Data: Marginal Tabulations of the 1938–63 Interviews Conducted by the Institute for Sex Research* (Bloomington: Indiana University Press, 1998), 33–35.

27. See Jones, *Alfred C. Kinsey*, 677–78, 685.

28. Gathorne-Hardy, *Sex the Measure of All Things*, 214.

29. Instances of this representation of "Kinsey and the feminine" include Jones, *Alfred C. Kinsey*, 678, 685, 748–49; Gathorne-Hardy, *Sex the Measure of All Things*, 258, 314, 350; Vern Bullough, *Science in the Bedroom: A History of Sexology* (New York: Basic Books, 1994), 180; and Janice M. Irvine, *Disorders of Desire: Sexuality and Gender in Modern American Sexology*, revised and expanded edition (Philadelphia: Temple University Press, 2005), 52, 59–60.

30. Collaborators included founding gynecological researcher Robert Latou Dickinson (1861–1950), clinician and academic marriage counseling founder Emily Hartshorne Mudd (1898–1997), Planned Parenthood Federation medical director Mary Steichen Calderone (1904–98), infertility specialist Frances Shields (1893–1964), New York gynecologist Sophia J. Kleegman (1901–71), lawyer Harriet Fleischl Pilpel (1911–91), and Kinsey's first female research associate, criminal justice researcher Alice Withrow Field (1909–60), among others.

31. For fuller discussion of this point, see Jane Gerhard, *Desiring Revolution: Second-Wave Feminism and the Rewriting of American Sexual Thought, 1920 to 1982* (New York: Columbia University Press, 2001), 40–47, 61–65.

32. See Edmund Bergler, "The Problem of Frigidity," *Psychiatric Quarterly* 18 (1944): 374–90; Bergler, "Frigidity in the Female: Misconceptions and Facts," *Marriage Hygiene* 1 (1947): 16–21. See also Eduard E. Hitschmann and Edmund Bergler, "Frigidity in Women—Restatement and Reviewed Experiences," *Psychoanalytic Review* 36 (1949): 45–53.

33. By 1949 Kinsey was dismayed at negative reviews by psychoanalytic and some psychiatric clinical fraternities, including Drs. Lawrence Kubie, Robert Knight, Albert Hobbs, and R. Lambert, aimed at discrediting his project with his funders. For discussion of this professional opposition, see ACK to Dr. O. Spurgeon English (OSE), February 12, 1948; OSE to ACK, February 22, 1954; ACK to OSE, March 2, 1954; OSE to ACK, June 10,

1954; ACK to OSE, June 15, 1954; and OSE to ACK, June 18, 1954, all in ACKD, I: Correspondence, KILSC.

34. Instances here include Albert Ellis, "Female Sexual Response and Marital Relations," *Social Problems* 1 (April 1954): 154; and Albert Ellis, "Is the Vaginal Orgasm a Myth?," in *Sex, Society, and the Individual*, ed. Albert Ellis and A. P. Pillay (Bombay: International Journal of Sexology, 1953), 158. See also ACK to Edmund Bergler (EB), August 22, 1950, ACKD, I: Correspondence, KILSC.

35. These specialists, all of whom Kinsey thanked in the acknowledgments to the female volume, were Dr. John O. Haman (San Francisco fertility clinician and researcher), Dr. Francis J. Hector (British gynecologist), Sophia J. Kleegman (New York gynecologist), Dr. Earle M. Marsh (San Francisco gynecologist and psychoanalytic psychiatrist), Dr. Frances E. Shields (New York and Monterey gynecologist specializing in sterility), and Dr. Abraham Stone (gynecologist and director of the Margaret Sanger Clinical Research Bureau). See *SBHF*, xi.

36. ACK to WBP, July 31, 1950, ACKD, I: Correspondence, KILSC.

37. *SBHF*, 468.

38. See Frances E. Shields (FES) to ACK, December 15, 1950, and ACK to FES, February 19, 1951, ACKD, I: Correspondence, KILSC. See also ACK to Earle Marsh, October 22, 1951, ACKD, I: Correspondence, KILSC.

39. ACK to CGH, December 21, 1950, ACKD, I: Correspondence, KILSC.

40. FES, "Artificial Insemination as Related to the Female," *Fertility and Sterility* 1, no. 3 (1950): 271–80; and FES, "The Safe Period," *Trained Nurse and Hospital Review* 94 (1935): 217–18. Soon Kinsey had Shields collecting data on her patients. Especially interesting to him were the reproductive issues, their full range and variation, as well as methodological issues. See also ACK to FES, February 13, 1949, FES to ACK, July 28, 1949, and ACK to FES, September 8, 1949, all in ACKD, I: Correspondence, KILSC.

41. See Frank Ambrose Beach (FAB) to ACK, January 16, 1950, and ACK to FAB, January 15, 23, 1950, ACKD, I: Correspondence, KILSC.

42. He had met her in 1943 through Robert Latou Dickinson. See Alice Withrow Field (AWF) to Robert Latou Dickinson (RLD), December 15, 1943, ACKD, VIII: Manuscripts and Collections, Alice Withrow Field Papers, 1909–60 (AWFP), KILSC.

43. Field had completed a study of the New York Women's Court that focused on prostitutes and girls sent from the Wayward Minor Court between 1936 and 1944. A critic of police strategies, sexism, heterosexism, and racism, she enriched Kinsey's enquiries with extensive criminal justice and corrections contacts and daunting interviewing skills. Kinsey's early 1950s concepts of the regulation of sex offenders included both women and men. See ACK to AWF, April 2, 1946, February 2, March 24, and April 8, 1950, September 15 and November 23, 1951, and March 10, 1952, all in ACKD, I: Correspondence, KILSC. See also ACK, "Progress Report, Institute for Sex Research, Indiana University," March 15, 1952, 5, ACKD, VIII: Manuscripts and Collections, AWFP, KILSC.

44. See Estelle B. Freedman, "'Uncontrolled Desires': The Responses to the Sexual Psychopath, 1920–1960," *Journal of American History* 74 (1981): 96–97.

45. See, for instance, AWF to ACK, June 4, 1944, ACKD, VIII: Manuscripts and Collections, AWFP, KILSC.

46. See Karl Murdock Bowman's testimony on this point, quoting Kinsey, in California Legislature—Assembly, *Preliminary Report of the Subcommittee on Sex Crimes of the Assembly Interim Committee on Judicial System and Judicial Process (1949)* (Sacramento: Government Printing Office, 1950), 176.

47. ACK to Vincent Nowlis, August 4, 1953, ACKD, I: Correspondence, KILSC.

48. *SBHF*, 79, 510, 79–80, 655.

49. Robinson, *The Modernization of Sex*, 100.

50. *SBHF*, 302, 307, 354, 452–54, 511, 532.

51. On mass frigidity, see, for example, Eduard Hitschmann and Edmund Bergler, *Frigidity in Women: Its Characteristics and Treatment*, Nervous and Mental Disease Monograph Series No. 60 (Washington, DC: Nervous and Mental Disease Publishing Company, 1936); William S. Kroger and Charles Freed, "Psychosomatic Aspects of Frigidity," *JAMA: Journal of the American Medical Association* 143, no. 6 (June 1950): 526–32; Kroger and Freed, "The Cold Women," *Time*, June 26, 1950, 82.

52. *SBHF*, 378–80.

53. Ibid., 17–20.

54. Robinson, *The Modernization of Sex*, 108.

55. *SBHF*, 146.

56. Ibid., 138.

57. Ibid., 598, 640–41, 761, 422, 459, 293–94. See also ACK to CRA, January 23, 1946, and ACK to Dr. Catherine Bacon, March 6, 1951, ACKD, I: Correspondence, KILSC.

58. Robinson, *The Modernization of Sex*, 109–10.

59. Contemporary feminists offer diverse readings of the implications of Kinsey's work on women. The first mention of his critique of the dual orgasm model came in the early work of the women's liberation movement. See Anne Koedt, "The Myth of the Vaginal Orgasm," reprinted in *Feminism in Our Time: The Essential Writings, World War II to the Present*, ed. Miriam Schneir (New York: Vintage, 1968), 333–42. More critical views followed. See, for instance, Margaret Jackson, "Sexology and the Universalization of Male Sexuality," in *The Sexuality Papers*, ed. Lal Coveney et al. (London: Hutchinson, 1984), 69–84; Sheila Jeffreys, *AntiClimax: Feminist Perspectives on the Sexual Revolution* (London: Women's Press, 1990), 91–144; Lynn Segal, "Sensual Uncertainty, or Why the Clitoris Is Not Enough," in *Sex and Love: New Thoughts on Old Contradictions*, ed. Sue Cartledge and Joanna Ryan (London: Women's Press, 1983), 30–47. For a more genealogical approach that is attentive to context, see Leonore Tiefer, "A Feminist Perspective on Sexology and Sexuality," in *Feminist Thought and the Structure of Knowledge*, ed. Mary McCanney Gergen (New York: NYU Press, 1988), 16–26.

60. *SBHF*, 598, 640–41, 761.

61. ACK to CGH, December 21, 1950, ACKD I: Correspondence, KILSC.

62. See Kinsey's testimony as edited in *Abortion in the United States*, ed. Mary Steichen Calderone (New York: Hoebler, 1958), 151.

63. See, for instance, Bullough, *Science in the Bedroom*, 170; Irvine, *Disorders of Desire*, 63; and Robinson, *The Modernization of Sex*, 108.

64. See Louise Rosenzweig and Saul Rosenzweig, "Notes on Alfred C. Kinsey's Pre-sexual Scientific Work and the Transition," *Journal of the History of the Behavioral Sciences* 5 (1969): 173–81.

65. See Robinson, *The Modernization of Sex*, 100, 110, 113.

66. See, for instance, "Calls Kinsey's Sex Studies a Bad Influence: Assails Foundation's Use of Funds," *Chicago Daily Tribune*, May 20, 1954, B17; Rodney Crowther, "Two Foundations Deny Making Grants to Subversive Groups," *Sun*, August 5, 1954, 6.

67. See, for instance, Nate Haseltine, "Experts Evaluate Kinsey Sex Study," *Washington Post*, January 17, 1954, B1; Hans Zeisel, review of *Sexual Behavior in the Human Female* by Alfred C. Kinsey, Wardell B. Pomeroy, Clyde E. Martin, and Paul H. Gebhard, *University of Chicago Law Review* 21 (March 1954): 517–25.

68. ACK to OSE, June 15, 1954.

69. See ACK to EB, August 22, 1950, and EB to ACK, August 25 and 27, 1950, ACKD, I: Correspondence, KILSC.

70. Edmund Bergler and William S. Kroger, *Kinsey's Myth of Female Sexuality* (New York: Grune & Stratton, 1954), 82–83.

71. OSE to ACK, February 22, 1954.

72. James W. Reed, interview with Emily Hartshorne Mudd, Family Planning Oral History Project (1974), OH-1, 154, SL.

73. D. Kenneth Rose to ACK, December 2, 1947, and ACK to Dr. Kenneth Rose, December 9, 1947, ACKD, I: Correspondence, Planned Parenthood, KILSC; ACK to RLD, October 23, 1943, Dr. Christopher Tietze to ACK, February 28, 1948, and Dr. Abraham Stone to ACK, October 8, 1943, all in ACKD, I: Correspondence, KILSC.

74. ACK to William Vogt, November 21, 1951, ACKD, I: Correspondence, Planned Parenthood, KILSC.

75. MSC to ACK, February 1, 1954, ACKD, I: Correspondence, KILSC; and ACK to MSC, January 22, 1954, addendum, 1–2, MSCC, SL. In 1968 Calderone founded the Sexuality Information and Education Council of the United States (SIECUS), although she is most known for her central role in late 1960s controversies over sex education in public schools.

76. MSC to ACK, June 14, 1954, ACKD, I: Correspondence, Planned Parenthood, Arden House Conference, KILSC.

77. MSC to Laurence Saunders, November 18, 1953, ACKD, I: Correspondence, Planned Parenthood, Arden House Conference, KILSC.

78. MSC to ACK, June 14, 1954, ACKD, I: Correspondence, Planned Parenthood, Arden House Conference, KILSC.

79. ACK to MSC, July 6, 1954, ACKD, I: Correspondence, Planned Parenthood, Arden House Conference, KILSC.

80. ACK to Alan F. Guttmacher (AFG), February 23, 1956, ACKD, I: Correspondence, Planned Parenthood, Arden House Conference, KILSC.

81. AFG, "Summarizing Statement by the Abortion Committee, as Discussed by Members of Statement Committee Present at November 23, 1955 Meeting," ACKD, I: Correspondence, Planned Parenthood, Arden House Conference, KILSC.

82. ACK to AFG, February 23, 1956, ACKD, I: Correspondence, Planned Parenthood, Arden House Conference, KILSC.

83. Calderone, *Abortion in the United States*, 55–56; and Planned Parenthood Federation of America, *Abortion Conference* (Harriman, NY: PPFA, 1955), 1:71.

84. See ACK to AFG, February 23, 1956, ACKD, I: Correspondence, KILSC.

85. Departmental Committee on Homosexual Offences and Prostitution, "Notes of a meeting held at 53 Drayton Gardens, S.W. 10, on Saturday, 29th October, 1955 . . . Witness: Dr. Alfred C. Kinsey," Document No. CHP/93, Annex, 3, Home Office 345/9/93/3, National Archives of the United Kingdom.

86. ACK, "Notes of His European Trip of Late 1955, Dictated by Dr. Kinsey at Staff Meetings—England, 12/12/1955, 5–12," ACKD, IX: Alfred C. Kinsey Collection (ACKC), KILSC.

87. See M. F. Ashley Montagu, *Adolescent Sterility: A Study in the Comparative Physiology of the Infecundity of the Adolescent Organism in Mammals and Man* (Springfield, IL: C. C. Thomas, 1946); and see ACK, *Abortion*, draft typescript, July 27, 1956, 3–5, ACKD, IV: Drafts, KILSC. Pioneering research of Kinsey's colleagues John Haman, Robert Hotchkiss, Frances E. Shields, Sophia J. Kleegman, and, of course, the late Dickinson

established that by no means were women invariably "at fault" in childlessness. See, for instance, John O. Haman, "Medico-legal Aspects of Artificial Insemination," *Transactions of the American Society for the Study of Sterility* 18 (1947): 19–25; Frances E. Shields, "Artificial Insemination as Related to the Female," *Fertility and Sterility* 1, no. 3 (1950): 271–80; Robert S. Hotchkiss, Endre K. Brunner, and Philip Grenley, "Semen Analyses of Two Hundred Fertile Men," *American Journal of Medical Sciences* 196, no. 3 (1938): 362–84; Robert S. Hotchkiss, Asdrubal Baias Pinto, and Sophia J. Kleegman, "Artificial Insemination with Semen Recovered from the Bladder," *Fertility and Sterility* 6 (1955): 37–42; Sophia J. Kleegman, "Sterility," *American Journal of Surgery* 33, no. 3 (1936): 392–405; Kleegman, "Therapeutic Donor Insemination," *Fertility and Sterility* 5, no. 1 (1954): 7–30.

88. ACK, *Abortion* (1956), chap. 3, 6.
89. Ibid., 6–7, 13.
90. Ibid., 13.
91. Ibid.
92. Ibid., 14, 18.
93. Ibid., 18.
94. Ibid., 7, 8.
95. Ibid., 7.
96. ACK to HBW, May 17, 1956, ACKD, I: Correspondence, KILSC.
97. HBW to ACK, May 21, 1956, ACKD, I: Correspondence, KILSC.
98. "Kinsey Fights U.S. to Keep 'Obscene' Data," *New York Post*, August 2, 1956, 4; "Curbing Dr. Kinsey," *New York Post*, August 5, 1956; and "Don't Drop the Bars," *Times Union* (Albany, NY), August 7, 1956.

3. Finishing the Mission (1957–1965)

1. Alfred C. Kinsey (ACK), "The Right to Do Sex Research," typescript, 1956, Alfred Charles Kinsey Directorship, 1947–56 (ACKD), IV: Drafts, Kinsey Institute Library and Special Collections (KILSC).

2. Jonathan Gathorne-Hardy, *Sex the Measure of All Things: A Life of Alfred C. Kinsey* (Bloomington: Indiana University Press, 1998), 303, 436, 437.

3. Wardell B. Pomeroy, *Dr. Kinsey and the Institute for Sex Research* (New York: Harper & Row, 1972), 449.

4. Mary Steichen Calderone to ACK, November 16, 1954, ACKD, I: Correspondence, KILSC.

5. Harriet Pilpel, "Summary," June 16, 1959, 4, in Customs case documents compiled by Greenbaum, Wolff and Ernst, "*AD. 189–50: United States District Court of Southern New York, v. 31 Photographs, 4-3/4 Inches in Size and Various Pictures, Books and Other Articles. Institute for Sex Research, Inc. at Indiana University*," series B: 1957–81, Paul Henry Gebhard Directorship, 1957–81 (PHGD), VII: Operations Records, a. Legal, KILSC.

6. Institute for Sex Research, annual report, June 30, 1955, ACKD, VII: Operations Records, b. Annual Reports, KILSC.

7. Pomeroy, *Dr. Kinsey*, 449.

8. Ibid., 449–50.

9. "Studies in Human Sex Behavior: Progress Report, April 1, 1948," 2, ACKD, VII: Operations Records, b. Annual Reports, KILSC.

10. See the *Act for the Suppression of Trade in, and Circulation of, Obscene Literature and Articles of Immoral Use*, 42nd Cong., 3rd sess. (1873), chaps. 256–58, 598.

11. The text of the act reads: "All persons are prohibited from importing into the United States . . . any obscene book, pamphlet, paper, writing, advertisement, circular, print, picture, drawing, or other representation, figure, or image on or of paper or other material, or any cast, instrument, or other article which is obscene or immoral" (Tariff Act of 1930, pt. 2, sec. 305).

12. ACK to Mr. John Wise, May 12, 1954, ACKD, I: Correspondence, KILSC.

13. Gathorne-Hardy, *Sex the Measure of All Things*, 345–46. See also Kenneth R. Stephens, "*United States v. 31 Photographs*: Dr. Alfred Kinsey and Obscenity Law," *Indiana Magazine of History* 71 (December 1975): 299–318.

14. Pilpel, "Summary."

15. Nancy Seely, "Kinsey Fights U.S. to Keep 'Obscene' Data," *New York Post,* August 2, 1957, 4.

16. Judge Edmund Palmeri, "Order," October 31, 1957, 360, in Customs case documents compiled by Greenbaum, Wolff and Ernst, "*AD. 189–50: United States District Court of Southern New York, v. 31 Photographs, 4–3/4 Inches in Size and Various Pictures, Books and Other Articles. Institute for Sex Research, Inc. at Indiana University.*"

17. *Roth v. United States*, 354 U.S. 476, argued April 22, 1957, decided June 24, 1957. Until 1973 the courts upheld strict obscenity standards. Then, while upholding the *Roth* ruling on the First Amendment, they held that "obscenity" must be defined by community standards, which, Chief Justice Warren Burger wrote, had changed significantly during the sexual revolution. This ruling effectively justified what some lower courts had already been doing when they ruled against banning a variety of books, magazines, and films. *Miller v. California*, 413 U.S. 15, argued January 18–19, 1972, reargued November 7, 1972, decided June 21, 1973.

18. *United States v. Levine*, 82 F.2d 156, 157 (2d Cir. 1936).

19. Palmeri, "Order," 6–7, 8.

20. Ibid., 13, 14.

21. Paul H. Gebhard, Wardell B. Pomeroy, Clyde E. Martin, and Cornelia V. Christenson, *Pregnancy, Birth and Abortion (PBA)* (Westport, CT: Greenwood Press, 1958), 192.

22. Ibid., 5–6. Gebhard's view here did not correspond with Kinsey's.

23. Hal Wallen, "Now! A *New* Kinsey Report," *Cavalier* 6, no. 59 (May 1958): 6.

24. Ernest Havemann, "The New Kinsey Report: *Pregnancy, Birth and Abortion*," *McCall's*, March 1958, 34.

25. *PBA*, 191, 203, 210.

26. Ibid., 17–18.

27. Ibid., 93–94, 57.

28. Institute for Sex Research, annual reports, 1957, 3, and 1958, 4, PHGD, VII: Operations Records, b. Reports, KILSC.

29. Institute for Sex Research, "Annual Progress Report," April 1, 1957, PHGD, VII: Operations Records, b. Annual Reports, KILSC.

30. Philip Sapir to Paul H. Gebhard (PHG), June 18, 1957, PHGD, I: Correspondence, "NIMH," KILSC.

31. See Paul H. Gebhard's notes on consultants' advice prepared for a 1963 site visit by Public Health Service (PHS) staff and outside grant application reviewers. PHGD, VII: Operations Records, g. External Reviews, PHS Site Visit, KILSC (hereafter cited as "Site visit" with consultant's last name and page number).

32. PHG to Dr. William Caudill, January 9, 1962, PHGD, I: Correspondence, NIMH, 1960–66, KILSC.

33. As a compromise, after the NIMH site visit, Institute policy was to provide researchers with marginal tabulations but not access to the raw data. In practice, this was

untenable, given the amount of time it would have taken to calculate data for each individual researcher who requested them. Later, the final goal was achieved with the publication of *The Kinsey Data: Marginal Tabulations of the 1938–1963 Interviews Conducted by the Institute for Sex Research* (Bloomington: Indiana University Press, 1979).

34. Site visit, Clausen, 1, Strodtbeck, 1, 6–7, 9–12, 18–21, 42–46, Benjamin and Eberhard, 3.

35. Site visit, Strodtbeck, 15–16.

36. Ibid., 21.

37. See, for example, John D'Emilio, *Sexual Politics, Sexual Communities: The Making of a Homosexual Minority in the United States* (Chicago: University of Chicago Press, 1983); Jennifer Terry, *An American Obsession: Science, Medicine, and Homosexuality in Modern Society* (Chicago: University of Chicago Press, 1999); Henry L. Minton, *Departing from Deviance: A History of Homosexual Rights and Emancipatory Science in America* (Chicago: University of Chicago Press, 2001); David K. Johnson, *The Lavender Scare: Cold War Persecution of Gays and Lesbians* (Chicago: University of Chicago Press, 2004); and David Eisenbach, *Gay Power: An American Revolution* (New York: Carol and Graf Publishers, 2006).

38. Site visit, Clausen, 1, 2, 4, Strodtbeck, 36.

39. PHG, "Gebhard Era History, 1956–1982," 4, PHGD, IX: Paul H. Gebhard Papers, KILSC.

40. Site visit, Clausen, 6, Strodtbeck, 15, 20–23, 33.

41. Site visit, Lilienfeld, 1.

42. Site visit, ibid., 12, Strodtbeck, 13.

43. PHG to Philip Sapir, September 12, 1962, and November 28, 1966, PHGD, I: Correspondence, KILSC.

44. PHG to Sapir, October 13, 1963, PHGD, I: Correspondence, KILSC.

45. Site visit, Lilienfeld, 11–12.

46. Paul H. Gebhard, John H. Gagnon, Wardell B. Pomeroy, and Cornelia V. Christenson, *Sex Offenders: An Analysis of Types*, hereafter *SO* (New York: Harper and Row, 1965), 25.

47. For example, see Benjamin Karpman, "The Sexual Psychopath," *Journal of Criminal Law, Criminology, and Police Science* 42, no. 2 (1951): 184–98; and Karpman, *The Sexual Offender and His Offences: Etiology, Pathology, Psychodynamics, and Treatment* (New York: Julian Press, 1954).

48. See Philip Jenkins, "The Liberal Era, 1958–1976," in *Moral Panic: Changing Concepts of the Child Molester in Modern America* (New Haven, CT: Yale University Press, 1998), 94–117.

49. Eric Pace, "New Kinsey Report: Narcotics, Pornography Dismissed in Sex Crimes," *Courier Express* (Buffalo, NY), July 18, 1965; AP, "Drug-Sex Crime Link Rejected," *Baltimore Morning Sun*, July 18, 1965; "U.S. Sex Laws Harsh, Confusing," *Charleston Gazette*, August 3, 1965; and Dale Burgess, "Indiana U. Research Series Adds Report on Sex Offenders," *Elkhart Truth*, July 22, 1965.

50. *SO*, 8.

51. Ibid., 9.

52. Ibid., 15.

53. Alfred C. Kinsey, Wardell B. Pomeroy, and Clyde E. Martin, *Sexual Behavior in the Human Male* (*SBHM*) (Philadelphia: W. B. Saunders, 1948), 639.

54. *SO*, 873, 873–74, 875.

55. Ibid., 324.

4. Navigating Sexual Revolution (1966–1981)

1. See Edwin M. Schur and Hugo Adam Bedau, *Victimless Crimes: Two Sides of a Controversy* (Englewood Cliffs, NJ: Prentice-Hall, 1974); and John Dombrink, "Victimless Crimes and the 'Culture Wars' of the 1990s," *Journal of Contemporary Criminal Justice* 9 (March 1993): 30–40.

2. John Barbour, "New Kinsey Report Detects Conservative Sex Trend," *Los Angeles Times*, June 18, 1978, 2.

3. Alton Blakeslee, "Sexual Revolution Disproved," *Herald Journal*, December 29, 1967; Barbour, "New Kinsey Report Detects Conservative Sex Trend," 2; William Simon, quoted in John Leo, "Sex 'Revolution' Called a Myth: 1,200 Students Interviewed in Study by Kinsey Institute," *New York Times*, December 15, 1968.

4. Quoted in Bill Pittman, "I.U. Sex Institute Still Alive," *Indianapolis News*, September 16, 1976.

5. In *The Sexual Scene*, Simon and Gagnon argued that even though "in the last half century sex has moved from the dim background of American life to occupy nearly the entire center stage," there was little or no "revolutionary change" in anyone's behaviors. Even among the more "radical" segments of the population, there was little that could be considered new: the hippies' "postures" on sexuality were little different from those of their bohemian counterparts of the 1920s, and "one senses that there is more talk about wife-swapping," for example, "than there is wife-swapping, and that the rates of participation are extremely marginal." See William Simon and John Gagnon, eds., *The Sexual Scene* (Piscataway, NJ: Transaction Publishers, 1970), 1, 10.

6. Ibid., 3–4.

7. See Steven Marcus, *The Other Victorians: A Study of Sexuality and Pornography in Mid-Nineteenth-Century England* (New York: Basic Books, 1966).

8. Dr. Eugene Eoyang quoted in the *Herald Telephone*, December 22, 1980, A12; PHG, "Memo to Trustees and Advisory Board," November 18, 1974, 2, Paul Henry Gebhard Directorship, 1957–81 (PHGD), I: Correspondence, Advisory Board, Kinsey Institute Library and Special Collections (KILSC).

9. Alton Blakeslee, "Many Follow in Kinsey's Inquiring Footsteps," *Arizona Republic*, January 23, 1968, Alfred Charles Kinsey Directorship, 1947–56 (ACKD), VI: Newsclippings, e. Institute for Sex Research, KILSC.

10. Paul Henry Gebhard (PHG) to Alan P. Bell (APB), June 12, 1967, PHGD, I: Correspondence, KILSC.

11. John H. Gagnon (JHG) to APB, June 6, 1966, PHGD, I: Correspondence, KILSC.

12. JHG to APB, July 25, 1966, PHGD, I: Correspondence, KILSC.

13. APB to PHG, June 14, 1967, 3–4, PHGD, I: Correspondence, KILSC.

14. This began with the publication of Alfred C. Kinsey, Wardell B. Pomeroy, and Clyde E. Martin, *Sexual Behavior in the Human Male* (SBHM) (Philadelphia: W. B. Saunders, 1948), and Alfred C. Kinsey, Wardell B. Pomeroy, Clyde E. Martin, and Paul H. Gebhard, *Sexual Behavior in the Human Female* (SBHF) (Philadelphia: W. B. Saunders, 1953), highlighting the gap between prescriptions and behavioral realities. For Hefner, Puritanism was "as stultifying to the mind as communism" and was, by definition, antidemocratic and anti-American. The Puritan repression of sex mattered beyond the individual: sexuality was a "major civilizing influence on our world," implicating sexual freedom in the progress of the nation. See Hugh Hefner, "The Playboy Philosophy, Part 2," *Playboy* 10, no. 1 (January 1963); "Part 3," 10, no. 2 (February 1963); "Part 8," 10, no. 7 (July 1963); "Part 13," 10, no. 12 (December 1963).

15. See Helen Gurley Brown, *Sex and the Single Girl: An Unmarried Woman's Guide to Men* (New York: Pocket Books, 1962), 60, 223, 215. See also Julie K. Berebitsky, "The Joy of Work: Helen Gurley Brown, Gender, and Sexuality in the White-Collar Office," *Journal of the History of Sexuality* 15, no. 1 (January 2006): 89–127. Significantly, however, the Single Girl who could not learn to be sexy was probably neurotic in some way or another. If her relationship troubles were significant enough, or if she still could not enjoy sex when she wanted to, or if she was involved "with one heel after another," Brown urged her to visit "The Big Couch."

16. See Alan P. Bell and Martin S. Weinberg, *Homosexualities: A Study of Diversity among Men and Women* (New York: Simon and Schuster, 1978), 226–27.

17. William H. Masters and Virginia E. Johnson, *Human Sexual Response* (New York: Ishi Press International, 1966), v, vi; and Masters and Johnson, *Human Sexual Inadequacy* (New York: Ishi Press International, 1970), 1.

18. Similar discourses informed Mary Steichen Calderone's 1960s endeavors. Critical of Planned Parenthood's neglect of the sexual etiology of undesired pregnancy, in 1968 she founded the Sex Information and Education Council of the United States (SIECUS) "to establish man's sexuality as a health entity" with a focus on characteristics distinguishing it from, yet relating it to, human reproduction. See Mary Steichen Calderone, "Man's Sexuality as a Health Entity," *Osteopathic Physician*, May 1970, 1, Papers of Mary Steichen Calderone, 1904–71, MSS 179/279, Arthur and Elizabeth Schlesinger Library on the History of Women in America, Radcliffe Institute for Advanced Study, Harvard University, Cambridge, MA (SL).

19. See Paul A. Robinson, *The Modernization of Sex: Havelock Ellis, Alfred Kinsey, William Masters and Virginia Johnson* (Ithaca, NY: Cornell University Press, 1989), 160–65.

20. See, for instance, Erik H. Erikson, *Identity: Youth and Crisis* (New York: W. W. Norton, 1968); Abraham H. Maslow, *Toward a Psychology of Being* (Princeton, NJ: D. Van Nostrand Company, 1962).

21. William Simon (WS) and JHG, "Youth Cultures and Aspects of the Socialization Process. A Grant Proposal Submitted to the National Institute of Mental Health and the National Institute of Child Health and Human Development," 1, PHGD, II: Projects and Grants, g. Youth Cultures and Aspects of the Socialization Process, KILSC.

22. David J. Callen to JHG, September 15, 1965, PHGD, I: Correspondence, KILSC.

23. WS and JHG, "Youth Cultures," 13–16.

24. Jane Brody, "More Coeds Find Less Guilt in Sex," *New York Times*, December 30, 1967.

25. WS and JHG, "Youth Cultures," 1. The NICHHD, which funded the Youth Study, was established by President Kennedy as part of a broad effort to understand and treat problems related to "mental retardation." Kennedy prioritized intellectual disabilities, specifically tasking the PHS with supporting projects on clinical treatments for those with intellectual disabilities and psychological development problems.

26. PHG, "Gebhard Era History, 1956–1982," 5, PHGD, IX: Paul H. Gebhard Papers, KILSC.

27. PHG to AJB, January 12, 1967, 1, PHGD, I: Correspondence, KILSC.

28. PHG to Dr. J. George Harrar, July 1, 1968, PHGD, I: Correspondence, KILSC.

29. Joseph L. Sutton to PHG, "Reorganization," February 9, 1967, PHGD, I: Correspondence, KILSC.

30. AJB to PHG, January 14, 1967, PHGD, I: Correspondence, KILSC; and PHG, "Gebhard Era History," 5–6.

31. PHG, "Gebhard Era History," 6.

32. PHG to Cliff Travis, October 5, 1970, PHGD, I: Correspondence, KILSC.

33. PHG, "Gebhard Era History," 8.

34. The Mattachine Society included supporting research into homosexuality as part of its mission statement and manifesto. The *Mattachine Review*, *One*, *One Quarterly*, and the *Ladder* all contained articles on the homophile movement's relationship with sex research. For historians' treatment of the ways that homosexuality was newly visible in the United States, see John D'Emilio, *Sexual Politics, Sexual Communities: The Making of a Homosexual Minority in the United States, 1940–1970* (Chicago: University of Chicago Press, 1983); John D'Emilio and Estelle Freedman, *Intimate Matters: A History of Sexuality in America* (New York: Harper and Row, 1988); Roy Cain, "Disclosure and Secrecy among Gay Men in the United States and Canada: A Shift in Views," *Journal of the History of Sexuality* 2, no. 1 (1991): 25–45; Vern L. Bullough, *Science in the Bedroom: A History of Sex Research* (New York: Basic Books, 1994); Robert O. Self, *All in the Family: The Realignment of American Democracy since the 1960s* (New York: Hill and Wang, 2012).

35. Henry L. Minton, *Departing from Deviance: A History of Homosexual Rights and Emancipatory Science in America* (Chicago: University of Chicago Press, 2002), 236.

36. Ibid., 236–37; Evelyn Hooker et al., *National Institute of Mental Health Task Force on Homosexuality: Final Report and Background Papers* (Washington, DC: Government Printing Office, 1972).

37. JHG to APB, April 28, 1966, PHGD, I: Correspondence, KILSC.

38. See Colin J. Williams and Martin S. Weinberg, *Homosexuals and the Military: A Study of Less than Honorable Discharge* (New York: Harper and Row, 1971); Williams and Weinberg, "Being Discovered: A Study of Homosexuals in the Military," *Social Problems* 18, no. 2 (1970): 409–23; and Williams and Weinberg, "The Military: Its Processing of Accused Homosexuals," *American Behavioral Scientist* 14, no. 2 (1970): 203–17.

39. PHG, "Patterns of Adjustment in Deviant Populations," application for research grant, October 1, 1965, 3–4, "Homosexual Proposal," and "Chicago Deviance," PHGD, II: Projects and Grants, e. Patterns of Adjustment in Deviant Populations, KILSC.

40. Ibid., 4.

41. Ibid., 9.

42. Ibid., 5, 6.

43. APB to PHG, January 14, 1967.

44. APB, untitled memo, August 1966, and APB to PHG, May 5, 1967, PHGD, I: Correspondence, KILSC.

45. APB to JHG, November 20, 1966, PHGD, I: Correspondence, KILSC.

46. "A Study of Deviant Socialization," research plan, undated, ca. 1967, 4, and "S.F. Study Proposal," PHGD, II: Projects and Grants, f. A Study of Deviant Socialization, KILSC. The Rotterdam Incomplete Sentences blank consisted of short, usually two-word, prompts and blanks, which the subject would fill in to make a complete sentence. It was a short test, averaging twenty minutes, so that it could be given in conjunction with the Institute's questionnaire. It shows variations in satisfaction in life, depression, and personality adjustment.

47. "A Study of Deviant Socialization," grant proposal draft, ca. 1968, PHGD, II: Projects and Grants, f. "A Study of Deviant Socialization," KILSC.

48. Alan P. Bell and Martin S. Weinberg, *Homosexualities: A Study of Diversity among Men and Women* (New York: Simon and Schuster, 1978), 51–52.

49. Ibid., 217–31.

50. Ibid., 22–23.

51. "Research Plan," undated draft proposal, "Attitude Study. Grant Materials," PHGD, II: Projects and Grants, h. "Attitudes towards Selected Forms of Deviant Behavior (1967–70)," KILSC.

52. Albert D. Klassen, "Attitudes towards Selected Forms of Deviant Behavior and Classification and Etiologies of Homosexuality," grant proposal adapted for internal circulation, October 1968, 13, PHGD, II: Projects and Grants, h. "Attitudes towards Selected Forms of Deviant Behavior (1967–70)," KILSC.

53. Ibid., 19.

54. Ibid., 17.

55. Hubert J. O'Gorman, introduction to *Sex and Morality in the U.S.*, by Albert D. Klassen, Colin J. Williams, and Eugene E. Levitt (Middletown, CT: Wesleyan University Press, 1989), xxiv.

56. Colin J. Williams, Eugene Levitt, and Albert Klassen, "American Sexual Standards," 1981, 3, PHGD, IV: Drafts, "Attitudes towards Selected Forms of Deviant Behavior (1967–70)," KILSC. After yet more delays due to a legal dispute between the Institute and Levitt and Klassen, this book was finally published as *Sex and Morality in the U.S.* (Middletown, CT: Wesleyan University Press, 1989), 217–19.

57. Williams, Levitt, and Klassen, "American Sexual Standards," 22–23.

58. Ibid., 12.

59. Ibid., 13.

60. Bell and Weinberg, *Homosexualities*, 53–61, 286–94.

61. Alan P. Bell, Martin S. Weinberg, and Sue Kiefer Hammersmith, *Sexual Preference: Its Development in Men and Women* (Bloomington: Indiana University Press, 1981), xii.

62. Wardell B. Pomeroy, *Dr. Kinsey and the Institute for Sex Research* (New York: Harper & Row, 1972), 455.

63. PHG to Dean Paul E. Klinge, March 10, 1970, PHGD, I: Correspondence, b. Indiana University Interdepartmental Correspondence, KILSC.

64. Levitt eventually produced a manuscript for the comic book study, "The Origins and Early Life of the Erotic Comic Book: America's Native Pornography," but it was rejected for publication. By that time, Levitt had agreed to remove PHG as an author and dissociate the work from the Institute.

65. PHG, "Copy of Memorandum Sent to Dean Joseph Sutton" for the advisory board, July 19, 1966, PHGD, I: Correspondence, Advisory Board, KILSC.

66. PHG to Cliff Travis, University Counsel, June 6, 1968, PHGD, I: Correspondence, Indiana University Interdepartmental Correspondence, KILSC.

67. David Smothers, "Sexual Permissiveness Thrives—25 Years after Kinsey," *Washington Post*, February 1, 1973, F3.

68. PHG, "Memo Regarding Intra-Institute Communication," undated, PHGD, I: Correspondence, ISR, KILSC.

69. PHG, annual report, 1971, 3, PHGD, VII: Operations Records, b. Reports, KILSC.

70. For an analysis of the exclusion of erotic materials from library catalogs in the 1970s, see Ruth Beasley, "Another Look at OCLC's Potential for Special Libraries," *Journal of the American Society for Information Services* 31 (July 1980): 300–301; for a broader treatment of erotic materials in libraries, see Albert Klassen, "Connoisseur and Gatekeeper of the Erotic in Print: The Public Librarian," *Focus on Indiana Libraries* 28, no. 1 (1974): 6–11; for a full analysis of the classification systems at the Kinsey Institute Library and Collections, see Liana Zhou, "Characteristics of Material Organization and Classification in the Kinsey Institute Library," *Cataloging and Classification Quarterly* 35, no. 3–4 (2003): 335–53.

71. Zhou, "Characteristics of Material Organization," 343.

72. Ibid., 345.

73. Mary Dogin, "Sex Research Has Mushroomed: IU Catalog Reflects Change," *Daily Herald* (Bloomington, IN), April 24, 1975.

74. PHG to Dean Homer Neal, February 22, 1978, 1, PHGD, I: Correspondence, KILSC.

75. Ruth Beasley and PHG, "Final Report: Training Seminar—Health Professionals Submitted to Experimental and Special Projects Branch Division of Manpower and Training," NIMH, September 20, 1978, KILSC.

76. *Herald Telephone*, December 22, 1980, A12.

77. PHG, "Letter to the Editor," typescript draft, n.d., PHGD, IX: Paul H. Gebhard Papers, Institute Correspondence and Documents—Other, KILSC.

78. PHG to ISR Trustees, "The State of the Institute," October 16, 1974, 2, PHGD, I: Correspondence, KILSC.

79. PHG, "Memo to Trustees and Advisory Board," November 18, 1974, 2.

80. PHG to ISR Trustees, "State of the Institute," October 16, 1974, 4.

81. See Bell and Weinberg, *Homosexualities*; Bell, Weinberg, and Hammersmith, *Sexual Preference*; and Albert D. Klassen, Colin J. Williams, and Eugene E. Levitt, *Sex and Morality in the U.S.: An Empirical Inquiry under the Auspices of the Kinsey Institute* (Middletown, CT: Wesleyan University Press, 1989).

82. PHG to ISR Trustees, "State of the Institute," October 16, 1974, 6.

83. Ibid., 7.

84. PHG, "Financial Report to Trustees, May 7, 1976," 4, PHGD, VII: Operations Records, b. Reports, KILSC.

85. PHG, "Memo to Trustees and Advisory Board," November 18, 1974, 2–3; and "AR, 1975—Addendum," 7, PHGD, VII: Operations Records, b. Reports, KILSC.

86. Kevin Scionti, "Funds Drop: Kinsey Institute Must Limit Services," *Indiana Daily Student*, November 11, 1977.

87. Sheldon Stryker et al., "Report of the Review Committee, Institute for Sex Research," February 26, 1980, 1, PHGD, VII: Operations Records, g. External Reviews, KILSC.

88. Ibid., 5.

89. PHG to Sesquicentennial Committee, March 10, 1971, PHGD, I: Correspondence, Indiana University N–Z, KILSC.

90. Ibid., 5.

91. Ibid., 1–2; John Money and Anke A. Ehrhardt, "Report on the Institute for Sex Research, Indiana University," January 10–11, 1980, 14, PHGD, VII: Operations Records, g. External Reviews, KILSC.

92. Stryker et al., "Report of the Review Committee," 5.

93. Money and Ehrhardt, "Report," 12–13.

94. Ibid., 3.

95. Ibid., 1.

96. Ibid., 5.

97. Ibid., 1, 16.

98. Ibid., 3, 9, 10.

99. John Money would later donate his records, now the John Money Collection, to the Kinsey Institute. Evidently, changes in the status of the library and archives after Gebhard's tenure were enough to convince Money of the relative safety of his records. See the John Money Collection, 204 boxes, John Bancroft Directorship, 1995–2003 (JBD), VIII: Manuscripts and Collections, KILSC.

100. PHG, "Director's Report for I.U.B. Research Review," January 1980, 8, PHGD, VII: Operations Records, g. External Reviews, KILSC. Indeed, the problem continues down to the present, the most serious leaking yet resulting from a broken water pipe in the roof that flooded the archival area of the Institute in June 2016 (damage still under assessment). Once again, the collections were closed to researchers, a situation still prevailing in the approach to the Institute's seventieth anniversary.

101. Stryker et al., "Report of the Review Committee," 10–11.

102. Money and Ehrhardt, "Report," 12.

103. Ibid., 13.

104. PHG, "Gebhard Response to Institute for Sex Research Review Committees," 1980, 1, PHGD, VII: Operations Records, g. External Reviews, KILSC.

105. Ibid., 1, 2.

106. Ibid., 1, 4.

107. Ibid., 2–3.

108. Ibid., 1–2.

109. PHG, "Kinsey Institute for Sex Research, Brief Annual Report for 1981," 1, PHGD, VII: Operations Records, b. Annual Reports, KILSC.

110. PHG, "Gebhard Era History," 13.

111. PHG, "Gebhard Response," 1.

5. Initiating Paradigm Shifts (1982–1993)

1. John Money and Anke A. Ehrhardt, "Report on the Institute for Sex Research, Indiana University," January 10–11, 1980, 11–13, Paul Henry Gebhard Directorship, 1957–81 (PHGD), VII: Operations Records, g. External Reviews, Kinsey Institute Library and Special Collections (KILSC).

2. On Anita Bryant, see, for example, "Anita Bryant Scores White House Talk with Homosexuals," *New York Times*, March 28, 1977; B. Drummond Ayres, "Miami Debate over Rights of Homosexuals Directs Wide Attention to a National Issue," *New York Times*, May 10, 1977.

3. See Paul Henry Gebhard (PHG) to Vice Chancellor Kenneth Gros Louis, August 27, 1987, Kenneth Gros Louis to PHG, August 31, 1987, PHG to June Machover Reinisch, September 13, 1988, and JMR to PHG, December 12, 1990, all in PHGD, IX: Paul H. Gebhard Papers, addendum I, KILSC.

4. See appendix B, "Selected Scholarly Works, Kinsey Institute Library and Special Collections."

5. See Ruth Beasley, "Current Status of Sex Research," *Journal of Sex Research* 11, no. 4 (November 1975): 336.

6. June Machover Reinisch (JMR), annual report, 1981, Kinsey Institute for Research in Sex, Gender, and Reproduction, 4, June Machover Reinisch Directorship, 1982–93 (JMRD), VII: Operations Records, b. Annual Reports, KILSC. Hereafter cited as JMR, annual report, plus the year date.

7. See Giovanna Breu, "As Did Kinsey, June Reinisch Takes the Plain Brown Wrapper Off the Study of Sex," *People Magazine* 22 (December 1984): 173–76. Reinisch brought diverse other professional experiences to the job, including training dolphins, skydiving, becoming a licensed pilot, singing with a rock group called the Seagulls, and working in the music recording industry as promotions director of Sly and the Family Stone for a year.

8. Money and Ehrhardt, "Report," 5. This international board of distinguished scientists, expert in the areas of sex, gender, and reproduction, advised the Institute on

research, conferences, collections, and information dissemination. Its members were Anke A. Ehrhardt and John Money, leaders in the field of sex and gender research who served as external reviewers of the Institute in 1980; John Bancroft, who became the next Institute director; Frank A. Beach, coauthor with Clellan S. Ford of the famous book *Patterns of Sexual Behavior* (1951) and a founder of behavioral endocrinology; John H. Gagnon, who after starting his career at the Institute was widely known for the concept of sexual scripts, privileging social over biological or psychological understandings of sexual behavior; David P. McWhirter, a psychiatrist and academic coauthor with his partner, Drew Mattison, of *The Male Couple* (1980); Leonard A. Rosenblum, noted primatologist and professor of psychiatry; and Robert T. Rubin, psychiatrist, neuroscientist, and editor of *Psychoneuro-endocrinology* (1982–91), who also served on the Institute's board of trustees.

9. Anke Ehrhardt specializes in the sexual and gender development of children, adolescents, and adults, serving as founding director of the HIV Center for Clinical and Behavioral Studies at the New York State Psychiatric Institute and Columbia University. John Money, director of the Psychohormonal Unit at Johns Hopkins Hospital, was a founder of sexual and gender identity studies, coining the terms "gender identity" and "gender role." On John H. Gagnon, see, for example, William Rimes, "John Gagnon, Who Linked Sexuality to Social Influences, Dies at 84," *New York Times*, April 11, 2016, A26. On Robert Rubin, see, for example, https://www.semel.ucla.edu/profile/robert-rubin.

10. JMR, annual report, 1984, 1.

11. For a more complete description of the United States/Denmark Prenatal Development Project, see June M. Reinisch, Erik L. Mortensen, and Stephanie A. Sanders, "The Prenatal Development Project," *Acta Psychiatrica Scandinavica*, Supplement 370 (1993): 54–61, Munksgaard, Copenhagen, Denmark.

12. June M. Reinisch and Stephanie A. Sanders, "Early Barbiturate Exposure: The Brain, Sexually Dimorphic Behavior, and Learning," *Neuroscience and Biobehavioral Reviews* 6 (1982): 311–19; Reinisch and Sanders, "Hormonal Influences on Sexual Development and Behavior," in *Sex and Gender—a Theological and Scientific Inquiry*, ed. M. F. Schwartz, A. S. Moraczewski, and J. A. Monteleone (St. Louis, MO: Pope John XXIII Medical-Moral Research and Education Center, 1983), 48–64; Reinisch and Sanders, "Prenatal Gonadal Steroidal Influences on Gender-Related Behavior," in *Progress in Brain Research*, vol. 61, ed. G. J. de Vries, J. P. C. DeBruin, H. B. M. Vylings, and M. A. Corner (Amsterdam: Elsevier, Science Publishers B.V., 1984), 407–15; Reinisch and Sanders, "Behavioral Influences of Prenatal Hormones," in *Handbook of Clinical Psychoneu-roendocrinology*, ed. C. B. Nemeroff and P. T. Loosen (New York: Guilford Press, 1987), 431–48; and Reinisch and Sanders, "Effects of Prenatal Exposure to Diethylstilbestrol (DES) on Hemispheric Laterality and Spatial Ability in Human Males," *Hormones and Behavior* 26, no. 1 (1992): 62–65. See also Stephanie A. Sanders and June M. Reinisch, "Behavioral Effects on Humans of Progesterone-Related Compounds during Development and in the Adult," *Current Topics of Neuroendocrinology*, vol. 5, ed. D. Ganten and D. Pfaff (Heidelberg: Springer-Verlag, 1985), 175–205; and Sanders and Reinisch, "Biological and Social Influences on the Endocrinology of Puberty: Some Additional Considerations," in *Adolescence and Puberty*, ed. John Bancroft and June M. Reinisch (New York: Oxford University Press, 1990), 50–62. And see June M. Reinisch, Mary Ziemba-Davis, and Stephanie A. Sanders, "Hormonal Contributions to Sexually Dimorphic Behavioral Development in Humans," *Psychoneuroendocrinology* 16, no. 1–3 (1991): 213–78.

13. Heather Boonstra, "Teen Pregnancy: Trends and Lessons Learned," *The Guttmacher Report on Public Policy*, February 2002, https://www.guttmacher.org/sites/default/files/pdfs/pubs/tgr/05/1/gr050107.pdf.

14. James Trussell, "Teenage Pregnancy in the United States," *Family Planning Perspectives* 20 (November–December 1988): 262–72.

15. JMR, annual report, 1985, app. F, 7. According to the 1986 annual report, Dr. Woodrow Meyer, Indiana state health commissioner, identified teen pregnancy and AIDS as two priority areas for Institute programs and research. Due to limited resources, attention shifted from teen pregnancy to AIDS.

16. In addition to this series, the Institute fostered interdisciplinary collaborative research projects through workshops and summer institutes for human sexuality professionals. A fifth Kinsey Institute Symposium in December 1988, "Sexuality and Disease: Metaphors, Perceptions, and Behavior in the AIDS Era," cochaired by John E. Boswell, Ralph Hexter, and June Reinisch, was never published due to the illness and untimely death of Boswell in 1994 from AIDS complications. See David W. Dunlap, "John E. Boswell, 47, Historian of Medieval Gay Culture, Dies," *New York Times*, December 25, 1994.

17. June Machover Reinisch, Leonard A. Rosenblum, and Stephanie A. Sanders, *Masculinity/Femininity: Basic Perspectives* (New York: Oxford University Press, 1987).

18. David P. McWhirter, Stephanie A. Sanders, and June Machover Reinisch, *Homosexuality/Heterosexuality: Concepts of Sexual Orientation* (New York: Oxford University Press, 1990); and Bancroft and Reinisch, *Adolescence and Puberty*.

19. On the HIV/AIDS crisis of the 1980s, see, for example, John D'Emilio and Estelle B. Freedman, *Intimate Matters: A History of Sexuality in America*, 3rd ed. (Chicago: University of Chicago Press, 2012); Victoria A. Harden, *AIDS at 30: A History* (Lincoln, NE: Potomac Books, Inc., 2012); Craig Timberg and Daniel Halperin, *Tinderbox: How the West Sparked the AIDS Epidemic and How the World Can Finally Overcome It* (New York: Penguin Books, 2012).

20. On ACT-UP, see, for example, D'Emilio and Freedman, *Intimate Matters*; Josh Gamson, "Silence, Death, and the Invisible Enemy: AIDS Activism and Social Movement 'Newness,'" *Social Problems* 36 (October 1989): 351–67; Peter F. Cohen, "'All They Needed': AIDS, Consumption, and the Politics of Class," *Journal of the History of Sexuality* 8 (July 1997): 86–115.

21. Centers for Disease Control, *Understanding AIDS*, US Department of Health and Human Services (Washington, DC: US Government Printing Office, 1988).

22. JMR, annual report, 1987, 3–4.

23. Bruce Voeller, June Machover Reinisch, and Michael Gottlieb, eds., *AIDS and Sex: An Integrated Biomedical and Biobehavioral Approach* (New York: Oxford University Press, 1990); Maria Eugenia Lemos Fernandes to June Reinisch, January 13, 1987, appended to JMR, annual report, 1988.

24. JMR, annual report, 1988, 56. Reinisch participated in "The AIDS Connection: An All-Night Dialogue," a five-hour live television program that generated more than sixty-five thousand calls, many seeking accurate AIDS information. As well, she served on the AIDS Policy Subcommittee of the National Advisory Mental Health Council (NIMH), the National Institute of Mental Health Acquired Immunodeficiency Syndrome Research Review Committee, the Mariposa Education and Research Foundation Institutional Review Board, and the Society for the Scientific Study of Sex AIDS Task Force. Meanwhile, Stephanie Sanders represented the Institute at the Midwestern AIDS Training and Education Center at Indiana University Medical School. A number of publications and policy recommendations followed "AIDS and Sex: An Integrated Biomedical and Biobehavioral Approach," a policy paper on sex research in the AIDS era for *American Psychologist*, and later the edited volume *The Evolution of Psychology: Fifty Years of the "American Psychologist."* See also June Machover Reinisch, Stephanie A. Sanders, and Mary

Ziemba-Davis, "The Study of Sexual Behavior in Relation to the Transmission of Human Immunodeficiency Virus: Caveats and Recommendations," in *The Evolution of Psychology: Fifty Years of the "American Psychologist,"* ed. Joseph M. Notterman (Washington, DC: American Psychological Association, 1997), 677–92, reprinted from *American Psychologist* 43, no. 11 (1988): 921–27.

25. Money and Ehrhardt, "Report," 10.

26. Douglas Freeman, collections annual report, 1984, 2, JMRD, VII: Operations Records, b. Annual Reports, KILSC.

27. Sheldon Stryker et al., "Report of the Review Committee, Institute for Sex Research," February 26, 1980, 10, PHGD, VII: Operations Records, g. External Reviews, KILSC.

28. Erwin J. Haeberle, for example, from the Institute for Advanced Study of Human Sexuality, created one of the first historical works on the history of the field of sexology that focused primarily on the late nineteenth and early twentieth centuries. Others such as Paul Jamison, a professor of anthropology at Indiana University, produced studies of penis length, while James H. Jones, who would later write a biography of Kinsey, used the collections for his dissertation and later published the work while he was a member of the history department at the University of Houston. See Erwin J. Haeberle, *The Birth of Sexology: A Brief History of Documents* (New York: United States Consortium for Sexology, 1983); and James H. Jones, "An Investigation of the History of the Institute and of Dr. Kinsey" (Ph.D. diss., Indiana University, 1972).

29. On the history of the removal of homosexuality from the *DSM*, see, for example, Ronald Bayer, *Homosexuality and American Psychiatry: The Politics of Diagnosis* (Princeton, NJ: Princeton University Press, 1987).

30. Examples of research associates from 1982 to 1985 include Erwin J. Haeberle, Institute for Advanced Study of Human Sexuality, San Francisco; Frederick Bunce, chair, Art Department, Indiana State University, Terre Haute; and James H. Jones, associate professor of history, University of Houston. See JMR, annual report, 1984, 11–13. Examples of research associates from 1985 include Jan Trost, professor of sociology at Uppsala University, Sweden; Helmuth Nyborg, professor at the Institute of Psychology and Cytogenetic Laboratory, University of Aarhus, Denmark; and Friedemann Pfafflin, assistant professor in the Department of Sex Research at the University of Hamburg, West Germany. See JMR, annual report, 1985, 18.

31. Works coming from the researchers involved in this program include Haeberle, *The Birth of Sexology*; and James H. Jones, *Alfred C. Kinsey: A Life* (New York: W. W. Norton & Company, 2004). Jones continued to work on the history of the Institute and biography of Kinsey well after he completed his doctorate at Indiana University.

32. Douglas Freeman, "Cataloging, Inventory, and Analysis of Resources," National Endowment for the Humanities, GM-22353–85, total direct costs (1985–86), $17,479.

33. See, for example, Bill Shaw, "Dr. Ruth's Got Nothing on Her," *Indianapolis Magazine*, December 1985, 87–92; Jo Durden-Smith and Dian De Simone, "Kinsey's June Reinisch and the Science of Sexual Identity," *Cosmopolitan*, February 1985, 122–29; Associated Press, "New Director Works, Writes to Restore Reputation of IU Sex Research Institute," *Post-Tribune*, January 20, 1985, E6; Lisa Hooker, "Reinisch Gives Inside Look at Kinsey Institute on Sex," *Herald-Telephone*, April 11, 1985, 4; Elizabeth Hall, "New Directions for the Kinsey Institute," *Psychology Today*, June 1986, 32–39; Nanci Hellmich, "Sexual Revolution Misses the Masses," *USA Today*, June 26, 1986, 5D; Beverly Beyette, "Former Rutgers Teacher Leads Kinsey into the '80s," *Courier-News*, May 29, 1986, B1–B2; Beverly Beyette, "Kinsey Institute's Reinisch Wants to Renew, Expand Sexual Studies," *Los Angeles Times*, May 18, 1986, 11–13.

34. JMR, annual report, 1984, 23.

35. JMR, annual reports, 1987, 72–75, 1988, 39–42, and 1989, 21–22.

36. JMR, annual report, 1990–92, 53.

37. On the Institute/Roper project, see, for example, Stephanie A. Sanders et al., "A Rejoinder: Intent and Purpose of the Kinsey Institute/Roper Organization National Sex Knowledge Survey," *Public Opinion Quarterly* 55, no. 3 (1991): 458–62.

38. June M. Reinisch and Ruth Beasley, *The Kinsey Institute New Report on Sex: What You Must Know to Be Sexually Literate (KINROS)* (New York: St. Martin's Press, 1990), 1–26.

39. On political stances of the Institute, see ibid., vii.

40. On the impact of HIV/AIDS and sexual knowledge, see, for example, ibid., vii, 1, 10–11, 463, and the chapters "The Sexual Adult," 76–99, "Sex with a Partner," 100–170, "Unfinished Development and Sexual Mismatches," 288–302, and "Sexually Transmitted Diseases," 463–510.

41. JMR, annual report, 1990–92, 4, 19–20.

42. Paul H. Gebhard to Ken Gros Louis, August 26, 1987, PHGD, IX: Paul H. Gebhard Papers, KILSC.

43. Edward J. Yee, "Management of Institute Questioned," *Indiana Daily Student*, October 10, 1988, 1; Daniel Golden, "Under the Covers at the Kinsey Institute: Controversy Steams Up America's Most Famous Sex-Research Center," *Boston Globe Magazine*, December 16, 1990, 37–38.

44. See, for example, Mary Ziemba-Davis, Scott Carroll, Thomas Albright, Sandra Stewart Ham, Craig Hill, Carolyn Kaufman, Elizabeth Roberge, Stephanie A Sanders, Kim Sare, Terry Sare, J. Susan Straub, Stacey Trainer, and Jana Wilson, "IU Institute Associates Dispute Claims of Letter Writer," *Indiana Daily Student*, November 2, 1988. And see *IDS* Editorial Board, "Following the Rules: Reinisch Should Be Given Review Letters," *Indiana Daily Student*, April 2, 1992. Later accounts offered more opinion, for instance, "Director of Kinsey Institute Is Urged to Resign," *New York Times*, December 24, 1988, sec. U.S., http://www.nytimes.com/1988/12/24/us/director-of-kinsey-institute-is-urged-to -resign.html; "Stalemate over Kinsey Institute's Director," *New York Times*, January 24, 1989, sec. Science, http://www.nytimes.com/1989/01/24/science/stalemate-over-kinsey -institute-s-director.html. For a retrospective perspective on these conflicts, see Claudia Dreifus, "Sitting in the Ultimate Hot Seat: The Kinsey Institute," *New York Times*, May 25, 1999, http://www.nytimes.com/1999/05/25/science/conversation-with-john-bancroft -sitting-ultimate-hot-seat-kinsey-institute.html.

45. See, for example, Golden, "Under the Covers"; Jo Ellen Meyers Sharp, "Kinsey Institute Falling behind Times in Study of Sexuality, Critics Say," *Indianapolis Star*, November 6, 1988; Sharp, "Kinsey Institute Chief Determined to Fight Accusations," *Indianapolis Star*, March 19, 1989; Yee, "Management of Institute Questioned," 1; JMR, annual report, 1988, app. O.

46. JMR, annual report, 1990–92, 5–6.

47. See Judith A. Reisman and Edward W. Eichel, *Kinsey, Sex, and Fraud: The Indoctrination of a People* (Lafayette, LA: Vital Issues Press, 1990). More information can be found at http://www.kinseyinstitute.org/about/controversy.html and in an article by Bancroft, "Alfred C. Kinsey & the Politics of Sex Research," *Annual Review of Sex Research* 15 (2004): 1–39.

48. A copy of the September 24, 1988, article in the *New York Post* can be found in JMR, annual report, 1988, app. G, 243.

49. Her other books include *Kinsey: Crimes and Consequences: The Red Queen and the Grand Scheme* (Crestwood, KY: Institute for Media Education, 1998); *Kinsey's Attic:*

Notes to Pages 147–152 · 211

34. JMR, annual report, 1984, 23.

35. JMR, annual reports, 1987, 72–75, 1988, 39–42, and 1989, 21–22.

36. JMR, annual report, 1990–92, 53.

37. On the Institute/Roper project, see, for example, Stephanie A. Sanders et al., "A Rejoinder: Intent and Purpose of the Kinsey Institute/Roper Organization National Sex Knowledge Survey," *Public Opinion Quarterly* 55, no. 3 (1991): 458–62.

38. June M. Reinisch and Ruth Beasley, *The Kinsey Institute New Report on Sex: What You Must Know to Be Sexually Literate (KINROS)* (New York: St. Martin's Press, 1990), 1–26.

39. On political stances of the Institute, see ibid., vii.

40. On the impact of HIV/AIDS and sexual knowledge, see, for example, ibid., vii, 1, 10–11, 463, and the chapters "The Sexual Adult," 76–99, "Sex with a Partner," 100–170, "Unfinished Development and Sexual Mismatches," 288–302, and "Sexually Transmitted Diseases," 463–510.

41. JMR, annual report, 1990–92, 4, 19–20.

42. Paul H. Gebhard to Ken Gros Louis, August 26, 1987, PHGD, IX: Paul H. Gebhard Papers, KILSC.

43. Edward J. Yee, "Management of Institute Questioned," *Indiana Daily Student*, October 10, 1988, 1; Daniel Golden, "Under the Covers at the Kinsey Institute: Controversy Steams Up America's Most Famous Sex-Research Center," *Boston Globe Magazine*, December 16, 1990, 37–38.

44. See, for example, Mary Ziemba-Davis, Scott Carroll, Thomas Albright, Sandra Stewart Ham, Craig Hill, Carolyn Kaufman, Elizabeth Roberge, Stephanie A Sanders, Kim Sare, Terry Sare, J. Susan Straub, Stacey Trainer, and Jana Wilson, "IU Institute Associates Dispute Claims of Letter Writer," *Indiana Daily Student*, November 2, 1988. And see *IDS* Editorial Board, "Following the Rules: Reinisch Should Be Given Review Letters," *Indiana Daily Student*, April 2, 1992. Later accounts offered more opinion, for instance, "Director of Kinsey Institute Is Urged to Resign," *New York Times*, December 24, 1988, sec. U.S., http://www.nytimes.com/1988/12/24/us/director-of-kinsey-institute-is-urged-to -resign.html; "Stalemate over Kinsey Institute's Director," *New York Times*, January 24, 1989, sec. Science, http://www.nytimes.com/1989/01/24/science/stalemate-over-kinsey -institute-s-director.html. For a retrospective perspective on these conflicts, see Claudia Dreifus, "Sitting in the Ultimate Hot Seat: The Kinsey Institute," *New York Times*, May 25, 1999, http://www.nytimes.com/1999/05/25/science/conversation-with-john-bancroft -sitting-ultimate-hot-seat-kinsey-institute.html.

45. See, for example, Golden, "Under the Covers"; Jo Ellen Meyers Sharp, "Kinsey Institute Falling behind Times in Study of Sexuality, Critics Say," *Indianapolis Star*, November 6, 1988; Sharp, "Kinsey Institute Chief Determined to Fight Accusations," *Indianapolis Star*, March 19, 1989; Yee, "Management of Institute Questioned," 1; JMR, annual report, 1988, app. O.

46. JMR, annual report, 1990–92, 5–6.

47. See Judith A. Reisman and Edward W. Eichel, *Kinsey, Sex, and Fraud: The Indoctrination of a People* (Lafayette, LA: Vital Issues Press, 1990). More information can be found at http://www.kinseyinstitute.org/about/controversy.html and in an article by Bancroft, "Alfred C. Kinsey & the Politics of Sex Research," *Annual Review of Sex Research* 15 (2004): 1–39.

48. A copy of the September 24, 1988, article in the *New York Post* can be found in JMR, annual report, 1988, app. G, 243.

49. Her other books include *Kinsey: Crimes and Consequences: The Red Queen and the Grand Scheme* (Crestwood, KY: Institute for Media Education, 1998); *Kinsey's Attic:*

The Shocking Story of How One Man's Sexual Pathology Changed the World (Nashville, TN: Cumberland House Publishing, 2005); *Sexual Sabotage: How One Mad Scientist Unleashed a Plague of Corruption and Contagion on America* (Washington, DC: World Net Daily Books, 2010); and *Stolen Honor, Stolen Innocence: How America Was Betrayed by the Lies and Sexual Crimes of a Mad "Scientist"* (Orlando, FL: New Revolution Publishers, 2012).

50. AAA Screening Service, *Glossary of Legal Terms for Civil and Criminal History*, 2, www.aaascreening.com/forms_and_info/LegalGlossary.pdf.

6. Turning Outward (1994–2016)

1. Dagmar Herzog, *Sex in Crisis: The New Sexual Revolution and the Future of American Politics* (New York: Basic Books, 2008), 61–73, 163–66.

2. James Davison Hunter, *Culture Wars: The Struggle to Define America* (New York: Basic Books, 1991); Richard Neuhaus, "'Culture Wars,'" *New York Times*, December 29, 1991, sec. Books, http://www.nytimes.com/1991/12/29/books/l-culture-wars-039691.html; Janny Scott, "At Appomattox in the Culture Wars," *New York Times*, May 25, 1997, http://www.nytimes.com/1997/05/25/weekinreview/at-appomattox-in-the-culture-wars .html.

3. Ethan Bronner, "Just Say Maybe; No Sexology, Please. We're Americans," *New York Times*, February 1, 1998, http://www.nytimes.com/1998/02/01/weekinreview/just-say -maybe-no-sexology-please-we-re-americans.html; and Claudia Dreifus, "Sitting in the Ultimate Hot Seat: The Kinsey Institute," *New York Times*, May 25, 1999, http://www .nytimes.com/1999/05/25/science/conversation-with-john-bancroft-sitting-ultimate-hot -seat-kinsey-institute.html.

4. For a discussion of the challenges religious and political conservatives have posed to sex research, education, and inclusion during the 1980s and 1990s, see, for example, Herzog, *Sex in Crisis,* 67–70, 104–105. On changes to the funding structure of the Institute in response to financial changes of Indiana University, see Julia R. Heiman (JRH), "Director's Capstone Report, 2004–2013," June 14, 2014, 7–9, Julia R. Heiman Directorship, 2004–13 (JRHD), VII: Operations, b. Annual Reports, Kinsey Institute Library and Special Collections (KILSC).

5. On the external review of the Institute, see JRH, "Director's Capstone Report," 7.

6. Rep. Steve Stockman, H.R. 2749, Child Protection and Ethics, 104th Cong., 1995.

7. For useful historical background on such panics, see Estelle B. Freedman, "'Uncontrolled Desires': The Responses to the Sexual Psychopath, 1920–1960," *Journal of American History* 74 (1981): 99–103.

8. See Robert H. Knight, "How Alfred C. Kinsey's Sex Studies Have Harmed Women and Children," http://concernedwomen.org/images/content/kinsey-women_11_03.pdf. For more on cycles of panic over crimes against children, see Philip Jenkins, *Moral Panic: Changing Concepts of the Child Molester in Modern America* (New Haven, CT: Yale University Press, 1998); Robert H. Knight, dir., *The Children of Table 34*, documentary, Family Research Council, 1994; and Judith A. Reisman and Edward W. Eichel, *Kinsey, Sex, and Fraud: The Indoctrination of a People* (Lafayette, LA: Vital Issues Press, 1990).

9. See John Bancroft (JB) to John Ryan, May 16, 1995, 1, John Bancroft Directorship, 1995–2003 (JBD), I: Correspondence, KILSC. See also "Amended and Restated Code of By-Laws of the Kinsey Institute for Research in Sex, Gender, and Reproduction," adopted September 6, 1996, JBD, VII: Operations, a. Legal, KILSC.

10. See JB to John Ryan, May 16, 1995, 2–4.

11. Alfred C. Kinsey, *Sexual Behavior in the Human Female*, reprint ed. (Bloomington: Indiana University Press, 1998); Kinsey, *Sexual Behavior in the Human Male*, reprint ed. (Bloomington: Indiana University Press, 1998). See Paul H. Gebhard and Alan B. Johnson, *The Kinsey Data: Marginal Tabulations of the 1938–1963 Interviews Conducted by the Institute for Sex Research*, reprint ed. (Bloomington: Indiana University Press, 1998).

12. Woody Burton's resolution was House Concurrent Resolution 16, introduced in 1998. See Tribune News Services, "House Questions Sex Funds," *Chicago Tribune*, January 22, 1998, http://articles.chicagotribune.com/1998-01-22/news/9801220072_1_kinsey-Institute-alfred-kinsey-indiana-house.

13. See, for example, John Bancroft, ed., *Researching Sexual Behavior: Methodological Issues* (Bloomington: Indiana University Press, 1997); Bancroft, ed., *The Role of Theory in Sex Research* (Bloomington: Indiana University Press, 2000); Bancroft, ed., *Sexual Development in Childhood* (Bloomington: Indiana University Press, 2003).

14. See, for example, JB, "KIRSGR Director's Report to the Board of Governors," October 1999, 9–10, and "KIRSGR Director's Report to the Board of Governors," November 2000, 20, JBD, VII: Operations, b. Reports, KILSC.

15. See, for example, John Bancroft, "The Menstrual Cycle and the Well-Being of Women," *Social Science and Medicine* 41 (September 1995): 785–91; Bancroft and D. Rennie, "Perimenstrual Depression: Its Relationship to Pain, Bleeding, and Previous History of Depression," *Psychosomatic Medicine* 57 (September 1995): 445–52; Bancroft, "Clinical Trials and Human Sexuality: Basic Concepts and Problems," *International Journal of Impotence Research* 10, Supplement 2 (May 1998): S4–S6, S24–S26. On pharmaceutical treatments for sexual dysfunction, see, for example, JB, "The Kinsey Institute for Research in Sex, Gender, and Reproduction Director's Report to the Board of Governors," October 1999, 3, JBD, VII: Operations Records, b. Annual Reports, KILSC. Institute researchers also worked with Eli Lilly on a drug to prevent postmenopausal bone loss in women and the sexual well-being of postmenopausal women (ibid., 4).

16. See, for example, Stephanie A. Sanders and June M. Reinisch, "Would You Say You 'Had Sex' If . . . ?," *Journal of the American Medical Association* 281, no. 3 (1999): 275–77; Richard Crosby, Stephanie Sanders, William Yarber, Cynthia Graham, and Brian Dodge, "Condom Use Errors and Problems among College Men," *Sexually Transmitted Diseases* 29, no. 9 (2002): 552–57.

17. On projects "not being worthy . . . of taxpayer funds," see "House Upholds Federal Grants for Sex Research," *Advocate*, July 12, 2003, http://www.advocate.com/news/2003/07/12/house-upholds-federal-grants-sex-research-9230; Benedict Carey, "Long after Kinsey, Only the Brave Study Sex," *New York Times*, November 9, 2004, F1.

18. Carey, "Long after Kinsey."

19. Interview in *Kinsey Today* 7 (Fall/Winter 2003).

20. On the congressional hearing on sex research, see, for example, www.cossa.org/CPR/congbriefing.htm.

21. Julia Heiman, Leslie LoPiccolo, and Joseph LoPiccolo, *Becoming Orgasmic: A Sexual Growth Program for Women* (New York: Prentice Hall, 1976).

22. "Indiana University Names New Director for the Kinsey Institute," *IU News Room*, press release, April 22, 2004, http://newsinfo.iu.edu/news-archive/1420.html.

23. On the political factors facing the Institute and the combining of the boards, see JRH, "Director's Capstone Report," 6–8. On the underfunding and understaffing of the Institute, see her appendix 7, "National External Review Committee Report," 366.

24. JRH, "Director's Capstone Report," 29.

25. Kimberly R. McBride et al., "Turning Sexual Science into News: Sex Research and the Media," *Journal of Sex Research* 44, no. 4 (2007): 347–58.

26. On the 10 Million Lives Project, see, for example, JRH, "Director's Capstone Report," 3; and Diane Anderson-Minshall, "A New Kinsey App Lets You Report Sexual Behavior," *Advocate*, September 5, 2012, http://www.advocate.com/arts-entertainment /internet/2012/09/05/new-kinsey-app-lets-you-report-sexual-behavior. See also www .kinseyreporter.org.

27. JRH, "Director's Capstone Report," 6.

28. On "having sex," see Stephanie A. Sanders, Brandon J. Hill, William L. Yarber, Cynthia A. Graham, Richard A. Crosby, and Robert R. Milhausen, "Misclassification Bias: Diversity in Conceptualisations about Having 'Had Sex,'" *Sexual Health* 7 (2010): 31–34. In 1998 the *Journal of the American Medical Association* fired its editor for publishing an article on the definitions of "having sex" that was construed to be in response to the sex scandal of former President Bill Clinton. See Andy Geller, "AMA Boots Editor over Sex Survey," *New York Post*, January 16, 1999, 4. The article in question was written by June Reinisch.

29. "The Masters and Johnson Collection," update, July 25, 2013, *Kinsey Institute Newsletter*, Fall 2011, http://www.indiana.edu/~kinsey/newsletter/fa112011 /mastersjohnson.html.

30. JRH, "Director's Capstone Report," 4.

31. For more information, see https://kinseyInstitute.org/about/profiles/john-money. php.

32. JRH, annual report, Kinsey Institute for Research in Sex, Gender, and Reproduction, 2006, 15, JRHD, VII: Operations Records, b. Reports, KILSC.

33. JRH, annual report, 2007, 20.

34. On the Juried Erotic Art Shows, see, for example, JRH, "Director's Capstone Report," 4.

35. During JRH's tenure, six Institute Juried Erotic Art Shows were held in addition to *Sex in the Cinema* (2006). Subsequent shows included *Sex Objects* (2006), *Kinsey Confidential* (2007), *Queer Projections* (2007), *iGuy(heLovesMeHeLovesMeNot.com)* (2008), *Women of Pleasure, Infinitely Variable* (2008), *Sex and Presidential Politics* (2008), *Pre-revolutionary Queer* (2009), *Eros in Asia* (2009), *Contemporary Art at the Institute* (2009), *The Shape of Us* (2009), *Private Eyes* (2010), *A Collector's Vision* (2010), *Nature & Nurture* (2009), *As See Them: Exotic and Erotic Images from Modern Alternative Process Photographers* (2010), *Storytellers* (2010), and *The Photographs of Len Prince* (2010). See JRH, "Director's Capstone Report," 4.

36. Ibid., 5. On the Wellcome exhibit, see https://wellcomecollection.org/exhibitions /Institute-sexology, and Wellcome Institute, *The Institute for Sexology* (London: Wellcome Trust, 2014).

37. Sanders served as interim director from 1993 to 1995 between Reinisch and Bancroft, for May 2004 between Bancroft and Heiman, and from November 2013 to October 2014 between Heiman and Carter.

38. Historians have adapted this term from psychoanalysis to characterize the sudden and reactive emergence of political organizations in response to a diametrically opposite development, for instance, employers' federations formed in response to the advent of unions, antisuffrage leagues formed in the wake of suffragette militancy, and the emergence of right-to-life lobbying groups in response to the medical legalization of abortion.

39. Personal communication, Herman B Wells to Judith A. Allen, October 12, 1993, Wylie Hall, Indiana University.

40. See Alfred C. Kinsey, Wardell B. Pomeroy, Clyde E. Martin, and Paul H. Gebhard, *Sexual Behavior in the Human Female (SBHF)* (Philadelphia: W. B. Saunders, 1953), 521–22.

41. Paul Henry Gebhard (PHG) to National Gay Task Force, October 25, 1977, Paul H. Gebhard Directorship, 1957–81 (PHGD), I: Correspondence, ISR, KILSC.

42. See PHG, "Gebhard Era History, 1956–1982," 12, PHGD, IX: Paul H. Gebhard Papers, KILSC. For erudite analysis of these developments nationally, see Robert O. Self, *All in the Family: The Realignment of American Democracy since the 1960s* (New York: Macmillan, 2012), esp. 9–11, 56, 130.

43. See Richard Rhoades, "Father of the Sexual Revolution," *New York Times,* November 2, 1997, http://www.nytimes.com/books/97/11/02/reviews/971102.02rhodest.html.

Conclusion: Looking Forward

1. Julia R. Heiman (JRH), "Director's Capstone Report, 2004–2013," June 14, 2014, app. 7, 366, Julia R. Heiman Directorship, 2004–13 (JRHD), VII: Operations, b. Annual Reports, Kinsey Institute Library and Special Collections (KILSC).

2. Ibid., 369.

3. Thomas D. Clark, typescript of interview with Herman B Wells (HBW), "Kinsey and the Kinsey Institute," Bloomington, January 1968, 6, 8, 13–15, Kinsey Institute for Sex Research, Indiana University Archives (IUA).

4. Ibid., 6–7.

1940–1949

KINSEY, Alfred C. "Criteria for a Hormonal Explanation of the Homosexual." *Journal of Clinical Endocrinology* 1 (1941): 424–28.

RAMSEY, Glenn Virgil. "The Sexual Development of Boys." *American Journal of Psychology* 56 (1943): 217–34.

RAMSEY, Glenn Virgil. "The Sex Information of Younger Boys." *American Journal of Orthopsychiatry* 13, no. 2 (1943): 347–53.

KINSEY, Alfred C. "Sex Behavior in the Human Animal." *Annals of the New York Academy of Science* 47, no. 5 (1947): 635–37.

KINSEY, Alfred C., Wardell B. Pomeroy, and Clyde E. Martin. *Sexual Behavior in the Human Male.* Philadelphia: W. B. Saunders, 1948.

RAMSEY, Glenn V., and Melita Seipp. "Public Opinions and Information Concerning Mental Health." *Journal of Clinical Psychology* 4, no. 4 (October 1948): 397–406.

KINSEY, Alfred C., Wardell Baxter Pomeroy, Clyde E. Martin, and Paul H. Gebhard. "Concepts of Normality and Abnormality in Sexual Behavior." In *Psychosexual Development in Health and Disease*, edited by Paul H. Hoch and Joseph Zubin, 11–32. New York: Grune and Stratton, 1949.

RAMSEY, Glenn Virgil. "Review: Sex Habits of American Men: A Symposium on the Kinsey Report." *Journal of Abnormal and Social Psychology* 44, no. 1 (1949): 145–49.

1950–1959

RAMSEY, Glenn V. "A Survey Evaluation of the Kinsey Report." *Journal of Clinical Psychology* 6, no. 2 (April 1950): 133–43.

RAMSEY, Glenn V. "Sexual Growth of Negro and White Boys." *Human Biology* 22, no. 2 (May 1950): 146–49.

BLAKE, Robert R., and Glenn V. Ramsey. *Perception: An Approach to Personality.* New York: Ronals Press, 1951.

RAMSEY, Glenn Virgil, and Mary Varley. "Censorship and the Kinsey Report." *Journal of Social Psychology* 33 (1951): 279–88.

KINSEY, Alfred C., Wardell B. Pomeroy, Clyde E. Martin, and Paul H. Gebhard. *Sexual Behavior in the Human Female.* Philadelphia: W. B. Saunders, 1953.

RAMSEY, Glenn V., et al. "Sex Information, Attitudes, and Behavior." In *The Adolescent: A Book of Readings*, edited by Jerome Seidman, 492–522. Fort Worth, TX: Dryden Press, 1953.

RAMSEY, Glenn Virgil. "Review of Sexual Behavior in the Human Female." *Journal of Abnormal and Social Psychology* 49, no. 1 (1954): 158–59.

KINSEY, Alfred C., Philip Reichert, David O. Cauldwell, and Eugene B. Mozes. "The Causes of Homosexuality: A Symposium." *Sexology* 21, no. 9 (1955): 558–62.

KINSEY, Alfred C. "Toward a Clarification of Homosexual Terminology." *Mattachine Review* 12, no. 4 (1956): 5–7.

KINSEY, Alfred C. "Music and Love as Arts." *High Fidelity*, July 1956, 27–28.

POMEROY, Wardell B. "Psychosurgery and Sexual Behavior." In *Studies in Topectomy*, edited by Nolan D. C. Lewis, Carney Landis, and H. E. King, 150–71. New York: Gene and Stratton, 1956.

KINSEY, Alfred C., Paul H. Gebhard, and Cornelia V. Christenson. "Hormonal faktorers betydning for den seksuelle adfærd." In *Samliv og samfund*, edited by H. Hoffmeyer, 230–58. Copenhagen: Hassings Forlag, 1957.

TIETZE, Christopher, and Clyde E. Martin. "Foetal Deaths, Spontaneous and Induced in the Urban White Population of the United States." *Population Studies* 11, no. 2 (1957): 170–76.

GEBHARD, Paul H., Wardell Baxter Pomeroy, Clyde E. Martin, and Cornelia V. Christenson. *Pregnancy, Birth and Abortion*. New York: Harper and Brothers Publishers, 1958.

1960–1969

POMEROY, Wardell B. "An Analysis of Questions on Sex." *Psychological Record* 10 (July 1960): 191–201.

LESER, Hedwig. "The Hirschfeld Institute for Sexology." In *Encyclopedia of Sexual Behavior*, vol. 2, edited by A. Ellis and A. R. Abarbanal, 967–70. New York: Hawthorne Books, 1961.

POMEROY, Wardell B. "Masturbation—Attitudes and Incidence." In *Sex Ways—in Fact and Faith*, edited by Evelyn M. Duvall and S. M. Duvall, 166–84. New York: Association Press, 1961.

POMEROY, Wardell B. "The Institute for Sex Research." In *Encyclopedia of Sexual Behavior*, vol. 2, edited by A. Ellis and A. R. Abarbanal, 970–75. New York: Hawthorne Books, 1961.

POMEROY, Wardell B. "The Reluctant Respondent." *Public Opinion Quarterly* 27, no. 1 (1962): 287–93.

CHRISTENSON, Cornelia V. "Premarital Pregnancies and Their Outcome." *Journal of the National Association of Women Deans and Counselors* 26 (January 1963): 29–33.

POMEROY, Wardell B. "Human Sexual Behavior." In *Taboo Topics*, edited by Norman L. Faberow, 22–23. New York: Atherton Press, 1963.

GEBHARD, Paul H., and John H. Gagnon. "Male Sex Offenders against Very Young Children." Paper presented at the Annual Meeting of the American Psychiatric Association, 1964.

GAGNON, John H. "Wonder Drugs, Fear of Venereal Disease, Infection and Sexual Contact." *Proceedings of the World Forum on Syphilis and Other Trepenamotoses*, 1964, 424–30. Washington, DC, September 4–12, 1962. US Government Printing Office, PHS Publications 997.

CHRISTENSON, Cornelia V., and John H. Gagnon. "Sexual Behavior in a Group of Older Women." *Journal of Gerontology* 20, no. 3 (1965): 351–56.

GAGNON, John H. "Female Child Victims of Sex Offenses." *Social Problems* 13, no. 2 (1965): 176–92.

GAGNON, John H. "Sexuality and Sexual Learning in the Child." *Psychiatry* 28 (1965): 212–28.

GEBHARD, Paul H. "Situational Factors Affecting Human Sexual Behavior." In *Sex and Behavior*, edited by Frank Beach, 483–95. New York: John Wiley, 1965.

GEBHARD, Paul H., John H. Gagnon, Wardell Baxter Pomeroy, and Cornelia V. Christenson. *Sex Offenders: An Analysis of Types*. New York: Harper and Row, 1965.

WEINBERG, Martin S. "Sexual Modesty, Social Meanings, and the Nudist Camp." *Social Problems* 12, no. 3 (1965): 311–18.

GEBHARD, Paul H. "Factors in Marital Orgasm." *Journal of Social Issues* 22, no. 2 (1966): 88–95.

GEBHARD, Paul H. "Homosexual Socialization." Proceedings of the World Congress of Psychiatry, Madrid. *Excerpta Medica International Congress Series*, No. 150, 1966, 1028–31.

MARCUS, Steven. *The Other Victorians: A Study of Sexuality and Pornography in Mid-Nineteenth-Century England*. Published as a volume in the Institute for Sex Research monograph series Studies in Sex and Society. New York: Basic Books, 1966.

WEINBERG, Martin S. "Becoming a Nudist." *Psychiatry: Journal of the Study of Interpersonal Processes* 29, no. 1 (1966): 240–51.

POMEROY, Wardell B. "Kinsey (Alfred Charles)." In *Nouveau dictionnaire de sexologie*, edited by Collectif et Servadio Emilio, 245–52. Paris: L'Or du Temps, 1967.

POMEROY, Wardell B., and Cornelia V. Christenson. *Characteristics of Male and Female Sexual Responses*. New York: Sex Information and Education Council, 1967.

GAGNON, John H., and William Simon, eds. *Sexual Deviance*. New York: Harper and Row, 1967.

GAGNON, John H., and William Simon. "The Sociological Perspective on Homosexuality." *Dublin Review* 510 (1967): 96–114.

GEBHARD, Paul H. "Normal and Criminal Sexual Behavior at Older Ages." *Beiträge zur Sexualforschung* 41, no. 2 (1967): 83–87.

SIMON, William, and John H. Gagnon. "Femininity in the Lesbian Community." *Social Problems* 15, no. 2 (1967): 212–21.

SIMON, William, and John H. Gagnon. "Homosexuality: The Formulation of a Sociological Perspective." *Journal of Health and Social Behavior* 8, no. 3 (1967): 177–85.

SIMON, William, and John H. Gagnon. "The Lesbians: A Preliminary Overview." In *Sexual Deviance*, edited by John H. Gagnon and William Simon, 247–82. New York: Harper and Row, 1967.

SIMON, William, and John H. Gagnon. "The Pedagogy of Sex." *Saturday Review* 91 (1967): 74–76.

WEINBERG, Martin S. "The Nudist Camp: Way of Life and Social Structure." *Human Organization* 26, no. 3 (1967): 91–99.

BELL, Alan P., R. M. Whitman (moderator), J. L. Titshoner, and S. Hornstein. "Foreplay." Roundtable discussion at the University of Cincinnati College of Medicine. *Medical Aspects of Human Sexuality* 2, no. 6 (1968): 9, 11–13.

CHRISTENSON, Cornelia V. "Kinsey, Alfred C." In *The International Encyclopedia of the Social Sciences*, edited by David L. Sills, vol. 14, 389–90. New York: Crowell-Collier, 1968.

GAGNON, John H. "Prostitution." In *International Encyclopedia of the Social Sciences*, vol. 15, 592–98. New York: Crowell-Collier, 1968.

GAGNON, John H. "Sexual Behavior: Deviation: Social Aspects." In *The International Encyclopedia of the Social Sciences*, edited by David L. Sills, vol. 14, 215–21. New York: Crowell-Collier, 1968.

GAGNON, John H., and William Simon. "Sex Talk—Public and Private." *ETC: A Review of General Semantics* 25, no. 2 (1968): 173.

GAGNON, John H., and William Simon. "Sexual Deviance in Contemporary America." *Annals of the American Academy of Political and Social Sciences* 376 (1968): 106–22. Philadelphia.

GAGNON, John H., and William Simon. "The Social Meaning of Prison Homosexuality." *Federal Probation* 32 (March 1968): 23–29.

GEBHARD, Paul H. "Human Sex Behavior Research." In *Perspectives in Reproduction and Sexual Behavior*, edited by M. Diamond, 391–410. Bloomington: Indiana University Press, 1968.

GEBHARD, Paul H. "Projects since the Kinsey Reports." *Medical Aspects of Human Sexuality* 2, no. 4 (1968): 51–55.

GEBHARD, Paul H., Jan Raboch, and Hans Giese. *Die Sexualität der Frau*. Reinbek bei Hamburg: Rowohlt Verlag, 1968.

RUBINGTON, Earl, and Martin S. Weinberg, eds. *Deviance: The Interactionist Perspective*. New York: Macmillan, 1968.

SIMON, William, and John H. Gagnon. "On Psychosexual Development." In *Handbook of Socialization Theory and Research*, edited by D. A. Goslin. New York: McGraw-Hill, 1968.

SONENSHEIN, David. "The Ethnography of Male Homosexual Relationships." *Journal of Sex Research* 4, no. 2 (1968): 69–83.

WEINBERG, Martin S. "Embarrassment: Its Variable and Invariable Aspects." *Social Forces* 46, no. 3 (1968): 382–88.

BELL, Alan P. "Adolescent Sexuality and the Schools." *North Central Association Quarterly* 43, no. 4 (1969): 342–47.

BELL, Alan P. "Attitudes towards Nudity by Social Class." *Medical Aspects of Human Sexuality* 3, no. 9 (1969): 101, 105–108.

BELL, Alan P. "Role Modeling of Fathers in Adolescence and Young Adulthood." *Journal of Counseling Psychology* 16, no. 1 (1969): 30–35.

BELL, Alan P. "The Scylla and Charybdis of Psychosexual Development." *Journal of Sex Research* 5, no. 2 (1969): 86–89.

ELIAS, J. E., and Paul H. Gebhard. "Sexuality and Sexual Learning in Childhood: Research and Possible Implications for Education." *Phi Delta Kappan* 1, no. 7 (1969): 401–405.

GEBHARD, Paul H. "Fetishism and Sadomasochism." *Science and Psychoanalysis* 15 (1969): 71–80.

GEBHARD, Paul H. "Why *Chant d'Amour* Was Banned." *Censorship Today* 2, no. 4 (1969): 17–19.

PECKHAM, Morse. *Art and Pornography*. Published as a volume in the Institute for Sex Research monograph series Studies in Sex and Society. New York: Basic Books, 1969.

WEINBERG, Martin S. "The Aging Male Homosexual." *Medical Aspects of Human Sexuality* 3, no. 12 (1969): 66–67, 72.

GEBHARD, Paul H. "Human Sex Behavior Research." In *Reproduction and Sexual Behavior*, edited by M. Diamond, 391–410. Bloomington: Indiana University Press, 1969.

GEBHARD, Paul H. "Misconceptions about Female Prostitutes." *Medical Aspects of Human Sexuality* 3, no. 3 (1969): 24–30.

1970–1979

BELL, Alan P. "Role Models in Young Adulthood: Their Relationship to Occupational Behaviors." *Vocational Guidance Quarterly* 18, no. 4 (1970): 280–84.

BELL, Alan P. "Role Modelship and Interaction in Adolescence and Young Adulthood." *Developmental Psychology* 2, no. 1 (1970): 123–28.

BOWIE, Theodore, and Cornelia V. Christenson, eds. *Studies in Erotic Art.* Published as a volume in the Institute for Sex Research monograph series Studies in Sex and Society. New York: Basic Books, 1970.

GAGNON, John H., and William Simon. "Prospects for Change in American Sexual Patterns." *Medical Aspects of Human Sexuality* 4, no. 1 (1970): 110–17.

GEBHARD, Paul H., Jan Raboch, and Hans Giese. *The Sexuality of Women.* London: Andre Deutsch Ltd., 1970.

GEBHARD, Paul H. "Postmarital Coitus among Widows and Divorcees." In *Divorce and After,* edited by Paul Bohannan, 82–96. New York: Doubleday, 1970.

GEBHARD, Paul H. Preface to *Studies in Human Sexual Behavior: The American Scene,* edited by A. Shiloh. Springfield, IL: C. C. Thomas, 1970.

GEBHARD, Paul H. "Sexual Motifs in Prehistoric Peruvian Ceramics." In *Studies in Erotic Art,* edited by Theodore Bowie and Cornelia V. Christenson, 109–44. New York: Basic Books, 1970.

GEBHARD, Paul H., Jan Raboch, and Hans Giese. *The Sexuality of Women.* Translated by Colin Bearne. New York: Stein and Day, 1970. Originally published as *Die Sexualität der Frau.*

WEINBERG, Martin S. "Homosexual Samples: Differences and Similarities." *Journal of Sex Research* 6, no. 4 (1970): 312–25.

WEINBERG, Martin S. "The Male Homosexual: Age Related Variations in Social and Psychological Characteristics." *Social Problems* 17, no. 4 (1970): 529–37.

WEINBERG, Martin S. "The Nudist Management of Respectability: Strategy for the Consequences of the Construction of a Situated Morality." In *Deviance and Respectability: The Social Construction of Moral Meanings,* edited by J. Douglas, 375–403. New York: Basic Books, 1970.

WILLIAMS, Colin, and Martin S. Weinberg. "Being Discovered: A Study of Homosexuals in the Military." *Social Problems* 18, no. 2 (1970): 409–23.

WILLIAMS, Colin, and Martin S. Weinberg. "The Military: Its Processing of Accused Homosexuals." *American Behavioral Scientist* 14, no. 2 (1970): 203–17.

BELL, Alan P., and Calvin S. Hall. *The Personality of a Child Molester: An Analysis of Dreams.* Chicago: Aldine, 1971.

CHRISTENSON, Cornelia V. *Kinsey: A Biography.* Bloomington: Indiana University Press, 1971.

GEBHARD, Paul H. "Human Sexual Behavior" (also the preface and appendix). In *Human Sexual Behavior: Variations in the Ethnographic Spectrum,* edited by D. Marshall and Richard Suggs. New York: Basic Books, 1971.

MARSHALL, Donald, and Richard Suggs, eds. *Human Sexual Behavior: Variations in the Ethnographic Spectrum.* Published as a volume in the Institute for Sex Research monograph series Studies in Sex and Society. New York: Basic Books, 1971.

WEINBERG, Martin S. "Nudists." *Sexual Behavior* 2, no. 5 (1971): 51–55.

WEINBERG, Martin S., and Earl Rubington, eds. *The Study of Social Problems: Five Perspectives.* New York: Oxford University Press, 1971.

WILLIAMS, Colin J., and Martin Weinberg. *Homosexuals and the Military: A Study of Less than Honorable Discharge.* New York: Harper and Row, 1971.

BELL, Alan P. "Human Sexuality: A Response." *International Journal of Psychiatry* 10, no. 1 (1971): 99–102.

CHRISTENSON, Cornelia V. "Kinsey—a Biography." *Medical Aspects of Human Sexuality* 6, no. 5 (1972): 136–73.

CHRISTENSON, Cornelia V. "Kinsey Revisited." *Review* 14, no. 3 (1972): 11–18. Indiana University Alumni Association of the College of Arts and Sciences.

GEBHARD, Paul H. "A Comparison of White-Black Offender Groups." In *Sexual Behavior: Social, Clinical and Legal Aspects*, edited by H. L. P. Resnik and M. E. Wolfgang, 89–130. Boston: Little, Brown, 1972.

GEBHARD, Paul H. "Incidence of Overt Homosexuality in the United States and Western Europe." In *National Institute of Mental Health Task Force on Homosexuality: Final Report and Background Papers*, edited by J. M. Livingood, 22–29. Washington, DC: Government Printing Office, 1972.

GEBHARD, Paul H. "Securing Sensitive Personal Information by Interviews." In *Selections from the Fifth and Sixth National Colloquia on Oral History*, edited by P. Olch and F. C. Pogue, 63–79. New York: Oral History Association, 1972.

POMEROY, Wardell B. "Alfred C. Kinsey: Man and Method." *Psychology Today* 5, no. 10 (1972): 33–40.

POMEROY, Wardell B. *Dr. Kinsey and the Institute for Sex Research*. New York: Harper & Row, 1972.

WEINBERG, Martin S., and Alan P. Bell. *Homosexuality: An Annotated Bibliography*. New York: Harper and Row, 1972.

WEINBERG, Martin S., and Colin J. Williams. "Fieldwork among Deviants: Social Relations with Subjects and Others." In *Research on Deviance*, edited by J. Douglas, 163–86. New York: Random House, 1972.

WILLIAMS, Colin J. "Opinion: Is There a Relationship between Homosexuality and Creativity?" *Sexual Behavior* 22 (1972): 47–48.

BELL, Alan P. "Adolescent Sexuality and the Schools." In *Contemporary Controversy*, 2nd ed., edited by M. Freedman and P. Davis, 279–86. New York: Macmillan, 1973. Reprinted from *North Central Association Quarterly* 43, no. 4 (1969): 342–47.

BELL, Alan P. *SIECUS Study Guide No. 2: Homosexuality*, rev. ed. New York: Sex Information and Education Council of the U.S., 1973.

CHRISTENSON, Cornelia V., and Alan B. Johnson. "Sexual Patterns in a Group of Older Never-Married Women." *Journal of Geriatric Psychiatry* 6, no. 1 (1973): 88–98.

GEBHARD, Paul H. "Sex Differences in Sexual Response." *Archives of Sexual Behavior* 2, no. 3 (1973): 201–203.

GEBHARD, Paul H. "Sexual Behavior of the Mentally Retarded." In *Human Sexuality and the Mentally Retarded*, edited by F. de la Crux and G. D. LaVeck, 29–49. New York: Brunner/Mazel, 1973.

HAMMERSMITH, Sue K., and Martin S. Weinberg. "Homosexual Identity: Commitment, Adjustment and Significant Others." *Sociometry* 36, no. 1 (1973): 56–79.

LEVITT, Eugene. "Excerpts of Sexual Terms." In *Psychology Encyclopedia*, edited by Nina Adams et al., 73–74. Guilford, CT: Dushkin Publishing Group, 1973.

WEINBERG, Martin S., and Earl Rubington, eds. *The Solution of Social Problems: Five Perspectives*. New York: Oxford University Press, 1973.

WEINBERG, Martin S., and Colin J. Williams. "Neutralizing the Homosexual Label." In *The Solution of Social Problems: Five Perspectives*, edited by Martin S. Weinberg and Earl Rubington, 287–98. New York: Oxford University Press, 1973.

BELL, Alan P. "Homosexualities: Their Range and Character." In *Nebraska Symposium on Motivation*, edited by J. K. Cole and R. Dienstbier, 1–26. Lincoln: University of Nebraska Press, 1974.

GEBHARD, Paul H. "Coping with Barriers to Sex Education and Sex Research." *WHO Meeting on Education and Treatment in Human Sexuality: The Training of Professionals*. Geneva. Background Paper No. 7, 1974.

GEBHARD, Paul H. "International Reference Service." *WHO Meeting on Education and Treatment in Human Sexuality: The Training of Professionals*. Geneva. Background Paper No. 8, 1974.

KLASSEN, Albert D. "Connoisseur and Gatekeeper of the Erotic in Print: The Public Librarian." *Focus on Indiana Libraries* 28, no. 1 (1974): 6–11.

LEVITT, Eugene E., and Albert D. Klassen. "Public Attitudes toward Homosexuality: Part of the 1970 National Survey by the Institute for Sex Research." *Journal of Homosexuality* 1, no. 1 (1974): 29–43.

WEINBERG, Martin S., and Colin J. Williams. *Male Homosexuals: Their Problems and Adaptations*. New York: Oxford University Press, 1974.

WILLIAMS, Colin J. "Comment on A. H. Gilbert's *The Africaine Courts-Martial: A Study of Buggery and the Royal Navy*." *Journal of Homosexuality* 1, no. 1 (1974): 111–23.

BEASLEY, Ruth. "Current Status of Sex Research." *Journal of Sex Research* 11, no. 4 (1975): 335–47.

BELL, Alan P. "Answers to Questions: What Percentage of Homosexuals Are Married?" *Medical Aspects of Human Sexuality* 9, no. 9 (1975): 106.

BELL, Alan P. "Answers to Questions: Why Do Homosexuals Seem So Much More Promiscuous and Sexually Active than Single Heterosexuals?" *Medical Aspects of Human Sexuality* 9, no. 2 (1975): 92–93.

BELL, Alan P. "The Homosexual Patient." In *Human Sexuality: A Health Practitioner's Text*, edited by R. Green, 55–72. Baltimore, MD: Williams and Wilkins, 1975.

BELL, Alan P. "Research in Homosexuality: Back to the Drawing Board." In *Sex Research: Future Directions*, edited by E. A. Rubinstein, R. Green, and E. Brecher. Proceedings of the conference held at the State University of New York at Stony Brook, June 5–9, 1975. *Archives of Sexual Behavior* 4, no. 4 (1975): 421–31.

BREWER, Joan S. "A Guide to Sex Education Books: Dick Active, Jane Passive." *Interracial Books for Children Bulletin* 6, no. 3–4 (1975): 1, 12–13.

INSTITUTE FOR SEX RESEARCH LIBRARY. *Catalog of the Social and Behavioral Sciences Monography Section of the Library of the Institute for Sex Research*. Boston: G. K. Hall, 1975.

GEBHARD, Paul H. "Comprehensive Sex Research Centers: Design and Operation Needs for Effective Functioning." In *Sex Research: Future Directions*, edited by E. A. Rubinstein, R. Green, and E. Brecher. Proceedings of the conference held at the State University of New York at Stony Brook, June 5–9, 1974. *Archives of Sexual Behavior* 4, no. 4 (1975): 447–57.

GEBHARD, Paul H. "Preparation for a Course on Human Sexuality." *Teaching of Psychology* 2, no. 1 (1975): 31–33.

WEINBERG, Martin S., and Colin J. Williams. "Gay Baths and the Social Organization of Impersonal Sex." *Social Problems* 23, no. 2 (1975): 124–36.

BEASLEY, Ruth A., comp. *International Directory of Sex Research and Related Fields*. Boston: G. K. Hall, 1976.

BELL, Alan P. "Homosexuality: An Overview." In *Male and Female: Christian Approaches to Sexuality*, edited by R. T. Barnhouse and U. T. Holmes III, 131–43. New York: Seabury Press, 1976.

BROOKS, JoAnn, and Helen C. Hofer. *Sexual Nomenclature: A Thesaurus.* Boston: G. K. Hall, 1976.

INSTITUTE FOR SEX RESEARCH LIBRARY. *Catalog of Periodical Literature in the Social and Behavioral Science Section, Library of the Institute for Sex Research, Including Supplement to Monographs, 1973–1975.* Boston: G. K. Hall, 1976.

GEBHARD, Paul H. "Proposed Model for a Course in Human Sexuality." In *Sex Education in Medicine*, edited by H. Lief and A. Karlen, 55–59. New York: Spectrum Publications, 1976.

POMEROY, Wardell B. "The Now of Kinsey's Findings." In *Sexuality Today—and Tomorrow*, edited by Sol Gordon and Roger Libby, 169–71. North Scituate, MA: Duxbury Press, 1976.

WEINBERG, Martin S. *Sex Research: Studies from the Kinsey Institute.* New York: Oxford University Press, 1976.

GEBHARD, Paul H. "The Acquisition of Basic Sex Information." *Journal of Sex Research* 13, no. 3 (1977): 148–69.

GEBHARD, Paul H. "Designated Discussion." In *Ethical Issues in Sex Therapy and Research*, edited by William H. Masters, Virginia E. Johnson, and Robert C. Kolodny, 11–19. Boston: Little, Brown, 1977.

GEBHARD, Paul H. "Sex Offenders." In *Handbook of Sexology*, edited by John Money and Herman Musaph, 1087–94. Amsterdam: Excerpta Medica, 1977.

IVKER, Barry. *An Anthology and Analysis of 17th and 18th Century French Libertine Fiction.* Monograph series Publishing on Demand. Ann Arbor: University Microfilms International, 1977.

RUBINGTON, Earl, and Martin S. Weinberg, eds. *The Study of Social Problems: Five Perspectives*, 2nd ed. New York: Oxford University Press, 1977.

BEASLEY, Ruth. "Training the Educator in Human Sexuality: Eight Years of Human Sexuality Programs for Professionals." In *Sex Education of the Professional*, edited by N. Rosenzweig and F. P. Pearsall, 203–12. New York: Grune and Stratton, 1978.

GEBHARD, Paul H. "Marital Stress." In *Society, Stress, and Disease*, vol. 3, edited by Levi Lennart, 100–112. New York: Oxford University Press, 1978.

GEBHARD, Paul H. "Anthropological Considerations in Sexuality Curriculum." In *Sex Education of the Professional*, edited by N. Rosenzweig and F. P. Pearsall, 103–11. New York: Grune and Stratton, 1978.

GEBHARD, Paul H. "Factors in Marital Orgasm." In *Handbook of Sex Therapy*, edited by J. LoPiccolo and L. LoPiccolo, 167–74. New York: Plenum, 1978.

GEBHARD, Paul H. "Stressor Aspects of Societal Attitudes to Sex Roles and Relationships." In *Society, Stress and Disease*, vol. 3, edited by L. Levi, 77–80. Proceedings of the symposium held in Stockholm, Sweden, May 29–June 3, 1972. Oxford: Oxford University Press, 1978.

BELL, Alan P., and Martin S. Weinberg. *Homosexualities: A Study of Diversity among Men and Women.* New York: Simon and Schuster, 1978.

BELL, Alan P. "The New Sex Education and Homosexuality." In *The New Sex Education*, edited by H. A. Otto, 325–35. Chicago: Association Press/Follett, 1978.

RUBINGTON, Earl, and Martin S. Weinberg, eds. *Deviance: The Interactionist Perspective.* 3rd ed. New York: Macmillan, 1978.

BREWER, Joan S. "The Library of the Institute for Sex Research, Inc." *INULA Quarterly* 10, no. 3 (1979): 5–7.

BREWER, Joan S., and R. W. Wright. *Sex Research: Bibliographies from the Institute for Sex Research*. Phoenix, AZ: Oryx Press/Neal-Schuman, 1979.

GEBHARD, Paul H., and Alan B. Johnson. *The Kinsey Data: Marginal Tabulations of the 1938–1963 Interviews Conducted by the Institute for Sex Research*. Philadelphia: W. B. Saunders, 1979.

1980–1989

BEASLEY, Ruth. "Another Look at OCLC's Potential for Special Libraries." *Journal of the American Society for Information Science* 31, no. 4 (1980): 300–301.

DOWNEY, Lois. "Intergenerational Change in Sex Behavior: A Belated Look at Kinsey's Males." *Archives of Sexual Behavior* 9, no. 4 (1980): 267–317.

GEBHARD, Paul H. "The Galton Lecture of 1978: Sexuality in the Post-Kinsey Era." In *Changing Patterns of Sexual Behavior*, edited by W. Armytage, A. Chester, and J. Peel, 45–88. London: Academic Press, 1980.

WEINBERG, Martin S., and Colin J. Williams. "Sexual Embourgeoisement: Social Class and Sexual Activity: 1938–1970." *American Sociological Review* 45 (1980): 33–48.

BELL, Alan P., Martin S. Weinberg, and Sue Kiefer Hammersmith. *Sexual Preference: Its Development in Men and Women*. Bloomington: Indiana University Press, 1981.

GEBHARD, Paul H. "Contribution No. 87." In *DSM-III Case Book*, edited by R. Spitzer et al., 121–22. Arlington, VA: American Psychiatric Association, 1981.

MARTIN, Clyde E. "Factors Affecting Sexual Functioning in 60–79-Year-Old Married Males." *Archives of Sexual Behavior* 10, no. 5 (1981): 399–420.

REINISCH, June Machover. "Prenatal Exposure to Synthetic Progestins Increases Potential for Aggression in Humans." *Science* 211, no. 4,487 (1981): 1171–73.

REINISCH, June Machover, and Raymond Charles Rosen. "The Growth and Diversity of Sex Research in the Past Decade: An Introduction to Selected Topics." *International Journal of Mental Health* 10, no. 2–3 (1981): 3–8.

RUBIN, Robert T., June M. Reinisch, and Roger F. Haskett. "Postnatal Gonadal Steroid Effects on Human Behavior." *Science* 211, no. 4,488 (1981): 1318–24.

RUBINGTON, Earl, and Martin S. Weinberg. *The Study of Social Problems: Five Perspectives*. 3rd ed. New York: Oxford University Press, 1981.

WEINBERG, Martin S., and Earl Rubington. *The Solution of Social Problems: Five perspectives*. 2nd ed. New York: Oxford University Press, 1981.

BREWER, Joan S. "A History of Erotic Art as Illustrated in the Collections of the Institute for Sex Research ('The Kinsey Institute')." In *Sexology: Sexual Biology, Behavior and Therapy*, edited by Z. Hoch and H. I. Lief, 318–27. Amsterdam: Excerpta Medica, 1982.

GEBHARD, Paul H. "Sexuality in a Cross-Cultural Perspective." In *Human Sexuality*, edited by William H. Masters, Virginia E. Johnson, and Robert C. Kolodny, 484–99. Boston: Little, Brown and Company, 1982.

REINISCH, June M., and Stephanie A. Sanders. "Early Barbiturate Exposure: The Brain, Sexually Dimorphic Behavior, and Learning." *Neuroscience and Biobehavioral Reviews* 6 (1982): 311–19.

REINISCH, June M. "Influence of Early Exposure to Steroid Hormones on Behavioral Development." In *Development in Adolescence: Psychological, Social, and Biological*

Aspects, edited by W. Everaerd, C. B. Hindley, A. Bot, and J. J. van der Werff ten Bosch. Boston: Martinus Nijhoff, 1983.

REINISCH, June M., and Stephanie A. Sanders. "Hormonal Influences on Sexual Development and Behavior." In *Sex and Gender—a Theological and Scientific Inquiry*, edited by M. F. Schwartz, A. S. Moraczewski, and J. A. Monteleone, 48–64. St. Louis, MO: Pope John XXIII Medical-Moral Research and Education Center, 1983.

HAEBERLE, Erwin J., ed. *The Birth of Sexology: A Brief History of Documents*. Printed for the Sixth World Congress of Sexology, May 22–27, Washington, DC, 1984.

HARRY, Joseph. *Gay Couples*. New York: Praeger Publishers, 1984.

HARRY, Joseph. "Gays and Lesbians Who Served Their Country." *Journal of Homosexuality* 10, no. 1–2 (1984): 117–25.

REINISCH, June M., and Stephanie Sanders. "Prenatal Gonadal Steroidal Influences on Gender-Related Behavior." In *Progress in Brain Research*, vol. 61, edited by G. J. de Vries, J. P. C. DeBruin, H. B. M. Vylings, and M. A. Corner, 407–15. Amsterdam: Elsevier, Science Publishers B.V., 1984.

SANDERS, Stephanie A. "Psychological Correlates of Menstrual Cycle Length and Variability." Ph.D. dissertation, Graduate Program in Psychology, Rutgers, The State University of New Jersey, New Brunswick, NJ. Dissertation Abstracts International, 46–02B, 696.

BREWER, Joan S., comp. *The Kinsey Interview Kit*. Bloomington, IN: Kinsey Institute for Research in Sex, Gender, and Reproduction, Inc., 1985.

CREWS, David, Linden T. Teramoto, and Hampton L. Carson. "Behavioral Facilitation of Reproduction in Sexual and Parthenogenic *Drosophila*." *Science* 227 (January 1985): 77–78.

HARRY, Joseph. "Defeminization and Social Class." *Archives of Sexual Behavior* 14, no. 1 (1985): 1–12.

REINISCH, June M. "The Kinsey Institute: Current Perspectives and New Directions." In *Proceedings of the 7th World Congress of Sexology*, edited by P. Kothari, 255–59. Bombay, India, 1985.

SANDERS, Stephanie A., and June M. Reinisch. "Behavioral Effects on Humans of Progesterone-Related Compounds during Development and in the Adult." In *Current Topics of Neuroendocrinology*, vol. 5, edited by D. Ganten and D. Pfaff, 175–205. Heidelberg: Springer-Verlag, 1985.

BREWER, Joan S. *Sex and the Modern Jewish Woman: An Annotated Bibliography*. Fresh Meadows, NY: Biblio Press, 1986.

REINISCH, June M., and Stephanie A. Sanders. "A Test of Sex Differences in Aggressive Response to Hypothetical Conflict Situations." *Journal of Personality and Social Psychology* 50 (1986): 1045–49.

PERSHING, Gwendolyn. "Sex and Scholarship: The Collections and Services of the Kinsey Institute for Research in Sex, Gender, and Reproduction." *Behavioral and Social Sciences Librarian* 6, no. 3–4 (1987): 129–38.

REINISCH, June M., Leonard A. Rosenblum, and Stephanie A. Sanders, eds. *Masculinity/Femininity: Basic Perspectives*. New York: Oxford University Press, 1987.

REINISCH, June M., and Stephanie A. Sanders. "Behavioral Influences of Prenatal Hormones." In *Handbook of Clinical Psychoneuroendocrinology*, edited by C. B. Nemeroff and P. T. Loosen, 431–48. New York: Guilford Press, 1987.

SANDERS, Stephanie A. "The Kinsey Institute for Research in Sex, Gender, and Reproduction." *American Psychological Association Division 44 Newsletter* 3, no. 1 (1987): 4, 8.

JAMISON, Paul L., and Paul H. Gebhard. "Penis Size Increase between Flaccid and Erect States: An Analysis of the Kinsey Data." *Journal of Sex Research* 24 (1988): 177–83.

REINISCH, June M. "Introduction to John Money's Commentary." *Journal of Psychology and Human Sexuality* 1, no. 1 (1988): 1–3.

REINISCH, June M., Stephanie A. Sander, and Mary Ziemba-Davis. "The Study of Sexual Behavior in Relation to the Transmission of Human Immunodeficiency Virus: Caveats and Recommendations." In *The Evolution of Psychology: Fifty Years of the "American Psychologist,"* edited by Joseph M. Notterman, 677–92. Washington, DC: American Psychological Association. Reprinted from *American Psychologist* 43, no. 11 (1988): 921–27.

REINISCH, June Machover, and Paul Cameron. "Kinsey Sex Surveys." *Science* 240, no. 4,854 (1988): 867.

HILL, Craig A., and Alan J. Christensen. "Affiliative Need, Different Types of Social Support, and Physical Symptoms." *Journal of Applied Social Psychology* 19, no. 16 (1989): 1351–70.

KLASSEN, Albert D., Colin J. Williams, and Eugene E. Levitt, eds. *Sex and Morality in the U.S.: An Empirical Enquiry under the Auspices of the Kinsey Institute.* Middletown, CT: Wesleyan University Press, 1989.

REINISCH, June M. Preface to *Sex and Morality in the U.S.: An Empirical Enquiry under the Auspices of the Kinsey Institute*, edited by Albert D. Klassen, Colin J. Williams, and Eugene E. Levitt, xii–xv. Middletown, CT: Wesleyan University Press, 1989.

1990–1999

BANCROFT, John, and June M. Reinisch. *Adolescence and Puberty.* New York: Oxford University Press, 1990.

HOOKER, E., and Mary Ziemba-Davis. "Homosexuality/Heterosexuality: Epilogue." In *Homosexuality/Heterosexuality: Concepts of Sexual Orientation*, edited by D. P. McWhirter, Stephanie A. Sanders, and June M. Reinisch, 399–401. New York: Oxford University Press, 1990.

McWHIRTER, David Paul, Stephanie A. Sanders, and June M. Reinisch, eds. *Homosexuality/Heterosexuality: Concepts of Sexual Orientation.* New York: Oxford University Press, 1990.

MORTENSEN, Erick L., June M. Reinisch, and T. W. Teasdale. "Intelligence as Measured by the WAIS and a Military Draft Board Group Test." *Scandinavian Journal of Psychology* 31 (1990): 315–18.

REINISCH, June M., and Ruth Beasley. *The Kinsey Institute New Report on Sex: What You Must Know to Be Sexually Literate.* New York: St. Martin's Press, 1990.

REINISCH, June M., Craig A. Hill, Stephanie A. Sanders, and Mary Ziemba-Davis. "Sexual Behaviors among Heterosexual College Students." *Focus: A Guide to AIDS Research and Counseling* 5, no. 4 (1990): 3.

REINISCH, June M., Stephanie A. Sanders, and Mary Ziemba-Davis. "Sexual Behavior and AIDS: Lessons from Art and Sex Research." In *AIDS and Sex: An Integrated Biomedical and Biobehavioral Approach*, edited by B. Voeller, J. M. Reinisch, and M. Gottlieb, 37–80. New York: Oxford University Press, 1990.

SANDERS, Stephanie A., and June M. Reinisch. "Biological and Social Influences on the Endocrinology of Puberty: Some Additional Considerations." In *Adolescence and*

Puberty, edited by John Bancroft and June M. Reinisch, 50–62. New York: Oxford University Press, 1990.

SANDERS, Stephanie A., June M. Reinisch, and David P. McWhirter. "Homosexuality/ Heterosexuality: An Overview." In *Homosexuality/Heterosexuality: Concepts of Sexual Orientation*, edited by David P. McWhirter, Stephanie A. Sanders, and June M. Reinisch, xix–xxvii. New York: Oxford University Press, 1990.

VOELLER, Bruce, June Machover Reinisch, and Michael Gottlieb, eds. *AIDS and Sex: An Integrated Biomedical and Biobehavioral Approach*. New York: Oxford University Press, 1990.

VOELLER, Bruce, June M. Reinisch, and Michael Gottlieb. "An Integrated Biomedical and Biobehavioral Approach to AIDS: An Introduction." In *AIDS and Sex: An Integrated Biomedical and Biobehavioral Approach*, edited by Bruce Voeller, June Machover Reinisch, and Michael Gottlieb, 3–10. New York: Oxford University Press, 1990.

HILL, Craig A. "Seeking Emotional Support: The Influence of Affiliative Need and Partner Warmth." *Journal of Personality and Social Psychology* 60, no. 1 (1991): 112–21.

MORTENSEN, Erik L., Anders Gade, and June M. Reinisch. "A Critical Note on Lezak's 'Best Performance Method' in Clinical Neuropsychology." *Journal of Clinical and Experimental Neuropsychology* 13, no. 2 (1991): 361–71.

PERSHING, Gwendolyn W. "Erotica Research Collections." In *Libraries, Erotica, Pornography*, edited by M. Cornog, 188–93. Phoenix, AZ: Oryx Press, 1991.

REINISCH, June M., Craig A. Hill, Mary Ziemba-Davis, and Stephanie A. Sanders. "Perceptions about Sexual Behavior: Findings from a National Sex Knowledge Survey—United States, 1989." *Morbidity and Mortality Weekly Report* 40, no. 15 (1991): 249–52.

REINISCH, June M., Leonard A. Rosenblum, Donald B. Rubin, and M. Fini Schulsinger. "Sex Differences in Behavioral Milestones during the First Year of Life." *Journal of Psychology and Human Sexuality* 4, no. 2 (1991): 19–36.

REINISCH, June M., Mary Ziemba-Davis, and Stephanie A. Sanders. "Hormonal Contributions to Sexually Dimorphic Behavioral Development in Humans." *Psychoneuroendocrinology* 16, no. 1–3 (1991): 213–78.

SANDERS, Stephanie A., Mary Ziemba-Davis, Craig A. Hill, and June M. Reinisch. "A Rejoinder: Intent and Purpose of the Kinsey Institute/Roper Organization National Sex Knowledge Survey." *Public Opinion Quarterly* 55, no. 3 (1991): 458–62.

BANCROFT, John. "Sexual Behaviour in Britain and France: As in Previous Research the Emphasis Is on Counting Rather than Understanding." *BMJ: British Medical Journal* 305, no. 6,867 (1992): 1447–48.

REINISCH, June M., and Stephanie A. Sanders. "Effects of Prenatal Exposure to Diethylstilbestrol (DES) on Hemispheric Laterality and Spatial Ability in Human Males." *Hormones and Behavior* 26, no. 1 (1992): 62–65.

REINISCH, June M., and Stephanie A. Sanders. "Prenatal Hormonal Contributions to Sex Differences in Human Cognitive and Personality Development." In *Handbook of Behavioral Neurobiology*, vol. 11, *Sexual Differentiation*, edited by H. Moltz, I. L. Ward, and A. A. Gerall, 221–43. New York: Plenum Publishing, 1992.

REINISCH, June M., Stephanie A. Sanders, Craig A. Hill, and Mary Ziemba-Davis. "High-Risk Sexual Behavior among Heterosexual Undergraduates at a Midwestern University." *Family Planning Perspectives* 24, no. 3 (1992): 116–45.

SANDERS, Stephanie A., and June M. Reinisch. "Psychological Correlates of Normal and Abnormal Menstrual Cycle Length." In *Menstrual Health in Women's Lives*, edited by A. J. Dan and L. L. Lewis, 131–46. Chicago: University of Illinois Press, 1992.

CRUMP, James. *George Platt Lynes: Photographs from the Kinsey Institute.* New York: Bulfinch Press/Little, Brown and Company, 1993.

BANCROFT, John. "Impact of Environment, Stress, Occupational, and Other Hazards on Sexuality and Sexual Behavior." *Environmental Health Perspectives* 101 (1993): 101–107.

REINISCH, June M. Preface to *George Platt Lynes: Photographs from the Kinsey Institute,* by James Crump, vii–viii. New York: Bulfinch Press/Little, Brown and Company, 1993.

REINISCH, June M., Erik L. Mortensen, and Stephanie A. Sanders. "The Prenatal Development Project." *Acta Psychiatrica Scandinavica,* Supplement 370 (1993): 54–61. Munksgaard, Copenhagen, Denmark.

HARTER, Margaret H. "Sexuality." In *American Library Association Guide to Information Access: A Complete Research Handbook and Directory,* edited by S. Whiteley. New York: Random House, 1994.

REINISCH, June M., and Margaret H. Harter. "Alfred C. Kinsey." In *Human Sexuality: An Encyclopedia,* edited by Vern L. Bullough and Bonnie Bullough, 333–38. New York: Garland Publishing, 1994.

SANDERS, Stephanie A. Preface to *Gay and Lesbian Stats,* edited by B. L. Singer and D. Deschamps, 7–8. New York: New Press, 1994.

WITKIN, Joel-Peter. *Harm's Way: Lust and Madness, Murder and Mayhem.* Altadena, CA: Twin Palms, 1994.

BANCROFT, John. "Are the Effects of Androgens on Male Sexuality Noradrenergically Mediated? Some Consideration of the Human." *Neuroscience and Biobehavioral Reviews* 19, no. 2 (1995): 325–30.

BANCROFT, John. "Effects of Alpha-2 Antagonists on Male Erectile Response." In *The Pharmacology of Sexual Function and Dysfunction,* edited by John Bancroft, 215–24. Amsterdam: Excerpta Medica, 1995.

BANCROFT, John. "From Behaviour Modifier to Behavioural Psychotherapist: The Personal Journey of a Sex Therapist." *Behavioural Cognitive Bulletin,* Royal College of Psychiatrists, 1995.

BANCROFT, John. "Sexual Problems in Diabetes." *Diabetes Reviews International* 3 (1995): 2–5.

BANCROFT, John. "Sexuality and Family Planning." In *Handbook of Family Planning and Reproductive Health Care,* edited by N. B. Loudon, A. F. Glasier, and A. Gebbie, 3rd ed., 339–62. Edinburgh: Churchill Livingston, 1995.

BANCROFT, John. "The Menstrual Cycle and the Well-Being of Women." *Social Science and Medicine* 41, no. 6 (1995): 785–91.

BANCROFT, John, and A. Cook. "The Neuroendocrine Response to D-fenfluramine in Women with Premenstrual Depression." *Journal of Affective Disorders* 36 (1995): 57–64.

REINISCH, June M., John Bancroft, and C. Graham. "Crisis Intervention." In *Introduction to the Psychotherapies,* 3rd ed., edited by S. Bloch, 116–36. Oxford: Oxford University Press, 1995.

BANCROFT, John, and N. Malone. "The Clinical Assessment of Erectile Dysfunction: A Comparison of Nocturnal Penile Tumescence Monitoring and Intracavernosal Injections." *International Journal of Impotence Research* 7 (1995): 123–30.

BANCROFT, John, M. Munoz, M. Beard, and C. Shapiro. "The Effects of a New Alpha-2 Adrenoceptor Antagonist on Sleep and Nocturnal Penile Tumescence in Normal Male

Volunteers and Men with Erectile Dysfunction." *Psychosomatic Medicine* 57 (1995): 345–56.

BANCROFT, John, and D. Rennie. "Perimenstrual Depression: Its Relationship to Pain, Bleeding, and Previous History of Depression." *Psychosomatic Medicine* 57, no. 5 (1995): 445–52.

CARANI, Caesar, A. R. M. Granata, John Bancroft, and P. Marrama. "The Effects of Testosterone Replacement on Nocturnal Penile Tumescence and Rigidity and Erectile Response to Visual Erotic Stimuli in Hypogonadal Men." *Psychoneuroendocrinology* 20, no. 7 (1995): 743–53.

DONOHUE, John, and Paul Gebhard. "The Kinsey Institute/Indiana University Report on Sexuality and Spinal Cord Injury." *Sexuality & Disability* 13, no. 1 (1995): 3–85.

DYE, Louise, Pamela Warner, and John Bancroft. "Food Craving during the Menstrual Cycle and Its Relationship to Stress, Happiness of Relationship, and Depression." *Journal of Affective Disorders* 34 (1995): 157–64.

GRAHAM, Cynthia A., Rebecca Ramos, John Bancroft, Caesar Maglaya, and Timothy M. M. Farley. "The Effects of Steroidal Contraceptives on the Well-Being and Sexuality of Women: A Double Blind, Placebo-Controlled, Two Centre Study of Combined and Progestogen-Only Methods." *Contraception* 52 (1995): 363–69.

GRANATA, Antonio, John Bancroft, Graziano Del Rio, and Caesar Carani. "Stress and the Erectile Response to Intracavernosal Prostaglandin E1 in Men with Erectile Dysfunction." *Psychosomatic Medicine* 57 (1995): 336–44.

GUTIERREZ, P., P. Langan, and John Bancroft. "Comparison of Home and Laboratory Based Monitoring of NPT Using the Rigiscan: A Preliminary Report." *International Journal of Impotence Research* 7 (1995): 137–46.

JANSSEN, Erick. "Activatie en inhibitie van de mannelijke genitale respons" [Activation and inhibition of the male genital response]. *Tijdschrift voor Seksuologie* 19 (1995): 283–91.

REINISCH, June M., Craig A. Hill, Stephanie A. Sanders, and Mary Ziemba-Davis. "High-Risk Sexual Behavior at a Midwestern University: A Confirmatory Survey." *Family Planning Perspectives* 27, no. 2 (1995): 79–82.

REINISCH, June M., Stephanie A. Sanders, Erik L. Mortensen, and D. B. Rubin. "Prenatal Exposure to Phenobarbital and Intelligence Deficits in Adult Human Males." *Journal of the American Medical Association* 274, no. 19 (1995): 1518–24.

REINISCH, June M., Stephanie A. Sanders, and Mary Ziemba-Davis. "Self-Labeled Sexual Orientation and Sexual Behavior: Considerations for STD-Related Biomedical Research and Education." In *Perspectives on Behavioral Medicine: Chronic Diseases*, edited by M. Stein and A. Baum, 241–57. New York: Lawrence Erlbaum, 1995.

SANDERS, Stephanie A., Erik L. Mortensen, and D. B. Rubin. "Prenatal Exposure to Phenobarbital and Intelligence Deficits in Adult Human Males." *Journal of the American Medical Association* 274, no. 19 (1995): 1518–24.

ZHOU, Liana Hong. "Su E Pian: A Unique Treasure at the Kinsey Institute Library." *Journal of Library and Information Science* 21, no. 5 (1995): 2–9.

BANCROFT, John. "Sex Therapy." In *Introduction to the Psychotherapies*, 3rd ed., edited by S. Bloch, 213–37. Oxford: Oxford University Press, 1996.

BANCROFT, John, and E. H. H. Cawood. "Androgens and the Menopause: A Study of 40- to 60-Year-Old Women." *Clinical Endocrinology* 45 (1996): 577–87.

BANCROFT, John, and C. Graham. "Crisis Intervention." In *Introduction to the Psychotherapies*, 3rd ed., edited by S. Bloch, 116–36. Oxford: Oxford University Press, 1996.

BANCROFT, John, and P. Gutierrez. "Erectile Dysfunction in Men with and without Diabetes Mellitus: A Comparative Study." *Diabetic Medicine* 13 (1996): 84–89.

KINSEY INSTITUTE FOR RESEARCH IN SEX, GENDER, AND REPRODUCTION LIBRARY. *Gender Affects*. Bloomington, IN: Fine Arts Gallery, 1996. Exhibition catalog.

KRAAIMAAT, F., A. Bakker, Erick Janssen, and J. Bijlsma. "Intrusiveness of Rheumatoid Arthritis on Sexuality in Male and Female Patients Living with a Spouse." *Arthritis Care and Research* 2 (1996): 120–25.

MORTENSEN, Erik L., June M. Reinisch, and Stephanie A. Sanders. "Psychometric Properties of the Danish 16PF and EPQ." *Scandinavian Journal of Psychology* 37 (1996): 221–25.

MORTENSEN, Erik L., June M. Reinisch, Stephanie A. Sanders, and D. B. Rubin. "Intelligensdefekter som senfølge af prænatal ekposition for phenobarbital-Fenemal." *Ugeskrift for Læger (Journal of the Danish Medical Association)* 158, no. 46 (1996): 6589–94.

SANDERS, Stephanie A. "Sexual Orientation." In *Dictionary of American History*, Supplement R, edited by Joan Ferrell and Robert H. Hoff. New York: Charles Scribner's Sons, 1996.

YAMASHIRO, Jennifer P. "Idylls in Conflict: Victorian Representations of Gender in Julia Margaret Cameron's Illustrations of Tennyson's *Idylls of the King*." In *Gendered Territory: Photographs of Women by Julia Margaret Cameron*, edited by D. Oliphant, 89–116. Austin: Harry Ransom Humanities Research Center at the University of Texas at Austin, 1996.

ZIEMBA-DAVIS, Mary, Stephanie A. Sanders, and June M. Reinisch. "Lesbians' Sexual Interactions with Men and Women: Behavioral Bisexuality and Risk for STD/HIV." *Journal of Women's Health: Research on Gender, Behavior, and Policy* 2, nos. 1–2 (1996): 59–72.

BANCROFT, John, ed. *Researching Sexual Behavior: Methodological Issues*. Bloomington: Indiana University Press, 1997.

BANCROFT, John. "Sexual Problems." In *Science and Practice of Cognitive Behaviour Therapy*, edited by D. Clark and C. Fairburn, 243–57. London: Oxford University Press, 1997.

GRAHAM, Cynthia A., and John Bancroft. "A Comparison of Retrospective Interview Assessment vs. Daily Ratings of Sexual Interest and Activity in Women." In *Researching Sexual Behavior: Methodological Issues*, edited by J. Bancroft, 227–36. Bloomington: Indiana University Press, 1997.

HARTER, Margaret. "The Cover." *Libraries & Culture: A Journal of Library History* 32, no. 2 (1997): 245–47. Feature on the Institute for Sex Research's bookplate designed by Dickinson, which was the cover design for the issue.

JANSSEN, Erick, M. Vissenberg, S. Visser, and W. Everaerd. "An In Vivo Comparison of Two Circumferential Penile Strain Gauges: Introducing a New Calibration Method." *Psychophysiology* 34 (1997): 717–20.

TOORIANS, W. F. T., Erick Janssen, E. Laan, L. Gooren, E. Giltay, P. Oe, A. Donker, and W. Evereard. "Chronic Renal Failure and Sexual Functioning: Clinical Status versus Objectively Assessed Sexual Response." *Nephrology Dialysis Transplantation* 12 (1997): 2654–63.

YAMASHIRO, Jennifer P. *Art of Desire: Erotic Treasures from the Kinsey Institute*. Bloomington, IN: Kinsey Institute, 1997. Exhibition catalog.

WU, Wei, John D. Bancroft, and J. W. Suttie. "Structural Features of the Kringle Domain Determine the Intracellular Degradation of under-γ -Carboxylated Prothrombin: Studies of Chimeric Rat/Human Prothrombin." *Proceedings of the National Academy of Sciences of the United States of America* 94, no. 25 (1997): 13654–60.

BANCROFT, John. "Alfred Kinsey's Work 50 Years Later." In *Sexual Behavior in the Human Female*, by Alfred C. Kinsey, Wardell B. Pomeroy, Clyde E. Martin, and Paul H. Gebhard. Bloomington: Indiana University Press, 1998.

BANCROFT, John. "Central Control and Inhibitory Mechanisms in Male Sexual Response." *International Journal of Impotence Research* 10, supplement 2 (1998): S40–S43.

BANCRFOT, John. "Clinical Trials and Human Sexuality: Basic Concepts and Problems." *International Journal of Impotence Research* 10, supplement 2 (1998): S4–6, S24–S26.

BANCROFT, John. "Kinsey." *Sexualities* 1 (1998): 85–87.

BANCROFT, John. "Sexual Disorders." In *Companion to Psychiatric Studies*, edited by Eve C. Johnstone, C. Freeman, and A. K. Zealley, 6th ed., 529–50. London: Churchill Livingstone, 1998.

BROSSCHOT, J., and Erick Janssen. "Continuous Monitoring of Affective-Autonomic Response Dissociation in Repressors during Negative Emotional Stimulation." *Personality and Individual Differences* 25, no. 1 (1998): 69–84.

ANDERSON, R. A., C. W. Martin, A. Kung, D. Everington, T. C. Pun, K. C. B. Tan, John Bancroft, K. Sundaram, A. J. Moo-Young, and D. T. Baird. "7a-Methyl-19-Nortestosterone (MENT) Maintains Sexual Behavior and Mood in Hypogonadal Men." *Journal of Clinical Endocrinology & Metabolism* 84, no. 10 (1999): 3556–62.

BANCROFT, John. "Cardiovascular and Endocrine Changes during Sexual Arousal and Orgasm." *Psychosomatic Medicine* 61 (1999): 290–91.

BANCROFT, John. "Central Inhibition of Sexual Response in the Male: A Theoretical Perspective." *Neuroscience and Biobehavioral Reviews* 23 (1999): 763–84.

BANCROFT, John. "Sexual Science in the 21st Century: Where Are We Going? A Personal Note." *Journal of Sex Research* 36 (1999): 226–29.

SANDERS, Stephanie A. "Midlife Sexuality: The Need to Integrate Biological, Psychological, and Social Perspectives." *SIECUS Report* 27, no. 3 (1999): 3–7.

SANDERS, Stephanie A., and June M. Reinisch. "Would You Say You 'Had Sex' If. . . ?" *Journal of the American Medical Association* 281, no. 3 (1999): 275–77.

2000–2009

BANCROFT, John. "Die Medikalisierung sexueller Probleme von Frauen." *Zeitschrift für Sexualforschung* 13 (2000): 69–76.

BANCROFT, John. "Effects of Alpha-2 Blockade on Sexual Response: Experimental Studies with Delequamine (RS15385)." *International Journal of Impotence Research* 12, supplement 1 (2000): S64–S69.

BANCROFT, John. "Helping People with Sexual Problems." *Medical Aspects of Human Sexuality* 1, no. 1 (2000): 8–9.

BANCROFT, John. "Psychogenic Erectile Dysfunction: A Theoretical Approach." *International Journal of Impotence Research* 12, supplement 3 (2000): S46–S48.

BANCROFT, John, and Erick Janssen. "The Dual Control Model of Male Sexual Response: A Theoretical Approach to Centrally Mediated Erectile Fysfunction." *Neuroscience and Biobehavioral Reviews* 24 (2000): 571–79.

GEER, J., and Erick Janssen. "The Sexual Response System." In *Handbook of Psychophysiology*, edited by J. T. Cacioppo, L. G. Tassinary, and G. G. Berntson, 315–41. New York: Cambridge University Press, 2000.

GOLDSTEIN, I., John Bancroft, F. Guiliano, J. P. W. Heaton, R. W. Lewis, T. F. Lue, K. E. McKenna, H. Padma-Nathan, R. Rosen, B. D. Sachs, R. T. Segraves, and W. D. Steers. "Male Sexual Circuitry." *Scientific American* 283, no. 2 (2000): 70–75.

GRAHAM, Cynthia A., Erick Janssen, and Stephanie A. Sanders. "Effects of Fragrance on Female Sexual Arousal and Mood across the Menstrual Cycle." *Psychophysiology* 37 (2000): 76–78.

HEIMAN, Julia R. "Medical Advances and Human Sexuality: Introduction and Comment." *Journal of Sex Research* 37, no. 3 (2000): 193–94.

JANSSEN, Erick, W. Everaerd, M. Spiering, and J. Janssen. "Automatic Processes and the Appraisal of Sexual Stimuli: Toward an Information Processing Model of Sexual Arousal." *Journal of Sex Research* 37, no. 1 (2000): 8–23.

ROZENMAN, D., and Erick Janssen. "Sexual Function after Hysterectomy." *Journal of the American Medical Association* 283, no. 17 (2000): 2238–39.

SQUIERS, C., J. P. Yamashiro, B. Stirratt, and J. A. Wolin. *Peek: Photographs from the Kinsey Institute*. Santa Fe: Arena Editions, 2000.

YAMASHIRO, Jennifer Pearson. "In the Realm of the Sciences: The Kinsey Institute's 31 Photographs." In *Porn 101: Erotica, Pornography, and the First Amendment*. New York: Prometheus, 1999–2000.

YARBER, William L., R. A. Crosby, and Stephanie A. Sanders. "Understudied HIV/STD Risk Behaviors among a Sample of Rural South Carolina Women: A Descriptive Pilot Study." *Health Education Monograph* 18 (2000): 1–5.

BANCROFT, John, Cynthia A. Graham, and Carol McCord. "Conceptualizing Women's Sexual Problems." *Journal of Sex & Marital Therapy* 27, no. 2 (2001): 95–104.

BANCROFT, John, and Erick Janssen. "Psychogenic Erectile Dysfunction in the Era of Pharmacotherapy: A Theoretical Approach." In *Male Sexual Function: A Guide to Clinical Management*, edited by J. Mulcahy, 79–89. Totowa, NJ: Humana Press, 2001.

SANDERS, Stephanie A., Cynthia Graham, Jennifer Bass, and John H. Bancroft. "A Prospective Study of the Effects of Oral Contraceptives on Sexuality and Well-Being and Their Relationship to Discontinuation." *Contraception* 64, no. 1 (2001): 51–58.

BANCROFT, John. "The Medicalization of Female Sexual Dysfunction." *Archives of Sexual Behavior* 31 (2002): 451–55.

BANCROFT, John. "Biological Factors in Human Sexuality." *Journal of Sex Research* 39, no. 1 (2002): 15–21.

BANCROFT, John. "Sexual Arousal." In *Encyclopedia of Cognitive Science*, edited by Lynn Nadel, vol. 3, 1165–68. London: Nature Publishing Group, 2003.

BANCROFT, John. "Promoting Responsible Sexual Behaviour: Leading Comment." *Sexual and Relationship Therapy* 17 (2002): 9–12.

BANCROFT, John. Foreword to *Sex and the Internet: A Guidebook for Clinicians*, edited by A. Cooper, ix–xii. New York: Brunner-Routledge, 2002.

BANCROFT, John. "Sexual Effects of Androgens in Women: Some Theoretical Considerations." *Fertility and Sterility* 77, supplement 4 (2002): 555–59.

CROSBY, Richard, Stephanie A. Sanders, William Yarber, Cynthia Graham, and B. Dodge. "Condom Use Errors and Problems among College Men." *Sexually Transmitted Diseases* 29, no. 9 (2002): 552–57.

GEBHARD, Paul. "In Memoriam: Wardell B. Pomeroy." *Archives of Sexual Behavior* 31, no. 2 (2002): 155–56.

GRAHAM, Cynthia A. "Methods for Obtaining Menstrual Cycle Data in Menstrual Synchrony Studies." *Journal of Comparative Psychology* 116, no. 3 (2002): 313–15.

GRAHAM, Cynthia A. "Sexual Side Effects of Oral Contraceptives: Clinical Considerations." *Medical Aspects of Human Sexuality*, March 2002, 1–6.

HEIMAN, Julia R. "Sexual Dysfunction: Overview of Prevalence, Etiological Factors, and Treatments." *Journal of Sex Research* 39, no. 1 (2002): 73–78.

JANSSEN, Erick. "Psychophysiological Measures of Sexual Response." In *Handbook for Conducting Research on Human Sexuality*, edited by M. W. Wiederman and B. E. Whitley, 139–71. Mahwah, NJ: Erlbaum, 2002.

JANSSEN, Erick, H. Vorst, P. Finn, and John Bancroft. "The Sexual Inhibition (SIS) and Sexual Excitation (SES) Scales: I. Measuring Sexual Inhibition and Excitation Proneness in Men." *Journal of Sex Research* 39, no. 2 (2002): 114–26.

JANSSEN, Erick, H. Vorst, P. Finn, and John Bancroft. "The Sexual Inhibition (SIS) and Sexual Excitation (SES) Scales: II. Predicting Psychophysiological Response Patterns." *Journal of Sex Research* 39, no. 2 (2002): 127–32.

JOHNSON, C., B. Stirratt, and John Bancroft. *Sex and Humor: Selections from the Kinsey Institute*. Bloomington: Indiana University Press, 2002.

LAAN, E., and Erick Janssen. "Beleefde Seks: Determinanten van seksuele gevoelens" [Experienced sex: Determinants of sexual feelings]. *De Psycholoog* 7–8 (2002): 370–76.

MORTENSEN, Erik, K. Michaelsen, Stephanie A. Sanders, and June M. Reinisch. "The Association between Duration of Breastfeeding and Adult Intelligence." *Journal of the American Medical Association* 287 (2002): 2365–71.

BANCROFT, John, J. Loftus, and J. S. Long. "Reply to Rosen and Laumann's (2003) 'The Prevalence of Sexual Problems in Women: How Valid Are Comparisons across Studies?'" *Archives of Sexual Behavior* 32, no. 3 (2003): 213–16.

BANCROFT, John. "Can Sexual Orientation Change? A Long-Running Saga. Peer Commentaries of Spitzer." *Archives of Sexual Behavior* 32, no. 5 (2003): 419–21.

BANCROFT, John, ed. *Sexual Development in Childhood*. Bloomington: Indiana University Press, 2003.

BANCROFT, John. "Androgens and Sexual Function in Men and Women." In *Androgens in Health and Disease*, edited by C. Bagatell and W. Bremner, 259–90. Totowa, NJ: Humana Press, 2003.

BANCROFT, John, Erick Janssen, D. Strong, L. Carnes, and J. S. Long. "Sexual Risk Taking in Gay Men: The Relevance of Sexual Arousability, Mood, and Sensation Seeking." *Archives of Sexual Behavior* 32, no. 6 (2004): 555–72.

BANCROFT, John, J. Loftus, and J. S. Long. "Distress about Sex: A National Survey of Women in Heterosexual Relationships." *Archives of Sexual Behavior* 32, no. 3 (2003): 193–209.

BANCROFT, John, Erick Janssen, D. Strong, L. Carnes, Z. Vukadinovic, and J. S. Long. "The Relation between Mood and Sexuality in Heterosexual Men." *Archives of Sexual Behavior* 32 (2003): 217–30.

BANCROFT, John, Erick Janssen, D. Strong, and Z. Vukadinovic. "The Relation between Mood and Sexuality in Gay Men." *Archives of Sexual Behavior* 32 (2003): 231–42.

CROSBY, Richard A., Stephanie A. Sanders, William L. Yarber, and Cynthia A. Graham. "Condom Use Errors and Problems: A Neglected Aspect of Studies Assessing Condom Effectiveness." *American Journal of Preventive Medicine* 24, no. 4 (2003): 367–70.

GRAHAM, Cynthia A., J. A. Catania, R. Brand, T. Duong, and J. A. Canchola. "Recalling Sexual Behavior: A Methodological Analysis of Memory Recall Bias via Interview Using the Diary as the Gold Standard." *Journal of Sex Research* 40, no. 4 (2003): 325–32.

GRAHAM, Cynthia A., Richard A. Crosby, Stephanie A. Sanders, and William L. Yarber. "Motivation of Self, Partner, and Couple to Use Male Condoms: Associations with Condom Use Errors and Problems." Special issue, *Health Education Monograph* 20, no. 2 (2003): 60–64.

GRAHAM, Cynthia A., John Bancroft, William L. Yarber, and Stephanie A. Sanders. "The Kinsey Institute as a Center for Graduate Education in Human Sexuality." In *Handbook of Sexuality Research Training Initiatives*, edited by G. Herdt, D. Di Mauro, and R. Parker. New York: Social Science Research Council, 2003.

GRAHAM, Cynthia A. "Methodological Issues Involved in Adult Recall of Childhood Sexual Experiences." In *Sexual Development in Childhood*, edited by John Bancroft, 67–76. Bloomington: Indiana University Press, 2003.

JANSSEN, Erick, D. Carpenter, and Cynthia A. Graham. "Selecting Films for Sex Research: Gender Differences in Erotic Film Preference." *Archives of Sexual Behavior* 32, no. 3 (2003): 243–51.

McCORD, Carol, and Stephanie A. Sanders. "Talking about Sex in HIV-Related Counseling and Health Care Settings." *Focus: A Guide to AIDS Research and Counseling* 18, no. 6 (2003): 1–4.

SANDERS, Stephanie A., Cynthia A. Graham, William L. Yarber, and Richard A. Crosby. "Condom Use Errors and Problems among Young Women Who Put Condoms on Their Male Partners." *Journal of the American Medical Women's Association* 58, no. 2 (2003): 95–98.

STIRRATT, B., and Catherine Johnson. *Feminine Persuasion: Art and Essays on Sexuality.* Bloomington: Indiana University Press, 2003.

BANCROFT, John, Erick Janssen, Lori Carnes, David Goodrich, David Strong, and J. Scott Long. "Sexual Activity and Risk Taking in Young Heterosexual Men: The Relevance of Sexual Arousability, Mood, and Sensation Seeking." *Journal of Sex Research* 41, no. 2 (2004): 181–92.

BANCROFT, John, and Zoran Vukadinovic. "Sexual Addiction, Sexual Compulsivity, Sexual Impulsivity or What? Toward a Theoretical Model." *Journal of Sex Research* 41, no. 3 (2004): 225–34.

BANCROFT, John, Erick Janssen, L. Carnes, D. A. Strong, D. Goodrich, and J. S. Long. "Sexual Activity and Risk Taking in Young Heterosexual Men: The Relevance of Personality Factors." *Journal of Sex Research* 41, no. 2 (2004): 181–92.

BANCROFT, John. "Alfred C. Kinsey and the Politics of Sex Research." *Annual Review of Sex Research* 15 (2004): 1–39.

CROSBY, Richard A., William L. Yarber, Stephanie A. Sanders, and Cynthia A. Graham. "Condom Use as a Dependent Variable: A Brief Commentary about Classification of Inconsistent Users." *AIDS and Behavior* 8, no. 1 (2004): 99–103.

CROSBY, Richard A., Cynthia A. Graham, William L. Yarber, and Stephanie A. Sanders. "If the Condom Fits, Wear It: A Qualitative Study of Young African-American Men." *Sexually Transmitted Infections* 80 (2004): 306–309.

GRAHAM, Cynthia A., Stephanie A. Sanders, R. R. Millhausen, and K. R. McBride. "Turning On and Turning Off: A Focus Group Study of the Factors That Affect Women's Sexual Arousal." *Archives of Sexual Behavior* 33, no. 6 (2004): 527–38.

HOFFMAN, H., Erick Janssen, and S. L. Turner. "Classical Conditioning of Sexual Arousal in Women and Men: Effects of Varying Awareness and Biological Relevance of the Conditioned Stimulus." *Archives of Sexual Behavior* 33, no. 1 (2004): 1–11.

MESTON, C., R. Levin, M. Sipski, E. Hull, and Julian Heiman. "Women's Orgasm." *Annual Review of Sex Research* 15 (2004): 173–257.

SUH, D. D., C. C. Yang, Y. Cao, Julia R. Heiman, P. A. Garland, and K. R. Maravilla. "MRI of Female Genital and Pelvic Organs during Sexual Arousal: Initial Experience." *Journal of Psychosomatic Obstetrics and Gynecology* 25, no. 2 (2004): 153–62.

YARBER, William L., Cynthia A. Graham, Stephanie A. Sanders, and Richard A. Crosby. "Correlates of Condom Breakage and Slippage among University Undergraduates." *International Journal of STD and AIDS* 15, no. 7 (2004): 467–72.

VITZTHUM, Virginia J., Hilde Spielvogel, Jonathan Thornburg, and Cynthia M. Beall. "Interpopulational Differences in Progesterone Levels during Conception and Implantation in Humans." *Proceedings of the National Academy of Sciences of the United States of America* 101, no. 6 (2004): 1443–48.

BANCROFT, John. "The Endocrinology of Sexual Arousal." *Journal of Endocrinology* 186, no. 3 (2005): 411–27.

BANCROFT, John, L. Carnes, and Erick Janssen. "Unprotected Anal Intercourse in HIV-Positive and HIV-Negative Gay Men: The Relevance of Sexual Arousability, Mood, Sensation Seeking, and Erectile Problems." *Archives of Sexual Behavior* 34, no. 3 (2005): 299–305.

BANCROFT, John, L. Carnes, Erick Janssen, D. Goodrich, and J. S. Long. "Erectile and Ejaculatory Problems in Gay and Heterosexual Men." *Archives of Sexual Behavior* 34 (2005): 285–97.

BANCROFT, John, D. Herbenick, T. Barnes, R. Hallam-Jones, K. Wylie, Erick Janssen, and members of BASRT. "The Relevance of the Dual Control Model to Male Sexual Dysfunction: The Kinsey Institute/BASRT Collaborative Project." *Sexual and Relationship Therapy* 20, no. 1 (2005): 13–30.

BANCROFT, John. "Normal Sexual Development." In *The Juvenile Sex Offender*, edited by H. L. Barbaree and W. M. Marshall. New York: Guilford, 2005.

CROSBY, Richard, William Yarber, Stephanie Sanders, and Cynthia Graham. "Condom Discomfort and Associated Problems with Their Use among University Students." *Journal of American College Health* 54, no. 3 (2005): 143–47.

FORTENBERRY, J. D., M'H Temkit, W. Tu, Cynthia Graham, B. Katz, and D. Orr. "Daily Mood, Partner Support, Sexual Interest, and Sexual Activity among Adolescent Women." *Health Psychology* 24, no. 3 (2005): 252–57.

MARAVILLA, K. R., Y. Cao, Julia R. Heiman, C. Yang, P. A. Garland, B. T. Peterson, and W. O. Carter. "Noncontrast Dynamic Magnetic Resonance Imaging for Quantitative Assessment of Female Sexual Arousal." *Journal of Urology* 172 (2005): 162–66.

MOORE, D. R., and Julia R. Heiman. "Women's Sexuality in Context: Relationship Factors and Female Sexual Functioning." In *Female Sexual Dysfunction*, edited by I. Goldstein, C. Meston, S. Davis, and A. Traish, 63–84. New York: Parthenon, 2005.

MORTENSEN, Erik L., K. F. Michaelsen, Stephanie A. Sanders, and June M. Reinisch. "A Dose-Response Relationship between Maternal Smoking during Late Pregnancy and Adult Intelligence in Male Offspring." *Pediatric and Perinatal Epidemiology* 19 (2005): 4–11.

MUELENHARD, C. L., and Z. D. Peterson. "Wanting and Not Wanting Sex: The Missing Discourse of Ambivalence." *Feminism and Psychology* 15 (2005): 15–20.

PRAUSE, N., J. Cerny, and Erick Janssen. "The Labial Photoplethysmograph: A New Instrument for Assessing Genital Hemodynamic Changes in Women." *Journal of Sexual Medicine* 2, no. 1 (2005): 58–65.

STRONG, D., John Bancroft, L. Carnes, L. Davis, and J. Kennedy. "The Impact of Sexual Arousal on Sexual Risk-Taking: A Qualitative Study." *Journal of Sex Research* 42, no. 3 (2005): 185–91.

VITZTHUM, Virginia J., and Karin Ringheim. "Hormonal Contraception and Physiology: A Research-Based Theory of Discontinuation Due to Side Effects." *Studies in Family Planning* 36, no. 1 (2005): 13–32.

YARBER, William L., R. R. Milhausen, Richard A. Crosby, and M. R. Torabi. "Public Opinion about Condoms for HIV and STD Prevention: A Midwestern State Telephone Survey." *Perspectives on Sexual and Reproductive Health* 37, no. 3 (2005): 148–54.

DAVIS, K. D., J. Norris, W. H. George, J. Martell, and Julia R. Heiman. "Men's Likelihood of Sexual Aggression: The Influence of Alcohol, Sexual Arousal, and Violent Pornography." *Aggressive Behavior* 32 (2006): 581–89.

DAVIS, K. D., J. Norris, W. H. George, J. Martell, and Julia R. Heiman. "Rape-Myth Congruent Beliefs in Women Resulting from Exposure to Violent Pornography: Effects of Alcohol and Sexual Arousal." *Journal of Interpersonal Violence* 21, no. 9 (2006): 1208–23.

DIAMOND, L. E., D. C. Earle, Julia R. Heiman, R. C. Rosen, M. A. Perelman, and R. Harning. "An Effect on the Subjective Sexual Response in Premenopausal Women with Sexual Arousal Disorder by Bremelanotide (PT-141), a Melanocortin Receptor Agonist." *Journal of Sex Medicine* 3, no. 4 (2006): 628–38.

GEORGE, W. H., K. C. Davis, J. Norris, Julia R. Heiman, R. L. Schacht, S. A. Stoner, and K. F. Kajumulo. "Alcohol and Erectile Response: The Effects of High Dosage in the Context of Demands to Maximize Sexual Arousal." *Experimental and Clinical Psychopharmacology* 4 (2006): 461–70.

GRAHAM, Cynthia A., Stephanie A. Sanders, and R. R. Milhausen. "The Sexual Excitation/Sexual Inhibition Inventory for Women: Psychometric Properties." *Archives of Sexual Behavior* 35, no. 4 (2006): 1–13.

GRAHAM, Cynthia A., Richard A. Crosby, William L. Yarber, Stephanie A. Sanders, K. R. McBride, R. R. Millhausen, and J. N. Arno. "Erection Loss in Association with Condom Use among Young Men Attending a Public STI Clinic: Potential Correlates and Implications for Risk Behavior." *Sexual Health* 3, no. 4 (2006): 255–60.

GRAHAM, Cynthia A., Richard A. Crosby, William L. Yarber, Stephanie A. Sanders, K. R. McBride, R. R. Millhausen, and J. N. Arno. "Condom-Associated Erection Loss among Men Who Have Sex with Women Attending a Public STI Clinic." *Sexual Health* 3 (2006): 1–6.

GRAHAM, Cynthia A., Richard A. Crosby, Stephanie A. Sanders, and William L. Yarber. "Assessment of Condom Use in Men and Women." *Annual Review of Sex Research* 16 (2006): 20–52.

HEIMAN, Julia R., M. Gittelman, R. Costabile, A. Guay, A. Friedman, A. Heard-Davison, C. Peterson, J. Dietrich, and D. Stephens. "Topical Alprostadil (PGE) for the Treatment of Female Sexual Arousal Disorder: In-Clinic Evaluation of Safety and Efficacy." *Journal of Psychosomatic Obstetrics & Gynecology* 27, no. 1 (2006): 31–41.

JANSSEN, Erick, N. Prause, and J. Geer. "The Sexual Response." In *Handbook of Psychophysiology*, 3rd ed., edited by J. T. Cacioppo, L. G. Tassinary, and G. G. Berntson. New York: Cambridge University Press, 2006.

KUFFEL, S. W., and Julia R. Heiman. "Effects of Depressive Symptoms and Experimentally Adopted Schemas on Sexual Arousal and Affect in Sexually Healthy Women." *Archives of Sexual Behavior* 35, no. 2 (2006): 163–77.

LYKINS, A., Erick E. Janssen, and Cynthia Graham. "The Relationship between Negative Mood and Sexuality in Heterosexual College Men and Women." *Journal of Sex Research* 43, no. 2 (2006): 136–43.

LYKINS, Amy D., Erick Janssen, and Cynthia A. Graham. "The Relationship between Negative Mood and Sexuality in Heterosexual College Women and Men." *Journal of Sex Research* 43, no. 2 (2006): 136–43.

MUSTABSKI, B., and John Bancroft. "Sexual Dysfunction." In *Psychopharmacogenetics*, edited by P. Gorwood and M. Hamon, 479–94. New York: Springer, 2006.

PRAUSE, N., and Erick Janssen. "Blood Flow: Vaginal Photoplethysmography." In *Female Sexual Dysfunction*, edited by I. Goldstein, C. Meston, S. Davis, and A. Traish, 359–67. New York: Parthenon, 2006.

RELLINI, A. H., C. R. Meston, and Julia R. Heiman. "Sexual Abuse, Sexuality, and Sexual Self-Schemas." *Journal of Consulting and Clinical Psychology* 74, no. 2 (2006): 229–36.

ROSEN, R., Erick Janssen, M. Wiegel, John Bancroft, A. Althof, J. Wincze, R. T. Segraves, and D. Barlow. "Psychological and Interpersonal Correlates in Men with Erectile Dysfunction and Their Partners: Predictors of Pharmacotherapy Outcome." *Journal of Sex and Marital Therapy* 32, no. 3 (2006): 215–34.

ROSEN, R., Julia R. Heiman, and Erick Janssen. "The Bolger Conference on PDE-5 Inhibition and HIV Risk: Implications for Health Policy and Prevention." *Journal of Sex Medicine* 3 (2006): 960–75.

SANDERS, Stephanie A., Cynthia A. Graham, William L. Yarber, Richard A. Crosby, B. Dodge, and R. R. Milhausen. "Women Who Put Condoms on Male Partners: Correlates of Condom Application." *American Journal of Health Behavior* 30, no. 5 (2006): 460–66.

AUBIN, S., R. E. Berger, Julia R. Heiman, and M. A. Ciol. "The Association between Sexual Function, Pain, and Psychological Adaptation of Men Diagnosed with Chronic Pelvic Pain Syndrome Type III." *Journal of Sexual Medicine* 5, no. 3 (March 2008): 657–67.

BROTTO, L. A., and Julian R. Heiman. "Mindfulness in Sex Therapy: Applications for Women with Sexual Difficulties Following Gynecologic Cancer." *Sexual and Relationship Therapy* 22, no. 1 (2007): 3–11.

CROSBY, Richard, William Yarber, Stephanie Sanders, Cynthia Graham, K. McBride, R. R. Milhausen, and J. N. Arno. "Men with Broken Condoms: Who and Why?" *Sexually Transmitted Infections* 83, no. 1 (2007): 71–75.

DAVIS, K. C., C. S. Hendershot, W. H. George, J. Norris, and Julia R. Heiman. "Alcohol's Effects on Sexual Decision Making: An Integration of Alcohol Myopia and Individual Differences." *Journal of Studies on Alcohol and Drugs* 68, no. 6 (2007): 843–51.

GRAHAM, Cynthia A., John Bancroft, H. A. Doll, T. Greco, and A. Tanner. "Does Oral Contraceptive-Induced Reduction in Free Testosterone Adversely Affect the Sexuality or Mood of Women?" *Psychoneuroendocrinology* 32, no. 3 (2007): 246–55.

HEARD-DAVIDSON, A. R., S. W. Kuffel, and Julia R. Heiman. "Genital and Subjective Measurement of the Time Course Effects of an Acute Dose of Testosterone vs. Placebo in Postmenopausal Women." *Journal of Sexual Medicine* 4, no. 1 (January 2007): 209–17.

HEIMAN, Julia R. "Orgasmic Disorders in Women." In *Principles and Practice of Sex Therapy*, 4th ed., edited by S. R. Leiblum, 84–123. New York: Guilford, 2007.

HEIMAN, Julia R., and K. R. Maravilla. "Female Sexual Response Using Serial MR Imaging with Initial Comparisons to Vaginal Photoplethysmography: Overview and Evaluation." In *The Psychophysiology of Sex*, edited by Erick Janssen, 363–68. Bloomington: Indiana University Press, 2007.

HEIMAN, Julia, D. Talley, J. Bailen, T. Oskin, S. Rosenberg, C. Pace, D. Creanga, and T. Bavendam. "Sexual Function and Satisfaction in Heterosexual Couples When Men Are Administered Sildenafil Citrate (Viagra®) for Erectile Dysfunction: A Multicentre, Randomised, Double-Blind, Placebo-Controlled Trial." *BJOG: An International Journal of Obstetrics and Gynecology* 114, no. 4 (2007): 437–47.

HURD, P. L., and Sari M. van Anders. "Latitude, Allen's and Bergmann's Rules, and Digit Rations: A Comment on Loehlin et al." *Archives of Sexual Behavior* 36 (2007): 139–41.

JANSSEN, Erick, ed. *The Psychophysiology of Sex*. Bloomington: Indiana University Press, 2007.

JANSSEN, Erick. "Sexual Motivation and Arousal: Discussion Paper." In *The Psychophysiology of Sex*, edited by Erick Janssen, 363–68. Bloomington: Indiana University Press, 2007.

JANSSEN, Erick, and John Bancroft. "The Dual-Control Model: The Role of Sexual Inhibition and Excitation in Sexual Arousal and Behavior." In *The Psychophysiology of Sex*, edited by Erick Janssen, 197–222. Bloomington: Indiana University Press, 2007.

LAAN, E., and Erick Janssen. "How Do Men and Women Feel? Determinants of Subjective Experience of Sexual Arousal." In *The Psychophysiology of Sex*, edited by Erick Janssen, 278–90. Bloomington: Indiana University Press, 2007.

McBRIDE, Kimberly R., M. Reece, and S. A. Sanders. "Predicting Negative Outcomes of Sexuality Using the Compulsive Sexual Behavior Inventory." *International Journal of Sexual Health* 19, no. 4 (2008): 51–62.

McBRIDE, Kimberly R., Stephanie A. Sanders, Erick Janssen, Maria Elizabeth Grabe, Jennifer Bass, Johnny V. Sparks, Trevor R. Brown, and Julia R. Heiman. "Turning Sexual Science into News: Sex Research and the Media." *Journal of Sex Research* 44, no. 4 (2007): 347–58.

PETERSON, Zoë D., and Erick Janssen. "Ambivalent Affect and Sexual Response: The Impact of Co-occurring Positive and Negative Emotions on Subjective and Physiological Responses to Erotic Stimuli." *Archives of Sexual Behavior* 36, no. 6 (2007): 793–807.

PETERSON, Zoë D., and Charlene L. Muehlenhard. "Conceptualizing the 'Wantedness' of Women's Consensual and Nonconsensual Sexual Experiences: Implications for How Women Label Their Experiences with Rape." *Journal of Sex Research* 44, no. 1 (2007): 72–88.

PRAUSE, Nichole, and Cynthia A. Graham. "Asexuality: Classification and Characterization." *Archives of Sexual Behavior* 36, no. 3 (2007): 341–56.

RIMMERMAN, Neta, H. V. Hughes, Heather B. Bradshaw, M. X. Pazos, K. Mackie, A. L. Prieto, and J. M. Walker. "Compartmentalization of Endocannabinoids into Lipid Rafts in a Dorsal Root Ganglion Cell Line." *British Journal of Pharmacology* 153, no. 2 (October 2007): 380–89.

RUBIO, Marina, Douglas McHugh, Javier Fernández-Ruiz, Heather Bradshaw, and J. Michael Walker. "Short-Term Exposure to Alcohol in Rats Affects Brain Levels of

Anandamide, Other N-acylethanolamines and 2-arachidonoyl-glycerol." *Neuroscience Letters* 421, no. 3 (2007): 270–74.

RUPP, Heather A., and Kim Wallen. "Relationship between Testosterone and Interest in Sexual Stimuli: The Effect of Experience." *Hormones and Behavior* 51, no. 5 (2007): 581–89.

RUPP, Heather A., and Kim Wallen. "Sex Differences in Viewing Sexual Stimuli: An Eye Tracking Study in Men and Women." *Hormones and Behavior* 51, no. 4 (2007): 524–33.

SCHACHT, Rebecca L., William H. George, Julia R. Heiman, Kelly Cue Davis, Jeanette Norris, Susan A. Stoner, and Kelly F. Kajumulo. "Effects of Alcohol Intoxication and Instructional Set on Women's Sexual Arousal Vary Based on Sexual Abuse History." *Archives of Sexual Behavior* 36, no. 5 (2007): 655–65.

ŠTULHOFER, Aleksandar, Cynthia A. Graham, Ivana Božicevic, Krešimir Kufrin, and Dean Ajdukovic. "HIV/AIDS Related Knowledge, Attitudes, Beliefs and Sexual Behaviors as Predictors of Condom Use in a Nationally Representative Sample of Young Croatian Adults, 18–24." *International Family Planning Perspectives* 33, no. 2 (2007): 58–65.

VAN ANDERS, Sari M. "Grip Strength and Digit Ratios Are Not Correlated in Women." *American Journal of Human Biology* 19, no. 3 (2007): 437–39.

VAN ANDERS, Sari, and Peter B. Gray. "Hormones and Human Partnering." *Annual Review of Sex Research* 18, no. 1 (2007): 60–93.

VAN ANDERS, Sari, Lisa Dawn Hamilton, Nicole Schmidt, and Neil V. Watson. "Associations between Testosterone Secretion and Sexual Activity in Women." *Hormones and Behavior* 51, no. 4 (2007): 477–82.

VAN ANDERS, Sari, Lisa Dawn Hamilton, and Neil V. Watson. "Multiple Partners Are Associated with Higher Testosterone in North American Men and Women." *Hormones and Behavior* 51, no. 3 (2007): 454–59.

VAN ANDERS, Sari M., and Neil V. Watson. "Ability- vs. Chance-Determined Competition Outcomes: Effects on Testosterone in Humans." *Physiology and Behavior* 90, no. 4 (2007): 634–42.

VAN ANDERS, Sari M., and Neil V. Watson. "Testosterone Levels in Women and Men Who Are Single, in Long-Distance Relationships, or Same-City Relationships." *Hormones and Behavior* 51, no. 2 (2007): 286–91.

VAN ANDERS, Sari M., and Peter B. Gray. "Hormones and Human Partnering." *Annual Review of Sex Research* 18 (2007): 60–93.

YARBER, William L., Richard A. Crosby, Cynthia A. Graham, Stephanie A. Sanders, Janet Arno, Rose M. Hartzell, Kimberly McBride, Robin Milhausen, Lindsay Brown, Laurie J. Legocki, Martha Payne, and Alexis Rothring. "Correlates of Putting Condoms on after Sex Has Begun and of Removing Them before Sex Ends: A Study of Men Attending an Urban Public STD Clinic." *American Journal of Men's Health* 1, no. 3 (2007): 190–96.

YARBER, William L., Richard Crosby, Cynthia A. Graham, Stephanie A. Sanders, Rose M. Hartzell, and Scott Butler. "'Do You Know What You Are Doing?': College Students' Experience with Condoms." *American Journal of Health Education* 38, no. 6 (2007): 322–31.

BROTTO, Lori A., Julia R. Heiman, Barbara Goff, Benjamin Greer, Gretchen M. Lentz, Elizabeth Swisher, Hisham Tamimi, and Amy Van Blaricom. "A Psychoeducational Intervention for Sexual Dysfunction in Women with Gynecologic Cancer." *Archives of Sexual Behavior* 37, no. 2 (2008): 317–29.

CARPENTER, Deanna, Erick Janssen, Cynthia Graham, Harrie Vorst, and Jelte Wicherts. "Women's Scores on the Sexual Inhibition/Sexual Excitation Scales (SIS/SES): Gender Similarities and Differences." *Journal of Sex Research* 45, no. 1 (2008): 36–48.

CROSBY, Richard, Robin Milhausen, Stephanie A. Sanders, Cynthia Graham, and William Yarber. "Two Heads Are Better than One: The Association between Condom Decision-Making and Condom Use Errors and Problems." *Sexually Transmitted Infections* 84, no. 3 (2008): 198–201.

CROSBY, Richard, Robin Milhausen, William Yarber, Stephanie Sanders, and Cynthia Graham. "Condom 'Turn Offs' among Adults: An Exploratory Study." *International Journal of STD & AIDS* 19, no. 9 (2008): 590–94.

CROSBY, Richard, Laura F. Salazar, William L. Yarber, Stephanie A. Sanders, Cynthia A Graham, and Janet N. Arno. "Theory-Based Approach to Understanding Condom Errors and Problems Reported by Men Attending an STI Clinic." *AIDS and Behavior* 12, no. 3 (2008): 412–18.

CROSBY, Richard, William L. Yarber, Stephanie A. Sanders, Cynthia A. Graham, and Janet N. Arno. "Slips, Breaks, and 'Falls': Condom Errors and Problems Reported by Men Attending an STI Clinic." *International Journal of STD & AIDS* 19, no. 2 (2008): 90–93.

DAVIS, Kelly Cue, Jeanette Norris, William H. George, Joel Martell, and Julia R. Heiman. "Men's Likelihood of Sexual Aggression: The Influence of Alcohol, Sexual Arousal, and Violent Pornography." *Aggressive Behavior* 32, no. 6 (2008): 581–89.

GERRESSU, Makeda, Catherine H. Mercer, Cynthia A. Graham, Kaye Wellings, and Anne M. Johnson. "Prevalence of Masturbation and Associated Factors in a British National Probability Survey." *Archives of Sexual Behavior* 37, no. 2 (2008): 266–78.

HARRIS, Juliette M., Lynn F. Cherkas, Bernet S. Kato, Julia R. Heiman, and Tim D. Spector. "Normal Variations in Personality Are Associated with Coital Orgasmic Infrequency in Heterosexual Women: A Population-Based Study." *Journal of Sexual Medicine* 5, no. 5 (2008): 1177–83.

HEIMAN, Julia R. "Treating Low Sexual Desire—New Findings for Testosterone in Women." *New England Journal of Medicine* 359, no. 19 (2008): 2047–49.

HIGGINS, Jenny A., Susie Hoffman, Cynthia A. Graham, and Stephanie A. Sanders. "Relationships between Condoms, Hormonal Methods, and Sexual Pleasure and Satisfaction: An Exploratory Analysis from the Women's Well-Being and Sexuality Study." *Sexual Health* 5, no. 4 (2008): 321–30.

HU, S. Shu-Jung, H. B. Bradshaw, J. S.-C. Chen, B. Tan, and J. M. Walker. "Prostaglandin E2 Glycerol Ester, an Endogenous COX-2 Metabolite of 2-arachidonoylglycerol That Produces Hyperalgesia and Modulates N F Kappa B Activity." *British Journal of Pharmacology* 153, no. 7 (2008): 1538–49.

HUANG, Susan M., Hyosang Lee, Man-Kyo Chung, Yin Yu, Heather B. Bradshaw, Pierre A. Coulombe, J. Michael Walker, and Michael J. Caterina. "Overexpressed TRPV3 Ion Channels Skin Keratinocyte Modulate Pain Sensitivity via Prostaglandin E2." *Journal of Neuroscience* 28, no. 51 (2008): 13727–37.

JANSSEN, Erick, Kimberly R. McBride, William Yarber, Brandon J. Hill, and Scott M. Butler. "Factors That Influence Sexual Arousal in Men—a Focus Group Study." *Archives of Sexual Behavior* 37, no. 2 (2008): 252–65.

LYKINS, Amy D., Marta Meana, and Gregory P. Strauss. "Sex Differences in Visual Attention to Erotic and Non-erotic Stimuli." *Archives of Sexual Behavior* 37, no. 2 (2008): 219–28.

McBRIDE, Kimberly R., Michael Reece, and Stephanie A. Sanders. "Using the Sexual Compulsivity Scale to Predict Outcomes of Sexual Behavior in Young Adults." *Journal of Sexual Addiction & Compulsivity* 15, no. 2 (2008): 97–115.

McBRIDE, Kimberly R., Michael Reece, and Stephanie Sanders. "Predicting Negative Outcomes of Sexuality Using the Compulsive Sexual Behavior Inventory." *International Journal of Sexual Health* 19, no. 4 (2008): 51–62.

MIDDLETON, Laura S., Stephanie W. Kuffel, and Julia R. Heiman. "Effects of Experimentally Adopted Sexual Schemas on Vaginal Response and Subjective Sexual Arousal: A Comparison between Women with Sexual Arousal Disorder and Sexually Healthy Women." *Archives of Sexual Behavior* 37, no. 6 (2008): 950–61.

NURNBERG, H. George, Paula L. Hensley, Julia R. Heiman, Harry A. Croft, Charles Debattista, and Susan Paine. "Sildenafil Treatment of Women with Antidepressant-Associated Sexual Dysfunction." *Journal of the American Medical Association* 300, no. 4 (2008): 395–404.

PETERSON, Zoë D., and Charlene L. Muehlenhard. "What Is Sex and Why Does It Matter? A Motivational Approach to Exploring Individuals' Definitions of Sex." *Journal of Sex Research* 44, no. 3 (2008): 256–68.

PRAUSE, Nicole, Erick Janssen, and William P. Hetrick. "Attention and Emotional Responses to Sexual Stimuli and Their Relationship to Sexual Desire." *Archives of Sexual Behavior* 37, no. 6 (2008): 934–49.

REECE, M., Debbie Herbenick, P. Monohan, Stephanie A. Sanders, M. Temkit, and William Yarber. "Breakage, Slippage, and Acceptability Outcomes of a Condom Fitted to Penile Dimensions." *Sexually Transmitted Infections* 84, no. 2 (2008): 143–49.

RIMMERMAN, Neta, Heather B. Bradshaw, H. Velocity Hughes, Jay Shih-Chieh Chen, Sherry Shu-Jung Hu, Douglas McHugh, Eivind Vefring, Jan A. Jahnsen, Eric L. Thompson, Kim Masuda, Benjamin F. Cravatt, Summer Burstein, Michael R. Vasko, Anne L. Prieto, and J. Michael Walker. "N-palmitoyl Glycine, a Novel Endogenous Lipid That Acts as a Modulator of Calcium Influx and Nitric Oxide Production in Sensory Neurons." *Molecular Pharmacology* 74, no. 1 (2008): 213–24.

RUPP, Heather A., and Kim Wallen. "Sex Differences in Response to Visual Sexual Stimuli: A Review." *Archives of Sexual Behavior* 37, no. 2 (2008): 206–18.

SAND, Michael S., William Fisher, Raymond Rosen, Julia Heiman, and Ian Eardley. "Erectile Dysfunction and Constructs of Masculinity and Quality of Life in the Multinational Men's Attitudes to Life Events and Sexuality (MALES) Study." *Journal of Sexual Medicine* 5, no. 3 (2008): 583–94.

SANDERS, Stephanie A., Cynthia A. Graham, and Robin R. Milhausen. "Predicting Sexual Problems in Women: The Relevance of Sexual Excitation and Inhibition." *Archives of Sexual Behavior* 37, no. 2 (2008): 241–51.

SANDERS, Stephanie A., William L. Yarber, Richard A. Crosby, and Cynthia A. Graham. "Starting Late, Ending Early: Correlates of Incomplete Condom Use among Young Adults." *Health Education Monograph* 25, no. 2 (2008): 45–50.

SYRJALA, Karen L., Brenda F. Kurland, Janet R. Abrams, Jean E. Sanders, and Julia R. Heiman. "Sexual Function Changes during the Five Years after High-Dose Treatment and Hematopoietic Cell Transplantation for Malignancy, with a Hematopoietic Cell Transplantation for Malignancy, with Case-Matched Controls at Five Years." *Blood* 111, no. 3 (2008): 989–96.

VITZTHUM, Virginia J. "Evolution and Endocrinology: The Regulation of Pregnancy Outcomes." In *Medicine and Evolution: Current Applications, Future Prospects*, edited by Sarah Elton and Paul O'Higgens, 99–126. Boca Raton: CRC Press, 2008.

YANG, Claire C., Yun Y. Cao, Y. Q. Guan, Julia R. Heiman, S. W. Kuffel, B. T. Peterson, and Kenneth R. Maravilla. "Influence of PDE5 Inhibitor on MRI Measurement of Clitoral Volume Response in Women with FSAD: A Feasibility Study of a Potential Technique for Evaluating Drug Response." *International Journal of Impotence Research* 20 (2008): 105–10.

YARBER, William L., Robin R. Milhausen, Richard A. Crosby, Cynthia A. Graham, and Stephanie A. Sanders. "Is Growing Up in a Rural Area Associated with Less HIV/STD-Related Risk? A Brief Report from an Internet Sample." *Health Education Monograph* 25, no. 2 (2008): 34.

VITZTHUM, Virginia J. "Evolutionary Models of Women's Reproductive Functioning." *Annual Review of Anthropology* 37 (2008): 53–73.

BANCROFT, John, Cynthia A. Graham, Erick Janssen, and Stephanie A. Sanders. "The Dual Control Model: Current Status and Future Directions." *Journal of Sex Research* 46, no. 2–3 (2009): 121–42.

BROTTO, Lori A., Julia R. Heiman, and Deborah L. Tolman. "Narratives of Desire in Mid-age Women with and without Arousal Difficulties." *Journal of Sex Research* 46, no. 5 (2009): 387–98.

CROSBY, Richard A., William L. Yarber, Stephanie A. Sanders, and Cynthia A. Graham. "Is Phosphodiesterase Type 5 Inhibitor Use Associated with Condom Breakage?" *Sexually Transmitted Infections* 85 (2009): 404–405.

HERBENICK, Debbie, Michael Reece, Stephanie A. Sanders, Brian Dodge, Annahita Ghassemi, and J. Dennis Fortenberry. "Prevalence and Characteristics of Vibrator Use by Women in the United States: Results from a Nationally Representative Study." *Journal of Sexual Medicine* 6, no. 7 (2009): 1857–66.

HIGGINS, Jenny A., Amanda E. Tanner, and Erick Janssen. "Arousal Loss Related to Safer Sex and Risk of Pregnancy: Implications for Women's and Men's Sexual Health." *Perspectives on Sexual and Reproductive Health* 41, no. 3 (2009): 150–57.

JANSSEN, Erick. "Sex in Established Relationships." In *Encyclopedia of Human Relationships*, 3 vols., edited by Harry T. Reis and Susan Sprecher, vol. 1, 1444–47. Thousand Oaks, CA: Sage, 2009.

JANSSEN, Erick, David Goodrich, John V. Petrocelli, and John Bancroft. "Psychophysiological Response Patterns and Risky Sexual Behavior in Heterosexual and Homosexual Men." *Archives of Sexual Behavior* 38, no. 4 (2009): 538–50.

KOPPEL, Jeremy, Heather B. Bradshaw, Terry E. Goldberg, Houman Khalili, Philippe Marambaud, Michael J. Walker, Mauricio Pazos, Marc L. Gordon, Erica Christen, and Peter Davies. "Endocannabinoids in Alzheimer's Disease and Their Impact on Normative Cognitive Performance: A Case-Control and Cohort Study." *Lipids in Health and Disease* 8, no. 2 (2009).

PETERSON, Zoë D., Erick Janssen, and Julia Heiman. "The Association between Sexual Aggression and HIV Risk Behavior in Heterosexual Men." *Journal of Interpersonal Violence* 25, no. 3 (2010): 538–56.

PETERSON, Zoë D., Jeffrey M. Rothenberg, Susan Bilbrey, and Julia R. Heiman. "Sexual Functioning Following Elective Hysterectomy: The Role of Surgical and Psychosocial Variables." *Journal of Sex Research* 47, no. 6 (2010): 513–27.

REECE, Michael, Debbie Herbenick, Stephanie A. Sanders, Brian Dodge, Annahita Ghassemi, and J. Dennis Fortenberry. "Prevalence and Characteristics of Vibrator Use by Men in the United States." *Journal of Sexual Medicine* 6, no. 7 (2009): 1867–74.

RIMMERMAN, Neta, Heather B. Bradshaw, A. Basnet, B. Tan, T. S. Widlanski, and J. M. Walker. "Microsomal Omega-Hydroxylated Metabolites of N-arachidonoyl

Dopamine Are Active at Recombinant Human TRPV1 Receptors." *Prostaglandins and Other Lipid Mediators* 88, no. 1–2 (2009): 10–17.

RUPP, Heather A., Giliah R. Librach, Nick C. Feipel, Ellen D. Ketterson, Dale R. Sengelaub, and Julia R. Heiman. "Partner Status Influences Women's Interest in the Opposite Sex." *Human Nature* 20, no. 1 (2009): 93–104.

RUPP, Heather A., Thomas W. James, Ellen D. Ketterson, Dale R. Sengelaub, Erick Janssen, and Julia R. Heiman. "Neural Activation in the Orbitofrontal Cortex in Response to Male Faces Increases during the Follicular Phase." *Hormones and Behavior* 56, no. 1 (2009): 66–72.

RUPP, Heather A., Thomas W. James, Ellen D. Ketterson, Dale R. Sengelaub, Erick Janssen, and Julia R. Heiman. "The Role of the Anterior Cingulate Cortex in Women's Sexual Decision Making." *Neuroscience Letters* 449, no. 1 (2009): 42–47.

RUPP, Heather A., Thomas W. James, Ellen D. Ketterson, Dale R. Sengelaub, Erick Janssen, and Julia R. Heiman. "Women's Neural Activation in Response to Masculinized versus Feminized Male Faces: Mediation by Hormones and Psychosexual Factors." *Evolution and Human Behavior* 30, no. 1 (2009): 1–10.

RUPP, Heather A., and Kim Wallen. "Sex-Specific Content Preferences for Visual Sexual Stimuli." *Archives of Sexual Behavior* 38, no. 3 (2009): 417–26.

SANDERS, Stephanie A., Robin R. Milhausen, Richard A. Crosby, Cynthia A. Graham, and William L. Yarber. "Do Phosphodiesterase Type 5 Inhibitors Protect against Condom-Associated Erection Loss and Condom Slippage?" *Journal of Sexual Medicine* 6, no. 5 (2009): 1451–56.

ŠTULHOFER, Aleksandar, Cynthia A. Graham, Ivana Božicevic, Krešimir Kufrin, and Dean Ajdukovic. "An Assessment of HIV/AIDS Vulnerability and Related Sexual Risks in a Nationally Representative Sample of Young Croatian Adults." *Archives of Sexual Behavior* 38, no. 2 (2009): 209–25.

VITZTHUM, Virginia J., Jonathan Thornburg, and Hilde Spielvogel. "Seasonal Modulation of Reproductive Effort during Early Pregnancy in Humans." *American Journal of Human Biology* 21, no. 4 (2009): 548–58.

VITZTHUM, Virginia J., Carol M. Worthman, Cynthia M. Beall, Jonathan Thornburg, Enrique Vargas, Mercedes Villena, Rudy Soria, Esperanza Caceres, and Hilde Spielvogel. "Seasonal and Circadian Variation in Salivary Testosterone in Rural Bolivian Men." *American Journal of Human Biology* 21, no. 6 (2009): 762–68.

2010–2017

CROSBY, Richard A., Cynthia A. Graham, Robin A. Milhausen, Stephanie Sanders, and William L. Yarber. "Condom Use Errors/Problems Survey (CUES)." In *Handbook of Sexuality-Related Measures*, 3rd ed., edited by T. D. Fisher, C. M. Davis, W. L. Yarber, and S. L. Davis, 153–59. New York: Routledge, 2010.

CROSBY, Richard A., Cynthia A. Graham, Robin A. Milhausen, Stephanie A. Sanders, and William L. Yarber. "Correct Condom Use Self-Efficacy Scale (CCUSES)." In *Handbook of Sexuality-Related Measures*, 3rd ed., edited by T. D. Fisher, C. M. Davis, W. L. Yarber, and S. L. Davis, 160–61. New York: Routledge, 2010.

CROSBY, Richard A., Cynthia A. Graham, William L. Yarber, and Stephanie A. Sanders. "Problems with Condoms May Be Reduced for Men Taking Ample Time to Apply Them." *Sexual Health* 7, no. 1 (2010): 66–70.

CROSBY, Richard A., William L. Yarber, Cynthia A. Graham, and Stephanie Sanders. "Does It Fit Okay? Problems with Condom Use as a Function of Self-Reported Poor Fit." *Sexually Transmitted Infections* 86 (2010): 36–38.

DODGE, Brian, Michael Reece, Debbie Herbenick, Vanessa Schick, Stephanie A. Sanders, and J. Dennis Fortenberry. "Sexual Health among U.S. Black and Hispanic Men and Women: A Nationally Representative Study." *Journal of Sexual Medicine* 7, Supplement s5 (2010): 330–45.

FERGUSON, David M., Balakrishna Hosmane, and Julia R. Heiman. "Randomized, Placebo-Controlled, Double-Blind, Parallel Design Trial of the Efficacy and Safety of Zestra® in Women with Mixed Desire/Interest/Arousal/Orgasm Disorders." *Journal of Sex & Marital Therapy* 36, no. 1 (2010): 66–86.

FORTENBERRY, J. Dennis, Vanessa Schick, Debbie Herbenick, Stephanie A. Sanders, Brian Dodge, and Michael Reece. "Sexual Behaviors and Condom Use at Last Vaginal Intercourse: A National Sample of Adolescents Ages 14 to 17 Years." *Journal of Sexual Medicine* 7, Supplement s5 (2010): 305–14.

GILMORE, Amanda K., Rebecca L. Schacht, William H. George, Jacqueline M. Otto, Kelly C. Davis, Julia R. Heiman, J. Norris, and K. F. Kajumulo. "Assessing Women's Sexual Arousal in the Context of Sexual Assault History and Acute Alcohol Intoxication." *Journal of Sexual Medicine* 7, no. 6 (June 2010): 2112–19.

GRAHAM, Cynthia A., Stephanie A. Sanders, and Robin A. Milhausen. "The Sexual Excitation/Sexual Inhibition Inventory for Women (SESII-W)." In *Handbook of Sexuality-Related Measures*, 3rd ed., edited by T. D. Fisher, C. M. Davis, W. L. Yarber, and S. L. Davis, 239–41. New York: Routledge, 2010.

HASSETT, J. M., H. A. Rupp, and K. Wallen. "Social Segregation in Male, but Not Female Yearling Rhesus Macaques (*Macaca mulatta*)." *American Journal of Primatology* 72, no. 87 (2010): 87–92.

HEIMAN, Julia R. "Alfred C. Kinsey's Legacy and the Kinsey Institute for Research in Sex, Gender and Reproduction." In *Routledge Handbook of Sexuality, Health and Rights*, edited by P. Aggleton and R. Parker, 37–44. London: Routledge, 2010.

HERBENICK, Debbie, Michael Reece, Stephanie A. Sanders, Brian Dodge, A. Ghassemi, and J. Dennis Fortenberry. "Women's Vibrator Use in Romantic Relationships: Results from a Nationally Representative Survey in the United States." *Journal of Sex & Marital Therapy* 36, no. 1 (2010): 49–65.

HERBENICK, Debbie, Michael Reece, Vanessa Schick, Stephanie A. Sanders, Brian Dodge, and J. Dennis Fortenberry. "An Event-Level Analysis of the Sexual Characteristics and Composition among Adults Ages 18 to 59: Results from a National Probability Sample in the United States." *Journal of Sexual Medicine* 7, supplement s5 (2010): 346–61.

HERBENICK, Debbie, Michael Reece, Vanessa Schick, Stephanie A Sanders, Brian Dodge, and J. Dennis Fortenberry. "Sexual Behavior in the United States: Results from a National Probability Sample of Men and Women Ages 14–94." *Journal of Sexual Medicine* 7, Supplement s5 (2010): 255–65.

HERBENICK, Debbie, Michael Reece, Vanessa Schick, Stephanie A. Sanders, Brian Dodge, and J. Dennis Fortenberry. "Sexual Behaviors, Relationships, and Perceived Health Status among Adult Women in the United States: Results from a National Probability Sample." *Journal of Sexual Medicine* 7, Supplement s5 (2010): 277–90.

HERBENICK, Debbie, Michael Reece, Vanessa Schick, Stephanie A. Sanders, Brian Dodge, and J. Dennis Fortenberry. "Pubic Hair Removal among Women in the United

States: Prevalence, Methods, and Characteristics." *Journal of Sexual Medicine* 7, no. 10 (October 2010): 3322–30.

HILL, Brandon J., Q. Rahman, D. A. Bright, and Stephanie A. Sanders. "The Semantics of Sexual Behavior and Their Implications for HIV/AIDS Research and Sexual Health: U.S. and U.K. Gay Men's Definitions of Having 'Had Sex,'" *AIDS Care* 16 (2010): 1–7.

HIROTA, Y., T. Daikoku, S. Tranguch, H. Xie, H. Bradshaw, and S. K. Dey. "Uterine-Specific Deficiency Confers Premature Uterine Senescence and Promotes Preterm Birth in Mice." *Journal of Clinical Investigation* 120, no. 3 (2010): 803–15.

McBRIDE, K., Michael Reece, and Stephanie A. Sanders. "Cognitive and Behavioral Outcomes of Sexual Behavior Scale." In *Handbook of Sexuality-Related Measures*, 3rd ed., edited by T. D. Fisher, C. M. Davis, W. L. Yarber, and S. L. Davis, 148–50. New York: Routledge, 2010.

MILHAUSEN, Robin R., Cynthia A. Graham, and Stephanie A. Sanders. "The Sexual Excitation/Sexual Inhibition Inventory for Women and Men (SESII-W/M)." In *Handbook of Sexuality-Related Measures*, 3rd ed., edited by T. D. Fisher, C. M. Davis, W. L. Yarber, and S. L. Davis, 247–49. New York: Routledge, 2010.

PETERSON, Z., Erick Janssen, and E. Laan. "Women's Sexual Responses to Heterosexual and Lesbian Erotica: The Role of Stimulus Intensity, Affective Reaction, and Sexual History." *Archives of Sexual Behavior* 39 (2010): 880–97.

PRAUSE, N., and Julia R. Heiman. "Reduced Labial Temperature in Response to Sexual Films with Distractors among Women with Lower Sexual Desire." *Journal of Sexual Medicine* 7, no. 2, part 2 (2010): 951–63.

REECE, Michael, Debbie Herbenick, Stephanie A. Sanders, Brian Dodge, A. Ghassemi, and J. Dennis Fortenberry. "Prevalence and Predictors of Testicular Self-Exam among a Nationally Representative Sample of Men in the United States." *International Journal of Sexual Health* 22, no. 1 (2010): 1–4.

REECE, Michael, Debbie Herbenick, Vanessa Schick, Stephanie A. Sanders, Brian Dodge, and J. Dennis Fortenberry. "Background and Considerations on the National Survey of Sexual Health and Behavior (NSSHB) from the Investigators." *Journal of Sexual Medicine* 7, Supplement s5 (2010): 243–45.

REECE, Michael, Debbie Herbenick, Vanessa Schick, Stephanie A. Sanders, Brian Dodge, and J. Dennis Fortenberry. "Condom Use Rates in a National Probability Sample of Males and Females Ages 14 to 94 in the United States." *Journal of Sexual Medicine* 7, Supplement s5 (2010): 266–76.

REECE, Michael, Debbie Herbenick, Vanessa Schick, Stephanie A. Sanders, Brian Dodge, and J. Dennis Fortenberry. "Sexual Behaviors, Relationships, and Perceived Health among Adult Men in the United States: Results from a National Probability Sample." *Journal of Sexual Medicine* 7, Supplement s5 (2010): 291–304.

REECE, Michael, Debbie Herbenick, Brian Dodge, Stephanie A. Sanders, Annahita Ghassemi, and J. Dennis Fortenberry. "Vibrator Use among Heterosexual Men Varies by Partnership Status: Results from a Nationally Representative Study in the United States." *Journal of Sex & Marital Therapy* 36, no. 5 (October 2010): 389–407.

SANDERS, Stephanie A., Brandon J. Hill, William L. Yarber, Cynthia A. Graham, Richard A. Crosby, and Robin R. Milhausen. "Misclassification Bias: Diversity in Conceptualizations about Having 'Had Sex.'" *Sexual Health* 7, no. 1 (2010): 31–34.

SANDERS, Stephanie A., Michael Reece, Debbie Herbenick, Vanessa Schick, Brian Dodge, and J. Dennis Fortenberry. "Condom Use during Most Recent Vaginal

Intercourse Event among a Probability Sample of Adults in the United States." *Journal of Sexual Medicine* 7, Supplement s5 (2010): 362–73.

SCHACHT, Rebecca L., William H. George, Kelly C. Davis, Julia R. Heiman, Jeanette Norris, Susan A. Stoner, and Kelly F. Kajumulo. "Sexual Abuse History, Alcohol Intoxication, and Women's Sexual Risk Behavior." *Archives of Sexual Behavior* 39, no. 4 (2010): 898–906.

SCHICK, Vanessa, Debbie Herbenick, Michael Reece, Stephanie A. Sanders, Brian Dodge, Susan E. Middlestadt, and J. Dennis Fortenberry. "Sexual Behaviors, Condom Use, and Sexual Health of Americans over 50: Implications for Sexual Health Promotion for Older Adults." *Journal of Sexual Medicine* 7, Supplement s5 (2010): 315–29.

WALLEN, K., and H. A. Rupp. "Women's Interest in Visual Sexual Stimuli Varies with Menstrual Cycle Phase at First Exposure and Predicts Later Interest." *Hormones and Behavior* 57, no. 2 (2010): 263–68.

AMICK, Erick E., Brandon J. Hill, and Stephanie A. Sanders. "The Brief Condom Attitudes Scale: Assessing Attitudes and Behavioral Intentions for Condom Use among Heterosexual College-Aged Men and Women." *Proceedings from the HIV/STD Prevention in Rural Communities Sharing Successful Strategies Conference, Brief Reports* 7 (September 2011): 11–16.

BANCROFT, John, J. Scott Long, and Janice McCabe. "Sexual Well-Being: A Comparison of U.S. Black and White Women in Heterosexual Relationships." *Archives of Sexual Behavior* 40, no. 4 (2011): 725–40.

CARPENTER, Jeffrey P., Justin R. Garcia, and J. Koji Lum. "Dopamine Receptor Genes Predict Risk Preferences, Time Preferences, and Related Economic Choices." *Journal of Risk and Uncertainty* 42, no. 3 (2011): 233–61.

CERNY, J., and Erick Janssen. "Patterns of Sexual Arousal in Homosexual, Bisexual, and Heterosexual Men." *Archives of Sexual Behavior* 40, no. 4 (2011): 687–97.

DREBER, Anna, David G. Rand, Nils Wernerfelt, Justin R. Garcia, Miguel G. Vilar, J. Koji Lum, and Richard Zeckhauser. "Dopamine and Risk Choices in Different Domains: Findings among Serious Tournament Bridge Players." *Journal of Risk and Uncertainty* 43, no. 1 (2011): 19–38.

FISHER, Maryanne L., Daniel J. Kruger, and Justin R. Garcia. "Understanding and Enhancing the Role of the Mass Media in Evolutionary Psychology Education." *Evolution: Education and Outreach* 4, no. 1 (2011): 75–82.

GARCIA, Justin R., Glenn Geher, Benjamin Crosier, Gad Saad, Daniel Gambacorta, Laura Johnsen, and Elissa Pranckitas. "The Interdisciplinary Context of Evolutionary Approaches to Human Behavior: A Key to Survival in the Ivory Archipelago." *Futures* 43, no. 8 (2011): 749–61.

GEORGE, William H., Kelly C. Davis, Julia R. Heiman, Jeanette Norris, Susan A. Stoner, Rebecca L. Schacht, Christopher S. Hendershot, and Kelly F. Kajumulo. "Women's Sexual Arousal: Effects of High Alcohol Dosages and Self-Control Instructions." *Hormones and Behavior* 59, no. 5 (2011): 730–38.

GRAHAM, Cynthia A., Richard A. Crosby, Robin R. Milhausen, Stephanie A. Sanders, and William L. Yarber. "Incomplete Use of Condoms: The Importance of Sexual Arousal." *AIDS and Behavior* 15, no. 7 (2011): 1328–31.

HEIMAN, Julia R., J. Scott Long, Shawna N. Smith, William A. Fisher, Michael S. Sand, and Raymond C. Rosen. "Sexual Satisfaction and Relationship Happiness in Midlife and Older Couples in Five Countries." *Archives of Sexual Behavior* 40, no. 4 (2011): 741–53.

HEIMAN, Julia R., Heather Rupp, Erick Janssen, Sarah K. Newhouse, Marieke Brauer, and Ellen Laan. "Sexual Desire, Sexual Arousal, and Hormonal Differences in Premenopausal US and Dutch Women with and without Low Sexual Desire." *Hormones and Behavior* 59, no. 5 (2011): 772–79.

HERBENICK, Debbie, Michael Reece, Devon Hensel, Stephanie A. Sanders, Kristen Jozkowski, and J. Dennis Fortenberry. "Association of Lubricant Use with Women's Sexual Pleasure, Sexual Satisfaction, and Genital Symptoms: A Prospective Daily Diary Study." *Journal of Sexual Medicine* 8, no. 1 (2011): 202–12.

HERBENICK, Debbie, Michael Reece, Vanessa Schick, Kristen Jozkowski, Susan E. Middlestadt, Stephanie A. Sanders, Brian Dodge, Annihita Ghassemi, and J. Dennis Fortenberry. "Beliefs about Women's Vibrator Use: Results from a Nationally Representative Probability Survey in the United States." *Journal of Sex & Marital Therapy* 37, no. 5 (2011): 329–45.

HERBENICK, Debbie, Vanessa Schick, Michael Reece, Stephanie A. Sanders, and J. Dennis Fortenberry. "The Female Genital Self-Image Scale (FGSIS): Results from a Nationally Representative Probability Sample of Women in the United States." *Journal of Sexual Medicine* 8, no. 1 (2011): 158–66.

HILL, Brandon J., Erick E. Amick, and Stephanie A. Sanders. "Condoms and US College-Aged Men and Women: Briefly Assessing Attitudes toward Condoms and General Condom Use Behaviors." *Sexual Health* 8 (2011): 372–77.

HILL, Brandon J., Erick E. Amick, and Stephanie A. Sanders. "Variations in Young Men's and Women's Condom Attitudes, Behavioral Intentions, and Use with Different Types of Sexual Partners." *Proceedings from the HIV/STD Prevention in Rural Communities Sharing Successful Strategies Conference, Brief Reports* 7 (September 2011): 25–29.

JANSSEN, Erick, and Jerome A. Cerny. "In Search of Something Our Study Was Not About: Response to Bailey et al." *Archives of Sexual Behavior* 40, no. 6 (2011): 1297–1300.

JANSSEN, Erick. "Sexual Arousal in Men: A Review and Conceptual Analysis." *Hormones and Behavior* 59, no. 5 (May 2011): 708–16.

MACAPAGAL, Katherine R., Heather A. Rupp, and Julia R. Heiman. "Influences of Observer Sex, Facial Masculinity, and Gender Role Identification on First Impression of Men's Faces." *Journal of Social, Evolutionary, and Cultural Psychology* 5, no. 1 (2011): 92–105.

MACAPAGAL, Katheryn R., Erick Janssen, Daniel J. Fridberg, Peter R. Finn, and Julia R. Heiman. "The Effects of Impulsivity, Sexual Arousability, and Abstract Intellectual Ability on Men's and Women's Go/No-Go Task Performance." *Archives of Sexual Behavior* 40, no. 5 (October 2011): 995–1006.

MARK, Kristen P., Erick Janssen, and Robin R. Milhausen. "Infidelity in Heterosexual Couples: Demographic, Interpersonal, and Personality-Related Predictors of Extradyadic Sex." *Archives of Sexual Behavior* 40, no. 5 (October 2011): 971–82.

MILHAUSEN, Robin R., Stephanie A. Sanders, Richard A. Crosby, William L. Yarber, Cynthia A. Graham, and Jessica Wood. "A Novel, Self-Guided, Home-Based Intervention to Promote Condom Use among Young Men: A Pilot Study." *Journal of Men's Health* 8, no. 4 (December 2011): 274–81.

NAGOSKI, Erin, Erick Janssen, David Lohrmann, and Eric Nichols. "Risk, Individual Differences, and Environment: An Agent-Based Modeling Approach to Sexual Risk-Taking." *Archives of Sexual Behavior* 41, no. 4 (2012): 849–60.

NOAR, Seth M., Elizabeth M. Webb, Stephanie K. Van Stee, Colleen A. Redding, Sonja Feist-Price, Richard A. Crosby, and Adewale Troutman. "Using Computer Technology for HIV Prevention among African Americans: Development of a Tailored Information Program for Safer Sex (TIPSS)." *Health Education Research* 26, no. 3 (2011): 393–406.

REHMAN, Uzma, Erick Janssen, Sarah New House, Julia Heiman, Amy Holtzworth-Munroe, Erin Fallis, and Eshkol Rafaeli. "Marital Satisfaction and Communication Behaviors during Sexual and Nonsexual Conflict Discussions in Newlywed Couples: A Pilot Study." *Journal of Sex and Marital Therapy* 37, no. 2 (2011): 94–103.

RELLINI, Alessandra H., Samantha Elinson, Erick Janssen, and Cindy M. Meston. "The Effect of Pre-existing Affect on the Sexual Responses of Women with and without a History of Childhood Sexual Abuse." *Archives of Sexual Behavior* 41, no. 2 (2011): 329–39.

ROBBINS, Cynthia, Vanessa Schick, Michael Reece, Debbie Herbenick, Stephanie A. Sanders, Brian Dodge, and J. Dennis Fortenberry. "Prevalence, Frequency, and Associations of Masturbation with Other Sexual Behaviors among Adolescents Living in the United States of America." *Archives of Pediatric and Adolescent Medicine* 165, no. 12 (2011): 1087–93.

TOPPING, A. A., Robin R. Milhausen, Cynthia A. Graham, Stephanie A. Sanders, William L. Yarber, and Richard A. Crosby. "A Comparison of Condom Use Errors and Problems for Heterosexual Anal and Vaginal Intercourse." *International Journal of STD & AIDS* 22, no. 4 (2011): 204–208.

BRAUER, Marieke, Matthias van Leeuwen, Erick Janssen, Sarah Newhouse, Julia R. Heiman, and Ellen Laan. "Automatic Affective Associations with Sexual Stimuli in Women with Hypoactive Sexual Desire Disorder." *Archives of Sexual Behavior* 41 (2012): 891–905.

CLAYTON, Anita H., Nancy N. Maserejian, Megan K. Connor, Liyuan Huang, Julia R. Heiman, and Raymond C. Rosen. "Depression in Premenopausal Women with Hypoactive Sexual Desire Disorder (HSDD): Baseline Findings from the HSDD Registry for Women." *Psychosomatic Medicine* 74, no. 3 (March 2012): 305–11.

CROSBY, Richard A., S. M. Noar, S. Head, and E. Webb. "Condoms and Other Barrier Methods of STI and HIV Prevention." In *Sexually Transmitted Infections*, 2nd ed., edited by S. Gupta and B. Kumar, 117–33. Amsterdam: Elsevier, 2012.

CROSBY, Richard A., Lydia A. Shrier, Richard J. Charnigo, Chandra Weathers, Stephanie A. Sanders, Cynthia A. Graham, Robin A. Milhausen, and William L. Yarber. "A Prospective Event-Level Analysis of Condom Use Experiences Following STI Testing among Patients in Three US Cities." *Sexually Transmitted Diseases* 39, no. 10 (2012): 756–60.

FISHER, Maryanne L., Kerry Worth, Justin R. Garcia, and Tami Meredith. "Feelings of Regret Following Uncommitted Sexual Encounters in Canadian University Students." *Culture, Health & Sexuality* 14, no. 1 (2012): 45–57.

FREDERICK, D. A., T. A. Reynolds, M. R. Fales, and Justin R. Garcia. "Physical Attractiveness: Dating, Mating, and Social Interaction." In *Encyclopedia of Body Image and Human Appearance*, vol. 2, edited by T. F. Cash, 629–35. San Diego: Academic Press, 2012.

GARCIA, Justin R., Chris Reiber, Sean G. Massey, and Anne M. Merriwether. "Sexual Hookup Culture: A Review." *Review of General Psychology* 16, no. 2 (2012): 161–76.

GRAHAM, Cynthia A. "Condom Use in the Context of Sex Research." Special issue, *Sexual Health* 9 (2012): 103–108.

GRAY, Peter B., and Justin R. Garcia. "Aging and Human Sexual Behavior: Biocultural Perspectives—a Mini-Review." *Gerontology* 6, no. 5 (2012): 446–52.

HEYWOOD, L. L., and Justin R. Garcia. "Fashion as Adaptation: The Case of American Idol." In *Fashion Talks: Undressing the Power of Style*, edited by Shira Tarrant and Marjorie Jolles, 67–82. New York: SUNY Press, 2012.

HILL, Brandon J., Erick E. Amick, and Stephanie A. Sanders. "Variations in Young Men's and Women's Attitudes and Intentions to Use Condoms with Different Types of Sexual Partners." *Journal of the Association of Nurses in AIDS Care* 23 (2012): 454–59.

JOZKOWSKI, Kristen N., and Stephanie A. Sanders. "Health and Sexual Outcomes of Women Who Have Experienced Forced or Coercive Sex." *Women & Health* 52 (2012): 101–18.

LYKINS, Amy D., Erick Janssen, Sarah Newhouse, Julia R. Heiman, and Eshkol Rafaeli. "The Effects of Similarity in Sexual Excitation, Inhibition, and Mood on Sexual Arousal Problems and Sexual Satisfaction in Newlywed Couples." *Journal of Sexual Medicine* 9 (2012): 1360–66.

LYSAKER, Paul H., Molly A. Erickson, Kathryn R. Macapagal, Chloe A. Tunze, Emily Gilmore, and Jaime M. Ringer. "Development of Personal Narratives as a Mediator of the Impact of Deficits in Social Cognition and Social Withdrawal on Negative Symptoms in Schizophrenia." *Journal of Nervous and Mental Disease* 200 (2012): 290–95.

MACAPAGAL, Kathryn R., Jaime M. Ringer, Shannon E. Woller, and Paul H. Lysaker. "Personal Narratives, Coping, and Quality of Life in Persons with HIV." *Journal of the Association of Nurses in AIDS Care* 23 (2012): 361–65.

NAGOSKI, Emily, Erick Janssen, David Lohrmann, and Eric Nichols. "Risk, Individual Differences, and Environment: An Agent-Based Modeling Approach to Sexual Risk Taking." *Archives of Sexual Behavior* 41 (2012): 849–60.

NGUYEN, Hong V., Kelly H. Koo, Kelly C. Davis, Jacqueline M. Otto, Christian S. Hendershot, Rebecca L. Schacht, William H. George, Julia R. Heiman, and Jeanette Norris. "Risky Sex: Interactions among Ethnicity, Sexual Sensation Seeking, Sexual Inhibition, and Sexual Excitation." *Archives of Sexual Behavior* 41, no. 5 (2012): 1231–39.

NOAR, Seth M., Elizabeth M. Webb, Stephanie K. Van Stee, Sonja Feist-Price, Richard Crosby, and Adewale Troutman. "Conversations with Low Income, African-American Men and Women: Critical Reflections on Sexuality and Risk Behavior." In *Communicating about HIV/AIDS: Taboo Topics and Difficult Conversations about HIV/AIDS*, edited by M. U. D'Silva, J. L. Hart, and K. L. Walker. Cresskill, NJ: Hampton Press, 2012.

NOAR, Seth M., Elizabeth Webb, Stephanie van Stee, Sonja Feist-Price, Richard A. Crosby, Jessica Fitz Willoughby, and Adewale Troutman. "Sexual Partnerships, Risk Behaviors, and Condom Use among Low Income Heterosexual African Americans: A Qualitative Study." *Archives of Sexual Behavior* 41, no. 4 (2012): 959–70.

RUPP, Heather, Thomas James, Ellen Ketterson, Dale Sengelaub, Beate Ditzen, and Julia Heiman. "Lower Sexual Interest in Postpartum Women: Relationship to Amygdala Activation and Intranasal Oxytocin." *Hormones and Behavior* 63 (2012): 114–21.

SANDERS, Stephanie, William Yarber, Erin Kaufman, Richard A. Crosby, Cynthia Graham, and Robin Milhausen. "Condom Use Errors and Problems: A Global View." *Sexual Health* 9, no. 1 (February 2012): 81–95.

SATINSKY, Sonya, Michael Reece, Stephanie A. Sanders, Barbara Dennis, Shaowen Bardzell. "An Assessment of Body Appreciation and Its Relationship to Sexual Function in Women." *Body Image: An International Journal of Research* 9, no. 1 (January 2012): 137–44.

STRANG, Emily, Zoë D. Peterson, Yvette N. Hill, and Julia R. Heiman. "Discrepant Responding across Self-Report Measures of Men's Coercive and Aggressive Sexual Strategies." *Journal of Sex Research* 50, no. 5 (February 2012): 458–69.

CAMERON, Nicole M., and Justin R. Garcia. "Maternal Effect and Offspring Development." In *Evolution's Empress: Darwinian Perspectives on the Nature of Women*, edited by Maryanne L. Fisher, Justin R. Garcia, and Rosemarie S. Chang, 133–50. New York: Oxford University Press, 2013.

FISHER, Maryanne L., Justin R. Garcia, and Rosemarie S. Chang, eds. *Evolution's Empress: Darwinian Perspectives on the Nature of Women*. New York: Oxford University Press, 2013.

CARVALHO, Joana, Ana Quinta-Gomes, Pedro Laja, Cátia Oliveira, Sandra Vilarinho, Erick Janssen, and Pedro Nobre. "Gender Differences in Sexual Arousal and Emotional Responses to Erotica: The Effect of Type of Film and Instructions." *Archives of Sexual Behavior* 42, no. 6 (2013): 1011–19.

CLASS, Quetzal A., Johan Verhulst, and Julia Heiman. "Postpartum 'Depression': Exploring the Heterogeneity of Clinical Presentation and Functional Impairment." *Journal of Reproductive and Infant Psychology* 31, no. 2 (2013): 183–94.

CROSBY, Richard A., Robin R. Milhausen, Kristen P. Marks, William L. Yarber, Stephanie A. Sanders, and Cynthia A. Graham. "Understanding Problems with Condom Fit and Feel: An Important Opportunity for Improving Clinic-Based Safer Sex Programs." *Journal of Primary Prevention* 34 (April 2013): 1–2.

CROSBY, Richard, Lydia A. Shrier, R. Charnigo, Stephanie A. Sanders, Cynthia A. Graham, Robin R. Milhausen, and William L. Yarber. "Negative Perceptions about Condom Use among a Clinic Population: Comparisons by Gender, Race, and Age." *International Journal of STD & AIDS* 24, no. 2 (February 2013): 100–105.

GILMORE, Amanda K., William H. George, Hong V. Nguyen, Julia R. Heiman, Kelly C. Davis, and Jeanette Norris. "Influences of Situational Factors and Alcohol Expectancies on Sexual Desire and Arousal among Heavy-Episodic Drinking Women: Acute Alcohol Intoxication and Condom Availability." *Archives of Sexual Behavior* 42, no. 6 (August 2013): 949–59.

GRAY, Peter B., and Justin R. Garcia. *Evolution and Human Sexual Behavior*. Cambridge, MA: Harvard University Press, 2013.

HARRIS, Amy L., and Virginia J. Vitzthum. "Darwin's Legacy: An Evolutionary View of Women's Reproductive and Sexual Functioning." *Journal of Sex Research* 50, nos. 3–4 (2013): 207–46.

HEIMAN, Julia R., Liana Zhou, Catherine Johnson-Roehr, and Jennifer Bass. "The Kinsey Institute Collections: Respecting and Conducting Scholarship on Sexology." *Sexuologie* 20, no. 1–2 (2013): 41–43.

HERBENICK, Debbie, Devon J. Hensel, Nicole K. Smith, Vanessa Schick, Michael Reece, Stephanie A. Sanders, and J. Dennis Fortenberry. "Pubic Hair Removal and Sexual Behavior: Findings from a Prospective Daily Diary Study of Sexually Active Women in the United States." *Journal of Sexual Medicine* 10, no. 3 (2013): 678–85.

HERBENICK, Debbie, Vanessa Schick, Michael Reece, Stephanie A. Sanders, and J. Dennis Fortenberry. "The Development and Validation of the Male Genital Self Image Scale: Results from a Nationally Representative Probability Sample of Men in the United States." *Journal of Sexual Medicine* 10, no. 6 (2013): 1516–25.

HERBENICK, Debbie, Vanessa Schick, Michael Reece, Stephanie A. Sanders, Nicole K. Smith, Brian Dodge, and J. Dennis Fortenberry. "Characteristics of Condom and Lubricant Use among a Nationally Representative Probability Sample of Adults Ages

18 to 59 in the United States." *Journal of Sexual Medicine* 10, no. 2 (February 2013): 474–83.

JANSSEN, Erick, Kathryn Macapagal, and Brian Mustanski. "Individual Differences in the Effects of Mood on Sexuality: The Revised Mood and Sexuality Questionnaire (MSQ-R)." *Journal of Sex Research* 50, no. 7 (2013): 676–87.

JOZKOWSKI, Kristen N., Debbie Herbenick, Vanessa Schick, Michael Reece, Stephanie A. Sanders, and J. Dennis Fortenberry. "Women's Perceptions about Lubricant Use and Vaginal Wetness during Sexual Activities." *Journal of Sexual Medicine* 10, no. 2 (February 2013): 484–92.

MASSEY, Sean G., Ann M. Merriwether, and Justin R. Garcia. "Modern Prejudice and Same-Sex Parenting: Shifting Judgments in Positive and Negative Parenting Situations." *Journal of GLBT Family Studies* 9, no. 2 (2013): 129–51.

MILHAUSEN, Robin R., Alexander McKay, Cynthia A. Graham, Richard A. Crosby, William L. Yarber, and Stephanie A. Sanders. "Prevalence and Predictors of Condom Use among a National Sample of Canadian University Students." *Canadian Journal of Human Sexuality* 22, no. 3 (2013): 142–51.

VITZTHUM, Virginia J. "Fifty Fertile Years: Anthropologists' Studies of Reproduction in High Altitude Natives." *American Journal of Human Biology* 25, no. 2 (2013): 179–89.

WOOD, Jessica R., Robin R. Milhausen, Jessica M. Sales, Cynthia R. Graham, Stephanie A. Sanders, Ralph J. DiClemente, and Gina M. Wingood. "Arousability as a Predictor of Sexual Risk Behaviours in African American Adolescent Women." *Sexual Health* 10, no. 2 (2013): 160–65.

CROSBY, Richard A., Cynthia A. Graham, Robin R. Milhausen, Stephanie A. Sanders, William L. Yarber, Ivy Terrel, and Ryan Pasternak. "Desire to Father a Child and Condom Use: A Study of Young Black Males at Risk of Sexually Transmitted Infections." *International Journal of STD & AIDS* 54, no. 2 (2014): s62–s63.

CROSBY, Richard A., Robin Milhausen, Cynthia A. Graham, William L. Yarber, Stephanie A. Sanders, Richard Charnigo, and Lydia A. Shrier. "Condom Use Motivations and Selected Behaviors with New versus Established Sex Partners." *Sexual Health* 11, no. 3 (2014): 252–57.

CROSBY, Richard A., Robin Milhausen, Stephanie A. Sanders, Cynthia A. Graham, and William L. Yarber. "Condoms Are More Effective When Applied by Males: A Study of Young Black Males in the United States." *Annals of Epidemiology* 24 (2014): 868–70.

CROSBY, Richard A., Robin R. Milhausen, Stephanie A. Sanders, Cynthia A. Graham, and William L. Yarber. "Condom Use Errors and Problems: A Study of High-Risk Young Black Males Residing in the Southern United States." *International Journal of STD & AIDS* 25, no. 13 (2014): 943–48.

CROSBY, Richard, Lydia A. Shrier, Richard Charnigo, Stephanie A. Sanders, Cynthia A. Graham, Robin Milhausen, and William L. Yarber. "Being Drunk and High during Sex Is Not Associated with Condom Use Behaviors: A Study of High-Risk Young Black Males." *Sexual Health* 11, no. 1 (2014): 84–86.

CROSBY, Richard A., Lydia Shrier, Richard Charnigo, Stephanie A. Sanders, Cynthia A. Graham, Robin A. Milhausen, and William L. Yarber. "Likelihood of Condom Use When STDs Are Suspected: Results from a Clinic Sample." *Health Education and Behavior* 41, no. 14 (2014): 449–54.

DODGE, Brian, Vanessa Schick, Debbie Herbenick, Michael Reece, Stephanie A. Sanders, and J. Dennis Fortenberry. "Frequency, Reasons for, and Perceptions of Lubricant Use among a Nationally Representative Sample of Self-Identified Gay and Bisexual Men in the United States." *Journal of Sexual Medicine* 11, no. 10 (2014): 2396–405.

EMETU, Roberta E., Alexandra Marshall, Stephanie A. Sanders, William L. Yarber, Robin R. Milhausen, Richard A. Crosby, and Cynthia A. Graham. "A Novel, Self-Guided, Home-Based Intervention to Improve Condom Use among Young Men Who Have Sex with Men." *Journal of American College Health* 62, no. 2 (2014): 118–24.

GEORGE, William H., Kelly Cue Davis, N. Tatiana Masters, Angela J. Jacques-Tiura, Julia R. Heiman, Jeanette Norris, Amanda K. Gilmore, Hong V. Nguyen, Kelly F. Kajumulo, Jacqueline M. Otto, and Michele P. Andrasik. "Sexual Victimization, Alcohol Intoxication, Sexual-Emotional Responding, and Sexual Risk in Heavy Episodic Drinking Women." *Archives of Sexual Behavior* 43, no. 4 (2014): 645–58.

GARCIA, Justin R., Elisabeth A. Lloyd, Kim Wallen, and Helen E. Fisher. "Variation in Orgasm Occurrence by Sexual Orientation in a Sample of U.S. Singles." *Journal of Sexual Medicine* 11, no. 11 (2014): 2645–52.

GRAHAM, Cynthia A., Richard A. Crosby, Robin A. Milhausen, Stephanie A. Sanders, and William L. Yarber. "Condom-Associated Erection Loss: A Study of High-Risk Young Black Males Residing in the Southern United States." *American Journal of Men's Health* 10, no. 2 (2014): 141–45.

HERBENICK, Debbie, Vanessa Schick, Michael Reece, Stephanie A. Sanders, and J. Dennis Fortenberry. "Women's Use and Perceptions of Lubricants: Prevalence and Characteristics in a Nationally Representative Sample of U.S. Adults." *Journal of Sexual Medicine* 11, no. 3 (2014): 642–52.

HIGGINS, Jenny A., Nicole K. Smith, Stephanie A. Sanders, Vanessa Schick, Debbie Herbenick, Michael Reece, Brian Dodge, and J. Dennis Fortenberry. "Dual Method Use at Last Sexual Encounter: A Nationally Representative, Episode-Level Analysis of U.S. Men and Women." *Contraception* 90, no. 4 (2014): 399–406.

HILL, Brandon J., Erick Janssen, Peter Kvam, Erick E. Amick, and Stephanie Sanders. "The Effect of Condoms on Penile Vibrotactile Sensitivity Thresholds in Young, Heterosexual Men." *Journal of Sexual Medicine* 11, no. 1 (2014): 102–106.

HOFFMAN, Heather, David Goodrich, Molly Wilson, and Erick Janssen. "The Role of Classical Conditioning in Sexual Compulsivity: A Pilot Study." *Sexual Addiction & Compulsivity: The Journal of Treatment & Prevention* 21, no. 2 (2014): 75–91.

JANSSEN, Erick, Stephanie A. Sanders, Brandon J. Hill, Erick Amick, Drake Oversen, Peter Kvam, and Kara Ingelhart. "Patterns of Sexual Arousal in Young, Heterosexual Men Who Experience Condom-Associated Erection Problems (CAEP)." *Journal of Sexual Medicine* 11, no. 9 (2014): 2285–91.

LORENZ, Tierney. "Religiosity and Sexual Attitudes." In *Encyclopedia of Quality of Life and Well-Being Research*, edited by Alex C. Michalos, 5477–81. Dordrecht: Springer Science, 2014.

LORENZ, Tierney, and Sari van Anders. "Interactions of Sexual Activity, Gender, and Depression with Immunity." *Journal of Sexual Medicine* 11, no. 4 (2014): 966–79.

LORENZ, Tierney, Bonnie McGregor, and Elizabeth Swisher. "Relationship Satisfaction Predicts Sexual Activity Following Risk-Reducing Salpingo-oophorectomy." *Journal of Psychosomatic Obstetrics & Gynecology* 35, no. 2 (2014): 62–68.

MARK, Kristen P., Debbie Herbenick, J. Dennis Fortenberry, Stephanie Sanders, and Michael Reece. "The Object of Sexual Desire: Examining the 'What' in 'What Do You Desire?'" *Journal of Sexual Medicine* 11, no. 11 (2014): 2709–19.

MASTERS, N. Tatiana, William H. George, Kelly Cue Davis, Jeanette Norris, Julia R. Heiman, Angela J. Jacques-Tiura, Amanda K. Gilmore, Hong V. Nguyen, Kelly F.

Kajumulo, Jacqueline M. Otto, and Cynthia A. Stappenbeck. "Women's Unprotected Sex Intentions: Roles of Sexual Victimization, Intoxication, and Partner Perception." *Journal of Sex Research* 51, no. 5 (2014): 586–98.

MILHAUSEN, Robin R., Alexander McKay, Cynthia A. Graham, Richard A. Crosby, William L. Yarber, and Stephanie A. Sanders. "Prevalence and Predictors of Condom Use in a National Sample of Canadian University Students." *Canadian Journal of Human Sexuality* 22, no. 3 (2014): 142–51.

OLIVEIRA, Cátia, Pedro Laja, Joana Carvalho, Ana Quinta Gomes, Sandra Vilarinho, Erick Janssen, and Pedro J. Nobre. "Predictors of Men's Sexual Response to Erotic Film Stimuli: The Role of Affect and Self-Reported Thoughts." *Journal of Sexual Medicine* 11, no. 11 (2014): 2701–2708.

PETERSON, Zoë D., Erick Janssen, David Goodrich, and Julian R. Heiman. "Physiological Reactivity in a Community Sample of Sexually Aggressive Young Men: A Test of Competing Hypotheses." *Aggressive Behavior* 40, no. 2 (2014): 152–64.

REECE, Michael, Debbie Herbenick, Vanessa Schick, Stephanie Sanders, and J. Dennis Fortenberry. "Men's Use and Perceptions of Commercial Lubricants: Prevalence and Characteristics in a Nationally Representative Sample of U.S. Adults." *Journal of Sexual Medicine* 11, no. 5 (2014): 1125–35.

RUPP, Heather, Thomas W. James, Ellen Ketterson, Dale Sengelaub, Beate Ditzen, and Julia Heiman. "Amygdala Response to Negative Images in Postpartum vs. Nulliparous Women and Intranasal Oxytocin." *Social Cognitive and Affective Neuroscience* 9, no. 1 (January 2014): 48–54.

SAMSON, Lelia, and Erick Janssen. "Sexual and Affective Responses to Same- and Opposite-Sex Stimuli in Heterosexual and Homosexual Men: Assessment and Manipulation of Visual Attention." *Archives of Sexual Behavior* 43, no. 5 (2014): 917–30.

SANDERS, Stephanie A., Brandon J. Hill, Richard A. Crosby, and Erick Janssen. "Correlates of Condom Associated Erection Problems (CAEP) in Young, Heterosexual Men: Condom Self-Efficacy, Perceptions, and Motivations." *AIDS and Behavior* 18, no. 1 (2014): 128–34.

SHEPPARD, Paula, Susan B. Schaffnit, Justin R. Garcia, and Rebecca Sear. "Fostering Relations: First Sex and Marital Timings for Children Raised by Kin and Non-kin Carers." *Evolution and Human Behavior* 35, no. 3 (2014): 161–68.

SHEPPARD, Paula, Justin R. Garcia, and Rebecca Sear. "A Not-So-Grim Tale: How Childhood Family Structure Influences Reproductive and Risk-Taking Outcomes in a Historical U.S. Population." *PLOS ONE* 9, no. 3 (2014): e89539.

VILARINHO, Sandra, Pedro Laja, Joana Carvalho, Ana L. Quinta-Gomes, Cátia Oliveira, Erick Janssen, and Pedro J. Nobre. "Affective and Cognitive Determinants of Women's Sexual Response to Erotica." *Journal of Sexual Medicine* 11, no. 11 (2014): 2671–78.

ALLEN, Judith A. "KINSEY, Alfred Charles (23 June, 1894–25 August, 1956), Entomologist and Zoologist, Pioneer Sex Researcher, 1947 Founder of the Institute for Sex Research at Indiana University." In *Indiana's 200: The People Who Helped to Shape the Character of the Hoosier State*, edited by Linda Guigan and James St. Clair. Indianapolis: Indiana Historical Society, 2015.

BELL, Aleeca F., C. S. Carter, Colin D. Steer, Jean Golding, John M. Davis, Alana D. Steffen, Leah H. Rubin, Travis S. Lillard, Steven P. Gregory, James C. Harris, and Jessica J. Connelly. "Interaction between Oxytocin Receptor DNA Methylation and Genotype Is Associated with Risk of Postpartum Depression in Women without

Depression in Pregnancy." *Frontiers in Genetics* 6, no. 243 (July 2015), doi:10.3389/fgene.2015.00243.

COE, Kathryn, Justin R. Garcia, and Ryan O. Begley. "Commentary: Art, Aesthetics, and Evolution." *ASEBL Journal* 11, no. 2 (2015): 41–42.

CROSBY, Richard, Cynthia Graham, Robin R. Milhausen, Stephanie A. Sanders, William L. Yarber, and Lydia Shrier. "Associations between Rushed Condom Application and Condom Use Errors and Problems." *Sexually Transmitted Infections* 91, no. 4 (June 2015): 275–77.

CROSBY, Richard A., Leandro Mena, William L. Yarber, Cynthia A. Graham, Stephanie A. Sanders, and Robin R. Milhausen. "Condom Use Errors and Problems: A Comparative Study of HIV-Positive versus HIV-Negative Young Black MSM." *Sexually Transmitted Diseases* 42, no. 11 (2015): 634–36.

GARCIA, Justin R., Michelle J. Escasa-Dorne, Amanda N. Gesselman, and Peter B. Gray. "Individual Differences in Women's Salivary Testosterone and Estradiol Following Sexual Activity in a Non-laboratory Setting." *International Journal of Sexual Health* 27, no. 4 (2015): 406–17.

GARCIA, Justin R., Susan M. Seibold-Simpson, Sean G. Massey, and Ann M. Merriwether. "Casual Sex: Integrating Social, Behavioral, and Sexual Health Research." In *Handbook of the Sociology of Sexualities*, edited by John DeLamater and Rebecca F. Plante, 203–22. Dordrecht, the Netherlands: Springer, 2015.

GARFIELD, Lindsey, Carmen Giurgescu, C. Sue Carter, Diane Holditch-Davis, Barbara L. McFarlin, Dorie Schwertz, Julia S. Seng, and Rosemary White-Traut. "Depressive Symptoms in the Second Trimester Relate to Low Oxytocin Levels in African-American Women: A Pilot Study." *Archives of Women's Mental Health* 18, no. 1 (2015): 123–29.

GARFIELD, Lindsey, Diane Holditch-Davis, C. Sue Carter, Barbara L. McFarlin, Dorie Schwertz, Julia S. Seng, Carmen Giurgescu, and Rosemary White-Traut. "Risk Factors for Postpartum Depressive Symptoms in Low-Income Women with Very Low-Birth-Weight Infants." *Advances in Neonatal Care* 15, no. 1 (2015): E3–E8.

GOUIN, Jean-Philippe, Hossein Pournajafi-Nazarloo, and C. Sue Carter. "Changes in Social Functioning and Circulating Oxytocin and Vasopressin following the Migration to a New Country." *Physiology and Behavior* 139 (2015): 67–72.

GRAY, Peter B., Justin R. Garcia, Benjamin S. Crosier, and Helen E. Fisher. "Dating and Sexual Behavior among Single Parents of Young Children in the United States." *Journal of Sex Research* 52, no. 2 (2015): 121–28.

GRAY, Peter B., Shelly L. Volsche, Justin R. Garcia, and Helen E. Fisher. "The Roles of Pet Dogs and Cats in Human Courtship and Dating." *Anthrozoös* 28, no. 4 (2015): 673–83.

GREGORY, Rebecca, Hu Cheng, Heather A. Rupp, Dale R. Sengelaub, and Julia R. Heiman. "Oxytocin Increases VTA Activation to Infant and Sex Stimuli in Nulliparous and Postpartum Women." *Hormones and Behavior* 69 (March 2015): 82–88.

HILL, Brandon J., Stephanie A. Sanders, Richard Crosby, Kara N. Ingelhart, and Erick Janssen. "Condom-Associated Erection Problems (CAEP): Behavioral Responses and Attributions in Young, Heterosexual Men." *Sexual Health* 12, no. 5 (2015): 397–404.

JANKOWIAK, William R., Shelly Volsche, and Justin R. Garcia. "Is the Romantic-Sexual Kiss a Near Human Universal?" *American Anthropologist* 117, no. 3 (2015): 535–39.

JONASON, Peter K., Justin R. Garcia, Gregory D. Webster, Norman P. Li, and Helen E. Fisher. "Relationship Dealbreakers: Traits People Avoid in Potential Mates." *Personality and Social Psychology Bulletin* 41, no. 12 (2015): 1697–1711.

KENKEL, William M., Jason R. Yee, Stephen W. Porges, Craig F. Ferris, and C. Sue Carter. "Cardioacceleration in Alloparents in Response to Stimuli from Prairie Vole Pups: The Significance of Thermoregulation." *Behavioural Brain Research* 286 (June 2015): 71–79.

KRUGER, Daniel J., Maryanne L. Fisher, Carey J. Fitzgerald, Justin R. Garcia, Glenn Geher, and Amanda E. Guitar. "Sexual and Emotional Aspects Are Distinct Components of Infidelity and Unique Predictors of Anticipated Distress." *Evolutionary Psychological Sciences* 1, no. 1 (2015): 44–51.

LANCASTER, Katie, C. Sue Carter, Hossein Pournajafi-Nazarloo, Themistoclis Karaoli, Travis S. Lillard, Allison Jack, John M. Davis, James P. Morris, and Jessica J. Connelly. "Plasma Oxytocin Explains Individual Differences in Neural Substrates of Social Perception." *Frontiers in Human Neuroscience* 9, no. 132 (2015): doi:10.3389/fnhum.2015.00132.

LORENZ, Tierney, Bonnie McGregor, and Virginia J. Vitzthum. "Presence of Young Children at Home May Moderate Development of Hot Flashes during the Menopausal Transition." *Menopause* 22, no. 4 (2015): 448–52.

LORENZ, Tierney K., Gregory E. Demas, and Julia R. Heiman. "Interaction of Menstrual Cycle Phase and Sexual Activity Predicts Mucosal and Systemic Humoral Immunity in Healthy Women." *Physiology of Behavior* 152, part A (December 2015): 92–98.

LORENZ, Tierney K., Julia R. Heiman, and Gregory E. Demas. "Sexual Activity Modulates Shifts in TH1/TH2 Cytokine Profile across the Menstrual Cycle: An Observational Study." *Fertility and Sterility* 104, no. 6 (2015): 1513–21.

LORENZ, Tierney K., Carol M. Worthman, and Virginia J. Vitzthum. "Links among Inflammation, Sexual Activity, and Ovulation: Evolutionary Trade-Offs and Clinical Implications." *Evolution, Medicine, and Public Health*, no. 1 (2015): 304–24.

MILICH, Krista M., Caroline Deimel, Frankia S. Schaebs, Jonathan Thornburg, Tobias Deschner, and Virginia J. Vitzthum. "Links between Breast Cancer and Birth Weight: An Empirical Test of the Hypothesized Association between Size at Birth and Premenopausal Adult Progesterone Concentrations." *Hormones & Cancer* 6, no. 4 (2015): 182–88.

PULVERMAN, Carey S., Tierney A. Lorenz, and Cindy M. Meston. "Linguistic Changes in Expressive Writing Predict Psychological Outcomes in Women with History of Childhood Sexual Abuse and Adult Sexual Dysfunction." *Psychological Trauma* 7, no. 1 (2015): 50–57.

SANDERS, Stephanie, Brandon J. Hill, Erick E. Janssen, Cynthia A. Graham, Richard A. Crosby, Robin R. Milhausen, and William L. Yarber. "General Erectile Functioning among Young, Heterosexual Men Who Do and Do Not Report Condom-Associated Erection Problems (CAEP)." *Journal of Sexual Medicine* 12, no. 9 (2015): 1897–904.

SWARTZENDURBER, Andrea, Sarah H. Murray, Jessica M. Sales, Robin R. Milhausen, Stephanie A. Sanders, Cynthia A. Graham, Ralph J. DiClemente, and Gina M. Wingood. "The Influence of Sexual Arousability on Partner Communication Mediators of Condom Use among African American Female Adolescents." *Sexual Health* 12, no. 4 (2015): 322–27.

VITZTHUM, Virginia J. "Fitness." In *International Encyclopedia of Human Sexuality*, edited by Patricia Whelehan and Anne Bolin, 708. Hoboken, NJ: Wiley Press, 2015.

WEISMAN, Omri, Esben Agerbo, C. Sue Carter, James C. Harris, Niels Uldbjerg, Tine B. Henriksen, Malene Thygesen, Preben B. Mortensen, James F. Leckman, and Søren

Dalsgaard. "Oxytocin-Augmented Labor and Risk for Autism in Males." *Behavioral Brain Research* 284 (May 2015): 207–12.

CARTER, C. Sue, and Stephen W. Porges. "Neural Mechanisms Underlying Human-Animal Interactions: An Evolutionary Perspective." In *The Social Neuroscience of Animal-Human Interactions*, edited by Lisa S. Freund, Sandra McCune, Layla Eposito, Nancy R. Gee, and Peggy McCardle, 89–105. Washington, DC: American Psychological Association, 2016.

CROSBY, Richard A., Cynthia A. Graham, Leandro Mena, William L. Yarber, Stephanie A. Sanders, Robin R. Milhausen, and Angelica Geter. "Circumcision Status Is Not Associated with Condom Use and Prevalence of Sexually Transmitted Infections among Young Black MSM." *AIDS & Behavior* 20, no. 11 (2016): 2538–42.

CROSBY, Richard A., Cynthia A. Graham, William L. Yarber, Stephanie A. Sanders, Robin R. Milhausen, and Leandro Mena. "Measures of Attitudes toward and Communication about Condom Use: Their Relationships with Sexual Risk among Young Black MSM." *Sexually Transmitted Diseases* 43, no. 2 (2016): 94–98.

FALES, Melissa R., David A. Frederick, Justin R. Garcia, Kelly A. Gildersleeve, Martie G. Haselton, and Helen E. Fisher. "Mating Markets and Bargaining Hands: Mate Preferences for Attractiveness and Resources in Two National U.S. Studies." *Personality and Individual Differences* 88 (January 2016): 78–87.

GARCIA, Justin R., and Helen E. Fisher. "Why We Hook Up: Searching for Sex or Looking for Love?" In *Gender, Sex, and Politics: In the Streets and between the Sheets in the 21st Century*, edited by Shira Tarrant, 238–50. New York: Routledge, 2016.

KENKEL, William M., and C. Sue Carter. "Voluntary Exercise Facilitates Pair-Bonding in Male Prairie Voles." *Behavioral Brain Research* 296 (January 2016): 326–30.

MASSEY, Suena H., Stephanie A. Schuette, Hossein Pournajafi-Nazarloo, Katherine L. Wisner, and C. Sue Carter. "Interaction of Oxytocin Level and Past Depression May Predict Postpartum Depressive Symptom Severity." *Archives of Women's Mental Health* 19, no. 5 (2016): 799–808.

PERRY, Adam N., C. Sue Carter, and Bruce S. Cushing. "Chronic Social Isolation Enhances Reproduction in the Monogamous Prairie Vole (*Microtus ochrogaster*)." *Psychoneuroendocrinology* 68 (June 2016): 20–28.

RUBIN, Leah H., Jessica J. Connelly, James L. Reilly, C. Sue Carter, Lauren L. Drogon, Hossein Pournjafi-Nazarloo, Anthony C. Ruocco, Sarah K. Keedy, Ian Matthew, Neeraj Tandon, Godfrey D. Pearlson, Brett A. Clementz, Carol A. Tamminga, Elliot S. Gershon, Matcheri S. Keshavan, Jeffrey R. Bishop, and John A. Sweeney. "Sex and Diagnosis Specific Associations between DNA Methylation of the Oxytocin Receptor Gene with Emotion Processing and Temporal-Limbic and Prefrontal Brain Volumes in Psychotic Disorders." *Biological Psychiatry: Cognitive Neuroscience and Neuroimaging* 1, no. 2 (2016): 141–51.

YEE, Jason R., William M. Kenkel, Jessie L. Frijling, Sonam Dodhia, Kenneth G. Onishi, Santiago Tovar, Maha J. Saber, Gregory F. Lewis, Wensheng Liu, Stephen W. Porges, and C. Sue Carter. "Oxytocin Promotes Functional Coupling between Paraventricular Nucleus and Both Sympathetic and Parasympathetic Cardioregulatory Nuclei." *Hormones and Behavior* 80 (April 2016): 82–91.

YEE, Jason R., William M. Kenkel, P. Kulkarni, K. Moore, A. M. Perkeybile, S. Toddes, J. Amacker, C. Sue Carter, and C. F. Ferris. "BOLD fMRI in Awake Prairie Voles: A Platform for Translational Social and Affective Neuroscience." *NeuroImage* 138 (September 2016): 221–32.

ALILUNAS, Peter. *Smutty Little Movies: The Creation and Regulation of Adult Video.* Oakland: University of California Press, 2013.

BECK, William Edward, and Peter Farrer. *Happenings: The Story of Bessie.* Liverpool: Karn, 2012.

BENOKRAITIS, Nijole V., John J. Macionis, and Peter Urmetzer. *Seeing Ourselves: Classic, Contemporary, and Cross-Cultural Readings in Sociology.* Toronto: Pearson Education, 2013.

BONDS-RAACKE, Jennifer M. *Thinking Critically about Social Psychology.* Dubuque, IA: Kendall Hunt, 2015.

BROPHY, Sarah, and Janice Hladki. *Embodied Politics in Visual Autobiography.* Toronto: University of Toronto Press, 2014.

BROTTMAN, Mikita. *Funny Peculiar: Gershon Legman and the Psychopathology of Humor.* Hillsdale, NJ: Analytic Press, 2004.

BULLOUGH, Vern L. *Science in the Bedroom: A History of Sex Research.* New York: Basic Books, 1995.

BURR, Vivien. *Gender and Psychology.* London: Routledge, 2014.

CANADAY, Margot. *The Straight State: Sexuality and Citizenship in Twentieth-Century America.* Princeton, NJ: Princeton University Press, 2011.

CARL, John D. *Think Sociology.* Upper Saddle River, NJ: Prentice Hall, 2010.

CARROLL, Janell L. *Sexuality Now: Embracing Diversity.* Boston: Cengage Learning, 2016.

CARTER, Lakeita. *Reflecting Humanity: Biological, Psychological, and Sociological Perspectives.* Dubuque, IA: Kendall Hunt, 2015.

CHAUNCEY, George. *Gay New York: Gender, Urban Culture, and the Making of the Gay Male World, 1890–1940.* New York: Basic Books, 1995.

CHURCH, David. *Disposable Passions: Vintage Pornography and the Material Legacies of Adult Cinema.* New York: Bloomsbury, 2016.

CICCARELLI, Saundra K., and Glenn E. Meyer. *Psychology.* Upper Saddle River, NJ: Pearson Prentice Hall, 2006.

CICCARELLI, Saundra K., and J. Noland White. *Psychology: An Exploration.* Boston: Pearson, 2013.

COLLIGAN, Colette. *A Publisher's Paradise: Expatriate Literary Culture in Paris, 1890–1960.* Amherst: University of Massachusetts Press, 2014.

DAVIS, Stephen F., and Joseph J. Palladino. *Psychology*. Upper Saddle River, NJ: Prentice Hall, 2010.

D'EMILIO, John. *Sexual Politics, Sexual Communities: The Making of a Homosexual Minority in the United States, 1940–1970*. Chicago: University of Chicago Press, 1998.

D'EMILIO, John, and Estelle B. Freedman. *Intimate Matters: A History of Sexuality in America*. New York: Harper and Row, 1988.

DENNIS, Donna J. *Licentious Gotham: Erotic Publishing and Its Prosecution in Nineteenth-Century New York*. Cambridge, MA: Harvard University Press, 2009.

DRUCKER, Donna J. "'Building for a Life-Time of Research': Letters of Alfred Kinsey and Ralph Voris." *Indiana Magazine of History* 106, no. 1 (March 2010): 71–101.

——. *The Classification of Sex: Alfred Kinsey and the Organization of Knowledge*. Pittsburgh, PA: University of Pittsburgh Press, 2014.

——. "Keying Desire: Alfred Kinsey's Use of Punched-Card Machines for Sex Research." *Journal of the History of Sexuality* 22, no. 1 (2013): 105–25.

——. *The Machines of Sex Research Technology and the Politics of Identity, 1945–1985*. Dordrecht: Springer, 2014.

——. "Male Sexuality and Alfred Kinsey's 0–6 Scale: Toward 'a Sound Understanding of the Realities of Sex.'" *Journal of Homosexuality* 57, no. 9 (2010): 1105–23.

——. "Marking Sexuality from 0–6: The Kinsey Scale in Online Culture." *Sexuality & Culture: An Interdisciplinary Quarterly* 16, no. 3 (2012): 241–62.

——. "'A Most Interesting Chapter in the History of Science': Intellectual Responses to Alfred Kinsey's *Sexual Behavior in the Human Male*." *History of the Human Sciences* 25, no. 1 (February 2012): 75–98.

——. "'A Noble Experiment': The Marriage Course at Indiana University, 1938–1940." *Indiana Magazine of History* 103, no. 3 (2007): 231–64.

DUFFY, Michael, dir. *Sex: A Horizon Guide*. Documentary. London: BBC4, 2013.

EISNER, Shiri. *Bi: Notes for a Bisexual Revolution*. Berkeley, CA: Seal Press, 2013.

EKINS, Richard, and Dave King, eds. *Virginia Prince: Pioneer of Transgendering*. Binghamton, NY: CRC Press, 2006.

FARRER, Peter. *Cross Dressing since the War: Selections from "Justice Weekly" 1955–1972*. Liverpool: Karn Publications Garston, 2011.

FELDMAN, Robert S. *Understanding Psychology*. New York: McGraw-Hill, 2013.

FOSTER, Thomas. *Sex and the Eighteenth-Century Man: Massachusetts and the History of Sexuality in America*. Boston: Beacon Press, 2007.

FRIEDMAN, Mack. *Strapped for Cash: A History of American Hustler Culture*. Los Angeles: Alyson Books, 2003.

GALUPO, M. Paz, Renae C. Mitchell, Ashley L. Grynkiewicz, and Kyle S. Davis. "Sexual Minority Reflections on the Kinsey Scale and the Klein Sexual Orientation Grid: Conceptualization and Measurement." *Journal of Bisexuality* 14, no. 3–4 (2014): 404–32.

GARTON, Stephen. *Histories of Sexuality: Antiquity to Sexual Revolution*. London: Routledge, 2004.

GATHORNE-HARDY, Jonathan. *Sex the Measure of All Things: A Life of Alfred C. Kinsey*. Bloomington: Indiana University Press, 2000.

GERTZMAN, Jay A. *Samuel Roth, Infamous Modernist*. Gainesville: University Press of Florida, 2013.

GHEROVICI, Patricia. *Please Select Your Gender: From the Invention of Hysteria to the Democratizing of Transgenderism*. New York: Routledge/Taylor & Francis Group, 2010.

GILBERT, James Burkhart. *Men in the Middle: Searching for Masculinity in the 1950s.* Chicago: University of Chicago Press, 2005.

GILLIS, Melissa, and Andrew Jacobs. *Introduction to Women's and Gender Studies: An Interdisciplinary Approach.* New York: Oxford University Press, 2016.

GLASS, Loren. *Counterculture Colophon: Grove Press, the "Evergreen Review," and the Incorporation of the Avant-Garde.* Stanford, CA: Stanford University Press, 2013.

GREENBERG, Jerrold S., Clint E. Bruess, and Sara B. Oswalt. *Exploring the Dimensions of Human Sexuality.* Burlington, MA: Jones and Bartlett Learning, 2014.

GRIFFEY, E., and B. Reay. "Sexual Portraits: Edward Melcarth and Homoeroticism in Modern American Art." *History Workshop Journal* 73, no. 1 (2012): 66–94.

GRIFFITH, Marie R. "The Religious Encounters of Alfred C. Kinsey." *Journal of American History* 95, no. 2 (2008): 349–77.

HALLER, John S., and Robin M. Haller. *The Physician and Sexuality in Victorian America.* Urbana: University of Illinois Press, 1974.

HEGARTY, Peter. *Gentlemen's Disagreement: Alfred Kinsey, Lewis Terman, and the Sexual Politics of Smart Men.* Chicago: University of Chicago Press, 2013.

HERRING, Scott. *Another Country: Queer Anti-urbanism.* New York: New York University Press, 2010.

——. "Out of the Closets, into the Woods: 'RFD,' 'Country Women,' and the Post-Stonewall Emergence of Queer Anti-urbanism." *American Quarterly* 59, no. 2 (2007): 341–72.

HILLSTROM, Laurie Collier. *The Stonewall Riots.* Detroit: Omnigraphics, 2016.

HIRSCH, Debra. *Redeeming Sex: Naked Conversations about Sexuality and Spirituality.* Downers Grove, OH: InterVarsity Press, 2015.

HOROWITZ, Helen Lefkowitz. *Rereading Sex: Battles over Sexual Knowledge and Suppression in Nineteenth-Century America.* New York: Knopf, 2002.

IGO, Sarah Elizabeth. *The Averaged American: Surveys, Citizens, and the Making of a Mass Public.* Cambridge, MA: Harvard University Press, 2007.

INSEL, Paul M., and Walton T. Roth. *Wellness Worksheets.* New York: McGraw-Hill, 2006.

IRVINE, Janice M. *Disorders of Desire: Sex and Gender in Modern American Sexology.* Philadelphia: Temple University Press, 1990.

JAGOSE, Annamarie. *Orgasmology.* Durham, NC: Duke University Press, 2013.

JOHNSON, Colin R. *Just Queer Folks: Gender and Sexuality in Rural America.* Philadelphia: Temple University Press, 2013.

JONES, James H. *Alfred C. Kinsey: A Public/Private Life.* New York: W. W. Norton & Company, 2004.

KERBER, Linda K., Jane Sherron De Hart, Cornelia Hughes Dayton, and Judy Tzu-Chun Wu. *Women's America: Refocusing the Past.* New York: Oxford University Press, 2015.

KIMMEL, Michael S., and Rebecca F. Plante. *Sexualities: Identities, Behaviors, and Society.* New York: Oxford University Press, 2004.

KING, Bruce M. *Human Sexuality Today.* Upper Saddle River, NJ: Pearson Education/ Prentice Hall, 2005.

KNOX, David, and Caroline Schacht. *Choices in Relationships: An Introduction to Marriage and the Family.* Belmont, CA: Wadsworth, 2013.

KOERTGE, Noretta. *Scientific Values and Civic Virtues.* New York: Oxford University Press, 2005.

KON, Igor S. *Sexual Revolution in Russia.* New York: Free Press, 1995.

KUEFLER, Mathew. *The History of Sexuality Sourcebook*. Orchard Park, NY: Broadview Press, 2007.

KUNZEL, Regina G. *Criminal Intimacy: Prison and the Uneven History of Modern American Sexuality*. Chicago: University of Chicago Press, 2008.

LAHOOD, Grant, dir., John Keir, prod., and Mani Bruce Mitchell. *Intersexion*. Kibirnie, Wellington, NZ: Ponsby Productions and Frameline (Firm), 2012.

LITTAUER, Amanda H. *Sex Anarchy: Women, Girls, and American Sexual Culture in the Mid-Twentieth Century*. Chapel Hill: University of North Carolina Press, 2015.

LOGHAN, Cheryl A. *Hormones, Heredity, and Race: Spectacular Failure in Interwar Vienna*. New Brunswick, NJ: Rutgers University Press, 2013.

LYONS, Andrew P., and Harriet Lyons. *Sexualities in Anthropology*. Oxford: Wiley-Blackwell, 2011.

MACIONIS, John J. *Social Problems*. Boston: Prentice Hall, 2010.

MARCUS, Steven. *The Other Victorians: A Study of Sexuality and Pornography in Mid-Nineteenth-Century England*. 1966; Piscataway, NJ: Transaction Publishers, 2008.

McINERNY, Thomas K. *American Academy of Pediatrics Textbook of Pediatric Care*. Elk Grove, IL: American Academy of Pediatrics, 2017.

McLAREN, Angus. *Twentieth-Century Sexuality: A History*. Malden, MA: Wiley-Blackwell, 1999.

MEYEROWITZ, Joanne. *How Sex Changed: A History of Transsexuality in the United States*. Cambridge, MA: Harvard University Press, 2004.

MILLER, Allison. "Am I Normal? American Vernacular Psychology and the Tomboy Body, 1900–1940." *REPRESENTATIONS*, no. 122 (2013): 23–50.

MILLER-YOUNG, Mireille. *A Taste for Brown Sugar: Black Women in Pornography*. Durham, NC: Duke University Press, 2014.

MINTON, Henry L. *Departing from Deviance: A History of Homosexual Rights and Emancipatory Science in America*. Chicago: University of Chicago Press, 2002.

MIRACLE, Tina S., Andrew W. Miracle, and Roy F. Baumeister. *Human Sexuality: Meeting Your Basic Needs*. Upper Saddle River, NJ: Prentice Hall, 2003.

MONSON, Ander. *Letter to a Future Lover: Marginalia, Errata, Secrets, Inscriptions, and Other Ephemera Found in Libraries*. Minneapolis, MN: Graywolf Press, 2015.

MÙÑOZ, Lisa Speicher. *Difference, Inequality, and Change: Social Diversity in the U.S.* Dubuque, IA: Kendall Hunt, 2011.

PASSET, Joanne. *Sex Variant Woman: The Life of Jeanette Howard Foster*. Reprint ed. New York: Da Capo Press, 2008.

PETTIT, Alexander, Janine Barchas, Deborah Needleman Armintor, Kevin Lee Cope, Lena Olsson, and Rictor Norton. *Eighteenth-Century British Erotica II*. London: Pickering & Chatto, 2004.

PETTIT, Michael. "The Queer Life of a Lab Rat." *History of Psychology* 15, no. 3 (2012): 217–27.

PIERCE, Jennifer Burek. *What Adolescents Ought to Know: Sexual Health Texts in Early Twentieth-Century America*. Amherst: University of Massachusetts Press, 2011.

PUKALL, Caroline. *Human Sexuality: A Contemporary Introduction*. New York: Oxford University Press, 2013.

RATHUS, Spencer A. *Human Sexuality in a World of Diversity*. Upper Saddle River, NJ: Prentice Hall, 2013.

REAY, Barry. *New York Hustlers: Masculinity and Sex in Modern America*. New York: Manchester University Press, 2010.

REUMANN, Miriam G. *American Sexual Character: Sex, Gender, and National Identity in the Kinsey Reports*. Berkeley: University of California Press, 2005.

RYLE, Robyn. *Questioning Gender: A Sociological Exploration*. Thousand Oaks, CA: SAGE/Pine Forge Press, 2012.

SAVIN-WILLIAMS, Ritch C. *The New Gay Teenager*. Cambridge, MA: Harvard University Press, 2006.

SCHWARTZ, Mary Ann, and Barbara Marlene Scott. *Marriages and Families: Diversity and Change*. Upper Saddle River, NJ: Prentice Hall, 2003.

SEARS, James T. *Behind the Mask of the Mattachine: The Hal Call Chronicles and the Early Movement for Homosexual Emancipation*. New York: Harrington Park Press, 2006.

SIGEL, Lisa Z. *Making Modern Love: Sexual Narratives and Identities in Interwar Britain*. Philadelphia: Temple University Press, 2012.

SILVERMAN, Gillian D. *Bodies and Books: Reading and the Fantasy of Communion in Nineteenth-Century America*. Philadelphia: University of Pennsylvania Press, 2012.

SIMMONS, Christina. *Making Marriage Modern: Women's Sexuality from the Progressive Era to World War II*. Oxford: Oxford University Press, 2009.

SLOBODA, Stacey. *Chinoiserie: Commerce and Critical Ornament in Eighteenth-Century Britain*. Manchester: Manchester University Press, 2014.

SMITH, Barbara. *The Psychology of Sex and Gender*. Boston: Pearson/Allyn and Bacon, 2007.

SPRING, Justin. *Secret Historian: The Life and Times of Samuel Steward, Professor, Tattoo Artist, and Sexual Renegade*. New York: Farrar, Straus and Giroux, 2011.

SPURLOCK, John C. *Youth and Sexuality in the Twentieth-Century United States*. New York: Routledge, 2016.

STEWART-WINTER, Timothy. *Queer Clout: Chicago and the Rise of Gay Politics*. Philadelphia: University of Pennsylvania Press, 2016.

STRUB, Whitney. *Perversion for Profit: The Politics of Pornography and the Rise of the New Right*. New York: Columbia University Press, 2011.

STRYKER, Susan. *Queer Pulp: Perverted Passions from the Golden Age of the Paperback*. San Francisco: Chronicle Books, 2001.

TERRY, Jennifer. *An American Obsession: Science, Medicine, and Homosexuality in Modern Society*. Chicago: University of Chicago Press, 1999.

THIO, Alex. *Deviant Behavior*. Boston: Allyn & Bacon, 2006.

TURNER, Trude Cooke, Azar Etesamypour-King, and La Keita D. Carter. *Multicultural Psychology: Reflecting Humanity*. Dubuque, IA: Kendall Hunt, 2013.

WADE, Carole, and Carol Tavris. *Invitation to Psychology*. Upper Saddle River, NJ: Pearson, 2014.

WATSON, Mary Ann, Suki Montgomery, and Michael Myers. *Your Sexuality Workbook*. Dubuque, IA: Kendall Hunt, 2003.

WEITEN, Wayne, and Margaret A. Lloyd. *Psychology Applied to Modern Life: Adjustment in the 21st Century*. Belmont, CA: Wadsworth, 2003.

WILLIAMS, Brian K., Stacey C. Sawyer, and Carl M. Wahlstrom. *Marriages, Families, Intimate Relationships: A Practical Introduction*. Boston: Pearson, 2013.

ZASTROW, Charles, and Karen Kay Kirst-Ashman. *Understanding Human Behavior and the Social Environment*. Boston: Cengage, 2013.

impotence, *see* sexual dysfunction

Indiana Daily Student, 126, 151

Indiana University, xi, 1, 2, 5, 8, 12, 14, 17, 26–27, 31–32, 70–72, 82, 86, 90, 97, 119, 123, 126–127, 129–131, 134, 138, 140, 151–153, 156, 175, 178, 179, 193n40; Archives, ix, xiii; board of trustees of, 5, 8, 60, 69, 74, 78, 146, 182, 184, 193n40; marriage course, offering of (1938–1942), 90; merger with the Kinsey Institute, 69, 110, 126, 137, 142, 143, 148, 154, 156, 158, 161–162, 184–187; Morrison Hall, space and conditions for Kinsey Institute collections, 103, 104, 123, 130, 138, 145–148, 183; Office of Research and Graduate Development, 126, 129, 131

Institute for Sex Research, x, 4, 6, 8, 17; advisory board, 90, 111, 119, 120, 184, 202n8, 205n65, 206n79, 206n84; articles of incorporation, 32–33, 69; bookplate for, 36; collections: erotic and sex-related art, objects and printed materials, 8, 82, 183, and customs case (*United States of America v. 31 Photographs*, 1957), 5, 8, 38, 60, 69–71, 74, 78, 80, 97, 120, 127, 129, 131, 184, 186; external grants and foundation support, 26, 86, 87, 91, 97, 100, 103, 110, 125–127, 137; founding of, 2, 6, 14, 16, 31, 32, 35, 36; and Indiana University, 2, 4, 5, 8, 12, 14, 17; library and librarians, 27, 29–32, 35, 47, 75–76, 80, 88, 92, 110–111, 119–125, 126–131, 135; naming of, 131; and National Institute of Mental Health (1962) site visit, 86, 92, 97, 184, 200n13, 201n34; publications of: *Catalog of Social and Behavioral Sciences, Monograph Section of the Library of the Institute for Sex Research* (1975), *Catalog of Periodical Literature in the Social and Behavioral Sciences Section, Library of the Institute for Sex Research* (1976), and *Sexual Nomenclature: A Thesaurus* (1976), 122; research projects of :"Attitudes towards Selected Forms of Deviant Behavior" (1967–70), 112, 116, 117, 118–119, 125, 205nn51–52, 205n56, data retrieval project (1963–68), 88, 92, 119, 120, 124, 125, "Patterns of Adjustment in Deviant Populations (1965–70)," 101, 112–113, 115–117, 119, 120, 125, 203n16, "A Study of Deviant Socialization" (1968–71), 112, 115, 204n31, 204n39, 204n46, and "Youth Culture and Aspects of Socialization" (1967–70), 99, 103, 105, 107, 113, 125, 203n21, 203n23, 203n25; reviews of: (external, 1980), 126, 127, 128, 130, 133, 137, 145, (internal, 1980), 126, 130, Studies in Sex and Society, Institute Monographs Series, 102; Summer Institute symposia, 124; teaching offered by, 155; trustees of, 124. *See also:* Alfred C. Kinsey Institute for Sex Research; Kinsey Institute for Research in Sex, Gender and Reproduction; Kinsey Institute

intergenerational sexuality, 12, 22, 50, 95, 118, 134, 152, 158, 177, 212n8. *See also:* sex offences and offenders

Janssen, Erick, 11, 162, 164, 169

Johnson, Alan Blaine, 84

Johnson, Virginia, 10, 107, 108, 144, 171, 172, 187

Jones, James H., 6, 190nn13–14, 192n30, 194n10, 195n27, 195n29, 210n27, 201nn30–31

Jorgensen, Christine, 77

Kinsey, Alfred Charles, iv, viii, xi, xiv, 1, 2, 3, 4, 5–8, 10, 11, 13, 14, 16, 17, 18, 19, 21–32, 35–36, 37–56; biographies of, ix, 5–6, 7, 11; book draft by, *Abortion* (1956), 8, 39, 63, 64, 66, 71, 84; claimed misogyny of, 44, 58; and class, education, and "social level" differences in sexual behavior, 2–5, 17, 22, 23, 38, 44, 50, 55, 56, 64, 67, 83, 123, 182, 209n20; and collections of publications, art, objects and films, 13–14, 17; correspondence with general public, 1, 2, 38, 42–44, 52, 70, 150, 189n1; FBI investigation of, 70–71; gall wasp research of, 5, 13, 18, 19, 27, 35, 50, 59, 180, 193n34; and Indiana University, ix, xi, 1, 2, 5, 8; lecture at University of California at Berkeley (1949), 53; and McCarthyism, 5; and race, 1, 22, 64; "A Scientist's Responsibility in Sex Instruction" (1943, unpublished lecture), 1; and "sex history" interviews, interviewing,

JUDITH A. ALLEN is Ralph Walter Professor of History at Indiana University, Associate Editor of the *Journal of American History*, and a senior research fellow of the Kinsey Institute. A social and cultural historian, she specializes in the histories of sexuality, feminism, interpersonal crimes, and population change in Anglophone cultures. She is the author of *The Feminism of Charlotte Perkins Gilman: Histories/Sexualities/Progressivism*.

HALLIMEDA E. ALLINSON is a doctoral candidate in the Department of History at Indiana University. Her dissertation is entitled "Public Sexuality: Erotic Desire, Identity Categories, and the 'Sexual Revolution,' 1920–1979." Currently, she serves as a historical consultant to the Kinsey Institute.

ANDREW CLARK-HUCKSTEP is a doctoral candidate in the Department of History at Indiana University. His dissertation on the history of sexological approaches to identity is entitled "Diagnosed with Sex: Rethinking Social Science, Sexology, and Identity, 1880–1970." He has served as an editorial assistant at the *Journal of American History* and is also a historical consultant to the Kinsey Institute.

BRANDON J. HILL is Executive Director of the Center for Interdisciplinary Inquiry and Innovation in Sexual and Reproductive Health (Ci3) in the Department of Obstetrics and Gynecology at the University of Chicago and Research Fellow at the Kinsey Institute for Research in Sex, Gender, and Reproduction at Indiana University. His interdisciplinary research explores the ways in which sex, gender, race/ethnicity, and the social environment influence disparities in sexual and reproductive health among adolescents and young adults. His publications address factors contributing to poor health, including sexually transmitted infections and HIV, among sexual and gender minorities of color. He oversees the development of digital and game-based interventions to improve the sexual and reproductive health of adolescents and young adults.

STEPHANIE A. SANDERS is Peg Zeglin Brand Chair of Gender Studies, Provost Professor in the College of Arts & Sciences, and Senior Scientist at the Kinsey Institute, Indiana University. She served as Associate Director and two terms as Interim Director of the Kinsey Institute. Her research addresses sexual behavior; sexuality, sexual identity, and gender relations; sex differentiation; gender difference in psychological and physical development, especially as affected by prenatal hormones and drugs; women's health and well-being; and biopsychological perspectives on debates in feminist theory.

LIANA H. ZHOU is Director of the Kinsey Institute Library and Special Collections, where she is responsible for the collections chronicling more than two thousand years of human history and diverse understandings of human sexuality. She leads the effort to organize, develop, and preserve the library and collection archives to ensure continued access by researchers around the world.